# FURNITURE

## A Practical Guide
## for Collectors

D0027142

John
Obbard

**COLLECTOR BOOKS**
*A Division of Schroeder Publishing Co., Inc.*

# Searching for a Publisher?

We are always looking for knowledgeable people considered to be experts within their fields. If you feel that there is a real need for a book on your collectible subject and have a large comprehensive collection, contact Collector Books.

Cover design by Beth Summers
Book design by Karen Smith
Drawings by Brenda Bechtel

# Contents

# Acknowledgments

Early handmade furniture is so diverse and complex that every book on the subject is to some measure a joint effort, and I would be less than honest if I did not acknowledge the help that went into writing this small field guide on American furniture.

First off, I would like to thank Brenda Bechtel for preparing the more than 400 illustrations that are scattered throughout the text. Brenda worked tirelessly for more than half a year, often with the aid of a magnifying glass, to translate the often less than perfect auction catalog photographs into detailed line drawings. Many of these drawings, particularly those of major pieces, are little works of art in themselves, and it is a pity that they have had to be reduced in size for publication.

Permission to make drawings from their catalogs was generously provided by Skinner, Inc., and Christie, Manson and Woods International. The color transparencies and slides used in designing the cover were provided by Skinner, Inc., by Edwin C. Ahlberg, and by Pleasant Bay Antiques.

The many excellent books on American period furniture, particularly those on museum and historical society collections, were invaluable sources of information. They provided both additional data and verified much of the informative detail found throughout this book.

Much credit should also go to Lisa Stroup, editor of Collector Books, and to Billy Schroeder, president of Schroeder Publishing, for backing this somewhat old-fashioned field guide, and to Karen Smith for the design and layout that does so much toward making this type of book easy to read and use.

Finally, I would like to thank my dear wife, Evelyn, for her support and patience during the many years of writing, and rewriting, that went into this book. For hours on end all she saw of her husband was the back of this head as he slaved away at the computer, an experience shared, I'm sure, by many others whose spouses have been captured by the computer, or worse yet, by the Internet.

# Introduction

*"...we may gather together souvenirs of the olden days that
lie so far away under a softening haze of happy illusion."*
— Henry Hammond Taylor

This small book is a primer on collecting early American furniture, whether the reader is starting from scratch or improving upon an existing family collection. It provides some essential background, suggests where and how to start, what to watch out for; then covers the styles and types of old furniture one is most likely to encounter in the marketplace. For those fortunate to obtain some old furniture through gift or inheritance, it will aid in understanding just what has come into the home, how old it is, which are the better pieces, and perhaps, where the pieces may have been made.

Among the many books on antique furniture, this field guide is unusual in that it is not written by a professional, that is, not by a fine arts auctioneer, an antiques dealer, or a specialist in period furniture; but by what the trade would consider to be an amateur — the collector — and a very average collector at that. As such, it reflects the viewpoint and the experience of most collectors. It is also unusual in that while covering American furniture, it includes some English and Continental products, principally mirrors, that are often found on the market. In a survey for the beginner there is no purpose in omitting Americana that you will see all the time simply because it started life on the other side of the Atlantic.

The many figures illustrate the more common furniture made in America between the last quarter of the 17th century and the first quarter of the 19th century; the pieces you are most likely to see at the better dealers, shows, and auctions. For both completeness and historical importance, I've also included some unusual pieces, but here I've been careful to indicate they are either uncommon or rare, for we need to know not only what was produced during this time, but more importantly, what we might expect to find in the marketplace.

The small pen and ink drawings not only provide convenient nesting of the illustrations among the text, but also best show the elements of style and form without distracting the eye with the details of the particular example, one that otherwise might be very similar to an example seen by the reader. Books on old furniture generally illustrate the very finest in each form, and while this laudably shows the subject to best effect, it is likely to confuse and discourage the average collector who seldom sees such pieces except in museums, and in any event, could not begin to afford them should they come on the market.

When beginning, you may be perplexed by old furniture. There will be things you have never seen before, not only because old furniture is different from modern, but because long years of production have seen a diversity of types and styles, some no longer in use, or even applicable to today's home. Here even reference books may not be much help. You will see something at a show or auction, then search in vain to find a similar example among the books in your local library. After a while, though, you will not only build a mental file of what you have seen, but will come to know what to expect in old furniture. You will also come to rely on indications of age and wear, construction methods and style, in determining what is genuinely old and what is not. Be patient, and that day will come when you just look at a piece of furniture across a room and it will say to you, "period" or "reproduction," "Boston" or "Philadelphia." With more experience it may even say "Lancaster County" or "North Shore."

Before getting started, we need to know what is meant by the word period as it is used to describe old furniture, for understanding the use of this term is fundamental to understanding our subject. As the word implies, it simply refers to the time or period in which an object was made. For example, furniture made in the time of Thomas Chippendale was made in that period, and is spoken of as being "of the period," or more simply, "period." A chair made in the Chippendale style in the 1750s would then be a "Chippendale period chair" or a "chair of the Chippendale period," although in practice, such chairs are often simply identified as "Chippendale."

However, successful styles are very long lived, often being revived many years after initially going out of fashion. This leads to an important distinction, as well as to an endemic problem in collecting period furniture, for fine chairs in the Chippendale style were being made right up through the following century. Such a chair, dating from perhaps the 1880s, would now be very much antique, but would not be of the Chippendale period, which ended a century earlier. It would be an antique chair in the Chippendale style, or a "Chippendale style" chair. This later production is commonly identified as either "Colonial

# Introduction

Revival," or "second period," or "Centennial" furniture. Similarly, there is also Queen Anne style, Hepplewhite style, and Sheraton style furniture. Further on, we will discuss period and style in more detail, as it has an important bearing on the availability, quality, and price of old furniture.

Period furniture is usually identified as being antique furniture, but here we need to be careful, for while period furniture is indeed antique furniture, not all antique furniture is period. When the United States Customs Office adopted the 100 year rule in 1930, a cut-off date of 1830 coincided approximately with the last of the classic furniture periods. Antique furniture was indeed period furniture. Now, however, we are on the edge of the second millennium, and the 100 year rule will include most of the Victorian era, and while such furniture has indeed become antique, it would not be considered period unless we were to group the many eclectic revivals of this time into their own period. In practice, antique dealers and auction houses often treat Victorian furniture as a separate category apart from period furniture. Dealers tend to specialize in either one or the other, and the larger auction firms hold separate auctions for each.

To the serious collector, though, the primary determinate is not so much age or period, but that period furniture was created before the advent of the factory system by craftsmen using only hand tools, starting with no more than the rough boards from the mill or sawyer. Far more than any particular time or style, and far more than even age, this is what gives period furniture its unique character and value. After the 1830s the introduction of power tools for planing, mortising, and dovetailing largely replaced handcraftsmanship, and although fine work continued to be done on the best grades of furniture, the average piece now becomes far more the product of the factory and the machine. With the demise of the cabinetmaker's trade, furniture loses much of its individuality and charm. It also loses most of its appeal to the collector. If this definition sounds arbitrary and disqualifies your grandmother's Victorian marble top table, I ask you to be patient. With some looking, and hopefully, a little collecting, you will soon come to appreciate the difference between handwork and machine work, between the product of the shop and the product of the factory.

In every book on antiques there is the question of what names to use, for terms have changed a great deal in the past 200 years. What we now call candlestands, highboys, and sewing tables were then called snap stands, high chests of drawers, and work tables. At the risk of appearing ignorant among my peers, I've chosen to use the popular terms, for this is a book for the beginner. Later, when we get to specific furniture types, we'll cover the old, and perhaps more "proper" names.

Also, authors differ as to whether the names of styles, notably Baroque and Rococo, should or should not be capitalized. At some risk of seeming old-fashioned, I have chosen the former, not only to bring these important terms to the reader's attention, but also in memory of a time in which writers, lacking the computer's boldface and italics, as well as our more rigid rules of grammar, capitalized every word requiring the least emphasis. The Declaration of Independence contains literally hundreds of capitalized words.

Little mention is made of monetary values in this book, although I would be the first to admit that initial cost and the hope for subsequent gain is a major factor in all collecting. Then why not some prices? Well, first off, the price of art varies widely with time and fashion, and nothing will make a book obsolete so fast as quoting current prices. Secondly, cost is a very poor guide in collecting early furniture. Unlike coins and dolls, which were mass produced and have a great many almost identical examples, there is too much diversity in old hand-made furniture, much of which has seen some repair and restoration, to quote more than a very wide range of values. Even the price of standard forms can easily vary by several orders of magnitude. Within the past few years, Queen Anne dining room tables have sold at auction for less than $3,000, and for over $145,000, and only a large color photograph would give some indication of the significant differences between these two examples. As with the other arts, the feel for market value is something that comes only with time and experience. In addition, it should be emphasized that cost, while unquestionably a major determinate, should be one of the lessor factors affecting purchase, for it can lead the mind away from far more important criteria. This book then, is not a price guide.

You will find that building a furniture collection is a long-time activity. The decision to purchase is made when the desired quality does not exceed the available funds on something that can be used in the home, and this is not apt to be often. However, you will also find that collecting tends to become a wonderful lifelong interest, and while perhaps slacking during the summer months, picks up again when the nights get cool, the leaves begin to turn, and there is a smell of wood smoke in the air. Not too surprisingly, this is when many auctions are scheduled.

While some acquire old furniture in the course of generations of family ownership, collecting remains a very democratic activity — open to anyone with the interest, the time, and a little extra income. That a fortunate few grow up among old things should in no way discourage the absolute novice. Many, indeed the majority, of fine collections are started from scratch, often by something as innocuous as wandering into a shop to shelter from a passing shower. Nor should collecting be limited to Americans of long standing, for we are a nation of immigrants. Not only have some notable collectors and dealers been first generation Americans, but among our most famous cabinetmakers there are a number that learned their trade abroad, in England, in Scotland, and in France. As we will discuss at the end, in the long run none of us are as much collectors as we are stewards, and with some reading and care, you can be as good a steward as any.

Collecting period furniture is in many ways a very private avocation. Only dealers, curators, and fellow collectors really understand the time and money you are willing to invest in something old and worn when the new and perfect could be had for so much less. Most of your friends will know little about old furniture, even though they may think your acquisitions are very pretty. To add insult, your children may think it funny old stuff and wonder why the money could not be spent on something important, like a new car, or at least a large screen TV. In recompense, I can only suggest your efforts will be rewarded by the beauty you bring into your home, by a modest pride that you are doing things a bit differently than others, and by the knowledge that you are, in some small way, maintaining and protecting your children's legacy.

Finally, most books on antiques contain occasional factual errors, and I'm sure that this small volume will not be the exception. Most of what I write of has been confirmed by experience, but I'm sure that a few errors will have crept in. In advance then, I apologize for any errors in fact or omission, and hope they will not lead the reader into other errors of his or her own.

Cummaquid, Massachusetts, 1998

# Chapter 1

## The Furniture Trade

We will start with a look at the furniture trade, for all the arts, whether painting, or music, or literature, are better understood and appreciated if there is some knowledge of the period that produced them. In a like manner, knowing something of the life and times of the turner, the joiner, and the cabinetmaker is important to our understanding of period furniture, perhaps all the more so in that the decorative arts have a very practical aspect not found in the other arts. Here we will discover that many of the unique and the distinctive characteristics of old furniture are normal outgrowths of the economy and the technology of the period, and are, in fact, logical and reasonable in light of the times.

Aside from what has been gleaned from surviving account or day books, court records, and newspaper advertisements, remarkably little is left to tell us about the many thousands of men and boys that worked in the furniture trades. There are only a handful of pictures that even show us their appearance, and most of these postdate the American Revolution when simple portraiture of all kinds became fairly common. In truth, cabinetmaking was little different from the many other trades of the period, and even successful cabinetmakers were not in the class of merchants, doctors, judges, and generals. As one writer so aptly put it, they were below the level of historical scrutiny.

It is fashionable now to view the cabinetmaker as an artist, and indeed, it is easy to think this when we see the best of Boston, Philadelphia, and Newport high style furniture that graces so many important collections. These indeed appear to be works of art, particularly when viewed in a museum setting. They are, however, a small minority among period furniture, and it is a mistake if these few lead us to somehow separate cabinetmaking from the many other 18th century trades, for cabinetmakers should not be seen as something unique apart from the general run of their period and society. This distorts both our view of their lives and their very real contribution to our civilization. Cabinetmaking was just one of many crafts that could produce, in the right hands, and under favorable circumstances, a high quality of design and workmanship. The best craftsmen had an eye for proportion, were skilled in their craft, and were aided by a long and rich tradition. It is very doubtful that they were seen as artists. In a time when handwork was the norm in so much of life, and many artists were employed in simple portrait, sign, and coach painting, there was perhaps less distinction than now between artisan and artist, particularly in America where there was less specialization than in Europe, and where many, such as Paul Revere, worked in a variety of trades. As John Singleton Copley lamented, "the people generally regard [painting] no more than other useful trade...like that of a carpenter, tailor, or shoemaker, not as one of the most noble arts of the world...."

When considering antiques, we should also remember that the present tends to simplify and idealize the past. There is always a golden age. With this comes a belief in and yearning for a time of simplicity and certainty in our daily life that probably never existed, and the appeal of early furniture is a part of this. When viewing a grand collection, it is easy to imagine that this was a better time and that everything looked this way. Sadly, this is not so. Houses then as now had their share of bric-a-brac and cheap furniture, but we do not see this now because time has swept most all this dross away.

Woodworking is an ancient trade. Although Joseph of Nazareth may first come to mind, carpentry, and to some limited extent, cabinetmaking, were well established crafts by the time of the Egyptians. Tombs from this period have yielded beautifully made gilded furniture with neatly made dovetail and mortise-and-tenon joints. The Romans were experienced in both veneering and joinery. The writer Pliny noted that paneled doors could be had in "Greek, Campanian, or Sicilian styles." In England, where there was ample wood and much timber construction, carpentry, carving, and turning were common trades by the late middle ages. From house carpentry developed the trade of joiner who "joined" wood with mortise-and-tenon joints to form the handsome oak paneling we see in Elizabethan buildings. The early paneled chests and wainscot chairs are much the same construction applied to furniture.

The joiner, or joyner as it was then spelled, made case furniture by mounting thin panels in grooves between vertical stiles and horizontal rails. This provided a relatively light, strong construction that compensated for the expansion of wood and permitted making large furniture from the somewhat narrow split or rived oak planks. Paneled construction required additional tools and skills, and the joiner's work developed into a separate craft from carpentry. The difference in the crafts is very evident when we compare the relatively simple products of the carpenter with the beautifully made chests of the joiner. From this early period have come the surnames of Carpenter, Joiner, Turner, and Sawyer, as well as those from other trades — Wheelwright, Cartwright, and Smith.

During the second half of the 17th century a new method of building case furniture was introduced from the Continent that eliminated the need for paneling and provided wide flat surfaces for decoration. Boards were edge glued together to form panels which were then joined at the ends with dovetails to produce a large open box which was then fitted with drawers set between spacers or blades. This was the beginning of modern furniture, and almost to this day is the way furniture is made. Until wide boards of mahogany were available, the sides and top of the case, as well as the drawer fronts, were made up of oak or pine and then veneered in walnut or other cabinet woods. This new construction required new techniques in gluing, veneering, and joining, and gave rise to a new craft, that of the cabinetmaker.

The transition to cabinetmaking spread slowly from the major urban centers, and in rural areas cabinetmakers usually engaged in joinery and carpentry to supplement their income. In America until 1725, or thereabouts, furniture was still made by turners and joiners rather than by chairmakers and cabinetmakers, and even after cabinetmaking replaced joinery in the urban centers, turning continued to be a separate trade. The well known William Savory of Philadelphia listed himself as a joiner as late as 1760. Late in the century Duncan Fife, joiner, arrived from Scotland and settled in Albany. A few years later he moved down the Hudson to growing New York City and set up shop as Duncan Phyfe, cabinetmaker.

The furniture trades in America followed the European three level guild system of apprentice, journeyman, and master. Boys would be apprenticed in their early teens, once they had learned to read and write and do some arithmetic. In return for essentially free labor, the apprentice received room, board, and training in the craft. The quality of all three probably varied widely, but must have been reasonably good in

America as labor was scarce and there was little to keep a young man from moving on if poorly treated. Newspapers of this period carry advertisements for runaway apprentices, offering rewards for their return, but they may not have been very effective. America was a big country and work was available everywhere.

The contract with the master included a provision that the apprentice be taught the "mysteries" of the craft. As you learn more about period furniture, and perhaps undertake some repair or restoration, you'll realize that these mysteries must have been the techniques involved in leveling boards, laying out joints, putting down veneer, and applying finishes; and the dozens of little shortcuts that let the work come along quickly and easily. Hundreds of years later, subtle reminders of these mysteries still remain to the discerning eye. They are a part of the charm of old furniture.

After an apprenticeship, which was nominally for seven years, but which seems to have become less in America as the 18th century drew to a close, a qualified apprentice would graduate to journeyman. The journeyman was skilled in all aspects of his craft, equal to the master except for the lack of his own shop. For the average journeyman, the step up to master was not easy. One would have to obtain a shop, additional tools, workmen, and then customers. To get started, journeymen often formed short term partnerships, which were dissolved when the business permitted, each partner then advertising for an apprentice. Another approach, still a common road to advancement, was to marry into the master's family. Sometimes the necessary capital would be provided by a patron or sponsor, who presumably would be paid back, with interest, when the new business was established. Many cabinetmakers probably remained journeymen all their lives. Some undoubtedly preferred to remain in this simpler and perhaps more secure position. In addition, larger shops almost certainly had openings for a foreman or a senior journeyman to tend to the details of running the shop while the owner concentrated on new business.

In time some masters rose to the economic and social level of merchants, buying wholesale from other cabinetmakers, selling through showrooms, and shipping furniture up and down the coast to other merchants. The Philadelphia cabinetmaker William Savory appears to have been one of these, which may be one reason why a number of his chairs are labeled.

---

To any who have labored for weeks over a project at home, the rate in which furniture was produced with nothing but muscle power and hand tools may be surprising. It is all the more impressive when we remember that the cabinetmaker started with just the rough boards from the mill. For example, a Pembroke table required three and a half days to make, a chest of drawers five days, a simple lowboy six days, and a flat top highboy about thirteen days. One of the lovely Boston blockfront chests of drawers took about three weeks, and cost $70. These times are, of course, for one craftsman to do the whole job. However, even in small shops the work was divided up among the workmen. The neat dovetail drawer joints we so admire were done by an experienced apprentice, who could do perhaps 12 drawers a day — a dovetail joint in 15 minutes, a drawer in an hour! Where now we carefully lay out each dovetail, he would simply scribe the depth and then cut the dovetails by eye, perhaps using a little template on the wider joints.

To save time, patterns of thin wood and paper were used in every shop. A chairmaker would have bundles of chair patterns hanging from nails in the overhead beams. There would be a pattern for the stiles and rear legs, the front legs, the crest rail, the splat, and perhaps the seat rails if they were shaped. A blockfront chest of drawers typically used three patterns: one for the blocking, one for the top, and one for the legs. Nothing was ever laid out if a pattern would do. A turner's shop, then called a turnery, would have a number of marking gauges consisting of battens with nails driven through to project out the other side. After working the billet down to a round, the turner would force the gauge against the rotating stock to indicate the location of cuts. Calipers were only used to fix the diameter of the ends of legs and the tenoned ends of stretchers. Everything else was turned by eye once the cuts had been located, a practice that can lead to an enchanting asymmetry in old turnings.

The spur to these shortcuts was that income was directly proportional to production. The more a craftsman could produce, the greater the income. This made for remarkable economy of effort. Furniture of all sorts was efficiently produced in shops we would consider tiny and miserably equipped. As we will see later, a salient characteristic of old furniture is that nothing unessential was ever done, even on the grandest pieces. Time spent doing something unnecessary just reduced income.

From long experience, cabinetmakers and chairmakers acquired a wonderful knowledge of the types and characteristics of wood and how to turn each variety to best advantage. A Windsor chair would be made of four or five different kinds of wood, each chosen for a particular set of characteristics and each at a different level of seasoning. Chair legs were commonly turned green and then fitted with seasoned stretchers so the joint would tighten as the leg seasoned. They are almost stronger now than when new. Later, when we get into the construction of old furniture, we'll see more examples of the way in which design was tailored to the always present expansion and contraction of the wood.

Veneering, now often associated with cheap furniture, was then a sign of superior craftsmanship and quality work. The veneer was normally applied to well seasoned pine, which was found to hold glue well. The base or ground had to be absolutely fair if the veneered surface was to be smooth, for any little dips or ridges would show through the finished surface as the glue dried and pulled the veneer down. Large sheets of cross-grained veneer were dampened to make them flat and supple, the hot glue spread on the warmed ground, the veneer applied, and all excess glue squeezed out before the glue had a chance to cool and set — a difficult task routinely done so well that much veneered furniture is still in good condition hundreds of years later.

Repair work typically accounted for a third to a half of the cabinetmaker's business. Furniture was relatively more expensive than now, and was returned to the local cabinetmaker for repairing and refinishing. Being fastened by pins and water-soluble glues, it was not difficult to take apart, and most finishes were simple and easily touched up. There is some evidence that case pieces were also returned for upgrading, being cleaned up and given "modern" brasses; for it is not uncommon to find chests of drawers with replaced brasses that are also very much period. Although the dedicated collector dislikes repairs, it is likely that many of the repairs now found in old furniture may in themselves be quite early.

Surviving account books show that rural cabinetmakers did a lot of outside work, apparently because small towns could not provide enough work to support a full time cabinetmaker. In addition to farming, they built corner cupboards and made moldings, windows, and doors, work now done by a finish carpenter. They also made a great many coffins, which makes sense when we consider that cabinetmakers are first and foremost skilled woodworkers.

When we think of old time cabinetmaking, we all tend to visualize the craftsmen at work cutting dovetails, or perhaps fitting tenons into mortises, but by far the most common labor, and by far the most tiresome, would have been the planing required to level down planks and work up moldings. In a time of standardized, dressed lumber, it is easy to forget that the cabinetmaker, if not actually cutting planks in his own shop, started with no more than the rough stock from the mill, which had to be planed and scraped to an acceptably level surface before any measuring or cutting. While secondary surfaces could be left somewhat rough, primary surfaces had to be very level indeed, particularly the tops of chests of drawers and tables which would show the slightest irregularity. Similarly, the stock for moldings had to be carefully leveled and squared before cutting the molding. While small moldings were then easily cut, thick moldings required much more effort, and large molding planes were often handled with the aid of a rope passed through the front stock, one man pushing the plane, and another, perhaps an apprentice, pulling on the rope. Both leveling stock and working out heavy moldings required a fair amount of muscle, particularly in the arms and shoulders, which is perhaps why cabinetmaking always seems to have been an exclusively male trade. Other trades requiring less effort, such as weaving, were followed by both men and women.

In this time the average shop, even in urban areas, was quite small. The Dominy establishment on Long Island, now carefully reassembled at Winterthur, is about 14 feet wide and 22 feet long. The shop of Christopher Townsend, home to some of the loveliest furniture ever made in this country, was a single 12 by 24 foot room. Normally benches would have been placed by the windows with the workman's tool boxes tucked underneath. Journeymen provided many of their own tools, which were kept in large dovetailed boxes. The master would have his own set of tools, and in addition, special purpose items such as the bigger saws and extra molding planes. Across one end of the shop there would be a fireplace or stove, not just for warmth and to drive off the damp, but also to heat the hide glue; and if a shop did veneering, to heat both the cauls used to hold down the veneer and the ground on which the veneer was laid.

---

The cabinetmaker's tools are notable both in their apparent simplicity and in their remarkable antiquity. However, for all their simplicity and age, they are specialized and quite sophisticated, and as any tool collector will tell you, very neatly made.

The hand saw dates from the Bronze Age, although it was not discovered until about the time of the Romans that setting teeth alternately left and right would make the kerf slightly wider than the blade and permit saws that cut when pushed rather than pulled. By early in the 18th century saws had developed into their modern form, and do not differ significantly from what are found today in any hardware store. The most common types employed by cabinetmakers were the panel, the bow, the keyhole and the backed saws shown in Figure 1-1. Panel saws, developed by the Dutch in the 17th century, were only used for rough cuts. As now, they were of two basic types, one with fine teeth for cross cuts and the other with large coarse teeth for ripping boards lengthwise.

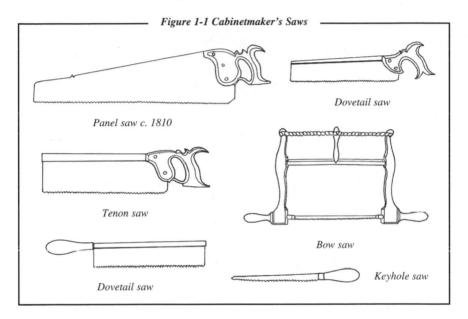

*Figure 1-1 Cabinetmaker's Saws*

Panel saw c. 1810

Dovetail saw

Tenon saw

Bow saw

Dovetail saw

Keyhole saw

The thin, accurate cuts required in cabinetmaking were made with back saws. Originally called backed saws, these have a thin steel blade stiffened with a brass or steel spline across the top of the blade. First developed by the Romans, these fine saws are indispensable for cabinet work. There were two basic types, a larger saw for cross cuts and tenons, and a very fine little saw with an open handle for cutting dovetails. A cabinetmaker would typically have a half dozen or so with different teeth for different jobs. A specialized version had the handle offset from the blade and no set to the teeth. It was used for cutting off mortise pins flush with the surrounding wood.

The plane was also an early development. The Romans used a variety of smoothing, jack, and molding planes, some with iron soles not too unlike a modern plane. The many planes used by the 18th century cabinetmaker fall into three general categories: those used for smoothing down surfaces, those used for shaping moldings, and those used for cutting tongues, grooves, and rabbets. Collectively, they are quite the most pretty and interesting of the cabinetmaker's tools, and are the most sought by the collector of old tools.

**13**

Planes for cutting down and smoothing wood are called bench planes. Rough stock from the mill was first taken down to the desired thickness with the jack or fore plane. Generally about 15" long, the fore plane was given a convex blade with a considerable crown, which allowed quick and easy leveling in a series of shallow scoops. If the board were to be used in an out of the way spot such as the back of a chest, this is all that was done. However, if a smooth surface was desired, the cabinetmaker would then use a try or trying plane to take out the marks left by the jack plane. This was a large plane, perhaps 22" long, with a wide body and a very slight crown to the blade. With a series of shallow cuts the cabinetmaker would "try the surface" until acceptably level, or if a primary surface, good enough that a steel scraper could then be used to finish up the job. When working in small areas or with a difficult grain such as tiger maple, the craftsman would use a small boat shaped smoothing plane which was kept very sharp and set to a very fine cut. Sometimes difficult cross grains would be taken down with a toothing plane followed by careful scraping. This odd looking plane had a toothed blade set vertically in the stock, and was normally used to rough up surfaces prior to veneering. When boards were to be joined edge to edge, it was necessary to make the sides perfectly level and straight. For this work a long (26") jointer would be used to get the edges absolutely true. The modern power tool which performs this function is still called a jointer.

Of molding planes there were a legion, for a different plane was required for each different shape of molding. Even the least of cabinetmakers would have a couple of dozen in his kit. The most common were the shaping planes, either rounds or hollows, which were used to work up simple curves. These were normally sold in sets of in ¼" increments in radius. For more detailed shapes individual planes were used in which the reverse of the desired shape was worked into the blade and sole. Because a molding plane can only make one shape, even a small shop needed a host of such planes. When working up a complex molding, the cabinetmaker would first remove as much wood as possible with saws and bench planes before going to the molding plane, for they were difficult to sharpen.

Planes for cutting rabbets can be identified by the open body that lets the blade come right to the side of the plane. When cutting a rabbet across the grain the blade must be at an angle to avoid breaking out the wood, hence we have planes called skewed rabbets. Because these joints vary in both width and depth, a rabbeting plane was developed that had both an adjustable fence to determine the width of the rabbet and an adjustable depth gauge to limit the depth of the cut. In addition, there were all sorts of special planes employed for mitre joints, for tongue and groove joints, for panel fielding, and the like. It is little wonder that so many old planes are found in antique shops.

Cabinetmakers employed a variety of drills, the more common of which are shown in Figure 1-3. The only type no longer seen in hardware stores is the spoon bit, which looks something like an old fashioned marrow scoop with a sharp end. Although not an easy tool to work with, it was used right up into the 19th century. Later, when we get to the identification of old furniture, we'll touch on the very characteristic round bottom hole left by this drill. The center bit, which was developed in the 16th century, has experienced a renaissance as a wood bit for high speed electric drills. The modern twist bit with cutting scribers and a screw point is technically called a Scotch bit.

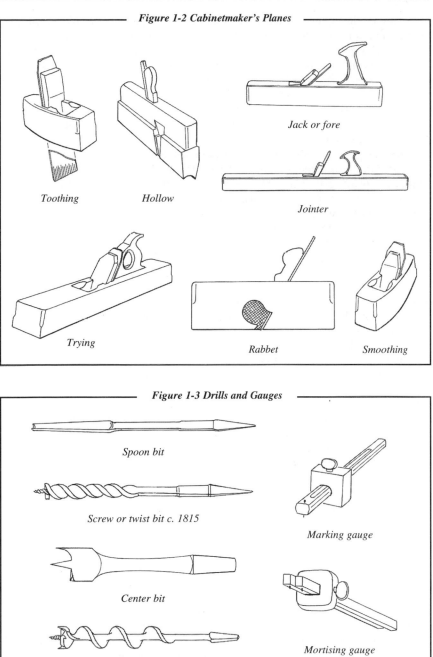

**Figure 1-2 Cabinetmaker's Planes**

Toothing

Hollow

Jack or fore

Jointer

Trying

Rabbet

Smoothing

**Figure 1-3 Drills and Gauges**

Spoon bit

Screw or twist bit c. 1815

Center bit

Modern Scotch bit

Marking gauge

Mortising gauge

In common with other cabinetmaker's tools, it also is not all that modern, having appeared in the first decades of the 19th century.

In addition to all these cutting tools, there were a number of measuring and scribing tools, of which the most handsome are the wooden marking gauges, squares, and mortising gauges. The mortising gauge was similar to the marking gauge except that it had two adjustable staves, allowing both sides of a mortise to be marked at once. A cabinetmaker might have a number of gauges, each set up for a different scribe line, so that the gauges would not have to be reset, and the same lines would always be identical on a job.

Lastly, it might be mentioned that factory-made sandpaper did not arrive until the 1870s. When the cabinetmaker needed a smooth surface, he first planed it as evenly as possible with a sharp plane adjusted to a very fine set. Then any remaining ridges were taken down with a steel scraper, and finally a little sanding might be done with dried sharkskin. Sandpaper as we know it was not introduced until about the turn of the 18th century, and then was made up in the shop using heavy paper, glue, and fine sand. However, with really sharp tools and careful fitting, there was little need for much sanding.

---

From quite early on, furniture making developed into a major Colonial industry. There was an abundance of good timber, much falling water to power sawmills, and a long, deeply indented coast that made it easy to move goods among settled areas. With the exception of easily shipped specialty items such as caned chairs, clock works, barometers, and looking glasses, American-made furniture predominated in the Middle Atlantic and New England colonies. It was both cheaper and better endured the vicissitudes of our climate. The industry in this period was largely urban. Not until the 19th century did manufacturing move inland along the rivers where falling water provided the power for early factory production.

Within a hundred years of the first New England settlement, Boston was a thriving cabinet and chair making center. Leather seated side chairs were sold all up and down the coast and as far south as the Caribbean. Newport exported plain desks and tables in large quantities; simpler versions of the grand pieces we now associate with this small city. By 1740, Philadelphia chair making was flowering, and 20 years later so many Windsors were being exported that they were simply known as "Philadelphia chairs." Generally, these businesses were very small. The largest shop in New England had only seven benches.

These little shops employed a surprising number of cabinetmakers when we consider the small size of Colonial cities. Just prior to the Revolution there were about 150 cabinetmakers working in Boston, 50 active in Newport, 100 in New York, and 70 in Charleston. Philadelphia, which was then a city of 35,000, must of supported several hundred. It was the second biggest city in the British Empire.

There was a great deal more specialization in the furniture trades than is generally realized. When considering old furniture one thinks of cabinetmakers and chairmakers, but there were also clock case makers, looking glass makers, barometer makers,

Windsor chair makers and box makers; and to support them turners, carvers, gilders, upholsterers, polishers, and inlay makers. Production was often divided up between several trades. The popular Philadelphia claw-and-ball tea tables seem to have been the work of carvers who did the carving on the legs, turners who turned the columns, and cabinetmakers who made the tops and assembled the final table. If the customer requested a dished top, this skilled turning job might also have been sent out, as would a carved "pie crust" top.

Supporting these trades were merchants who imported tools, fabric, hardware, and fine cabinet woods. By 1800, cabinetmakers could buy cabinet woods from a "mahogany yard." In both England and on the Continent there was widespread manufacture of saws and planes; the forerunner of the modern machine tool industry. Upholstery material was very expensive prior to the introduction of mechanized weaving, and upholstering was solely an urban trade, the upholsterer actually commanding a higher wage than the cabinetmaker. Wing chairs would be purchased as a bare frame from the cabinetmaker and then completed by the upholsterer. Rural chairs, if not given rush seats, tend to have drop seats where the simple upholstering could be done by the chairmaker.

One of the more interesting specialties was that of inlay maker, who made both inlays and the associated holly and ebony stringing that was so popular during the Hepplewhite period. Inlays appear to have been both imported and made locally. Production here was also greater than one would think. The estate of Thomas Barrett of Baltimore listed hundreds of fans and shells at 7 to 25 cents each. Inlays from this period are beautifully made, with lovely fitting, shading, and coloring. When you examine old furniture, you will find that it is easy to tell the work of the professional inlay maker from that of the rural cabinetmaker who had to make do on his own. It is also easy to tell the modern reproduction after one has seen a few of the original. Because certain inlay patterns were popular in certain areas, and because an inlay maker dealt with many local cabinetmakers, it is sometimes possible to tell the source of a piece of furniture from the inlay.

To a considerable extent, marketing seems to have been not too different from the way we now purchase upholstered furniture, wherein one selects the style and the fabric, then waits for the order to be filled. Then as now, there must have been vexatious delays, for advertisements invariably included a statement to the effect that all orders would be "attended to promptly." Until the advent of warehouses and warerooms in the years following the Revolution, there was far less to show the customer, but this may not have been a problem in a time when there were only a few styles and successful designs were copied by just about everybody. An order for "six crooked-back chairs in black leather" or a "walnut chest of four drawers" might have provided quite enough description, all the more so if the customer was familiar with the cabinetmaker's work.

In addition, much furniture was produced on speculation when business was slack, for records not only indicate that it was made up for wholesale to other cabinetmakers or merchants, but advertisements for going out of business invariably identify for sale, not just the benches and the tools, but also a stock of furniture "at very favorable prices." In either event, the whole system by which furniture was made up to order, or to speculation, seems to have led to care in design and proportion, characteristics now much admired by collectors. It is an error to conclude that people then had unusually good taste; economic and market conditions may have simply favored good looking, well built furniture.

While the actual marketing is not clear, we do know that most furniture was made up from standard patterns, and that only special commissions were done to a different design, perhaps one selected from the design books by Chippendale, Hepplewhite, or Sheraton. Price books indicate that a standard design could be ordered with a wide variety of embellishments; tables with and without inlay, chairs in walnut or mahogany, with cabriole or straight legs, and with or without carving. Furniture made up for stock or speculation would have no more than perhaps a little stringing, and a minimum of carving, and that to a large measure the very fine work we now see in museums represent special orders from well-to-do clients. This suggests that much of the average grade of period furniture was nothing special at the time, and in fact, may not even have been the product of a specific order, particularly with the advent of warehouses and warerooms in the early years of the 19th century. However, this does not seem to have affected the quality of the workmanship, for you will find that the simpler furniture, although lacking inlay and carving, is generally well proportioned and well made.

Because furniture was often made up to order, one sometimes sees charming little individual features that must have been requested by the owner. In addition to some unusually small furniture that may have been made up to accommodate a diminutive person, or perhaps a narrow room, or a low ceiling, there are blockfronts in which each "block" forms a separate drawer, chests of drawers in which the bottom drawer is inexplicably split into several smaller drawers, and desks that have neither pigeonholes, nor prospect doors, nor document drawers, just four tiers of little drawers.

Brasses were imported and expensive, and there are a significant number of old blanket chests, high chests, and chests of drawers that have never had them. The intention may have been to fit brasses later as funds became available, for turned wooden knobs could have been had for little extra cost. To save money, furniture might also be purchased unfinished, or "in the white." The owner could then either paint it, perhaps with a homemade milk based paint; or brew up some stain in an old cooking pot, then finish the job off with several coats of wax.

Most sales, both rural and urban, were very local. The population was small, and there was little need for signatures or labels. Anyone could ask for the name of the cabinetmaker. Where one finds labels or brands, it is generally on products like Windsor chairs and Federal mirrors that were distributed over a wide area.

Unfortunately, the age of the cabinetmaker was not to last forever. By the turn of the 18th century, during the Federal Period in America and toward the close of the long and troubled life of George III in England, the age of the craftsman was drawing to a close. In cities, cabinetmakers' shops were growing larger and the tasks becoming increasingly specialized. With the change from a master with a few journeymen and apprentices to a manufacturer with many workers, there was less opportunity for a journeyman to own his own business. Indeed, the demand for journeymen themselves decreased as work was subdivided into simple repetitive tasks that a grown boy could be trained to do at far less cost. This was a period of labor unrest, of strikes among journeymen, and of price books that attempted, in great detail, to fix the prices of various types of furniture. Although probably not very successful, these books have provided scholars with a wonderful insight into the furniture trades.

This change first took place in the manufacture of turned chairs where identical parts lend themselves to mass production. They were already being made by the thousands in small shops. However, the early years of the 19th century saw something new, the development of small factories using water power to manufacture chairs. This first occurred in the production of Windsors, but was rapidly followed by Hitchcock type chairs. Within a few years the use of power saws, planers, and routers spread mass production to other forms of furniture, and the age of the cabinetmaker began to draw to a close. Although much handwork continued to be done on the finer pieces, most of the industry shifted from skilled craftsmanship in small shops to simple assembly operations in a factory, or a manufactory as they were called then. Industrialization was particularly rapid in America where there was a chronic a shortage of skilled labor. In England, where there was ample skilled labor, the furniture trades were slower to industrialize and much handwork continued to be done right up into the 20th century.

Perhaps the last to go were rural cabinetmakers, who may have been ruined not so much by the introduction of power equipment and production techniques as by the spread of railroads, which, for the first time provided rapid and economical land transportation. Even in Colonial times the urban shop with its greater specialization and production volume could make furniture at less cost. Now, however, this inexpensive furniture could be shipped anywhere, and the small town cabinetmaker had to find another trade; carpentry, farming, and in some cases, mortician. They were already making coffins.

# Chapter 2
## Understanding Period and Style

Because furniture was made at different times in different styles, and is primarily identified this way, we need to know something about period and style. The next chapter will also touch on period, but only as it applies to quality. Here, though, we will discuss period and style in American and English furniture as an historical and a technological narrative from the time of the Pilgrims until the introduction of factory production in the first half of the 19th century. Although our subject is American furniture, American and English styles are so intertwined that we cannot, and should not, discuss one without the other. This is a big subject for just one short chapter, so we will only touch on the highlights, the more common stylistic features you are likely to see in shops and at auctions. Even so, 300 years is a long time, so do not feel inadequate if at first it is confusing. If you wish, read this chapter in sections, going on to other topics should you tire or begin to lose track of events and styles. Remember though, to come back later, for a real understanding of period and style is very necessary to successful collecting.

Period is just the time in which a style was popular. Normally, periods are identified by the reign of a king or a queen or by an historical period. Therefore, we have Elizabethan, Jacobean, William and Mary, Queen Anne, and four king George's in England;

and Pilgrim Century, Colonial, and Federal in America. English and American periods do not coincide. For example, the long reign of George III covers the last half of the Colonial period in America and much of the following Federal period. In addition, commencing about the middle of the 18th century, furniture periods are also identified by the names of cabinetmakers, architects, and writers who publicized different styles. Thus, we have Adam, Chippendale, Hepplewhite, and Sheraton styles. These also tend to overlap reigns and historical periods. To simplify all this, some scholars now prefer to identify the major periods by their characteristic style as being either Baroque, Rococo, or Neoclassical, with further divisions into early and late, and the use of additional terms such as Greco-Roman Revival. However, this is of little help to the beginner collector, for not only do dealers and auctioneers not use these terms, but styles in art and architecture do not translate easily into domestic furnishings, and you will find no more than a suggestion of Baroque or Rococo among the average grade of American furniture.

To help put this in prospective, we might employ a time line (2-1) to show when American furniture periods started and ended, or more correctly, tapered off, for while styles have reasonably clear beginnings, they tend to close out in an indeterminate fashion. Much of the best work of a period, exhibiting an exuberance, a naturalness, and a certain charming naiveté, is produced early in the period. Thereafter, the style tends to loose boldness and becomes lighter and simpler, finally tapering off in simple rural survival pieces. You will notice in this figure that styles are a great deal more long-lived than some dealers would like to admit. The old jingle that: "American Revolution fought and won; The style of Chippendale is done" is only true in a limited sense. While the Rococo of Thomas Chippendale was out of fashion after the Revolution, a great deal of work continued to be done in this style, some of it for very well off clients. We will see later that the popular New England oxbow-front desks and chests of drawers, which are Chip-

**Figure 2-1 American Furniture Periods**

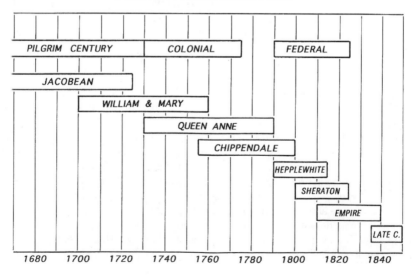

pendale in style, almost always postdate the Revolution. Because stylistic lag is common among early American furniture, the time line endeavors to illustrate not just when a style was in fashion, but rather, the extent of significant work in that style. Even here though, some elements of a style will continue to appear long afterward. For instance, among the illustrations of turned chairs in Chapter 9 you will see that the Spanish foot so typical of the William and Mary period is used in rural work well up into the 19th century.

The reverse also happens, for elements of a new style sometimes appear in an earlier style. This is particularly common among furniture made shortly after the Revolution when American cabinetmakers were still producing furniture in the Rococo style. Here we see Chippendale chairs with tapered Hepplewhite legs, and Chippendale mirrors with some patera or conch inlays. The presence of newer elements makes furniture relatively easy to date, for as was noted, the introduction of a new style is usually fairly well known.

In the discussion that follows, each major style is accompanied by an illustration of the more common period motifs typical to that period. Period motifs are the decorative features of the style that were popular during the period. As you gain experience, you will find that certain motifs occur again and again, not just in furniture, but in all sorts of objects made during the same period. For example, conch and paterna inlay is found not only in Neoclassical furniture, but also in clock cases, barometers, knife boxes, dressing mirrors, and tea caddies. The classical urn is found everywhere during the Federal period — even on tombstones. For the most part, these period motifs are easy to spot and provide us with handy clues as to age and to period.

### Jacobean

The earliest American furniture dates from the Jacobean period, the great majority from the latter years of the period during the reigns of Charles II and James II (1660 – 1688). Jacobean furniture is in many ways an extension of the preceding Tudor Gothic style. It includes paneled and carved chests, court cupboards, wainscot chairs, Cromwell and farthingale chairs, and a great many joint stools, for chairs are not yet common and most people sit on either a stool or a chest. Here we also see the introduction of upholstered chairs, chests of drawers decorated with mitered moldings, the long popular gateleg table, and the first desks, which are no more than slant lid boxes mounted on frames. Brass hardware comes into use, and elaborate twist turning, so popular during the following William and Mary period, first starts to be employed. Oak is the primary wood, although some elm, chestnut, and yew are found in English furniture. American furniture exhibits more diversity, and in addition to both red and white oak, we see the use of pine, ash, cedar, maple, poplar, and chestnut.

While the earliest American furniture postdates the reign of Elizabeth by at least half a century, both the court cupboard (16-11) and the joint stool (8-1) are Tudor Gothic, and may have been considered old-fashioned by the time they were being produced in America in the latter part of the 17th century. American examples are rare and seldom come on the market. However, the court cupboard is important as the first grand high style furniture made in a very new world.

This period is of particular interest to the collector of American furniture as it coincides with the arrival of large numbers of settlers in New England and Virginia. Here

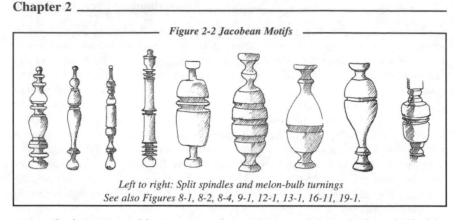

Figure 2-2 Jacobean Motifs

Left to right: Split spindles and melon-bulb turnings
See also Figures 8-1, 8-2, 8-4, 9-1, 12-1, 13-1, 16-11, 19-1.

we see the beginnings of furniture manufacturing in America. By the latter half of the 17th century the colonies are sufficiently established to start making a significant quantity of their own furniture. As you would expect, what little American furniture survives from this early period is very Jacobean in character, and is often identified as American only by analysis of the woods used in the construction. Although considered very old-fashioned in England, furniture that is essentially Jacobean in style continues to be made in America right up through the first quarter of the 18th century.

During this period most furniture is made of oak. The better case pieces employ paneled construction and are decorated first by carving and the inlay of lighter woods, and later by the use of applied moldings. Unfortunately, for all its strength and ease of splitting or riving, oak offers little to the cabinetmaker, for it is bound by a lack of color and by a coarse grain, which doesn't provide much figure or permit fine detail in carving. Examine almost any furniture from this period and you will see how the design is limited by this wood. By the end of the 17th century, there was little more that could be done in oak.

However, with the restoration of Charles II in 1660, a new method of construction is introduced from the Continent. Here a finely figured wood such as walnut is veneered over dovetail joined boards of a secondary wood. Now there is no need for paneling, and case work can be decorated with handsome figured veneers rather than with carvings and moldings. At first, veneering is over oak, but soon cabinetmakers discover that pine makes a better base, and this is the secondary wood we now find in most of these pieces. While walnut is quite the most common veneer during this period, cabinetmakers also use walnut burls, laburnum, and fruitwoods to obtain pretty effects. Another common technique, called oystering, employs elliptical pieces of veneer cut at an angle from cross-sections of small logs. Thus, we should be remember 1660 as the time when walnut first began to replace oak as the fashionable wood. The following 90 years, until about 1730, is often called the age of walnut or the walnut period.

The new dovetail construction had a revolutionary effect on design, for it reduced the mass and weight of case work by permitting both thin drawer sides and large, light cases. Within a relatively few years furniture went from being heavy and horizontal to being light and vertical, and we see the introduction of furniture that is basically just a stack of dovetailed boxes — the highboy, the chest on chest, and the secretary. Visit a museum and you can see this remarkable transition when you compare a Jacobean court cupboard (16-11) with a William and Mary highboy (15-9). In fact, it is the only major advance in furniture design following the development of paneled construction hundreds of years earlier. Nothing nearly as important is to follow until the introduction of wood working machinery and factory production in first half of the 19th century. While social and economic factors undoubtedly precipitated this change, there were at least two major technological contributors: improvements in tools, particularly saws, and the use of hide glue. With better saws it was easier to work out dovetails and to cut veneers in large pieces; and hide glue provided a strong adhesive with some elasticity to give with the expansion and contraction of wood. Three hundred years later it is still one of the best glues for furniture.

### William and Mary

Although these changes first began in 1660, it is not until the arrival of William of Orange from Holland in 1689 that they become common, and not until the early years of the 18th century that they are introduced into American furniture. The following William and Mary period is the first one from which a substantial amount of American furniture survives. It is also blessed with a number of stylistic features that make for easy identification; the most obvious being the round bun or turnip shaped feet on desks and chests of drawers; and the cup or trumpet turned legs on highboys and lowboys. These legs, which resemble either a pilsner glass or a muted trumpet, are doweled into a block glued to the bottom of the case, an inherently weak construction that needs the additional support of

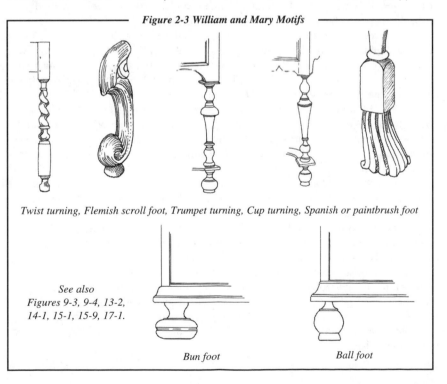

*Figure 2-3 William and Mary Motifs*

*Twist turning, Flemish scroll foot, Trumpet turning, Cup turning, Spanish or paintbrush foot*

*See also
Figures 9-3, 9-4, 13-2,
14-1, 15-1, 15-9, 17-1.*

*Bun foot*

*Ball foot*

stretchers. One of the charming features of this form is that the shape of the skirt is reflected in the shape of the stretcher — a nice touch that tends to tie together what would otherwise be a rather leggy design.

When you look at William and Mary desks and chests of drawers, you will notice a heavy molding around the base of the chest. This base molding is a common feature of case work from this period. To keep the foot from being hidden under the molding, it is given a short post, not too unlike the stem of a pumpkin. The post is then doweled into the bottom of the case.

In England, the large moldings of this period are typically built up with small pieces of walnut set cross grain to a pine base. The walnut was first glued to the backing, then shaped with a sharp molding plane set to a very fine cut. In America, where there is ample walnut, these moldings are simply made up from solid stock. Also, only the fronts of American case work from this period are veneered; the sides will be made up in the solid from walnut, maple, or a hard pine. In spite of this economy, veneering on American furniture from this period is not common. Even this early we can observe the effect of limited labor and almost unlimited wood on the design of American furniture.

The William and Mary period also sees the fashion for caned chairs with turned, scrolled and carved legs, and very high narrow backs with carved crests. Due to the labor in carving and caning, these are seldom American. The examples you see at Americana auctions will most likely be London made, even though they may have arrived here long before the Revolution. American chairmakers developed the banister-back chair as a cheaper and more hardy substitute.

Other features from this period are the use of the Spanish or paintbrush foot on chairs and tables, and twist turning on chairs, candlestands, tables, and clocks. Twist turning, a product of turning, then much filing and smoothing, was very popular, and like bun feet, it is found on much English and Continental furniture. However, being labor intensive, it is rarely found on American furniture.

The Spanish foot and the carved crests on chairs are associated with the Baroque style, although William and Mary American furniture from this period is so far from the massive English court furniture of this period that the association is fairly tenuous. Nevertheless, both William and Mary and the following Queen Anne styles are sometimes referred to as Baroque.

The William and Mary period is noteworthy for the introduction of new types of furniture. The 20 years following the landing of William of Orange in Devon sees the development of the highboy, the lowboy, the wing chair, the gaming or card table, the slant lid desk, and both drop front and slant front secretaries. The chest on chest is to follow within just a few years, and thereafter, among major pieces of furniture, only the cellaret sideboard and the modern pillar form dining table still await development.

This period also sees the general introduction of furniture brasses, only simple rural work still retaining wooden knobs. These early brasses are quite small by later standards. The thin cast backplates and key escutcheons, normally of a different pattern, are decorated with hand-chased designs, and no two are just alike. The handles, often just hollow cast teardrops, are fastened with cotterpins, a weak attachment that does not often survive.

## Queen Anne

The next major period commences about 1705 in England and perhaps 25 years later in America. Because the reign of Queen Anne (1702 – 1714) is short, English furniture is still in the Walnut period, and we continue to see the use of walnut veneering that had started in the previous century. In America, where there was ample walnut, this handsome wood is at first veneered, but then is more generally used in the solid. If we look at the time line, we see that the beginning of Queen Anne in America actually corresponds to the reign of George II in England, but over here we do not use the term Georgian, perhaps due to the problems that were to follow during the long reign of George III. Thus, Queen Anne is the last English ruler associated with American furniture periods until we get to Queen Victoria in the middle of the next century. After Queen Anne, American furniture is identified as Chippendale or Federal, but never as Georgian.

Queen Anne is a useful term, but something of a misnomer, for not only does her brief reign not correspond to the period of the style in America, but the term itself was not even used until 1880. Some authorities consider William and Mary to be Early Baroque, and Queen Anne to be Late Baroque, although these terms are not used in the antique business.

The most notable feature of this period is the cabriole leg, which first appears during the reign of William and Mary, but now is fully developed and comes into general use. We see the graceful curves of these legs in chairs, stools, highboys, lowboys, and tables; in fact, if you see a cabriole leg with a simple pad, trifid, or slipper foot, the style is almost certainly Queen Anne. Here we also see the introduction of the bracket foot on case furniture, on chests on chests, chests of drawers and secretaries. This simple, sturdy foot, which neatly frames the bottom of a square case, is common to this day.

Queen Anne chairs are notable for their curves. The back will be reverse curved, the crest rail rounded and slightly scooped, and the seat usually curved or balloon

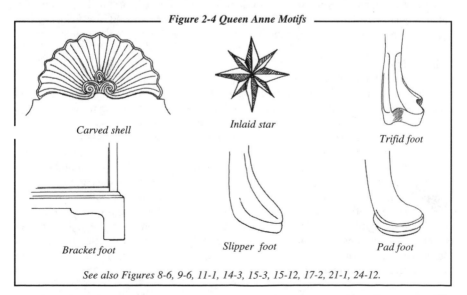

*Figure 2-4 Queen Anne Motifs*

*Carved shell*

*Inlaid star*

*Trifid foot*

*Bracket foot*

*Slipper foot*

*Pad foot*

*See also Figures 8-6, 9-6, 11-1, 14-3, 15-3, 15-12, 17-2, 21-1, 24-12.*

**25**

shaped. There is not a straight line in a high style Queen Anne chair. Better quality chairs will often have a carved shell centered in the crest rail, a popular Queen Anne motif that is also found in case work. Whatever the quality, Queen Anne chairs have in common a shallow "S" shaped back topped with a rounded crest rail that curves over to meet a solid splat, which, more often than not, is vase shaped.

During this period we see the introduction of the chest on chest, a form far more popular in England than America. The other large case furniture used for storing clothing, the highboy, is produced in both England and America, but ultimately proves to be much more successful in America. The bonnet topped highboy with its carved urn or flame finials is Queen Anne in style, even though many were made right up to the time of the Revolution, long after highboys had gone out of fashion in England.

With Queen Anne brasses get somewhat larger and begin to be fastened with posts rather than cotter pins, which is both stronger and permits a more comfortable bail or handle. Key escutcheons are now made in matching sets with the back plates, so the brasses don't look to have come from two different sources. The most typical of these brasses on American furniture is a simple "batwing" design.

About 1730, at the beginning of the Queen Anne period in America, mahogany starts to be shipped up from the Caribbean. With the arrival of this superb cabinet wood veneering is no longer necessary and falls into disuse. Walnut slowly ceases to be the fashionable wood, although it continues to be popular as a less expensive option, particularly in and around Philadelphia. Mahogany is a cabinetmaker's dream, providing, for the first time, really wide boards with beautiful figuring and minimum of warping and shrinkage. No longer is it necessary to veneer up secondary woods with thin sheets of walnut to obtain large surfaces that are both decorative and dimensionally stable. Now it is possible to fashion the sides of chests, the leaves of desks, and the tops of tables out of single boards. This move away from veneering is more pronounced in England where wide boards of walnut and cherry were not available, but we also see it in America where very little veneering is done after the first quarter of the century. Indeed, the following half century is notable for the almost complete absence of any veneer on furniture.

## Chippendale

The period that follows Queen Anne is probably the best known, being named after a successful London cabinetmaker, Thomas Chippendale, who inadvertently bestowed his name on a whole style of furniture by publishing a book of high style furniture designs in 1754. The *Gentleman and Cabinet-Maker's Director*, or the *Director* as it is often referred to now, was basically just an illustrated trade catalog of fashionable furniture, the sort of work that would have been turned out by any first rate London cabinetmaker. It was not even the first such publication, but now is the one we all remember.

The *Director* was very popular, going through a number of editions and being sold on both sides of the Atlantic; although in America only a few high style chairs can be actually traced to the drawings in his books. Chippendale furniture is most often associated with the claw-and-ball foot, which first appears in Queen Anne and Early Georgian furniture — but ironically, is not shown in the *Director*, apparently because it was out of fashion in England by this time. In America, though, the claw-and-ball foot is just becoming stylish, and it continues in popularity right up through the 18th century, even being used occasionally in the first decade of the 19th century. This now very Chippendale feature originated in the Orient as a symbol of the balance between good and evil, or as strength guarding purity from evil — a dragon's claw holding a pearl.

In some respects we can think of Chippendale as an enhanced Queen Anne, a Queen Anne with a Rococo flavor. Indeed, Chippendale is sometimes referred to as Rococo, although the association with the charming and exuberant Rococo that we see in palaces and churches in Germany and Austria is very minimal. However, in the grander English furniture, where the customer could pay for carving and gilding, we see more Rococo ornament, particularly in console tables and giltwood mirrors. Rococo is characterized by asymmetrical curves and naturalistic motifs such as shells, foliage, and rocks. A good way to spot Rococo is to look for a C-scroll shape, which as it sounds, looks much like the letter "C." However, carving and gilding is expensive, and in America we usually only see Rococo motifs in the crests of mirrors and in the splats of chairs.

In addition to the claw-and-ball foot, which tends to be larger and bolder than is found in earlier Queen Anne examples, the Chippendale style is most easily identified in the chairs, which loose many of the curves associated with Queen Anne, particularly the S-shape back and the round balloon seats, and now have simple curved backs, square seats, projections or "ears" at the ends of the crest rail, and pierced splats. More often than not, these chairs will not have a cabriole leg, but rather, will have the simpler

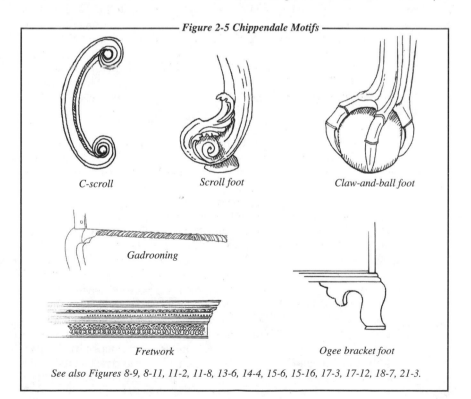

*Figure 2-5 Chippendale Motifs*

*C-scroll*          *Scroll foot*          *Claw-and-ball foot*

*Gadrooning*

*Fretwork*          *Ogee bracket foot*

*See also Figures 8-9, 8-11, 11-2, 11-8, 13-6, 14-4, 15-6, 15-16, 17-3, 17-12, 18-7, 21-3.*

and less expensive square molded Marlborough leg, which although lacking the claw-and-ball foot, is actually more definitive of Chippendale than the earlier Queen Anne cabriole leg. As a general rule, Chippendale furniture is both larger in scale and more ornate than Queen Anne. The ogee foot appears on chests and there is likely to be more carving on the better pieces. With Chippendale, wing chairs not only acquire claw-and-ball feet, but also serpentine backs, something we also see in sofas. The pierced, and often carved, chair splats appear in innumerable designs — ribbon, tassel, Gothic, and even Chinese; and in a complete departure, somewhat later in the period we also see the splats set sideways to form the very common ladder-back chairs.

As you would expect, brasses also get larger and more ornate, some of the very large mounts on high style American work almost outshining their hosts. During this period a simple bail handle with little cast rosettes around the posts is also popular. On some of the better pieces these bail handles acquire quite an ornate Rococo flavor. Many were once guilded, which may not be as extravagant as it sounds, for it kept them from tarnishing.

While the *Director* was not published until 1754, furniture one would call Chippendale was being produced in England by 1740, and thereafter the style remained in fashion until about 1780. In America, Chippendale style furniture does not appear until the 1750s, but then continues to be produced in limited quantities into the early years of the 19th century. However, Queen Anne is not discarded, and furniture we would consider to be very much Queen Anne in style continues to be made right up until the end of the century. The wonderful high style Newport block and shell furniture is as much Queen Anne as it is Chippendale.

For all the fame of this period, there are few innovations in furniture. Only the Pembroke table and the round tilt-top tea table are new, although there are now many more sofas and an increased popularity of the press, which is a chest on chest having the top section fitted with doors, behind which will be shelves or drawers.

### Adam

Almost no sooner had the *Director* been published than Rococo lost favor to a new style. Robert Adam, a Scottish architect, began designing public and private buildings that drew on the earlier English Palladian style as well as on the Roman ruins he had studied in Italy. However, they were a departure from prior classical work, not only in their light and airy feeling, but also in the harmonious relationship between the exterior of the building, the interior rooms, and the furniture. To do this, Robert and his brother James provided the client with a complete stylistically integrated home right down to the furniture, much the way Frank Lloyd Wright did in this century.

Adam furniture is a marked departure from Chippendale, being more delicate looking and somewhat classical in feeling. In addition to the use of lighter colored mahoganies, we see the introduction of satinwood, amboyna, and harewood veneers. The legs on Adam chairs are lighter than cabriole or molded Chippendale legs, being fluted and tapering, and having a small square foot. Many of the chairs are made of beech, then painted and gilded to harmonize with the rooms. Carving, often in the form of swags, is refined and delicate in keeping with similar forms found in the surrounding room paneling. Perhaps the most common innovation among more middle class furniture is the painting of delicate branches, leaves, and flowers on desk lids, cabinets, and table tops.

Robert and James Adam's work is important in the evolution of English furniture, for its Neoclassicism is a clear break with the earlier Rococo. It forms a bridge to the Hepplewhite and Sheraton styles which were to follow, and indeed, all three styles are often identified as Neoclassical. Interestingly, Neoclassicism gained popularity in a period most of us think of as belonging to Chippendale. Such was the overlap in styles that Chippendale's shop made a lot of Adam furniture, which makes sense if we remember that he was simply making high quality furniture "to the latest fashion."

Many Americans find the Adam style puzzling, and perhaps for good reason, for aside from a handful of high style painted and guilded chairs, there is almost no American furniture that can be identified with Adam.

## Hepplewhite

Adam furniture, with its carving, painting, and gilding, was limited to the well-to-do client. However, its neo-classical look was very popular, perhaps in reaction to 40 years of Rococo exuberance, or perhaps in response to a renewed interest in the classical at a time when the little Roman cities of Herculaneum and Pompeii were just emerging from sixteen centuries of slumber. In either event, Robert Adam soon had a host of imitators, many of whom worked out less expensive interpretations of the classical look. In 1788, the widow of George Hepplewhite, a London cabinetmaker and furniture designer, published a book of his designs, *The Cabinet-Maker and Upholster's Guide*. Like its famous precursor, this book was also something of a trade catalog of popular designs, and to complete the analogy, George Hepplewhite is also recorded as having made furniture for Robert Adam. However, the illustrations are far more practical, and it has been suggested that they may have been taken from actual products.

The Hepplewhite style is easy to tell from Chippendale, for it is a return to the linear, being characterized by straight vertical lines, gentle curves, and the use of contrasting inlay and veneer. The most notable feature is slender, tapering legs used on chairs, sideboards, and on all sorts of tables. On some of the better American furniture, and on many English examples, these legs end in a spade foot, a tapering square end that looks in profile something like a narrow garden spade. An easy rule to remember is that square legs are Chippendale, and tapered are Hepplewhite. In addition to tapering legs, on chests of drawers and secretaries we see the use of outswept French feet connected by a deeply valanced curved apron. By this time glass is less expensive and the fielded panels on secretaries and corner cupboards gives way to geometrically glazed doors. In addition to tapered legs, Hepplewhite chairs will normally have shield, oval, or hoop backs, sometimes with a Prince of Wales feather pattern on the splat. You will notice that these chairs are noticeably smaller and lighter than similar Chippendale chairs.

With Hepplewhite comes a return to veneering, but as in the past, mostly as a decorative treatment on the front of furniture, the sides and the tops of case work still being solid wood. Improved saws make it possible to cut thinner veneers in large sheets, so now we see dramatic drawer fronts of matching flitches of cross-grained mahogany. Along with veneer comes a return to inlay, the most common being stringing, patera patterns, and conch-shell medallions. There is very little carving except in the backs of chairs, which are often decorated with a delicate wheat sheaf pattern.

Furniture brasses also see major changes. Backplates and escutcheons are no longer castings, but now are thin raised brass stampings, normally elliptical in shape with pretty little designs worked into the center of the ellipse. The handles, also elliptical in shape to match the plates, fit into the posts from the outside rather than the inside as before. With this change in design comes the end of matching escutcheons. Now the area around the key hole will have either a small oval stamping, an inlayed piece of ivory, or just a little cast brass insert.

American Neoclassicism is notable in the use of period motifs to impart a classical feeling to both furniture and homes. The ellipse is immensely popular in all kinds of furniture, and you will find ellipses and circles worked into clock fronts, sideboards, chests, sofas, and card tables — just about everywhere there is a flat surface! Similarly, the classical urn is often found in the backs of chairs, in the columns of candlestands, and in the crests of mirrors. These motifs, and others, are also incorporated into

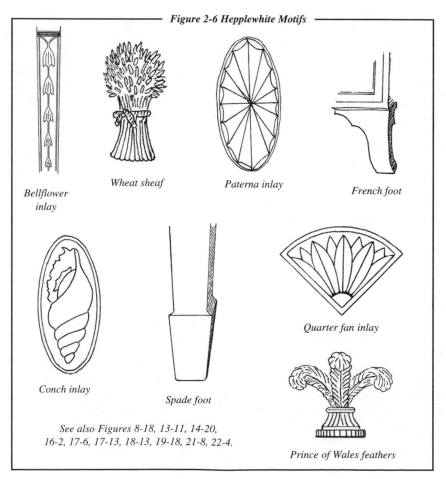

*Figure 2-6 Hepplewhite Motifs*

Bellflower inlay

Wheat sheaf

Paterna inlay

French foot

Conch inlay

Spade foot

Quarter fan inlay

Prince of Wales feathers

*See also Figures 8-18, 13-11, 14-20, 16-2, 17-6, 17-13, 18-13, 19-18, 21-8, 22-4.*

the trim of Federal houses, much in keeping with Robert Adam's idea that a house and its furnishings should be treated as an integrated unit.

The latter part of the 18th century sees the increasing use of a room set aside exclusively for meals, something that had previously existed only in very grand houses. With this comes the development of middle class furniture for this dining room, the cellaret sideboard, two and three section dining tables with folding leaves, and a great many more sets of side chairs. The cellaret sideboard is similar to a modern sideboard except that one end has a deep cellaret drawer for wine and liquor bottles; the other end a matching door with storage behind for platters and dishes. Its invention is credited to Thomas Shearer who, also in 1788, published *The Cabinet Makers London Book of Prices and Designs*. While we think of styles from this time as being defined in the famous books by Hepplewhite and Sheraton, they were concurrently being illustrated in this sort of price book. These books appear to have been what customers used when ordering furniture.

### Sheraton

Only a few years after George Hepplewhite's widow published his book, Thomas Sheraton published *The Cabinet-Maker and Upholsterer's Drawing-Book*. This was followed by the *The Cabinet Dictionary* in 1803. Sheraton, the last of the celebrated 18th century furniture designers, may also have worked a cabinetmaker, but apparently was not successful, as he seems to have been lived in poverty, supporting himself as a drawing master, what we might now call a commercial artist.

The Sheraton style is primarily a variation of Neoclassical, quite similar to Hepplewhite, but somewhat heavier in feeling and more monochromatic, with additional use of delicate Neoclassical carving for decoration on the backs of sofas and chairs, and at the tops of table legs. The tambour sliding doors found on desks and sideboards are also Sheraton. Quite the most pronounced feature, though, and the easiest way to tell Sheraton from Hepplewhite, is the use of turned and reeded legs on all types of furniture. Often these legs are set slightly outside the case and continue as pilasters on the corners of the case. Then the top is given half rounds, or "cookie corners" to receive the pilasters. The linearity that appeared with Adam now is applied to chairs, and Sheraton chairs typically have flat crest rails. The handles on drawers also change, and will typically be stamped brass rosettes, or a lions head with a pendant ring, or a stamped rectangular octagonal shape; the latter two more typically English than American. This gives us another handy rule: Federal furniture in which the drawer pulls are mounted on single posts will probably be Sheraton rather than Hepplewhite.

With Sheraton we see the first modern pillar type dining room tables, although they are not yet common, and the collector will see many more of the two or three section Hepplewhite tables, but now with turned and sometimes reeded legs. To remember the difference between reeding and fluting, think of reeding as a bundle of thin reeds glued lengthwise to the leg. Fluting is the reverse, the half round curve that is cut into the surface. It may also be a sign of earlier work, having been used on all types of furniture throughout the 18th century. Reeding and fluting are shown together in Figure 2-7.

In addition to cookie corners, Sheraton chests of drawers tend to be more ornate than Hepplewhite, and we see the introduction of small drawers on the top, and the

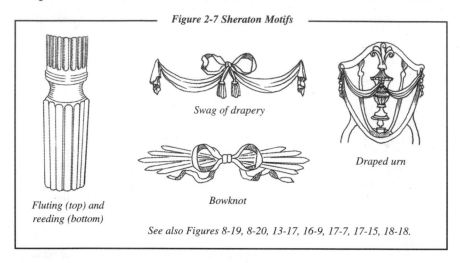

**Figure 2-7 Sheraton Motifs**

Swag of drapery

Draped urn

Bowknot

Fluting (top) and reeding (bottom)

See also Figures 8-19, 8-20, 13-17, 16-9, 17-7, 17-15, 18-18.

use of backboards or an attached mirror. The small drawers and mirror are in many ways just a fixed version of a dressing mirror, which has now been attached to the chest and given a bigger mirror. During this period the cellaret sideboard continues to be very popular, but now it is more common to keep silver in a compartmented drawer than in separate boxes, and Neoclassical knife urns and knife boxes decline in popularity. The charming little sewing or work tables, which first appear with Hepplewhite, become very popular and are found in almost every conceivable size and shape. Normally they are fitted with two shallow drawers for scissors and thread, then a bag underneath for scraps and yarn. Some are fitted with delightful little adjustable writing surfaces.

Lastly, the reader should be forewarned that just as Hepplewhite and Sheraton periods overlap in time, so also they frequently overlap in details of style. Tambour desks and Sheraton style chairs commonly have Hepplewhite legs, and elliptical drawer pulls are often found on Sheraton case work. It is not always easy to delineate the two styles, and for this reason, as well as to indicate the country of origin, dealers and auctioneers tend to use the term Federal rather than Hepplewhite and Sheraton in identifying American furniture from this period.

If you are still clear on this narrative, be patient, for after Sheraton there is but one more period to cover before the advent of the factory production and the end of period furniture. This last period gets a little more complicated than some of the others, as American and English designs now go more their own ways, and some new ideas are brought over from France.

### Empire and Regency

Just a few years after Sheraton, the turn of the century found all of Europe in turmoil; Louis XVI had lost his head, George III had lost his reason, and a young artillery officer from Corsica was leading the armies of France to victory all over the Continent. We realize now that this was the beginning of modern Europe, but then it must have been a period of wrenching change. Out of this came a new style, Empire, named for the empire which Napoleon established in the spring of 1804. In England, this period corresponds to the regency of the Prince of Wales, and is called Regency. In America, we usually call this period Empire, although some writers prefer to group Hepplewhite and Sheraton together as Neoclassicism, then identify Empire as either Classical Revival or Greco-Roman Revival. To help sort this all out, and because there is a lot of Regency furniture on the American market, we'll discuss English Regency and American Empire separately, for there are very real differences between the two styles.

Regency is normally dated from about 1800 to 1830, although the long and troubled reign of George III did not end until 1820, and the Prince of Wales was regent only during the last nine of these years. As in other periods, Regency is easiest to spot in chairs, which now get narrower, have either sabre or turned legs, and backs with curved horizontal splats. During this period the interest in things classical continues unabated, but instead of just a classical inspiration, furniture now embodies a more literal interpretation, and everywhere we see the use of Greek, Roman, and Egyptian motifs, the sabre leg chair itself being an adaptation of the Klismos chair that appears on Greek vases. The Regency style also sees much use of brass, not only as castors on all sorts of furniture, but also for inlay, and for galleries around the tops of tables and bookcases. Until now inlay has normally consisted of contrasting light woods such as holly and satinwood, but in Regency furniture, in addition to brass, ebony is used to provide a contrasting dark wood. The use of rosewood for veneering, which started a few year earlier, is now common, and continues to be employed right up through Victorian times, when even chairs and sofas are made of this hard, brittle tropical wood.

In addition to sabre-leg chairs, the most notable types of Regency furniture are the handsome dining tables, the equally handsome breakfast tables, and a new form, the circular center table. Pillar form tables, first introduced in the last decade of the 18th century, now become the common form of dining table. Later in the period they lose some of their earlier grace, the column becoming thicker and more ornate; the legs carved and scrolled. In center tables, the feet are generally attached to a square or triangular section which forms the base of the column. The whole feeling of this period is of increasing diversity in a furniture that is both heavier and more ornate than either Hepplewhite or Sheraton.

Regency furniture also includes the sofa table, the Canterbury, and the Davenport desk. These charming little desks, which originated in the 1790s, become popular during this period, then even more so during Victoria's reign, with the result that most examples on the market are Victorian rather than Regency. None of these forms were popular in America, although there are a few American sofa tables and canterburys.

Lastly, it should be noted that after George IV and Regency, and before Victoria, there is the brief reign of William IV. The most notable feature of these few late years are the chubby, tapering reeded legs used on tables and chairs. Dealers in English furniture treat the interval between 1830 and 1837 as a separate period, referring to it as William IV.

The Empire style is introduced in America about 1810, and thereafter continues to be popular until superseded by Victorian. Furniture from this period is sometimes identified as Greco-Roman Revival, but more often is called Classical Revival, or just Classical, the style being seen as a revival of the classicism introduced by Adam in the 1760s. Classical Revival and Classical are used interchangeably with Empire in auction catalogs, although Empire tends to be associated with early high style production in the major urban centers.

Because furniture is starting to be mass produced by the 1830s, the amount of fine, handcrafted American furniture from this time is more limited than the relative lateness of this period would suggest. Empire furniture is also limited because Philadelphia and Boston were slow to follow New York's lead in the new style. By this time New York is the largest city in America and is the leader in fashion and style, providing us with the two best known cabinetmakers of this period, Duncan Phyfe and Charles-Honore Lannuier.

In addition to a great many handsome sabre-leg chairs, Empire sees the introduction of the secretaire a abattant, Grecian sofas, sleigh beds, and a great many mirror-backed pier tables. Case furniture tends to become heavier and acquire more decoration. Sideboards, secretaries, and chests of drawers all grow large and ornate, many acquiring a pair of classical columns that end in either turned or paw feet. These columns in turn support an overhanging top drawer, which contributes to the already somewhat massive feeling.

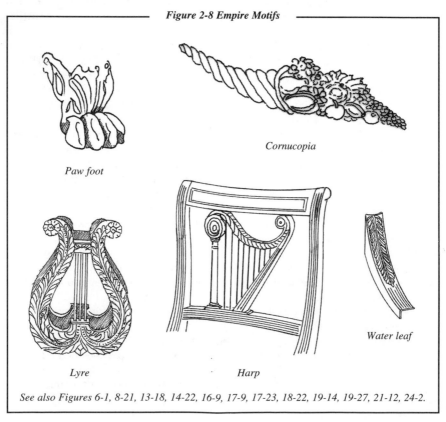

*Figure 2-8 Empire Motifs*

Paw foot

Cornucopia

Lyre

Harp

Water leaf

*See also Figures 6-1, 8-21, 13-18, 14-22, 16-9, 17-9, 17-23, 18-22, 19-14, 19-27, 21-12, 24-2.*

Empire furniture is also characterized by the use of gilded or ebonised half round turnings on clocks and mirrors. Brasses, in keeping with their hosts, grow larger. Now on single posts, they may be large stamped brass rosettes, pressed glass knobs, or just mushroom shaped wood turnings.

Just as Regency was followed by the minor period of William IV, Empire in America is followed by a period called Late Classicism, which runs from 1835 to about 1850. By this time most furniture is mass produced, leading to many thousands of Boston rockers and ogee mirrors. Case work is now characterized by sheets of thin mahogany veneered on a pine base. Because veneer can only curve in one direction, this furniture has a lot of flat surfaces, which does nothing to flatter its size. This period is also called pillar and scroll for the use of C- and S-scrolls which appear everywhere on inexpensive furniture. These were cut out on large bandsaws, then veneered up with mahogany, giving us the flat surfaces that make this furniture so easy to identify.

The best and most useful furniture of this late last period are generally the smaller items, particularly the handsome and comfortable chairs, which, in keeping with French practice, are given an attractive curved or gondola back that extends around to the sides (8-22). French Empire furniture was largely a court style, and these gondola-back chairs are one of the few places where some traces of French style is found among American furniture.

After Empire and Regency, period loses most of its significance. By the second quarter of the 19th century, most furniture, even if assembled and finished by hand, is designed for machine production. In rural areas handcraftsmanship will last just another few decades. In America, the 1820s see the divergence of urban and rural styles, one going the way of the machine, the other remaining the way of the craftsman, and it is among the latter that we still find some charming workmanship.

Before finishing, it should be noted that the major American furniture periods are sometimes identified simply as Pilgrim Century, Colonial, and Federal, an easy to understand division that is particularly useful due to the amount of style overlap in this country. If you look back at Figure 2-1, you will see that Queen Anne and Chippendale styles are both popular for most of the Colonial period, and that there is a similar overlap with Hepplewhite and Sheraton during the Federal period.

The Pilgrim Century is normally defined as the hundred years following the landing of these first settlers in New England, although very little furniture survives from this time, and most of what does is from the last 40 or so years of this period. Probably a lot of simple furniture was made in America during the 17th century; records show both carpenters and joiners arriving quite early on, but most of this early work was discarded as the economy improved and better was available.

The Colonial period begins with the introduction of the Queen Anne style in America in the 1730s, and ends with a bang on the town green in Lexington, Massachusetts, at six in the morning on the 19th of April, 1775. There follows eight long years of conflict, then a period in which the economy was depressed, so the Federal period doesn't really begin until about 1790. It then lasts only until about 1825 or so, quite the shortest of the these three periods, but the one from which the most furniture survives.

Because the onset of the American Revolution delayed the introduction of the Neoclassical style for almost two decades, there is another convenient way to visualize American furniture periods. They can be arranged as follows:
- Pilgrim Century – Jacobean
- Early Colonial – William and Mary and Queen Anne (Baroque)
- Late Colonial – Chippendale (Rococo)
- Early Federal — Hepplewhite and Sheraton (Early Neoclassical)
- Late Federal – Late Sheraton and Empire (Late Neoclassical)

To this we might add that Early Colonial could in turn be subdivided into Early Baroque (William and Mary) and Late Baroque (Queen Anne).

You will find that dealers and auctioneers use the term Pilgrim Century to describe very early work whose style is largely based on designs introduced by immigrant joiners from the south of England. Some of this work is Jacobean in style, other forms might be described as a rural Elizabethan. Federal is used for the years following the Revolution, and sometimes Late Federal if Empire or Classical in style. Furniture identified simply as Hepplewhite or Sheraton will usually be English. Colonial is often used to describe houses, but is seldom used in conjunction with old furniture. Instead, furniture from this period is usually described in relation to style. Thus, you will see illustrations of Queen Anne and Chippendale chairs, but not Colonial chairs. American furniture from all periods is normally also described by the use of source and primary wood, and in auction catalogs and advertisements you will see pieces identified as "Philadelphia Chippendale walnut side chair," "Massachusetts Queen Anne bonnet-top mahogany highboy," and "New England Federal Sheraton birch card table."

# Chapter 3

## Evaluating Quality

Quality is fundamental to a good collection. It should be the first thought in any purchase, large or small, for in collecting anything, quality is everything. Whether the subject is coins, old bottles, or period furniture, if your acquisitions are not of consistent merit, they will not long satisfy you, however cleverly they may have been acquired. As a collector, whatever your budget, quality should always be your primary consideration. Nothing will please you more, or earn more respect among your peers, than a collection with both focus and quality. You will find that stepping down to pick up a bargain is always a mistake. The piece you bought at such a low price will not be a bargain, for with time and experience its problems will become very evident. While you may have gotten the better of the seller, you have also cheated yourself.

Most collectors both buy and sell. As a collection is built, some items are sold and others are bought. This exchange provides an opportunity to upgrade. If something is replaced, always try to replace it with better. Very few of us are able to start at the top of the market, or even at the level we would wish, and in any event, our initial acquisitions will not be tempered by experience. Although we would not want to emulate

Francis Garvan, who sold off an entire collection of questionable English furniture before starting over with American furniture, there will be pieces for which we might substitute better, and when the opportunity arises, this should always be done. Not only should our collection grow over the years, it should also grow better.

In the art market there is a general correlation between price and quality. The more something costs, the better is likely to be its quality. However, there is also a general correlation between price and popularity, although the popularity may have little to do with real merit. In such a market, even ample funds are no guarantee of a sound collection. For most of us, though, the bigger challenge is obtaining quality on a limited budget. To do so, we must learn to identify quality when we see it, particularly in the average grade of period furniture. That is the subject of this chapter.

When the De Beers company markets diamonds, they talk about quality in terms of the four C's of color, carat weight, clarity, and cut. In a similar way, quality in antique furniture might be defined in terms of the four P's of period, provenance, proportion, and patina, if we also remember two other very important factors, construction and condition.

Let's review each of these six factors in turn, for all are important, and some are perhaps very new to the reader.

## Period

Period, as it relates to history and style, you now know all about. George Hepplewhite and Thomas Sheraton are familiar names. When Chippendale is mentioned, you know the reference is not to Chip 'n Dale of Saturday morning fame. However, period is also fundamental to quality, for not only is really old furniture uncommon, but to a considerable measure, each piece is unique, it is different from any other piece. More importantly, period work has a spontaneity, exuberance, and naiveté not found in the reproduction. It stands out in a room full of other furniture, for there is nothing else like it. Reproductions also stand out, but to the discerning eye, only as nice reproductions. When beginning, period furniture and good reproductions may look very much alike, but as you gain experience you will see that there is a world of difference. Even 19th century reproductions, many of them beautifully made and faithful in design and construction, will not appear quite right. Although by now in themselves antique, to the experienced collector, they are inescapably reproductions. They are just not the real thing.

## Provenance

Provenance is what we know about the past. Noah Webster states it is the "place of origin; source." Actually, there are two almost identical words; the English provenience and the French provenance. Both are derived from the Latin provenire, "to come forth; originate," but only the latter word is used with antiquities. In association with old furniture, provenance is any historical knowledge or documentation.

The amount and quality of provenance can vary from as little as the name of a past owner or a dealer to a long and complete history. The best is what we sometimes see on grand pieces, where there will be the original bill of sale from the cabinetmaker, then a continuous history of family ownership right down to the present time. Such a record might be considered the ultimate proof of authenticity. However, such complete histories are fairly rare. What we more commonly find in very good furniture is a recent history of ownership and a record of sale through dealers and auctions. For the average piece, though, it is unusual that anything is available beyond some limited family history, the most recent appraisal, the last bill of sale, or the occasional dealer's label. All of this, however, is indeed provenance, and should not be ignored.

Provenance encompasses all historical association. It includes not only family histories, but also owner's brands, labels left by dealers and repairers, and mention in account books, wills, and letters. Quite often one will find penciled or inked notes added by later family members; perhaps something to the effect that "This very old chest was owned by my great-great...." While disparaged by some, family histories have a way of being quite accurate, although it is not unusual for the piece to be ascribed to the wrong ancestor.

How much provenance actually contributes, or should contribute, to quality, is somewhat questionable. In earlier times much importance was attached to family histories, particularly if the original owner was a well known American. At this time scholarship in early furniture was much more limited, and an illustrious family history must have contributed not only to the collector's pride of ownership, but also to peace of mind that an expensive purchase was not a fake. However, rather than an uncertain family history, we might now prefer the certain knowledge that a piece had been handled by a well known dealer, particularly one that would not touch items that were modified, married, or had a significant amount of restoration. At a somewhat lesser level would be the sale by a notable auction house; lesser because their staff, while perhaps very knowledgeable, does not have the immediate fiduciary interest in quality. The staff might miss a replaced top, but a good dealer could not afford such an oversight.

## Proportion

Proportion is defined as the "proper relation between...parts," and also as "symmetry, harmony, or balance." Not surprisingly, the word comes from the Latin word for symmetry. Good proportion is achieved by design in which, as Albert Sack wrote, "each component blends into a harmonious whole." In such furniture, the size and shape of the individual elements, the legs, the case, the top, the carving, and the inlay, all come together to form a fully integrated design. Nothing seems to be out of size, out of place, or added as an afterthought. Good proportion is fundamental to quality, for nothing, neither beautiful inlay, nor elaborate carving, nor a lovely finish, will correct poor proportions. A dog in a mink coat is still a dog.

In past times, there seems to have been a lot of emphasis on pleasing lines and good proportion. Certainly there was a lot of interest in balance and symmetry. We see this in Philadelphia's Independence Hall, where large dummy windows were added to either side of the entrance just to keep the facade of the building symmetrical. Whether, as is often implied, our forbears had better judgment and taste is another question. I would suspect that the attention to balance and proportion seen in antique furniture is not only the product of long experience, but is also the natural outgrowth of a time in which furnishings were relatively expensive, were often made to order, and were expected to last a long time; all of which tended toward conservative design, pleasing lines, and good construction. We should also remember that our view of the past is skewed in that the better tends to survive the poorer. Far less of the common and the ordinary has survived.

In any event, cabinetmakers were aware of the elements that contributed to pleasing proportions and used them to the best effect. To avoid a top-heavy look, drawers were usually graduated in depth by an inch or so from top to bottom. Similarly, the upper sections of highboys and chests-on-chests were always set in by an inch or two. Where tiger maple was used for drawer fronts, the slant of the stripes was alternated from drawer to drawer to avoid the illusion of tilting to the left or to the right. The tops of candlestands and other small tables were kept as thin as possible, both to avoid top-heaviness and to provide a feeling of lightness. If thicker material were required, the top would be tapered under the edge to give the impression of a thinner top.

Cellaret sideboards present a problem, for they are basically just a large box raised on rather thin Neoclassical Hepplewhite or Sheraton legs. To break up the mass of the box, the front is normally curved and then inlaid with lighter woods. So common is this treatment that you will find rectangular sideboards to be quite rare except in small sizes where there is less mass to the box.

The thin Hepplewhite legs so common to Federal furniture can induce a top-heavy look if not treated correctly. To improve balance and avoid an illusion of tucking in, they were tapered just on the inside so that they actually splay out a little. Sometimes the whole leg is also splayed out a bit to provide a greater feeling of stability.

Poor proportions are particularly evident in candlestands and tea tables, for here the three basic elements, the legs, the column, and the top, are equally visible, and if one is not right, the whole design is compromised. All too often you will see legs that are too heavy or have a poor curve, columns with thick or uninspired turnings, and tops that are too thick, or perhaps too large for the base.

In tables and chairs with turned legs, and in chairs with turned stiles, much depends on the quality of the turnings. The best work will be both bold and crisp. In early turned chairs the medial stretcher across the front was the most visible turning, and this received the turner's best effort. A chair with a really bold medial stretcher is very likely to be a good chair. In a general way, within a style, the turnings progress from bold to less bold with the passage of time. The best work will be early in the period when the design is new and fashionable, the poorest when going out of fashion and under pressure to reduce cost. Compare early and late Windsor chairs and you will see this progression, and with this the difference that good turnings can make in the same basic type of chair.

Cabriole legs are a three-dimensional shape that requires real skill to get right. Watch out for legs that have high or fat knees, too much or too little curve, too thick or too thin ankles. A good cabriole leg should have a fairly high knee, a gradual taper from knee to ankle, and flat curves free from any excessive bow or bandiness.

Understanding and appreciating proportion requires some experience, and this short section will no more than get you started. In acquiring an eye for symmetry, there is no substitute for looking at a lot of old furniture, and for looking at it from various angles. Pieces with really good proportions look good from any angle, as you will note when visiting a museum. Auctions are also useful places to acquire a feeling for proportion, for at previews there will be a mixture of good and bad for comparison. For further reading, quite the most useful discussion is found in Albert Sack's *Fine Points of Furniture*, and in the subsequent *New Fine Points of Furniture*, the well known

"Good, Better, Best" books which have many hundreds of photos covering the good, the fair, and the poor among every major type of American furniture.

## Patina

Patina is the cumulative effect of age, sunlight, wear, and grime on old surfaces of wood and metal — and there is nothing quite like it. However well finished, a new piece of furniture, even a first class reproduction, will lack patina. Without it, not only will the object appear to be new, but it will lack much of the unique character we associate with period workmanship. To many collectors this one quality is preeminent; they will subordinate all else to it, and will not touch a piece that lacks a good patina. Patina is perhaps the most difficult of our six qualities to describe, for to a great extent, it is the look of age. Even more than proportion, patina must be seen and felt to be understood; although a good large scale color photograph of the sort you see in full page advertisements in *Antiques* magazine will give you an idea of what to look for.

Patina is the soft, warm, mellow look of age and wear, a delightful surface texture and color that comes with much time and polishing. With a good patina, we see charming variations in the color of the wood, lighter where there has been more polishing or exposure to sunlight, darker in corners where there is a buildup of old dust and wax. All over the surface there will be little random marks from long use, repairs, and minor accidents, so that the overall effect is one of continuous variation, much like the endless interleaving of order and variety that we find in nature.

However, patina is not limited to clear finishes. It includes both the color and the surface texture of all woods and metals. The unfinished bottom of an old pine drawer will have a patina that is very different from the drawer face, but which is just as important to the collector. Similarly, an old painted surface on a chest or cupboard, the weathered copper of a weathervane, and the worn surface of old silver or pewter, all have a cherished patina of their very own. Because patina normally requires years to acquire, and physically is a very thin layer of material, collectors are loath to do anything that will disturb it, for once gone, it is gone forever.

## Construction

Well made furniture is notable in the way it seems to withstand the effects of time and use. Good work will show some wear and shrinkage, but this will not affect the basic structure, and for the most part such pieces will be as sound and serviceable now as when they were made. It is not just that better furniture receives better care, for much utilitarian furniture, such as Windsor chairs, are quite sound and useable to this day.

Perhaps the best way to look for good construction is to understand the problems encountered by cabinetmakers in building strong and lasting furniture, and the solutions they developed within the available materials and technology. The cabinetmaker well understood the natural strengths and weaknesses of the materials at hand; the different kinds and characteristics of woods, the various types of joints and the best fastening methods. In particular, good construction involved compensating for the expansion and contraction of wood; something which all cabinetmakers understood, but did not always have the time to correct for in the best manner.

Most old case furniture is simply a large dovetailed box set on its side. Here the grain all runs the same way and the shrinkage will be just about the same all around. The problem arises with drawer slides and moldings, which run at right angles to this grain. If these are fastened too solidly, the sides can only split, or the slides and moldings push out, as the wood shrinks. To avoid this, in good work the drawer slides were sometimes locked into half dovetail slots without glue, so if the sides contracted, they would not split. Lacking this, slides would be set into slots and held in place with a minimum number of nails, the slot carrying most of the drawer load. The makers may have felt that mahogany was so stable a wood that the soft iron nails would provide enough give. Little did they anticipate the very dry air that was to come a century or more later with the introduction of central heating.

Cornices and the moldings to carry legs present a similar problem. One solution, perhaps the neatest, is not to attach them to the case at all. American Federal secretaries often have separate cornices, and English secretaries are sometimes made such that both the base and the cornice are separate sections; the whole secretary being in four parts, the frame, the desk, the bookcase, and the cornice molding.

Contrary to popular opinion, dust dividers between drawers do not tell us much. In England, they were felt to be such a mark of quality that even cheap, poorly made furniture was fitted with them. In this country they are not as common, and are perhaps more a sign of good work. For all this, they do not appear on a great deal of very good American furniture, so the lack of dividers has little bearing on quality; although conversely, their presence would suggest better than average work. A more useful indication on American furniture is the treatment of the top of the drawer sides. On good work these are often given a curved or molded edge rather than being left square, a nice little touch that has the additional virtue of being easy to spot.

Most of us will pull out a drawer and look at the dovetail joints, which in good work are very neatly made, particularly in front where they show whenever a drawer is opened. By itself, though, this is not much of a guide, for these joints were so common that most are reasonably well done. However, keep in mind that to make a really neat dovetail one needs a very fine saw, and the earlier a piece the fewer and cruder will be the dovetails, even on what was then felt to be first class work.

When furniture is made for the kitchen or shop, a simple nailed lap joint is often used. Even the Shakers used lap joints on workshop and laundry room furniture. Again though, lap joints are not just a sign of workaday furniture, for they were used everywhere in the 17th century before the adoption of the stronger dovetail joint.

Today we often see veneer as a sign of cheap construction, but in the past it was a mark of quality furniture. Veneer, which was hand cut and expensive, allowed the cabinetmaker to use pretty cross grains without the attendant structural problems; and to use woods, such as burls, that only came in small pieces. On some very good work, mahogany is even veneered on a mahogany base. It is not until the 19th century, when large thin sheets of veneer are used to make inexpensive furniture, that veneering becomes associated with cheap construction.

In addition to the use of figured veneers, Hepplewhite style furniture is often decorated with inlayed areas of different or contrasting woods. For best effect, these ellipses and panels need to be given a border; otherwise the eye tends to blend them into the surrounding surface. Examine this furniture and you'll see that the contrast is enhanced by a delicate little border that frames the inlay and sets it off from the mahogany background. On fine work, this border will not be just be an ebony, holly, or maple stringing, but will in itself be a complete little inlay of alternating light and dark woods. The care we see taken in setting the inlay gives us an easy check for quality work, for generally, the better the quality of the inlay, the better the quality of the piece.

When time and budget permitted, cabinetmakers used dense, close grain woods, not only for strength, but because they were less subject to shrinkage. The weight of these better cabinet woods is an indication of quality. When you handle furniture at auction previews, you will notice that some of the chairs, candlestands, and desk lids are unusually heavy, even by the normal standards of period furniture. All else being equal, these will probably be the better quality pieces.

In general, better furniture will be made with better woods, commencing with pine, poplar, and oak for simple country and kitchen pieces, then ascending through birch, beech, maple, and cherry for better, then walnut, mahogany, and satinwood for best. Remember though, that superior wood is no guarantee of a superior product, and that some magnificent work has been done with maple and cherry. One also has to keep in mind what was available, and fashionable, at different times. In England, much of the best work was done in oak until walnut became available at the end of the 17th century. Thereafter, we find oak used mostly in the simpler provincial pieces. Also, throughout the Connecticut River Valley, cherry was so popular that it was the fashionable wood.

Usually, the finer the hardware the finer the furniture, for a generous budget not only allowed for better woods and more care in construction, but also for the purchase of better brasses. Having said this, we should remember that much Colonial furniture, even good work, was fitted with inexpensive little brasses imported from Birmingham, which are not much bigger than the early William and Mary designs. Many of the replacements we see now are probably much grander than the originals ever were. However, better work did employ better mounts, and one can get a relative idea of the original cost of a piece by the quality of the brasses, provided, of course, that they are original. In addition to being larger, good brasses were sometimes silvered or gilded, but it is very rare to come across these brasses in their original state. On the really grand work you see in museums, the brasses get so large that they almost outshine the case. These large mounts must not have been common, for you will sometimes see that the plate behind a handle will have a keyhole, the cabinetmaker having substituted escutcheon plates for back plates that were evidently not available.

### Condition

If patina is motherhood to collectors, then surely original condition is the daughter, for the dedicated collector much cherishes, and will pay very dearly for, the original in old furniture. At auctions, furniture that is pretty much still all there, even if now in pieces, always fetches a premium. As you gain experience, you will more and more come to appreciate original workmanship. Simple age and a pretty finish will become less significant than the appeal of the unaltered and the unrestored. Ironically, the very same furniture in perfect condition, just out of the cabinetmakers shop, and with neither age, nor wear, nor patina, would be scorned. A time machine would do us no good at all.

How much importance to attach to condition is not always clear, for it is a function both of age and of rarity. In old and rare pieces, such as the well known Hadley chests, one would accept considerable restoration, for these very early chests have seen much use, and in any event, seldom come on the market. It would not be reasonable to expect a pristine Hadley chest. Similarly, many William and Mary chests of drawers lack their original feet, not surprising after three centuries of worm and damp floors. Here, it will take a fair amount of patience, and money, to get the original, but it is not an unreasonable quest; and the serious collector might not be satisfied with less. However, in acquiring one of the ubiquitous Federal bow-front chests, you should not have to settle for much less than pristine. A great many even have their original brasses, and show no more restoration than perhaps a few little pieces of veneer.

Both the amount and the type of restoration affect quality. For example, a replaced foot on a chest of drawers is not all that serious, for the opposite foot serves as a perfect model for the replacement. If well done, the new should be pretty much identical to the original foot. Much less desirable would be two new front or rear feet, even though perhaps enough remained to provide a good idea of what was lost. Far worse yet would be a completely replaced base, for not only is a considerable portion of the chest new, but there is no assurance that the restoration is anything like the original.

Restoration is a problem all collectors face sooner or later, for absolutely pristine condition can be very expensive. Perhaps such perfection is best left to the very grandest collections and to the beautiful full page color advertisements in *Antiques* magazine? In practice, we might follow the lead of museums, who have no difficulty with restoration so long as there is both a clear guide to the original and the restoration is well done. The key is in knowing just what the missing element looked like and how it was made. While any restoration is unfortunate, if a replaced foot brings a nice desk within reach, it should not be scorned. When considering a piece that has had some restoration, remember also that if the restoration is not good, it can usually be redone without any further damage or loss to the original structure.

Refinishing, which you would think would enhance not only condition, but also appearance and value, generally does just the opposite unless it is done with care. Aside from perhaps altering an old or even original finish, and maybe damaging the patina besides, refinishing is distrusted by dealers and collectors, for it is often a mask for major restoration. Similarly, painted surfaces may have a little skilled touch up or in painting with soluble paints, but should never be refinished, for the paint is a major part of the design. Much worse than simple refinishing, however, are the pieces one sometimes finds that have been scraped and sanded down to remove all signs of age and wear — to make them good as new again. Such refinishing not only ruins any hope of good quality, it also destroys much of the market value.

Perhaps the only thing worse than heavy refinishing are later design embellishments, or conversions to serve another use, for time will never heal these wounds. In furniture, embellishment normally takes the form of additional carving or inlay, either fraudulently performed to enhance value, or added during Victorian times when much old furniture was seen as too plain for modern taste. This is the same period when a great many lovely old silver teapots were "improved" with additional engraving.

Conversions come in endless flavors: spinet pianos will be converted to dressing tables and desks, tea caddies to knickknack boxes, knife boxes to stationary boxes, and toilet commodes to diminutive chests of drawers. Any furniture that no longer has a function is a candidate for conversion. Even if the result is good looking and far more useful than the original, such pieces are of little interest to the serious collector, and should be avoided, if for no other reason than that they will reduce the quality of your collection.

Another class of modifications are marriages. This is just as it sounds, some of the components of a piece of furniture that are now together did not start out life together. Here we find chests-on-chests with different upper and lower sections, desks with later bookcases, and tables with borrowed tops. Even if the individual pieces are all old, the piece itself is not in the least original. Marriages are fairly common among highboys, perhaps because the upper and lower cases had to be separated when moving to a smaller house, or perhaps because Americans are likely to divide up cherished possessions equally among children. Although shunned by the serious collector, there are good and bad highboy marriages, good when the upper section is consistent in size, wood, style, and region with the base, bad when a top is shoehorned into a reluctant base, or when a fan is added to a drawer to make things look better. Marriages among highboys are not as difficult as they might seem, for highboys made in same period and region can be remarkably similar. While any kind words for marriages will strike some as heresy, and indeed they should be avoided, a good marriage is much better than an oversized lowboy with a later top and a strange looking tall chest with a new base.

As a general rule, avoid antiques that are but fragments of the original: the highboy base, the secretary without its bookcase top, the dressing mirror missing its frame — even though the piece may be quite pretty and the cost very attractive. Such antiques are no particular asset to any collection. An exception, though, is the very old and the very rare, such as a Pilgrim Century blanket chest that has lost some height and the bottom drawer. Here age and rarity are their own merit, and though missing major components, such pieces have a quality all their own. You will find that these things are frequently left unrestored, even though similar work would provide a reasonable guide to the original. Restoration here may do little more than provide a mix of the very new and the very old. They are perhaps best just left alone.

As a special case among fragments, we should also consider pairs and sets of furniture which have become separated, because, while each piece may be in good or even perfect condition, each is actually but a part of the original concept. For example, highboys and lowboys were usually made up as a matching set, card tables were sold in pairs, or even in sets of four, and dining room chairs were produced in sets of two arm chairs and four or more side chairs. When together, such groupings are significantly more original than if separated, and as such, always bring a premium from the collector. While highboys, lowboys, and card tables can stand alone on their own merits, you will find that a single side chair, unless of unusual quality, will never do very well at an auction. It is all too obviously just a fragment of the original.

With these last words on condition we come to the end of this subject, having covered the more significant elements that combine to make for quality in old furniture. If this has not been the easiest chapter, it is quite the most important, for it is all the difference between a good collection that you enjoy and can be proud of, and a sorry hodgepodge that never ceases to bother you. Collecting on a limited budget inevitably requires concessions, but quality should not be one of them. Whether the level of your finances permits a grand big Massachusetts blockfront secretary, or just a simple New Hampshire country slant-lid desk, your purchase should always be of the period, exhibit good proportions, have a nice patina, and be pretty much all original. If there is some restoration, it should be correct and neatly done. Most of us must compromise on cost, but we need not compromise on quality.

# Chapter 4

## Antiques as an Investment

Although the subject of investment is seldom covered in books on period furni ture, and then perhaps only in passing, the cost in time, money, and effort, and the return on this investment, is a major factor in all collecting. As the reader may just be starting to collect, we should therefore examine investment, particularly as it applies to period furniture.

To start off, acquiring period furniture for no other reason than financial gain is an error, for not only is the real gain likely to be minimal, but also, it is the wrong approach, the wrong reason to collect. Worse yet, focusing on asset appreciation may distract us from other very real returns on our investment. However, since the hope of gain is at the heart of so much collecting, and is the first thing that may occur to your friends, we should cover this first. Then we'll touch on some other, and perhaps more important, returns on our investment.

That there is a long-term gain in the real value of antiques appears to be true, if only in that antiques are a limited commodity in a growing economy. However, the appreciation will usually be slow, prices rising irregularly in response to collecting trends and other economic activity. Studies of the market have observed, that in the long run, the best work in any field of art tends to appreciate the most. Those of us who cannot afford the best must make do with a slower rate of gain, but nevertheless, some gain is still there. To gain at all, though, we must collect wisely, always looking for real value and having the patience to wait out, or work around, the inflated prices that accompany surges in popularity or a particularly strong market.

Collections that appreciate the most are those that exhibit both focus and quality. After some initial and perhaps more or less random acquisitions, most successful collectors settle on a particular area of interest, then acquire a real knowledge of the subject. In period furniture the area might be a period such as Federal, a region such as the Connecticut River Valley, a genre such as Shaker, or a type such as painted furniture. The collection does not have be the very best in the field, or even all that expensive, but within its scope it must be consistent and of uniform quality. The market rewards this thoroughness, for such a collection will do exceptionally well when it is disbursed. At auctions you will see that good collections, even if not particularly grand, generally do much better than is warranted by the normal market value of the items themselves, for consistency suggests a prudent and knowledgeable collector, and with this a corresponding quality. Even very average lots among the collection will do well. Not only will the sum be greater that the parts, but the rising tide will, in some measure, lift all the boats.

All art is subject to changes in taste, to swings in fashion, and period furniture is no exception. The last 90 years have seen, in turn, enthusiasm and very high prices in Pilgrim Century, Federal, Connecticut, and Shaker furniture. In addition, different things become popular at different times. In the late 1980s, for instance, sideboards and card tables were much in demand. It is important to be aware of these distortions in the normal market. We do not want to buy high, and then perhaps have to sell low. Even if we are able to purchase the very best, our investment may still depreciate. Observers of the art market have noticed that taste tends to skip generations, and if you buy near the crest, it may be a very long wait before your particular market recovers. However, these changes in fashion also present opportunity to the contrarian investor, one who looks for things of intrinsic value that are under priced because they are currently out of fashion. If the area that interests you is not popular, but has real merit, in the long run it may prove to be a better than average investment.

Collectors and dealers are by nature incurable optimists, and you will hear all sorts of stories of things acquired at a fraction of their true worth, and of collections that have soared in value. Because the reader may just be starting to collect, we might review some of these tales, for they can lead to unreasonable expectations of financial gain.

Quite the most common example of gain is a comparison of prices then to prices now, and the inference that with a little patience the same good fortune awaits us. As further inducement, there always seems to have been some time in the not too distant past when lovely old furniture could be had for a song. Unfortunately, such proofs usually reflect more optimism than reality. For some reason, the examples always seem to coincide with a rising market, comparing an economic valley with an economic crest, going from a low point in the market to a high point in the market. The price indices which track the changes in various classes of art also seem to favor periods of rapid economic growth, with the additional bias in that they are based on prices at major auctions, which tends to be the better art that does exceptionally well in a strong market. This is not realistic. Any investment will look good if the starting point is a time when prices are depressed. Start in the Great Depression and everything is a winner. A more honest analysis might be a long-term running average, or perhaps a comparison of similar periods in economic cycles, such as the late 1920s with the late 1980s. With this we would also need a market basket of antiques, sort of a S&P 500, to even out trends in collecting and changes in fashion. Then we might be able to obtain a true measure of long-term appreciation — provided that we also compensated for the value of the dollar.

This leads to another caveat. In looking back, do not overlook changes in buying power. The last 50 years have seen almost continuous inflation. Stories of wonderful buys are a lot less wonderful if we remember that the dollar has lost about 90% of its face value since 1940. A chest of drawers bought then for $500 would have to sell now for over $4000 just to break even. This presumes that when young we even had $500 to spend on just one piece of furniture, and our decorating, in fact, was not based on the local Salvation Army store. That something could once be had for a song does little good if we could not afford the song.

In truth, buying antiques in the expectation of rapid appreciation is just speculation, somewhat classier sounding but really no different than trading in pork bellies on the Chicago exchange. Now there is nothing at all wrong in speculation, per se, for it is one of the driving forces behind our economy and the source of many fortunes. However, successful speculation in any market requires dedication and hard work, an intimate knowledge of the field, some talent, and a fair amount of luck. It is best left to professionals. All markets in art are subject to waves of enthusiasm and inflated prices. It takes a special kind of collector to make money in such an environment. Timing is everything. You must anticipate an area of rising prices, get in early, then get out early, selling off things you may have come to love. How many of us could do this? Always remember that speculative markets have few real winners. They are supported by the great mass of those who get in late, and then, get out late. They buy high — and sell low.

While on this subject, something might be said about the truly remarkable appreciation that occurs when something wonderful turns up, perhaps at a yard sale or in a small antiques shop, and none are aware of its real market value. Hardly a week seems to pass that the press does not report on such marvelous finds, even though we know in our hearts that they must be actually be very rare, and in any event, seldom involve furniture. At a more practical level, though, all collectors sometimes come across a very good buy, perhaps because something was not identified correctly, or because no dealer at an auction could use the piece. However, such serendipity does not happen every day, and it will take a long time to build a collection on nothing but bargains. In practice, most collections are made up of a few pieces that were very good buys, a majority that were obtained at a fair market price, and perhaps a few obtained at a premium because they were just too good to pass up.

Although the appreciation may not be as great as we might wish, period furniture does have the advantage of being a remarkably tax free investment. Our collection generates no interest or dividend income, is not reported to the Internal Revenue Service on one of those ubiquitous little 1099 forms, and is not subject to real estate or excise taxes, as are houses, autos, and boats. If things are sometimes sold to upgrade the collection, any increase in value might be subject to taxes on the gain, but this is very seldom done, perhaps because the real gain or loss would be difficult to determine. Most art simply does not have a clear value.

It might be mentioned here that while there is little tax burden, there is also very little the collector can do to deduct the expenses in maintaining a collection. A dealer can write off burglar alarms, humidity controls, and insurance as the costs of doing business, but the collector has little chance at these deductions because the Internal Revenue Service views collecting art as a hobby. This is a little discouraging, for there can be significant expenses to the active collector, but then, perhaps the less the government is involved in one's affairs the better?

From all this, you might think that old furniture is not a good investment. Well, that's not true. It depends on how you define investment, what the word really means to you. Actually, things from the past are a very good investment, but perhaps not the way some would have us believe. Collecting provides a variety of returns. Only some are monetary. It is the others that we should keep in mind, for to most of us, they are far more real than any financial windfall.

First off, in comparison to new furniture that starts to depreciate from the moment it is brought home, period furniture, particularly if obtained at fair market value at an auction, is a far better buy. In many ways it is not unlike real estate, which if purchased wisely, and then well maintained, does not lose value, and indeed, is very likely to gain value with time. If sold, the only cost to the homeowner is the broker's commission; and similarly, if antiques are sold at auction, the only cost to the collector is the auctioneer's commission, and in some cases, both are negotiable.

For most collectors, the search itself is one of the great pleasures in collecting old furniture. Hunting for something that is uncommon, in a market where there is much we cannot afford, is necessarily a long-term avocation, and one that is little limited by age. Over the years you will travel all over, see a great many lovely things, and get to meet a lot of people in an interesting business that is full of characters. Indeed, for some collectors the hunt itself is nine-tenths the pleasure.

There is a certain quiet pride in owning antique furniture, even though our Puritan consciences tell us that this is something that "goeth before the fall." Two hundred year old furniture in everyday use is not found in many households, and this sets one's home apart — which is perhaps what pride is all about — doing something a little differently or a little better than others. There is also satisfaction in a sound collection, in having the patience and the prudence to seek quality in the face of a limited budget and the constant temptation to compromise. In another sense, there is an honest enjoyment in understanding and appreciating things from the past, in taking good care of them, then passing them on to others, for in the long run, we are not so much owners as we are stewards.

Finally, period furniture is a joy to the eye and a pleasure to have in the home. Much of the enjoyment in collecting old furniture is that you get to live with it every day. Like an interest bearing account, it provides a continuous small return. It is not just something occasionally taken out of a cupboard or a drawer to show to other collectors and to honored guests. Wherever you turn there is the boldly turned stretcher, the gracefully shaped column, the delicate inlay, all to charm the eye and delight the senses. In the morning you can take a fresh shirt or blouse out of a Federal bowfront chest of drawers, comb your hair in front of little dressing mirror, and as you come down the stairs, check with the grandfather clock to see if you are running late. In the evening you can return home from the office and unwind in a lolling chair with a drink on the little snake-leg stand beside you, then at dinner, sit on Hepplewhite chairs at a Regency dining table.

It is a nice way to live.

# Identifying Period Workmanship

Now we must learn to recognize period workmanship. How do we tell the difference between a 200 year old chair and a good 1930s reproduction? More significantly, how do we tell the difference between this chair and a 100 year old Colonial Revival reproduction? This is important, not only in building a sound collection, but also because reproductions, whatever their age, are far less valuable than comparable period work. We do not want to pay for period, then bring home a reproduction. As we'll discover in this chapter, identifying period workmanship is not as difficult as it may seem, for once we know what to look for, old furniture generally tells us both its age and its source. However, there are times when the voice is not at all clear, and if in doubt, we should always seek the advice of someone more knowledgeable.

This will be a long chapter, for there is much to consider when dealing with old furniture. To help keep things straight, it is divided it into a series of topics, each covering a salient characteristic of period work. Therefore, we will examine in turn: dimensions, construction, tool marks, fastenings, hardware, finish, patina, wear, shrinkage, and yes, even smell.

Before getting started, it should be noted that in determining age and period, the reader should always consider the sum of the evidence. Not often does furniture survive two hundred or more years of use without some repairs and refastening. Thus, it is not uncommon to discover much later elements in genuine early work, and we must look past these to ascertain the real age. At an auction preview I once examined a little pine wall box which still retained most of its old red paint. The front was originally fastened with a couple of handsome early rose-headed nails. Sometime later, as the wood shrank, the front had pulled loose, and several small cut nails were added. Still later, the top of the backboard had broken and was repaired with a modern wire nail. Here we have much of the history of nails, and all within one small object! Yet this little box could be assigned to the late 18th or early 19th century, not only by the old red paint, but by its earliest fastenings — the rose-headed nails.

The other rule to keep in mind is that furniture must always be dated by its latest stylistic feature. For example, a chair with Queen Anne legs and a Chippendale back will not be earlier than Chippendale. It cannot be otherwise. Similarly, one of the popular Massachusetts serpentine-front desks having ball and claw feet, although Chippendale in style, if fitted with original Hepplewhite brasses, must be Federal rather than Colonial. It is important to keep this in mind, for such an imprimatur is attached to age that most of us instinctively seek out the earlier rather than the later in estimating age and period.

## Dimensions

When looking at old furniture, perhaps the first thing that catches the eye is the unusual size and proportions. Most typically, period furniture will be significantly larger in some aspect; it will be deeper, or wider, or higher — and sometimes, all three. Many pieces will be much bigger than what you would expect from the pictures you see in books. In addition, there will be none of the diminutive chests and tables now so commonly placed at the ends of sofas and beside beds. Low occasional tables, such as the ubiquitous coffee table, are also a modern development. Aside from a few forms, such as toilet commodes and children's furniture, there is very little that is either small or low in period furniture. For the most part, charming little furniture is not old furniture. Here then are some of the things to look for:

- The width and depth of Windsor chair seats varies greatly in period work. Early Philadelphia low-back and comb-back chairs typically have great wide seats, a full 6" wider than modern practice. Conversely, many old Windsors will have very shallow seats, seemingly designed for people with short legs.
- The seats of Queen Anne and Chippendale side chairs will be an inch or more lower than their modern counterparts; and Chippendale chairs, in particular, will also be a couple of inches wider, something you will notice if you try to fit a set of Chippendale chairs into a small dining room. Sometimes you will also see a slipper chair, a full sized chair with a seat only 12" to 14" high.
- Similarly, early wing chairs will seem a bit lower if lacking the original thick down cushion; and may be much bigger and wider. Some are so wide that they could comfortably seat a couple of children.
- Queen Anne and Chippendale chests of drawers are about modern height, but later Federal and Regency chests will normally be about 40" high, roughly as high as they are wide. Also common are tall chests of drawers having five, six and even seven drawers. These are typically country pieces, and will range from five to six feet high.
- Desks and secretaries vary a lot in size, many being quite large by modern standards. In addition, the writing surface is very often too high for comfort. There seems to be no common explanation for this, for you will be told variously that this height made for easier reading by candlelight, or that desks were frequently used while standing, or that a higher than normal chair was used, or that a thick pillow was used on the chair.
- Dowry chests are quite big, typically four or more feet long. Blanket chests are smaller, but still about 40" long.
- Hepplewhite and Sheraton sideboards will normally be three or four inches higher and deeper than their modern counterparts. Empire sideboards will be higher yet.
- Pembroke tables, which were used as breakfast tables, vary greatly in size. While some high style tables are quite small and modern looking, many are much bigger, perhaps 28" to 30" high, 35" long and 40" wide with the flaps up.
- Rectangular tray-top tea tables are much bigger than the modern reproductions now used as end tables. Period tables will be perhaps 26" high, 32" long and 20" deep.
- Candlestands, will usually be much higher than now, perhaps 26" to 29" to the top. Place a candle on one and you'll discover that this extra height brings the rather limited light of a candle in over the shoulder, even when the candle has burnt down to a stub.
- Tall case clocks, particularly those with the expensive eight-day brass works, were intended to be imposing pieces, and will often be eight or more feet high, too tall for many modern houses.

From this we see that both in size and in proportion, old furniture is apt to be very different from modern. Period furniture will also differ in various small ways from later reproductions whose design has been modified to suit current taste. While period in appearance, they are more contemporary in scale. These differences, both obvious and subtle, are a good way to spot genuine period furniture among the numerous reproductions seen in small antique shops.

## Construction

Quite the best way to identify old furniture is by determining how it was made. This is a dead giveaway, for handmade furniture is very different from the factory product of our times. It is also very different from modern handcrafted furniture in which power tools have been employed to reduce time and labor. With some experience you will discover that in making furniture entirely by hand, a trace of the craftsman inevitably remains in the work. While signatures and labels are rare, to a certain extent, every piece is "signed," not only by regional shop practices, but in the small variations among individual craftsmen. These little reminders of the past contribute much to the charm of antique furniture.

Perhaps the first thing you notice is that old furniture is made with great wide boards. The mahogany tops of tea tables, sideboards, and chests will typically be a single piece of wood. If made from smaller trees such as cherry and walnut, two pieces may be used, with sometimes a narrow filler in between. Never will you see a top made up from many narrow pieces of wood glued together. The sides of chests and desks will also be just one or perhaps two pieces of wood. Look at the backs and bottoms of American work and you will see that the secondary woods are very wide. It is not at all unusual for a pine or poplar back to be made from a single board. Windsor chair seats will also be made from a single wide plank; it is not until well into the 19th century that we see built up chair seats, and even these will be composed of just two or three pieces.

When looking at the wood, note that unless an unusually wide plank was required, boards were always quarter sawn. Such a board is cut radially from the center of the log. Think of a slice of pie. If a very narrow piece is cut so that the sides are almost parallel, that will correspond to the cross section of a quarter sawn board. When seen from the end, the annual rings will be at right angles, or almost so, to the side of the plank. Most such wood will not have a great deal of figure, although quarter sawn or rived oak shows a pretty figuring called rays, a bonus for having cut it to best advantage, for cut this way a board will be easiest to work and is least likely to shrink and warp. Logs are now usually plain sawn straight across the growth rings, which provides the most useable lumber and the widest boards, but at the cost of much more splitting and warping.

These wide boards give us an insight into what was once a very different countryside. The first settlers found themselves on the fringes of one of the greatest temperate forests the world has ever seen; one in which a squirrel could travel from Maine to Florida, and west to the Ohios, without ever having to touch the ground. Magnificent stands of oak, walnut, pine, and popular soared high into the air from a largely open forest floor, the first branches not appearing until far above the ground. This was indeed "the forest primeval, the murmuring pine and the hemlock." Two hundred years later it was all but gone.

After examining the wood, look at how the piece has been joined together, for this also will be very different from modern practice. The old time joiners and cabinet-makers, not having high speed precision cutting tools and modern fastening systems, employed a limited set of joints that were easy to lay out and suitable for pinning and gluing. The most common of these are shown in Figures 5-1. The joints that were used varied with the craftsman. A carpenter's work would be mostly limited to simple edge nailing, and rabbet, butt, and miter joints, while a joiner would be skilled in mortise-and-tenon work, and a cabinetmaker in all kinds of dovetails. More significantly, they built furniture this way. So pronounced is this difference that we might well refer to the age of the joiner as the age of the mortise-and-tenon joint, the age of the cabinet-maker as the age of the dovetail joint. Among these joints, the spline and the double rabbet are now rarely used, and the blind dovetail and the mortise-and-tenon have been replaced by doweling. Of all the cabinetmaker's dovetail joints, only the lapped dovetail still survives in some better furniture.

If the piece you are examining has a drawer, you are fortunate, for the easiest way to spot period workmanship is to look at how a drawer has been made. The earliest drawers have the sides nailed into a rabbeted front using a simple a half-lap joint, a simple construction that survived in country and kitchen pieces well into the 19th century, and in inexpensive furniture, right to this day. These early drawers were hung from rails, having thick sides with a slot that matched a runner that carried the drawer (5-2). This allowed the drawer to be hung with a minimum of framing, but aside from this, these drawers were not very successful, being very heavy and prone to jamb. Within just a few years they were superseded by a new type of drawer consisting of a dovetailed box that rested on slides, a design at once so perfect that they have continued in use right down to our time. A drawer made with dovetail joints allows a light but strong frame, for the sides no longer have to be thick to support the nailed lap joint; and the dovetail joints perfectly resist the natural tendency of the front to pull off when the drawer sticks.

*Figure 5-1 Cabinetmaker's Joints*

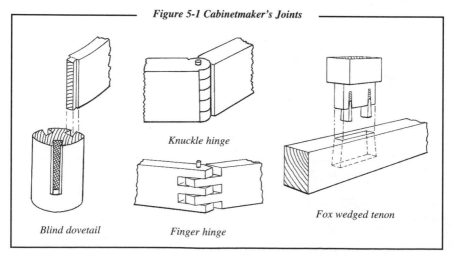

*Knuckle hinge*

*Fox wedged tenon*

*Blind dovetail*          *Finger hinge*

*Figure 5-1 Cabinetmaker's Joints*

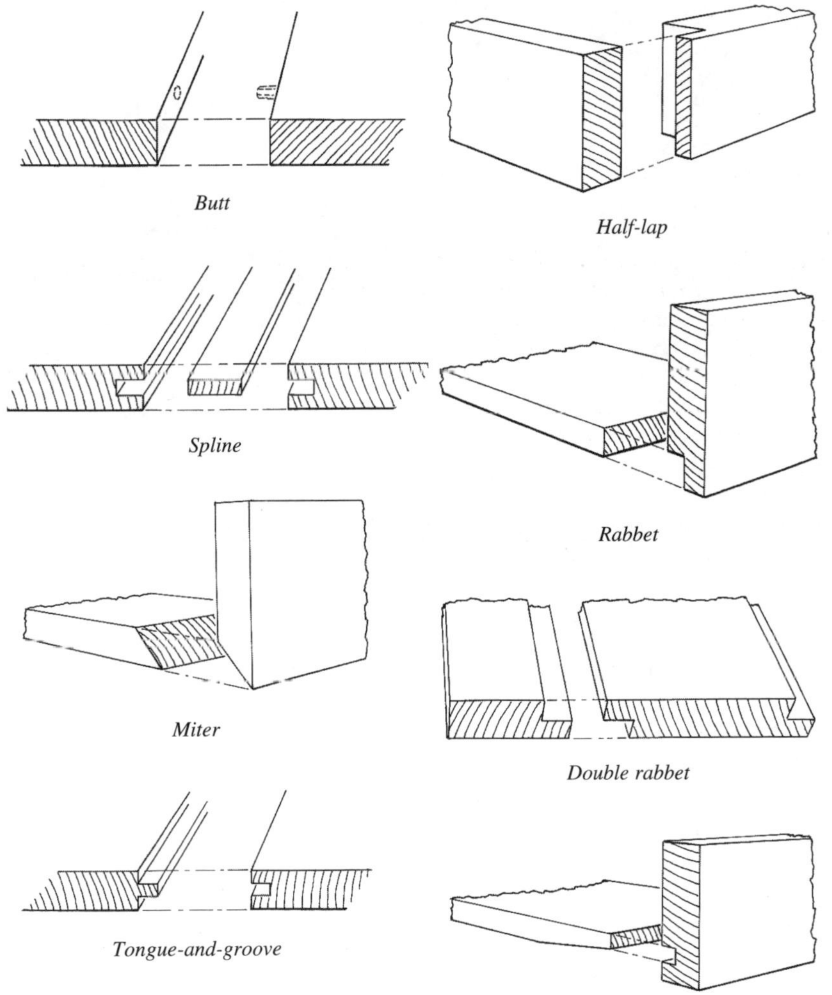

Butt

Half-lap

Spline

Rabbet

Miter

Double rabbet

Tongue-and-groove

Dado

Lap

Rule hinge

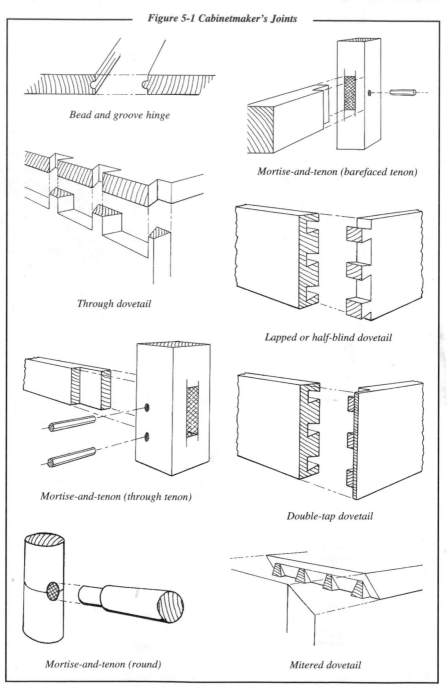

**Figure 5-1 Cabinetmaker's Joints**

Bead and groove hinge

Mortise-and-tenon (barefaced tenon)

Through dovetail

Lapped or half-blind dovetail

Mortise-and-tenon (through tenon)

Double-tap dovetail

Mortise-and-tenon (round)

Mitered dovetail

When we look at a dovetail joint on a drawer, we see that it is made of interlocking "pins" and dovetails . In handwork, the dovetails are invariably wider than the pins; they do not become equal in size until cut by machine about the middle of the 19th century. They will also be somewhat uneven in width, and across the base of the dovetail will be a thin line that was scribed by a marking gauge to indicate the depth of the dovetail. The earlier the work, the larger and fewer will be the dovetails. The first drawers had just one or two, often reinforced with a hand-wrought nail or two; later there will be four to six as shown in the figure. With time the pins get smaller and smaller, progressing from a hefty trapezoid on early work to a thin vee shape found in some later urban work. With time, and with better saws, the quality also improves, going from simple and rough to so neat and refined that it almost seems to be the product of a power tool. This progression from crude to fine, and from few to many, provides us with a rough measure of age, if we keep in mind that urban work will normally be more advanced than rural. However, it is not always this simple, for we also need to keep in mind that the quality of dovetail joints is likely to be poor in simple rural survival furniture. Here crude dovetails are not a sign of very early work, but rather, very late work. In addition, remember that in any one period dovetail joints are the product of many hands, and it is not at all unusual, even on major pieces, to observe overcut and poorly fitted joints.

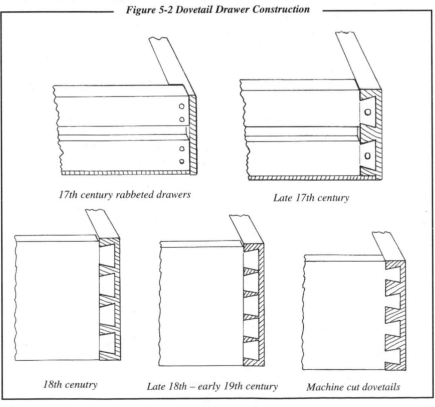

*Figure 5-2 Dovetail Drawer Construction*

*17th century rabbeted drawers*

*Late 17th century*

*18th cenutry*

*Late 18th – early 19th century*

*Machine cut dovetails*

**55**

The fronts of drawers also tell us of age, for they too were made very differently than now. The problem here was how to make a drawer that would stay tight and dust free in spite of wear and shrinkage. An associated problem was how to keep the veneer on a drawer from being damaged as it was closed, especially if the secondary wood shrank a bit more than the veneer. Ancillary to these problems there is a question of style, for drawers look best if they appear to stand slightly out from the surrounding case. Each drawer should, in effect, be "framed" within the case. Over the years these problems were handled in four different ways: by the use of contrasting veneers, by lipping the drawers, by the use of cockbeading, and by the use of a simulated cockbeading. With the aid of Figure 5-3, let's take a look at each of these solutions, for they are not only an interesting aspect of period work, but also help us to date old furniture.

Early veneered drawer fronts were commonly bordered with either a cross-band or herringbone pattern of contrasting wood which provided the desired framing and minimized the effects of shrinkage by making the edges from short pieces of veneer. The framed effect was then further enhanced by bordering the drawers with a single or double half-round molding applied to the face of the case. At first, drawer fronts were through dovetailed, a poor construction as glue would not hold well on the end grain of the dovetails. This ceased to be done by about 1700, and if you see a drawer made this way you are looking at very early work. The solution was to set the dovetails behind the drawer face by the use of the lapped or half-blind dovetail joint. Now there is no exposed end grain and all the veneer has a common base. More importantly, the dovetails are hidden so that the face of the drawer no longer must be veneered. So successful was this change that to this day — almost 300 years later — drawers are still made with these same lapped dovetails.

The next innovation was to lip the drawers. This not only provided the desired framing, but also allowed the drawer front to shrink without showing a gap and letting in dust. Lipped drawers first appear in England about 1720, then in America about 1740. At this time drawer fronts were often veneered, and English cabinetmakers devised a somewhat complex built up lip that both kept the front tight and protected the veneer. However, in America lipping was not used on veneered drawers, and here the lip was simply a shallow rabbet cut into the back of the drawer front. Now popularly called thumbnail-molding from the shape of the small molding worked into the edge of the lip, this design was so successful that it continued to be used right up into the early years of the 19th century. A charming feature of this practice is that usually only the top and sides of the drawer front were lipped, then the thumbnail molding was worked in on all four sides, giving the impression that the lip continues all the way around. Because the drawer rests evenly on the divider, there was no reason to add a lip across the bottom. This also avoided damage to the lipping when the drawer was lifted out and placed on a table or on the floor.

The problem with all lipped drawers is that the lip tends to break out at the corners, either from something sticking out when the drawer is closed, or by someone trying to pry open a stuck drawer. You will find that much old furniture has repairs to the thin and delicate lipping.

The final step was the introduction of cockbead molding, which also was introduced about 1720 in England, then gained in popularity as the century wore on and built up lipping fell into disuse. Cockbeading, or cocked bead molding as it is sometimes called, is a small rounded molding attached to all four edges of the drawer front. Typically, it will form a cap to the top of the drawer front and then be rabbeted into the sides and bottom as shown in the figure. By the middle of the 18th century this was the normal type of English drawer front, although it does not seem to have become common in America until after the Revolution. Both Hepplewhite and Sheraton drawer fronts are normally veneered, and the cockbead protects the edge of the veneer. You will find that cockbeading is often reinforced with small cut nails, particularly on the short side pieces that are fastened to the end grain of the drawer front.

When the cabinetmaker employed well seasoned mahogany, there was less need to allow for shrinkage. Thus, on much of the better American work, if the face of the drawer is not veneered, there will be no special treatment of drawer edges — they will simply be cut straight across. What you will see, however, is a simulated cockbeading, a small half round molding worked into the case sides and drawer rails. From a dis-

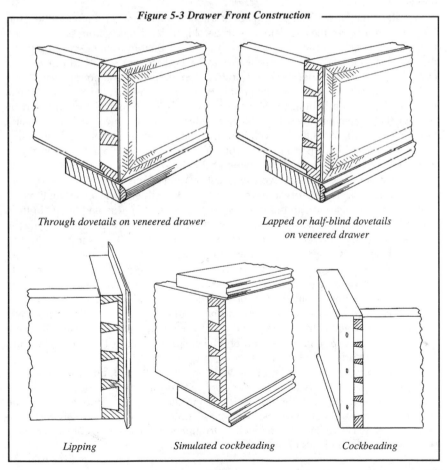

*Figure 5-3 Drawer Front Construction*

*Through dovetails on veneered drawer*

*Lapped or half-blind dovetails on veneered drawer*

*Lipping*

*Simulated cockbeading*

*Cockbeading*

tance, the drawers appear to be cockbeaded. This was also the normal treatment on chests with blocked and serpentine fronts where cockbeading would have been difficult to cut and fit.

While here, we should discuss the construction of curved drawer fronts, for special techniques were employed when the front could not be made up from a single thin board. If you look at block-front chests, you'll find that the drawer fronts are generally a great deal thinner than what you would think, the back having been cut away in profile with the pattern of the blocking. The backs of serpentine-front drawers are cut away in a similar manner. This extra labor was required if the drawers were not to be front heavy.

On bow-front chests of drawers we see a different construction. Here the fronts are either laminated from thin boards, or built up with neatly fitted blocks, or "bricks," which were then planed smooth before veneering. Look inside the drawer of an old bow-front chest and you will often be able to pick out the joints between the blocks. This was done not so much to save wood, as to avoid end grain, which is a poor ground for veneer.

Finally, something should be said about the bottoms of drawers before putting this subject to rest. Here the problem was threefold: to have the bottom light, but stiff enough not to sag and bind the drawer; to keep the bottom from opening up when the wood shrank; and to minimize the wear on both drawer sides and drawer rails over many thousands of openings and closings. On early work, the bottom was simply nailed (5-4A). Sometimes a thin runner of hardwood would be added to cover the nail heads and allow the bottom to clear the drawer blade. This was later improved by rebating the bottom into the sides, which provided a smooth drawer side and a neater looking job (5-4B). The difficulty with both methods, however, is that even if well seasoned wood is used, the bottom will eventually shrink and split. Something has to give when the bottom is locked into the frame of the drawer.

This problem was solved in two ways: first by running the grain of the drawer bottom from side to side rather than from front to back; and secondly, by fitting the bottom into dados or grooves in the sides of the drawer (5-4C). Running the grain from side to side reduced shrinkage by minimizing the width across the grain; and fitting the bottom into grooves allowed it to expend and contract with changes in humidity. To avoid sagging over this greater span, the bottom was sometimes divided into two sections with a muntin across the middle (5-4D), although these are not as common on American work because the thicker pine bottoms seldom require additional stiffening. At first drawer bottoms continued to be nailed at front and back, but later the front was also grooved and they were fastened only at the back. In effect, the bottom was now free to float within the frame of the drawer. However, not all drawers are made this way. On block-front furniture, and on Philadelphia furniture, the grain of the bottom continues to run from front to back.

After the Revolution the sides of drawers tend to get thinner, and when the sides are very thin it is necessary to provide not only additional bearing surface, but also to reinforce the joint between the drawer sides and the bottom, for the grooves in the sides of the drawer that receive the bottom will now be very shallow. This was done by adding battens or a line of thin blocking to stiffen the joint and to spread the wear between the sides and rails (5-4E).

This progression in drawer construction is not as straightforward as it may sound, particularly in the case of drawer bottoms, for small drawers that see little shrinkage and carry only small loads can be given almost any sort of bottom. Even on 19th century work the bottoms of small drawers may be just rebated into the sides, or simpler yet, just nailed directly on to the bottom. To properly evaluate drawer construction, we should always examine the larger drawers.

Now having looked at drawers from every angle, let's consider the case they served. Aside from pulling out a drawer, to really examine case furniture we must look in, look under, and look behind. First off, the backs of desks and chests of drawers were never finished, but left rough, either as cut from the mill, or more commonly, quickly smoothed down with a jack or fore plane. Even the most grand pieces of furniture will have simple, unfinished backs. Because secondary woods tend to shrink, it was common to overlap the joints to keep out the dust. Prior to about 1750 this was done by camfering and overlapping the edges; thereafter it was more common to employ a

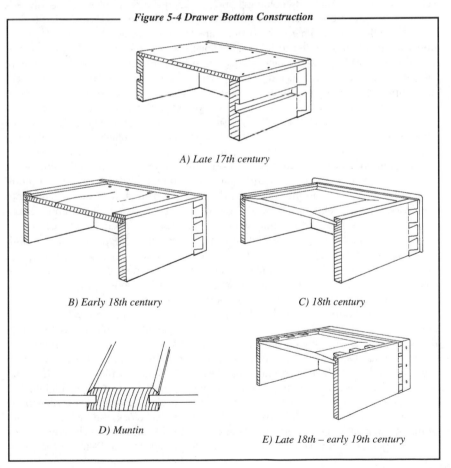

*Figure 5-4 Drawer Bottom Construction*

A) Late 17th century

B) Early 18th century

C) 18th century

D) Muntin

E) Late 18th – early 19th century

**59**

tongue-and-groove joint, although in much American furniture the boards are simply butted together. Fastening was sometimes done with wooden pins, but more commonly we will find rose or T-headed forged nails, and later, cut nails — very likely accompanied by a modern wire nail or two where a board has come loose. Backs do not acquire a smooth, finished look until the power planer arrives in the middle of the 19th century. Even here, many simpler pieces continue to use unplaned stock, and this is where you will sometimes see the characteristic curved marks of the circular saw.

We noted earlier that most case furniture is basically just a large box dovetailed together at the corners. Where the corners show, as in the tops of desks, lapped dovetails were normally used, but where they would be covered, the cabinetmaker simply used large through dovetails. These may be difficult to see from the bottom where they are often covered by framing and blocking, but they show nicely behind the upper molding on the unfinished tops of highboys and tall chests of drawers.

The dovetails that join the edges and corners of case work are usually easily concealed under tops, behind moldings, and inside drawers. However, the dividers between drawers present more of a problem, for they should be dovetailed to lock in the sides of the case, and here the dovetails are not so conveniently hidden. The Middle Atlantic colonies tended to follow the English practice of concealing joints, and would hide these dovetails behind a covering strip, a molding, or a quarter column. However, on much New England Colonial work, even on good work, these dovetails are simply left showing, a somewhat hasty solution that in some ways adds much charm to this early furniture. These exposed dovetails were handled one of three ways. The first, and most direct approach, was simply to extend the dovetail clear through the side of the case (5-5A). The disadvantage was that the dovetail showed on the side of the case, and since it was the end grain, it was very obvious. A neater solution, which required a little more work, was to stop the dovetail just short of the side of the case (5-5B). Better yet was to first cut a shallow dado in the case, then to use a shouldered dovetail that fit into the end of the dado (5-5C). The drawer runners fitted into the dado and were held in place by a couple of nails. Because the divider and the runners rested in the same groove, they would always stay in perfect alignment.

In the years following the Revolution American furniture becomes more sophisticated, and in Federal furniture, except for some rural work, we no longer see exposed dovetails on dividers. Here the dovetails are either stopped short of the front of the case, or hidden behind a thin covering strip, or concealed behind a corner molding such as the quarter columns that were so popular in the Delaware Valley.

Look at the bottom of an old desk or a chest of drawers and you will see that the apron and feet are just glued in place, then reinforced with glue blocks (5-5D). Often the blocks are roughly shaped with a chisel or a file so that they do not show. The square vertical block at the corner acts to reinforce the facing and actually carries much of the load of the case. Sometimes there will be a nail or two. Screws were not used, and if you see them, either the piece is not old, or they are a later addition. This is not the best construction, for the grain of the vertical block is at right angles to the grain of the facing. In the South, instead of a single vertical block, the foot may be supported by a small stack of horizontal blocks set at right angles to each other so that there is a good glue surface on both the front and the sides of the facing. Incidentally, these glue blocks were not clamped in place while the glue dried; they were just given a liberal coating of hot glue, then wiggled into position with enough pressure to force the air out and make a good bond. As the glue cooled and set up it would pull them firmly into place. While this was the normal construction, there were regional variations. In Boston the feet were glued to a strip of wood fastened to the underside of the case, and in Connecticut the feet were sometimes made up as a separate assembly, then nailed into place.

When examining a lowboy or a chest of drawers, pull out the top drawer and look under to see how the top has been attached. There were a number of ways this was done. Because the grain of the wood on the sides of lowboys is run horizontally so that it can be tenoned into the legs, or in Newport work, be dovetailed to the front and the back of the case, the top cannot be fastened with dovetails. Therefore, the tops of lowboys are normally either secured with hand cut wood pins, or fastened from the

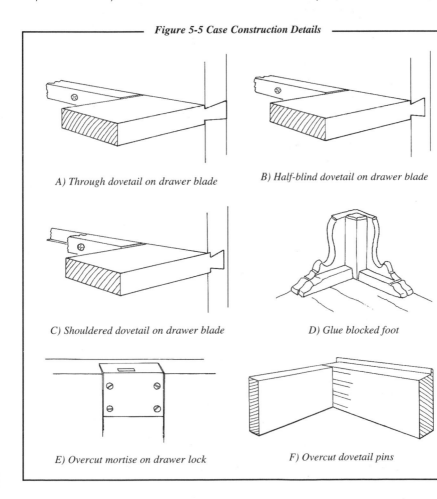

*Figure 5-5 Case Construction Details*

A) *Through dovetail on drawer blade*

B) *Half-blind dovetail on drawer blade*

C) *Shouldered dovetail on drawer blade*

D) *Glue blocked foot*

E) *Overcut mortise on drawer lock*

F) *Overcut dovetail pins*

underside with a row of blocking. Neither method is perfect, for the side to side grain of the top must shrink across the front to back grain of the sides. If the pins do not pull out, in time shrinkage across the grain of the top tends to loosen the blocks This may be why we so often see lowboys with restored tops.

The grain of the wood on the sides of chests of drawers runs vertically, and here the normal method is to first lap dovetail in a pair of rails at the front and back of the case. These both secure the top of the case and provide an attachmant for the top which is then fastened with screws driven up through the rails. Another, and more elegant solution, is to cut either a full or a half dovetail across the length of the upper edge of each side of the case, and a pair of similarly shaped slots in the underside of the top. Then the top is just driven on from the front. As it expands and contracts over the years, it can move back and forth in the slot.

The undersides of tables were also left unfinished, but unlike the backs of case work, the surface was worked down quite smooth so that it would rest evenly on the frame or bed of the table. The top was then secured one of three ways. In much early country work, the top was simply pegged to the rails with tapered wooden pins driven in from the top. Typically, these pins will be almost square in cross-section. Often you will find some later screws or nails added where pins have come loose. When better woods were used, the top was fastened from the underside with a row of glue blocks. This is a better fastening than it may sound, as there is not a great deal of shrinkage across the grain of the top, early dining tables being quite narrow with the leaves down. A variation was to screw cleats to the underside of the top. The cleats would be given short tenons that fitted into matching slots in the apron so that the top would be free to expand and contract. Then, as the cost of hardware came down, tops started to be fastened with screws driven up from the inside of the rails. To provide a level surface and to minimize screw length, a semicircular pocket would be chiseled out inside the rail (5-6A). Look under Pembroke and card tables and you will find that most all have their tops fastened this way. When the tops of tavern tables were not stiffened with breadboard ends, there will usually be a stretcher running across the grain and then notched into the frame of the table (5-6B). The top is then nailed to the stretcher. Also, the legs, rails, and stretchers of these rural tables will be joined with mortise-and-tenons, which you will spot when you notice the pins used to lock the joints.

The leaves on Pembroke tables (17-13) are usually supported by brackets that swing on wood hinges, although on simpler work you will find the use of wood pivots. On old tables the hinges will have five knuckles, and there will often be two brackets under each leaf. Nowadays there is usually just a single bracket, sometimes with just three knuckles.

Pillar form circular candlestands and tea tables employ a very different construction. First off, with a few late and rare exceptions, they always have just three legs. Four leg tables do not appear until an additional leg is required to support a large dining table. Not only do three legs always rest evenly on an uneven floor, but in a time when everything has to be worked up by hand, four legs would not be used when three would do. Turn over an old candlestand and you'll see that the three legs are joined to the column with a blind dovetail (5-1). Because this joint tends to break out when stressed, the column will either be somewhat heavier at the bottom, or be reinforced with strapping. The strapping may be a single triangular piece of iron, or three little overlapping straps. However, there are some stands in which the legs are simply mortised-and-tenoned into the column. Here the column is generally hexagonal at the bottom end, and will extend below the underside of the leg to provide sufficient stock at the lower end of the mortise. To keep the leg in place these joints are usually pinned. However, this method of construction is mostly limited to rural New Hampshire work, and is not common. On most modern candlestands the three or four legs are joined to the column with a pair of dowels, and if they have loosened a little, as is often the case, you will be able to see that the leg has not been fastened with a mortise-and-tenon joint. Also, a blind dovetail joint will not be evident at the base of the column.

Because furniture was generally kept along the sides of rooms when not in use, all but the simplest or smallest of these old pillar form tables incorporate a tilting mechanism. The other reason for this feature is that small tables could then double as firescreens. The tops of non-tilting tables will simply be nailed or screwed to a tapered board that is then mortised to the pedestal. The tops of tilting tables will be fastened to a pair of tapered cleats, generally with screws, but sometimes with rose-headed nails in early work. These in turn pivot on a hardwood block that is joined to the pedestal with a square tenon. It was common, particularly in the Middle Atlantic colonies, to fit tables with a "birdcage" mechanism so that the top would both rotate and tilt (5-6C).

Lastly, we should discuss chairs. Like tables, chairs are the domain of the mortise-and-tenon joint which was used fasten the stretchers to the legs, the seat rails to the front and back legs, and the crest rails to the stiles. As with tavern tables, you will often see pins used to lock the tenons in place. As a general rule, these pins are a useful guide to age, as they indicate the use of the mortise-and-tenon joint rather than the doweled joint which was introduced later in the 19th century at a time when furniture has become a factory product.

*Figure 5-6 Table Construction Details*

A) Screw pocket

B) Notched in stretcher

C) Birdcage mechanism

Another good indicator of age in a chair is the treatment of the back splat. When you examine a Queen Anne or a Chippendale chair, you'll notice that the edges of the splat are normally chamfered or beveled toward the back. This seems to have been done so that the outline of the splat would appear crisp and clear even when the chair was viewed at an angle. Most reproductions lack this little touch, and today it provides us with a handy clue to period workmanship. It also illustrates the attention to detail and perspective that characterizes so much period workmanship.

While looking at the back, see how the bottom of the splat is joined to the back rail. In high style chairs there will be a section known as a shoe which provides a graceful transition between the vertical splat and the horizontal rail. In period work the shoe is generally separate from the rail, what is called a detached or a two-part shoe. On drop seat chairs, the bottom of the splat is mortised into the top of the shoe with a simple barefaced tenon, the shoe then being glued to the top of the rail (5-7A). However, reproduction chairs normally employ an integral shoe which is just an extension of the back rail. The back rail and the shoe are fashioned from a single piece of wood. While there are exceptions, the majority of old chairs are not made this way. They will have a separate shoe.

On over-upholstered chairs, a different method was used because there is no way to fasten down the back of the fabric without having a row of exposed tacks across the front of the shoe. The solution here was to bring the splat right down into the rail, then to cut out the shoe so that it would pass in front of the splat (5-7B). The upholstery was tacked down to the top of the back rail before the shoe was fastened in place. The shoe was then fastened with just a couple of little headless nails so it wouldn't be hard to remove when the fabric needed replacing. From the front these chairs look as though the bottom of the splat is housed in the shoe, but tip the chair forward and you will see the splat passes behind the shoe. In effect, the shoe is not structural, it is just a fabric cover.

It was normal practice in the past to reinforce the joint between the seat rails and the legs with braces or blocking, particularly if the chair was not fitted with stretchers. While the method of reinforcement varied from one area to another, the point to remember is that original blocking will be fastened with glue, or with glue and nails, but never with screws. If you find corner blocks fastened with long screws, either the chair is not old, or as is often the case, the blocks have been replaced, or perhaps added later.

Should the chair be fitted with stretchers, you are in luck, for this is a good place to spot old construction. When there are cabriole legs, the turned stretchers will usually be tenoned into the front legs with a narrow rectangular tenon, which provides a strong joint and avoids weakening the ankle with a large round hole (5-7C). If the chair has straight legs, the stretchers will employ easily made barefaced tenons, and the outside of the stretchers will be flush with the outside of the legs (5-7D). Should the legs be molded, that is, curved in cross section, you may find that the stretchers are not quite flush. These flush stretchers are only found on period chairs — or on unusually faithful reproductions. Stretchers on modern chairs are fastened with dowels, and to leave sufficient room between the dowel and the outside of the leg, the stretcher must be set in a little. In addition, the stretcher may also be thickened to carry the dowel,

**Figure 5-7 Chair Construction**

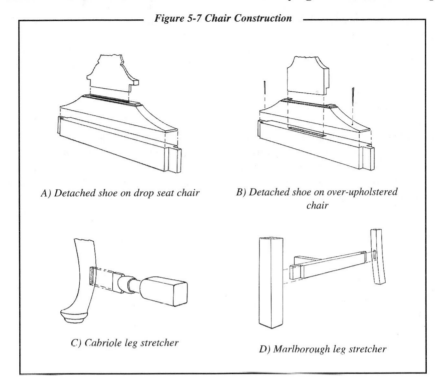

A) Detached shoe on drop seat chair

B) Detached shoe on over-upholstered chair

C) Cabriole leg stretcher

D) Marlborough leg stretcher

and will usually then be centered in the leg. While this detail may seem small, it is significant, and you will see it all the time.

While on the subject, is should be emphasized that dowels were almost never employed to join old furniture. Dowels did not come into common use until the second half of the 19th century, and if you find a chair fastened this way, it cannot be a period chair. A few chairmakers employed short hand cut dowels to fasten the crest rail to the stiles, but the seat rails will always be joined to the legs and stiles with mortise-and-tenon joints. Another exception is found in large table tops, where butt joints were often reinforced and kept true by use of short hand cut pegs set between the planks.

Now that we have covered specific things to look for, there remains to note a few construction features we find in all period furniture. First off, veneer was hand sawn, and unless refinished right down, will be a great deal thicker than what we see now. Prior to 1700 it was only available in fairly small pieces which may be as much as 1/10" thick. Later, as saws improved, it became possible to cut larger and thinner sheets, and by 1800 it was common to veneer up whole drawer fronts with sheets, or more properly, flitches, of mahogany veneer that were only 1/16" or so thick. After about 1850 veneer is machine cut and may be only 1/50" thick. Modern veneer is peeled from large logs in paper thin sheets, and is easy to tell from early work if you can find a little spot where it has lifted to reveal its extreme thinness.

Spade feet, which are found on some American and much English Hepplewhite style furniture, were normally worked out whole from the stock, which you can spot if you look carefully at a foot where the figure of the wood can be followed across the spade. However, this was not always so, for on some fine work the spade was built up with contrasting pieces of ebony or a darker mahogany — a nice finishing touch on a fine table or chair.

The larger case pieces, secretaries, highboys, and the like, will be made up of a number of component sections stacked on top of each other, sometimes then topped with a separate cornice. Although two sections are most common, some American secretaries were made in three sections, and there are English secretary bookcases with four sections; a frame that carried the legs, then the desk proper, then the bookcase top, and finally the cornice. Building furniture this way had a number of advantages, in addition to reducing problems with shrinkage: it made large furniture easier to handle in a small shop, easier to repair, easier to transport, and then easier to work up the narrow stair wells so common in old houses.

While touching on case furniture, it might be noted that if there are paneled doors, they are more likely to be fielded (beveled on the outside edges) in the 18th century and reverse fielded (beveled on the inside) in the 19th century. Also, the door hinges on secretaries will normally be mounted behind the frame so that only the pivots show from the front.

Period furniture is often quite heavy, even though the wood has had two centuries and more to dry out. This is due partly to the ample use of wood, and partly to the use of very close grain woods, particularly the dense mahoganies. You will notice this weight in things you are apt to move; in chairs, table leaves, and desk lids; and indeed, a quick way to check if a chair may be old is simply to pick it up.

Lastly, and perhaps most significantly, always remember that in an age of hand-craftsmanship a worker's time was literally money. The more produced, the more money to be earned. In such an environment a cabinetmaker would employ all sorts of little shortcuts, and would never do any work that was not absolutely necessary. Earlier in the section we noted the rough backs on case furniture and the unfinished bottoms of drawers; but this is only the tip of the iceberg, for as you study old furniture you will notice that cabinetmakers employed all kinds of shortcuts where they could save a little time and it would not be noticed. For example, lapped dovetails were never used where simple through dovetails would do, nor mitred dovetails where lapped would do. Only the surfaces that showed were ever given a finish. The tops of high chests, the undersides of tables, and the insides of drawers were invariably left bare. Desks and chests fitted with carved front feet will frequently have simpler rear feet. Even when there are ball and claw feet all around, the back of the rear feet that were out of sight against the wall were usually left uncarved. Similarly, fluting was often not extended to the rear of Sheraton sofa legs, the back of the leg will be left uncarved. Beds also illustrate this economy, for carving was normally limited to the posts at the foot of a bed. The back posts, covered by hangings, were just left as turned; and the headboard, hidden behind bolsters and pillows, will be of a simple shape and have no more than a minimum of finish. To save a little time, mortises for table hinges and drawer locks were often overcut so that only a few quick cuts with a chisel were needed to complete the mortise (5-5E), and similarly, the pins of the lapped dovetails on drawer fronts were sometimes partially cut with a saw, which can be seen on the insides of the drawers (5-5F). The shoulders of tenons were cut at slightly more than the required angle to assure a good fit at first try, which at times shows in the blind dovetail joints on candlestands. Aside from a few guide lines from a marking gauge, chair stretchers were quickly turned by eye, and as a result, often exhibit a delightful asymmetry.

These many little testimonies of calculated haste tell us something about the life of the cabinetmaker. They make the world then far more real to us than perfection ever would, and as you would suspect, are much loved by collectors. Much of the charm of old furniture lies not in the perfect, but in the imperfect, in these many small evidences of calculated haste. Somewhat like an artist, the cabinetmaker relied on visual effect rather than complete accuracy, knowing that the eye always fills in where necessary; much the way a painter gives the effect of leaves rather than painting every single one.

In retrospect, this section very briefly covers a large and diverse subject. Words such as "often," "normally," and "frequently" have been used generously, and for good reason, for in an age of handcraftsmanship one finds innumerable variations among normal practice. This section, long as it has been, covers only the most common features found in period construction. Among the thousands of individual craftsmen scattered up and down the eastern seaboard, there are endless little local variations in construction methods. They will keep scholars occupied for years.

### Toolmarks

Much of the charm of period furniture lies in the little reminders of handcraftsmanship left by the workmen so many years ago. Many are tool marks, still remaining faintly on primary surfaces because there was never enough time to work them completely out, and left untouched on secondary surfaces where they would not show. These echo the most commonly used cutting and marking tools, falling into nine general categories; those left by saws, planes, lathes, chisels, gouges, files and rasps, scribing tools and drills, and also, chalk and pencils, which we might not always think of as tools.

So much has been written about saw marks, or more correctly, kerf marks, that we'll confine this discussion to some general comments and a few significant dates. First off, saw marks are not as common as you might think, for generally the cabinetmaker quickly cleaned up rough mill stock, even when it was only to be used for back boards. However, we do find telltale marks on secondary surfaces when the mill stock was left unfinished, or where the marks were not entirely cleaned up.

All saws cut by means of either a back and forth reciprocating stroke or a continuous circular movement, the latter being a relatively modern technique. Early reciprocal saws, whether a panel saw, a bow saw, or the large pit saw, left irregular kerf marks that altered in depth and angle between cutting strokes as user tired or shifted position. Also, because of the way in which they were used, we would expect the marks left by pit saws to be at an angle to the grain of the wood. The large, coarse marks of these big saws are commonly ascribed to very early work, and most of them probably are, although pit saws were still in use in country districts in England right up through the 19th century. In

America, where there was ample falling water and a chronic shortage of labor, sawmills were common within 50 years of the first settlements; and when you see early kerf marks on American furniture, they will usually be the rough parallel marks of these water powered saws. Now long gone, evidence of their presence remains in the number of Saw Mill Runs and Saw Mill Roads that are found all up and down the East Coast.

Quite early on it was realized that a saw that cut by continuous motion would produce a cleaner and a faster cut by not losing position and time in the return stroke. Samual Miller patented a circular saw in 1777; and small hand powered circular saws were being used for inlay cutting by the end of the 18th century. However, large circular saws require both considerable power and high speed rotation, which was difficult to obtain from a water mill which does not turn at more than a few rpm. Thus, it was not until the development of economical high speed steam engines, about 1830, that the circular saw really caught on. The other continuous motion saw, the bandsaw, was patented in 1808, but also lagged in application, not coming into use until the 1840s. Its kerf marks also show the regularity of a power saw, but will be straight up and down across the grain. From this we see a general rule that saw marks on old furniture should be not be curved, and aside from the large marks of the old mill saws, should not be regular. These indicate later work, or perhaps some restoration.

Unlike saw marks, evidence of planing is common on period furniture. Most conspicuous will be the shallow curved mark left by the jack or fore plane on the unfinished back boards and the bottoms of drawers. On primary surfaces this rough planing was then followed by careful leveling with a long, straight-bladed trying plane, then by much scraping to achieve a satisfactory surface. In skilled hands this leveling was remarkably good, and at first glance primary surfaces will seem quite smooth and flat. However, if you pass a hand lightly over the surface, and across the grain, you will often feel the slight unevenness of a handworked surface, the hand being more sensitive than the eye. A word of caution is in order, however, for a good cabinetmaker could do wonders with a fine steel scraper, and some surfaces, particularly the tops of tables where even a slight ridge would show against a slanting light, were worked very smooth indeed. Here the telltale unevenness of handwork may not be felt, and may only show if you pass a light under the edge of a straightedge.

Another area where you can spot plane marks is along the edges of moldings. Sight along an old molding in a good light and you can sometimes see slight irregular marks left by the molding plane.

Power planing machines came into use about the same time as circular saws, but unless the cutters were very sharp they were apt to leave fine ripple marks across the grain of the wood. In good work these would be taken out with a trying plane set to a very fine cut — a remarkable exercise in cabinetmaking skill. Should you spot these slight ripples you'll know that you are not dealing with early work.

The significant aspect of hand or foot powered lathes is that they turned much more slowly than their modern counterparts. In treadle lathes the motion was also reciprocal, cutting only on the down stroke of the treadle. This low rotation rate tends to leave faint marks that spiral completely around a turning. They are particularly noticeable in the deep turnings, perhaps because of less wear here, or because the turner could not quickly remove them with a file. Incidentally, the "X" centering mark is the trademark of a modern lathe, and indicates new work, or perhaps a pieced out or replaced leg. The old lathes left a single shallow centering hole which you will sometimes see on the bottom of chair feet.

There is not much to say about chisel marks, for there are fewer than the common use of these tools would indicate. The cabinetmaker's most frequent use of chisels, cutting mortises and dovetails, leaves little evidence in the finished joint. However, chisel marks do show nicely on the insides of drawer fronts when a recess has been cut for the nuts of the pulls, on the backs of chairs when the splant has been beveled, and on the insides of the rails of tables when a pocket has been cut for the screw. Another place where we often see old chisel marks is where they were used for marking rather than cutting; in matching up with Roman numerals (I, II, etc.) bed rails and posts, and the drop seats in chairs. Even carefully made mortise-and-tenon joints require a little final fitting, and will not be quite interchangeable. Matching the joints by number made correct reassembly easy when the bed was delivered to the customer. Similarly, drop seats must be trimmed to fit individual chair frames, and were generally marked with matching numbers on the underside of the seat frame and then on the inside of the front or back seat rails. These numbers can sometimes tell us, hundreds of years later, about the size of the original set. A "XV" on a rail would indicate a very grand set indeed.

There are also few marks from carving tools, mostly because relatively little carving is found among period furniture. Carving requires considerable time to lay out and execute, and even a simple fan or pinwheel was an extra. While we see a lot of carving in museum collections, the great majority of surviving period furniture has none whatsoever. Not until carving machines were developed in Victorian times do we find much carving on average quality furniture. However, if you get the chance to look at some old carving, you will see that the tool marks are not all that noticeable. Carvers worked with very sharp tools and were careful to leave few obvious marks that would have to be cleaned up later. Indeed, very little sanding and finishing was done after the carving was completed. Where you may have to look for carving marks is in out of the way places where only quick shaping was needed and the work could be left in the rough. We find this in ornate mirrors and in the crests of William and Mary chairs where the design was first cut through and then carved. Here the back would be beveled with a few quick cuts, then left rough because it would not show.

Cabinetmakers employed files and rasps for all sorts of quick shaping, particularly on cabriole legs. However, these areas were then cleaned up with scrapers and sandpaper. Where you will find marks, though, is in out of the way places where there was no need to clean up the surface, particularly on the undersides of curved aprons which were first chiseled to shape, and on the inside of feet where the blocking was rounded off so as to not show.

The marks of old scratch awls are also less common than you would think, for they were usually employed to mark cuts, and the saw then removed the scribed line. The neat little hairline cuts we tend to assign to these tools are generally the work of their more specialized cousins, the depth and mortising gauges shown in Figure 1-3. They show in the marking the depth of drawer dovetails (5-2) and in marking the edge of mortise cuts in a mortise-and tenon joint (5-1). Sometimes it is possible to pick out traces of the center hole and arc left by the compass in laying out pinwheels and fans. We also see scribe marks left on chair turnings to locate mortise and drill holes, but again, these are perhaps the product of a marking gauge, which was used by the turner to assure that the position of the mortises would be identical from leg to leg and stile to stile. The turner would turn dozens of legs at a time, and all had to be interchangeable.

Drill holes may seem a little strange to classify as evidence of old tool marks, but they are a significant element in much old furniture. The important thing to remember here is that the modern gimlet-pointed wood drill did not come into use until about the middle of the 19th century. Shine a light into the hole made by one of these drills and you will see the very characteristic flat bottom with a deep groove around the outer edge cut by the fluke, and then a large gimlet screw hole on the center. Prior to the development of this drill, either the pod bit or the brad pointed bits shown in Figure 1-3 would have been used. The pod bit left a round bottomed hole; and the brad pointed bit a flat bottomed hole, but without the outer edge groove and the threaded gimlet hole of the modern twist bit. However, these characteristic drill marks are not easy to check without access to an X-ray machine, for it is not common to find period furniture that has pulled apart at the joints. Furniture in pieces, where we can easily check drill holes — and spot doweled joints — is likely to be modern work. Furniture that has survived several hundred years may have some fractures, but it is not likely to be pulled apart at the joints. The chair in pieces that you spot at the town dump may indeed be an old chair, but it is very unlikely to be a period chair.

Just as cabinetmakers would identify specific bed joints and chair seats with chiseled Roman numerals, they also used penciled numbers to distinguish between parts that required individual fitting up. These are most common on the backs or bottoms of small drawers of desks and dressing mirrors where drawers would have been interchangeable; and where the job would really be messed up if two drawers were inadvertently fitted for the same opening. In addition to the chiseled numerals linking chairs with their respective seats, the legs, rails, and backs of chairs will sometimes carry the same numbers as an aid in assembling the set. If the number seven (7) is used, it will usually be what we now think of as a European or Continental seven with a crossed staff. In addition to fitting drawers and assembling sets of chairs, we will also find shop marks used where parts might be interchanged or reversed. Written in script in pencil or chalk will be "L" and "R," "Top" and "Bottom," "Front" and "Back."

Sometimes these little casual notations offer insights into production practices. I've seen a Regency dressing mirror where the three small drawers and the corresponding case openings were marked "10," "11," and "12"; indicating that these little shaving mirrors were sometimes made in production runs of at least four at a time.

### Fastenings

After construction and tool marks, perhaps the next easiest thing to spot in old furniture are the fastenings the cabinetmaker used where carefully fitted joints and glue would not suffice: pins and wedges, hand wrought and cut nails, and handmade screws.

Any discussion of fastenings should begin with those made of wood, for they are almost certainly the oldest, wooden pins having been used to lock mortise-and-tenon joints in ancient Egypt. These pins should not be confused with the modern dowling that is sold in stock sizes. The old ones were cut from hardwoods with a small spokeshave or knife into a rough polygon that would jamb satisfactorily in the hole. On finer and later work, more care was taken to make them circular, and you may have to look closely to see that they are not quite round. When the inner side of a joint would not show, as in the upper rail of a tavern table, pins were often just broken off short, or sometimes just left untouched.

It is popularly thought that mortise-and-tenon joints were locked in place with a "draw bore pin." Here the hole through the tenon would be bored slightly nearer to the shoulder than the hole through the sides of the mortise. When the pin was driven in, the offset would tend to pull the tenon into the mortise. This technique was indeed used by joiners in making paneled chests from rather green wood where shrinkage across the grain of the stiles would tend to loosen the joints, but does not seem to have been employed by cabinetmakers who worked with seasoned wood. In any event, such pinning would require an extra marking and drilling operation in assembling every joint, which would seem out of keeping with the general economy of effort we see in period furniture.

Note here that we are discussing pins, not the plugs that one sees in so much contemporary furniture. Plugs are not fastenings; they are just little round inserts employed to hide fastenings. Remember that you pin a joint and plug a hole. Unlike pins, the grain of a plug is always parallel to the surface to blend in with the surrounding wood. Plugs, and the precision plug cutters that make them, are a modern development. When cabinetmakers needed to plug a hole, which was not common, they normally employed a little bit of colored beeswax.

In addition to locking joints, pins were also used for fastening in lieu of nails where there would not be a great deal of pull on the joint. Thus we see them employed to fasten down table tops, to pin on backboards, and to join together small drawers.

Among wood fastenings you will often find wedges used to lock joints. These are most commonly seen in Windsor chairs where the legs are brought up through the seat plank and then wedged to keep them tight. On bow-back Windsors, the spindles are similarly wedged where they pass through the bow, as also are the arm supports when they pass through the arms. The wedges will always be set at right angles to the grain to avoid splitting the surrounding wood. On some Windsors the legs do not come up through the seat. However, these are probably also wedged, but with the blind or fox wedge, a clever and somewhat insidious fastening that will be discussed when we get to repair and restoration.

If wooden pins are ancient, hand forged iron nails are not all that much newer, being found scattered around old Roman military camps. By the time of our interest, nail making was a well established trade. Nails could be made from any available iron, but the professional would normally start with nailer's rod. These were soft iron rods, perhaps 2' long and ¼" square. To make nails, the rods were first heated and pointed, then cut, put in a swage block and headed. The hammering resulted in a tough nail, that being almost pure iron, was very resistant to corrosion. Although tough, they seem now to have little temper, and are easily bent.

These simple nails were manufactured in large quantities; a few men and boys could produce several thousand a day. Like their modern counterparts, they were made in a wide variety of shapes and lengths from large spikes down to tiny headless brads. In old furniture you will see them in all sizes from about 3" long down to very small finishing nails; and with rose heads, T-heads, L-heads, and almost no head at all (5-8). They are commonly called rose-head nails, but the term is somewhat deceptive, for the four or five quick heading blows often produces a more square than round head, and in truth, many of the heads are pretty much shapeless. Whatever the shape of the head, the common characteristic of all hand forged nails is a roughly square shank tapering on all sides to a sharp point.

Toward the end of the 18th century a new method of manufacture was developed in which nails were "cut" from a strip of iron. The cut was made at a slight alternating angle to provide a taper, the width of the strip determining the length of the nail. If you associate names with dates, then remember that Ezekial Reed's cut-nail machine was developed in 1785. At first cut nails still had to be headed in a separate operation, which gives early examples a somewhat hand forged look; but by 1825 this also was being done by machine. Cut nails cost about a fifth of the hand forged variety, and by 1800 they were in common use, although hand forged nails continued to be used by some cabinetmakers, particularly in England, until about 1830. Their relative softness probably made them a superior furniture nail. Actually, cut nails are too brittle to clench an exposed point back over into the wood, so forged nails were used right up through the 19th century for boat and wagon work. Despite their brittleness, the sharp edges of cut nails hold very well, and they are still in use today for jobs that require a nail that will not back out. Whether headed or not, cut nails characteristically have a rectangular cross section that tapers on just two sides, then a blunt point at the end. Like the hand forged nail, the old ones are iron rather than steel, and thus quite rust resistant.

The modern wire nail is developed in the 1870s, acquiring its name from the large coils of steel wire that were fed into the nail making machine to be automatically pointed, cut, and headed. Early wire nails can be distinguished from their modern counterparts by bulbous and eccentric heads. The common wire nail, with the normal or "common" head, is found in reproduction furniture — and also here and there among the rose headed and cut nails in the backboards of old furniture. The small headed finishing variety appears just about everywhere in old furniture as the signature of a hasty repair job.

Before finishing, we should touch on upholstery nails, as they are perhaps the most common fastening on sofas and upholstered chairs. Old tacks, like early nails, had square shanks and handmade heads, and are not too unlike a very short hand forged nail. However, as upholstery became more common, so did the demand for upholstery nails, and by 1810 tack making machinery was in use. Thereafter, but for the lack of modern bluing, tacks are very similar to the ones you now find in a hardware store.

For many years, but particularly during the Federal period, it was popular to decorate the edges of the fabric on chairs and sofas with round-headed brass upholstery nails. These were cast in rows, then broken out and polished. In addition to their typical square shanks, you can sometimes still see the breaks on either side of the head where they once joined their neighbor. Modern upholstery nails are easy to spot as they have a very different construction, being made up of two pieces; a round wire shank spot welded or crimped to a stamped brass cap.

**Figure 5-8 Fastenings**

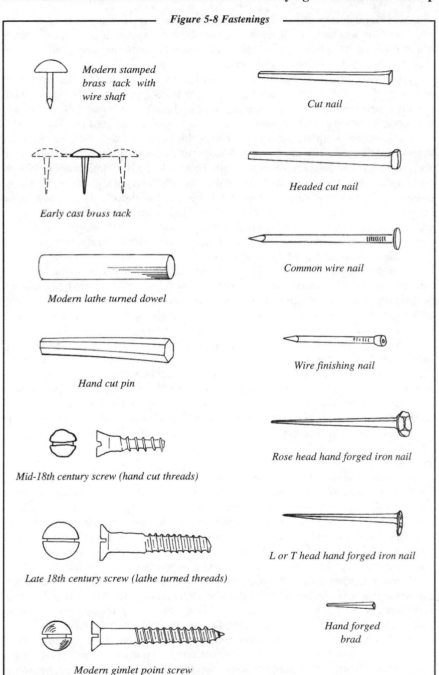

Modern stamped brass tack with wire shaft

Early cast brass tack

Modern lathe turned dowel

Hand cut pin

Mid-18th century screw (hand cut threads)

Late 18th century screw (lathe turned threads)

Modern gimlet point screw

Cut nail

Headed cut nail

Common wire nail

Wire finishing nail

Rose head hand forged iron nail

L or T head hand forged iron nail

Hand forged brad

73

Always remember that even if a nail is missing, you can tell much by the hole it has left; hand wrought nails will leave a square hole, cut a rectangular hole, and wire a round hole. As mentioned earlier, there will often be later fastenings, but here we should judge age by evidence of the earliest.

As you would think, screws are a relatively late development. The first mention of their use in furniture occurs in a book published in 1678, but they were employed considerably earlier in firearms where the high cost of the product justified the expense of this superior fastening. Early screw making was a laborious four step process in which the shank was first shaped by swaging, then roughly headed, after which the head was shaped and slotted, and finally the threads were cut. These early screws have blunt ends and are typically quite short, often no more than ¾" long. The threads will be deeply cut and the screwdriver slot may be quite thin, having been cut with a saw. Often the slot is very obviously off-center. As we don't ever want to disturb old screws, look for the off-center slots and heads that seem to have been shaped with a file. When examining old furniture, you will generally find that among every half dozen or so screws, one or two will have noticeably off-center slots. Modern machine made screws not only have wide centered slots, but the head will often show circular turning marks. Because of their high cost, very few screws are used in furniture until the middle of the 18th century. Then they start to appear in places where a short screw was effective and the better holding power justified the cost; in table and door hinges and in the cleats under table tops. However, in early work you may also see nails used in these locations, sometimes with a little leather washer under the head to provide a snug fastening.

In common with nails, efforts to increase production and reduce cost commenced in the latter years of the 18th century, continuing until the modern gimlet point screw was developed in 1850. By the end of this century lathes with a mechanical advance were used to cut threads, and by 1815 screws were being made mostly by machine, although still with blunt ends and without the characteristic turning marks we see in the heads of modern screws. Most of the original screws we find in period furniture will have regular lathe cut threads, blunt points, and handworked heads.

### Hardware

Now we come to a topic that everyone knows a little about, for there is hardly a book on old furniture that does not have a plate showing the styles of brasses associated with the different periods, and indeed, these are such a useful identifier of period that we'll also illustrate some of the more common designs (5-9). However, furniture hardware is not just limited to brasses, or mounts, as some prefer to call them, but also includes locks, hinges, castors, and window glass, and these we will cover also, for they are in some ways even more indicative of period workmanship.

Furniture hardware was obtained from merchants, some of whom may have specialized in this business, for by the end of the 18th century the various available styles and shapes of brasses were being illustrated in catalogs not too unlike the publications now available from Ball and Ball, Horton Brasses, and others. In America until 1820, or thereabouts, most brasses were imported from the industrial center of Birmingham, including the highly prized Federal pulls decorated with patriotic figures of eagles and thirteen stars. So dominant was Birmingham in the production of furniture hardware, that with few exceptions, the pulls and latches on American furniture will almost always be English and from Birmingham.

When examining brasses, as much as the shape, we need to look at the way they have been made and the way they are installed, for old designs are so commonly reproduced, that by itself, style is not much of a guide to age. Until rolled sheet brass became available in the last quarter of the 18th century, back plates and escutcheons were sand cast, then scraped and filed down to obtain a smooth finish. On many you will still see small inclusions from the casting, minute ripples left by the steel scraper, and file marks around the edges. The backs will show the fine pebbled look of the casting. William and Mary period brasses are very thin and are decorated by chasing, which is the art of creating patterns by cutting or hammering with specially shaped chisels (5-9A). Look closely at William and Mary period brasses and you'll notice that the patterns on no two plates are quite alike. Early pulls were first in the form of single small drops. Originally round and solid, they were later made half round and pear shaped; and if this latter shape, will always be hollow. A few years later, about 1700, the larger and easier to grasp bail handle is developed (5-9B). Whether drop or bail, they were fastened with long cotter pins passed through the drawer face and then clenched over into the back. This is a somewhat weak attachment and not many of these early brasses survive intact. Even if the pin did not pull out it would tend wear through where attached to the drop. Sometimes you will see furniture with genuine old brasses that have been given new heavier cotter pins. During this period the back plates of the pulls and the key escutcheons are treated as different design elements, and usually do not match. From a distance, though, the most noticeable thing about these early brasses is not the lack of matching plates and escutcheons, but that they seem too small for the furniture they serve.

Shortly after the turn of the century, about 1710, the post and bail pull is developed (5-7C). This innovation was so successful that it was never replaced by anything better, and is only now becoming outdated. Here the bails are fitted into the ends of posts or pommels which pass through the drawer face and are secured by nuts on the inner side. At first the bails pass clear through the posts; but later, as the bails are made heavier and stiffer, the holes extend only about ¾ the way through the posts. Period posts have square shanks, and the early nuts will be rough squares, almost like little threaded slugs, which is just about what they were. After 1770 you will also see the use of round slotted nuts which seem to have been tightened with a tool that fitted into the slot. Throughout the Queen Anne and Chippendale periods, the bail ends face outwards, the corresponding holes in the posts facing inwards. Although most cabinetmakers went to post and bail pulls, there is much style overlap in this time, and the old fashioned and less expensive cotter pin hardware continues to be used on rural work right up through the last half of the 18th century.

After William and Mary, back plates and escutcheons get both thicker and larger, and now are made in matching sets, or en suite. No longer do they seem too small for the furniture, although early Queen Anne brasses are still not very large. With these changes, chasing goes out of fashion and decoration is now obtained from shape alone, which becomes much more ornate. Better work from this era not only has fanciful Rococo shapes, but will have pierced or cut out centers (5-9D).

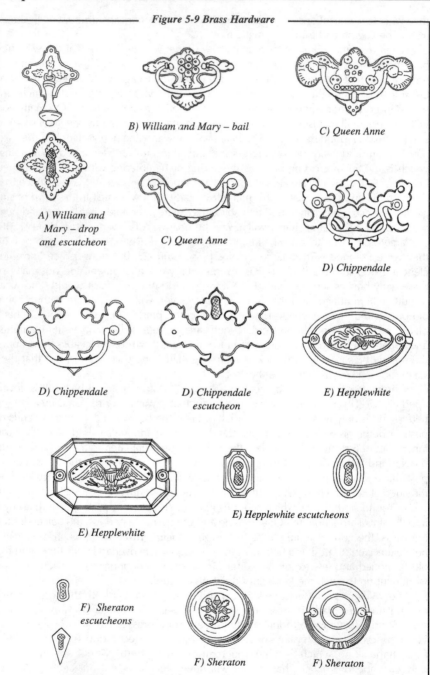

## Figure 5-9 Brass Hardware

B) William and Mary – bail

C) Queen Anne

A) William and
Mary – drop
and escutcheon

C) Queen Anne

D) Chippendale

D) Chippendale

D) Chippendale
escutcheon

E) Hepplewhite

E) Hepplewhite escutcheons

E) Hepplewhite

F) Sheraton
escutcheons

F) Sheraton

F) Sheraton

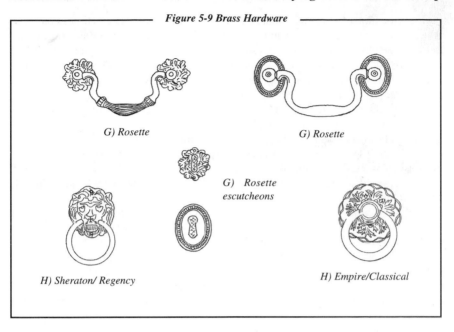

*Figure 5-9 Brass Hardware*

G) Rosette

G) Rosette

G) Rosette
escutcheons

H) Sheraton/ Regency

H) Empire/Classical

Chippendale brasses can become very grand indeed, and in fine collections you'll see secretaries and chests of drawers in which half the front seems to be covered with brass.

Another change we see during the middle of the 18th century is the introduction of brass with a higher copper content. Before this time brass has a larger proportion of zinc and is a slightly paler yellow, a feature much admired by those who collect old candlesticks. The difference is not all that great, but it shows if you hold some modern brass beside an old pull.

About 1780, the cost of brasses is greatly reduced by cutting the back plates and escutcheons directly out of rolled brass sheets, an innovation that lessens much of the character of the later Chippendale pulls, for now there is little to tell them from modern reproductions. Most of the Chippendale pulls you'll see on old furniture are made from these rolled plates, their unfortunate appearance not being helped in that a great many are too small — the result being a sort of William and Mary scale, but without William and Mary character. Another common feature of these inexpensive little export brasses is that the threaded posts are too short to extend beyond the inside face of the drawer, and the cabinetmaker will have chiseled out little depressions in order to put on the nuts. Dealers will tell you that this was done to protect the clothing from snagging, but I would suspect the real reason was that money could be saved by keeping the length of the threaded shaft to a minimum. On later Federal furniture, when thread cutting machinery had been developed, this practice is discontinued.

# Chapter 5

With the advent of Neoclassicism at the end of the 18th century, there is another major shift in the design and manufacture of brasses. Again these reflect advances in metalworking. Now thin rolled brass sheets are squeezed between a pair of steel dies to produce delicate raised backplates in which the ornamentation is in relief. These backplates are usually oval in shape, echoing the ellipses we see in so much Federal and Georgian furniture (5-9E). Since the raised shape is not suitable for an escutcheon, the large matching escutcheons are now replaced by small oval rosettes. Within a short time these new brasses are being made in literally hundreds of designs. Look closely at Hepplewhite brasses and you will see framed within the ellipse eagles, medallions, acorns, thistles, swags, beehives, and cornucopia — to name just a few. After the Revolution cabinetmakers frequently used these fashionable new brasses with furniture that is Chippendale in style, giving the impression of replaced brasses that are, in fact, very much original.

About this time you will also see the use of small turned ivory knobs on all sorts of small drawers and covers. Occasionally you will also see turned ivory or whalebone pulls used on chests of drawers in lieu of brasses, but not many of these have survived intact.

With the onset of Sheraton, hardly a decade later, there is yet another transition in style and design; this time a return to single pulls, but far different from the simple pear-shaped pulls of the William and Mary period. Two basic types become popular: a raised embossed knob and a flush ring (5-9F). Both are mounted on a large circular stamped rosette. A common variation of the ring pull, particularly in Regency England, is the use of a lion mask, the lion holding the brass ring in his mouth. Escutcheons from this time might be the small rosette we saw earlier, or inlayed ivory in a diamond shape, or simply a little cast brass insert in the shape of the key opening. Note here that in period work this insert will have a rounded bottom. Not until after about 1840 does the bottom edge of the insert become square, the way we see them on modern furniture.

Concurrent with all these brasses there is a design of quite another type. From early Queen Anne right up through Hepplewhite a simpler mount was used in which two small round or oval rosettes substituted for the single large back plate. This elegantly simple rosette or bail pull (5-9G) was popular on both sides of the Atlantic, and 200 years later it is still more attractive than a budget Chippendale pull. The treatment of the escutcheon is equally elegant, just a matching rosette pierced for a keyhole. You often find these brasses used as handles on tea caddies, for being symmetrical, they do not have a top or bottom side. Wherever used, you can tell something of age and period by looking at the fabrication and shape of the rosette; simple cast rounds are the earliest, then a figurative oval appears with Chippendale, and lastly, Hepplewhite rosette pulls will be stamped and are apt to be plain with little rope edges. Actually, rosette pulls do not always remain simple, and on fine furniture you will sometimes see ornate pulls that have a distinctly Victorian look. They appear to be late 19th century, but they are Rococo, and date from about the middle of the 18th century. To avoid polishing, many of these ornate brasses were also gilded.

Finally, there are the the Late Federal Classical brasses. Here the raised embossed knobs and ring pulls introduced earlier continue in popularity, but tend to get larger and more ornate, quite in keeping with the size and scale of much Empire furniture (5-9H). The increase in size seems to have been accompanied by a reduction in the thickness of the brass, for many of these ornate mounts are very thin and fragile, and fewer of the original have survived than the lateness of this period would suggest. This period also sees a return to the popularity of wooden pulls, but unlike 17th century designs, they are now wide and flat. They are fastened either with threaded post, or with a screw driven in from the inside of the drawer, for by this time screws are more common and much less expensive. Another popular pull of this period are glass knobs, which appear a few years before the Boston and Sandwich Glass Company started turning out their pressed glass in the 1820s. At first small objects may have been easier to make by this new method of forcing hot glass into an iron mold.

During all periods, pulls were also made of wood, and while these are most often found on rural and Shaker work, they were sometimes used on urban furniture. Sadly, most of the latter have long since been replaced with more "correct" brasses. Early wood pulls were small hardwood knobs, rarely more than an inch or so in diameter and perhaps 1½" long, but by the middle of the 18th century they had gotten broader and easier to grip. Whatever the shape, the salient characteristic of all old work is that knob is given a shaft which extends through the drawer face. Generally, they were just driven into a slightly undersize hole to provide a snug fit. Later, the shaft was sometimes threaded to provide more strength. The modern wood pull, which first appears about 1810, has no shaft and will be attached with a long screw that passes through the drawer and into the knob.

The period styles we have covered are not much help in determining age and period unless we are looking at the original brasses. Unfortunately, brasses are so easy to change and so often replaced that all should be approached with a fair amount of caution; although as you would surmise, the older the furniture the more likely they are to be replacements. After a careful look at the outside to see if the brasses appear untouched, the next thing to do is to open a drawer and have a close look at the inside. Even if there are no unused cotter pin clench marks or extra holes, the brasses may not be original if the new posts happen to have matched the original holes. To add to the confusion, replaced brasses may be either earlier or later in style than the originals; later if the change was made to modernize a piece with more contemporary mounts, or earlier if the intention was, perhaps fraudulently, to shift things back a bit. In the past, when far more furniture was repaired and refurbished than now, it seems to have been a common practice to update an old piece by giving it a new set of contemporary brasses, for it is not uncommon to find a chest fitted with genuine old brasses that do not seem to match the period. Actually, the client could select any style desired. The Victoria and Albert museum has a hardware catalog of 1790 that illustrates not only brasses of the 1790 period, but also William and Mary, Queen Anne, and Chippendale styles. One should be very careful in identifying original brasses.

Even if the original brasses are missing, we can often learn something of the original by examination of what is left. First off, consider that escutcheons are not subject to the pulling forces that eventually separate so many pulls. If anything original is left, it is most likely to be the escutcheons. Failing this, check the post holes and look for any marks remaining, however faintly, on the drawer faces. If there are clench marks from cotter pins, these are most certainly from the original pulls; and if only post holes, then the holes that appear square or squarish on the face of the drawer are probably the original, for as noted earlier, period pulls had square cast posts. The presence of earlier marks and holes themselves are indicative of period furniture. Should there be more than one set of holes that seem old, the set that are the closest together are likely to be the original because Chippendale brasses were generally somewhat bigger than Queen Anne.

Although furniture is frequently refinished when brasses are replaced, traces of the original mounts often remain on the drawer fronts. Look for an outline in the color of the wood, for filled in escutcheon pin holes, and for marks left by the brasses being forced into the surface of the wood. Rosette pulls, in particular, will often leave indentations under the rosettes and show marks where the bail contacted the unprotected drawer face.

Finally, we might note that for one rare class of period furniture all this discussion is a waste of time, for there is a significant amount of rural case work that has never been fitted with pulls. There are neither brasses, nor wooden knobs, nor keyholes. Nothing. These pieces have lipped drawers so the user can get a finger grip around the edge of the lipping. Even so, they must not have been easy to use. Why these few were left unfinished when simple wood pulls could have been had at so little extra cost, I'll leave to the reader. Perhaps they were not unfinished at all?

While we find relatively few fastenings in old furniture, this is more than offset by the number of locks. Indeed, the multiplicity of locks is a distinguishing characteristic of period furniture. Except for some simpler rural work, there will generally be a lock on almost every drawer. Locks, like everything else, were handmade, and the mechanical complication of even simple locks must have made them expensive hardware. In spite of this they were generally used on every drawer of any significance. This prodigality was not limited to the large case pieces; locks were fitted on writing boxes, tea caddies, spice chests, and table drawers — anywhere something of value might be stored away. To save money we sometimes see charming little workarounds; the use of wood spring locks, drop in pins, and little tilters to secure a drawer which could only be reached by opening a drawer or a lid which in turn was fitted with a lock.

Old locks are not easy to study, for there is not much to see except the case plate and the front plate. Early samples look a little crude and very much handmade, and may still retain a few of the rose headed nails used to secure them to the back of the drawer front. However, they will also appear to be quite professionally made, which is not surprising, for locksmithing had become its own trade by 1600. Lock design was quite standardized, and except for the presence of wrought iron nails or old screws with their off-center slots, 18th century locks look quite modern. By this time you will find locks with brass cases on better furniture; and later sometimes with a GR (George Rex), a WR (William Rex), or a VR (Victoria Regina) stamped on the case. Whatever their age, old locks always used a hollow shaft key which fitted over a centering post in the lock. Also, the handle or bow of genuine old keys will usually look rather thin and fragile.

These many locks tell us something of economic and social life in past times. Prior to the advent of power looms, clothing was much less plentiful and relatively more costly. Also, houses were much more crowded, sheltering grandparents, servants, and apprentices in addition to the large families normal to the period. It would have some of the smaller children sharing their bedroom, perhaps sleeping on trundle beds.

Quite apart from light-fingered servants, one's possessions needed protection from inquisitive little children. Carefully locking up a blouse or a pair of pants may seem strange to us now, but then it must have been thought very necessary, well worth the extra cost and trouble of locks.

Antique hinges are best described by illustration and a few general comments (5-10). Early hinges were made by blacksmiths. They were fashioned by doubling the plate over the hinge pin and then back on itself, forming, in effect, a thin iron sandwich. Being hand forged, they show hammer marks and will usually be thinner at the edges. At first they were fastened with nails rather than screws, the holes being simply punched rather than drilled and chamfered. Although later fastened with screws and somewhat less crude looking, hinges continued to be made this way into the early years of the 19th century. You most commonly see them on drop leaf tables and on the lids of early desks.

Cast brass butt hinges were developed about the middle the 18th century. If you look carefully at an old hinge you may be able to the marks left by a scraper or file, and the little surface irregularities or inclusions that are typical of early castings. On all these hinges the pin will pass clear through the butts; hinges cast in one piece with an internal pin are a 19th century development.

Cast iron butt hinges arrive later, not becoming common until the 1820s, perhaps 20 years after the cut nail. Like the cut nail, they rapidly displaced hand forging, and the great majority of antique furniture you examine will have either cast iron or cast brass hinges. The modern rolled plate hinge, where the ends circle over the pin, first appears in the 1820s, but does not become common until the middle of the century. It is probably safe to conclude that no rolled plate hinge is very old.

The simple staple or snipe hinge is nothing more complicated that a pair of large interlocking cotter pins with the ends clenched over into the wood to hold them in place. Although an ancient design, their simplicity and low cost kept them in use right up to about 1800. Because they tend to wear through, you will often see where they have been replaced with a pair of strap hinges. However, the holes, and sometimes the clenched over end of the snipes, will still remain.

Before leaving hinges, it should be noted that in addition to the wood pivots found in chest tills and tilt top candlestands, hinges were also made of leather, and although most of these have long since been replaced, you will find evidence of their past presence on inexpensive furniture, sometimes on table leaves, but more commonly on the tops of lift top chests.

The most interesting aspect of castors is that they are not a modern invention, which perhaps should not surprise us when we remember that in the past tables and chairs were moved almost every day. Swiveling castors were introduced in the early 1700s, first with boxwood wheels, then with more successful leather disk wheels about 1750, and finally with "modern" brass wheels about 1770. These early casters were mounted on a brass pad that was fastened with small screws to the bottom of the leg. About 1770, to fit the thin tapering classical legs then coming into style, casters start to be mounted on brass sockets with iron or brass rollers. Very few of the early boxwood casters survive, but you will occasionally come across a chair or table with its original leather wheel castors still in place. Perhaps because of the additional cost, castors are rare on American furniture until after the Revolution, at which time they become com-

**Figure 5-10 Hinges**

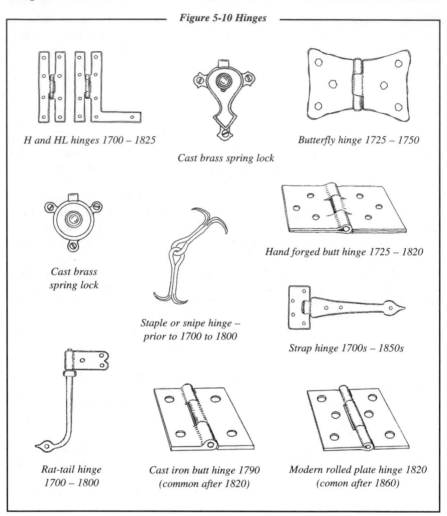

H and HL hinges 1700 – 1825

Cast brass spring lock

Butterfly hinge 1725 – 1750

Cast brass
spring lock

Staple or snipe hinge –
prior to 1700 to 1800

Hand forged butt hinge 1725 – 1820

Strap hinge 1700s – 1850s

Rat-tail hinge
1700 – 1800

Cast iron butt hinge 1790
(common after 1820)

Modern rolled plate hinge 1820
(comon after 1860)

mon on furniture that is normally moved around. The modern castor that fits inside a hole drilled in the bottom of the leg first appears about 1820, but it should look very different from the inexpensive stamped steel versions now found in hardware stores. The white ceramic castor is also a fairly recent arrival, appearing with Victorian furniture about the middle of the 19th century.

Finally, there is the glazing that was used in the doors of secretaries and cupboards. In the past window glass was made two ways: by blowing the molten glass into a globe and then working it into a large flat disk; or by blowing a cylinder, then cutting the cylinder lengthwise and rolling it out on a polished metal sheet. As you would expect, neither process avoided the visible imperfections that show on even small panes, and this is what most of us look for. However, this is not the only way to identify old glass. Although apparently colorless, if you put a piece of white card stock behind early glass you will frequently spot a yellow or blue tint caused by metallic impurities in the glass. Blowing also resulted in delicate, thin panes, which you can spot in mirrors by gently placing an object like a coin against the surface and noting how close the reflection appears to the mirrored surface. Lastly, old glass is frequently not quite flat; the whole pane will be slightly curved in one direction or another. You will see this if you look closely at old glazed doors and note that to seat the pane the glazier will have put putty on both sides of the glass. Glass that is both clear and flat does not appear until 1840, but even here it is likely to show some imperfections, for it was not until the 1870s that American manufacturers were able to produce quality plate glass.

**Finish**

Should we be lucky enough to find it, traces of an old finish are indicative of period work. Although the great majority of original finishes are long since gone, spotting old paint is not as difficult as you might think, for traces often remain in out of the way places. When you look at the many antiques that now have clear finishes, keep in mind that a great deal of this furniture was once painted. Only when the primary woods had a pretty color or figure, as in walnut, mahogany, or tiger maple; or could easily be stained up in imitation of something better, as was done with birch and maple, were clear finishes used. Even here, the finish was often nothing more than a light oiling to bring up the figure in the wood, followed by several coats of beeswax. All turned chairs, Windsor chairs, tavern tables, and the majority of dining tables, beds, chests, and stands were painted. If something of the original paint remains, and the color can be determined, it can provide a clue to age. From the 17th century on, red, yellow, and black paints were in common use. The pretty copper blue-green color we see on American furniture appears about the end of the 18th century. Milk based red, white, and pale gray shades are later, dating from perhaps the 1830s. Grain painting is also most likely to be 19th century.

Just as no two antiques are alike, so also will no two finishes be alike, not only because of years of sunlight and wear, but because paints were made up from scratch until the 1870s. In a very real sense, old painted surfaces are as handmade as are the furniture they cover. A wide variety of formulas were developed in an effort to combine pleasing color, easy application, and low cost. Many of these recipes included compounds of lead, mercury, and arsenic that we would never use now. In additional to conventional paints, cabinetmakers employed thin penetrating paints that colored the wood but let the grain show through. Some of the old reds, in particular, often look more like a thin red wash that was used to provide a reddish color to the surface, perhaps to be a "budget" mahogany. When looking at old finishes, remember that they are very much a product of age and are much changed from the original, that the dark brown greens, the gold mustards, and the mellow reds now so admired by collectors were originally much more bright and bold.

When paint remains, we will see that it has a very dry look and generally shows a myriad of little cracks. Oil paints oxidize slowly over the years as the natural oils dry out, and if scraped will come off in chips rather than flakes — but then you can hardly expect the dealer to scrape off a little paint to confirm this, any more than you will be invited to back out an old screw as so many books advise.

Should the paint be gone, it is still sometimes possible to see traces of the old red, worn so thin as to be no more than a very light red stain under later varnish or shellac. Perhaps because of less wear, the legs of tavern tables often show the lovely old red paint almost undisturbed. However, in many cases your search for old paint will have to be in out of the way places that years of wear, paint remover, and scraper have not yet reached; under chair seats, in the corners of panels, and at the edges of drawers. Traces of old paint in these places bespeaks of age.

If there is a deteriorated clear finish, it is possible to tell the type of finish, and indirectly the age of the piece, from the pattern of cracks that develop as the finish dries out. Shellac will separate into little circles that slowly darken and hide the figure of the wood until the whole surface looks rough and becomes almost black. As the oils dry out, varnish checks into squares that later deepen and develop into a characteristic alligatoring. Clear lacquer, a 20th century innovation, checks into rectangles. If the finish is still in good condition, shellac and varnish take considerable experience to tell apart, but lacquer, which is applied by spray gun, looks so mechanical and lifeless that it is easy to spot.

### Patina

Patina we have already discussed, and there is not much to add except to caution the reader that patina on exposed surfaces is no great evidence of age. English Victorian chests of drawers often have a beautiful patina from generations of diligent cleaning and waxing; and in contrast, there are 18th century American pieces so scraped down that nothing shows but a new coat of varnish over a new stain. However, if the finish is undisturbed, or restored with a gentle hand, patina is sign of considerable age, for it comes only with time.

Where patina provides a much surer record of age is on the unfinished surfaces, on the bottoms, the backs, and the insides of furniture. With time the exposed surfaces of secondary woods will slowly oxidize to a pale honey yellow, to a reddish tobacco brown, and on to shades of dark brown that are not far from black. The amount of darkening always proceeds in logical order from the surfaces most exposed to the surfaces least exposed. Thus the back boards will be the darkest, then the bottom boards, then the backs of drawers, then the sides of drawers, and finally the small interior drawers of desks and secretaries, which are so protected that they may look almost new. Look at small two drawer stands and you'll see that the bottom of the lower drawer, being more exposed to the air, is somewhat darker than the bottom of the upper drawer. The extra darkness we find on the backs of old pieces is probably in large part due to smoke. With an open fireplace in almost every room, there must have been a lot of smoke around at times. It would rise and spread across the ceiling, then be cooled upon reaching the outside walls and drift down across the backs of the furniture.

### Wear

The subject of wear is covered in most books, and frequently with such excellent illustrations, that in this section we'll only touch on the more obvious examples and then delve into some of the less common and perhaps more interesting aspects. Wear, to a greater or lessor degree, is the common lot of all old furniture. Any surface that is subject to repeated handling, cleaning, and movement will show some wear. Even very good furniture that has been well cared for will exhibit wear if you take the time to look for it. After all the years of use, we should not expect otherwise. Almost without exception, furniture that shows little or no wear is not old.

First off, all exposed edges will show some abrasion. This will vary from perhaps just a little gentle rounding on quality furniture to very considerable wear on rural work that has seen much hard use. Anything exposed to rough walls or feet, particularly the finials on chairs and the feet on chairs and tables, will exhibit chipping and abrasion. Similarly, table and chair stretchers within comfortable reach of feet will show wear, all the more so because dirt is quite abrasive. Very early tables and chairs typically have heavy stretchers set low down on the legs, and these often show much wear from generations of feet. I might suggest that this is not because our ancestors were a little uncouth and didn't know enough to keep their boots off the furniture, but simply because floors were unbelievably cold and drafty in the winter. Whenever possible, you kept your feet clear of the floor.

As mentioned earlier, furniture was moved around much more than now, most side chairs and many tables being moved every day. Before the advent of electricity — and indoor plumbing — it would also have made sense to put furniture back against the walls so it would not be tripped over in the dark. Thus it is common to find old chairs that not only show wear at the top of the stiles where they have rubbed against the wall, but also chairs that have lost an inch or two in height. The wear on legs is frequently not even. Wing chairs seem to loose more height at the rear, probably because they were just picked up at the front and dragged forward on the rear feet. Side chairs seem to have been tipped forward and dragged, perhaps by children who could not lift them, for often the front edges of the front feet will be rounded up. The feet of chairs that have been on rugs will have a dark polished look from years of picking up not only dirt, but also spilled tallow and candle wax.

While so obvious as to be easy to overlook, remember that seat rails and the frames of drop seats should show a myriad of tack holes, and repairs, from repeated recovering. Conversely, replaced rails are also an indication of age.

By now you probably know that the bottom of drawer sides often show considerable wear, developing a very characteristic bow shape when sighted along their length. The more wear, the more bow. What is interesting here is that the amount of wear will very from drawer to drawer depending on the amount of use, and I suppose, the weight of the contents. You see this particularly on tall furniture where the upper drawers typically show very little wear. Also, the drawer slides will show corresponding wear, and if made of a hard wood, be worn smooth and polished.

In addition to actual wear, there are many little reminders of long use that add much charm to old furniture. Here we have dark circles on table tops where water seeped through the unglazed bottom of a pot; fingernail marks at the edges of cabinet doors where a knob went missing for years; ink stains all over desks and writing boxes; mouse holes wherever food was stored or a drawer offered a safe home for the winter; oil from hands on the bottom of chair rails; sewing-bird pincushion clamp marks under the tops of candlestands, and finally, young people's initials cut into almost any level surface!

Like us, furniture is subject to the trials and vicissitudes of life. Much old furniture shows the effects of hard times in the past, and we see dents, strange gouges, and deep irregular scratches that defy a simple explanation. You will also find, either repaired or restored, just about anything that can be broken off — feet, legs, lids, and doors; and with this evidence of all kinds of amateur repairs using wire finishing nails and steel strap hinges.

Coming from a time of much open flame, it is not uncommon to find burn marks on old furniture where candles tipped, were hung on the backs of chairs, or were temporarily propped up in an open drawer and then forgotten. There is a magnificent secretary in the Metropolitan Museum of Art with a deep char mark on a door panel where a candle tipped in its socket. This must have been much more common in a time when candles were hand dipped and not all standard diameters. So common are burn marks that at times seems a wonder that anything has survived.

Generally, the older the furniture the greater the signs of wear. However, there are exceptions. Some old pieces inexplicably survive in almost pristine condition, perhaps because they went out of fashion and sat for years almost unused in a back hall. There is so little apparent wear that they almost seem to be reproductions, but they are not. While this is more true of better work which sees better care, there are also rural pieces that appear almost unused. By itself, just looking old and worn can be very misleading, for wear is very much a part of construction and environment. A 19th century pine kitchen table will typically show much more wear, and may appear a great deal older, than an 18th century mahogany dining table. Country furniture, which sees a lot of use and is frequently made of soft woods, will often look a great deal older than its actual age.

Somewhere we need to cover worm damage, and while this is more a sign of decay than wear, it is popularly associated with old and worn furniture. By themselves, worm holes are no particular sign of age, for in a suitable environment a dozen or so years will see a significant amount of damage. There is no reason why Victorian furniture should not be extensively wormed. Only perhaps in conjunction with the extensive wear in very old furniture that exposes their tunnels does worm damage contribute to a feel of authenticity. Most of the small holes you see are made by the grubs of two small beetles, Anobium punctatum or Xestobium bufovillosum. The female lays her eggs in an opening, perhaps in a crack or hole. After the eggs hatch, the larvae spend about two years tunneling through the wood, roughly following the grain. Then they bore a round exit hole and fly off to mate and repeat the cycle. The holes you see in furniture are these exit holes. Try to avoid wormed furniture, for generally there is a good deal more internal damage to the structure than the few exit holes would indicate. Some woods are more resistant than others. The beetles are fond of beech and walnut, but for some reason, do not like mahogany or the heart wood of oak. Aside from some early furniture which may have sat on damp floors, worm damage is not common in North America. However, what we do see in American furniture are the tunnels of the Chestnut borer (Agrilus bilineatus), which leaves a larger hole than the others, perhaps $\frac{3}{32}$" in diameter. This insect destroyed most of our chestnuts in the early 20th century, but the holes of the infestation appear much earlier.

## Shrinkage

Wood starts to lose moisture when cut and trimmed into logs, a process that is accelerates when the logs are then sawn into boards and billets. As the moisture content is reduced, the cells contract and the wood shrinks. The rate of loss, high at first, gradually tapers off over time, but never really stops, for even carefully dried and seasoned woods show a significant amount of shrinkage over the years. As a general rule, the harder and denser the wood, the less will be the shrinkage. Modern kiln dried woods also shrink, but by starting relatively dry, and being far younger, the shrinkage is usually a great deal less than what we find in period furniture.

The amount that wood shrinks depends on the run of the grain, or more correctly, the alignment of the cells in the tree. Radial shrinkage is always less than tangential, and longitudinal least of all. Think about the cracks that develop as a log dries out. They will always be in the direction of the grain and proceed from the bark in towards the heart of the tree. This is why cabinetmakers preferred quarter sawn wood. Cutting a plank this way minimized both shrinkage and warping, even though the radial shrinkage was still far more than the longitudinal shrinkage. To remember the way in which wood shrinks least, imagine placing your hand on a plank with the fingers parallel to the grain and slightly spread apart. Then bring the fingers together. Your hand will now be narrower, but your fingers will be just as long. This is how wood shrinks — mostly across the grain.

Now we know how wood shrinks, here are some of the many little things to look for:

- Legs, stiles, and stretchers were turned when the wood was still somewhat green; unseasoned wood being easier to turn and less likely to split. Because tangential shrinkage is greater than radial, such members will now be slightly out of round, and if not detected by feel, can be noted with a pair of calipers.
- The circular tops of tea tables and stands will always be out of round, sometimes by an inch or more in large tables.
- Similarly, anything square, such as table tops and Marlborough legs, will no longer be quite square, being somewhat narrower, either across the grain in a table top or in tangential direction in a leg.
- Splats in chairs shrink away from their mortise joints, sometimes by a ¼" or more, giving a false impression of somewhat sloppy workmanship.
- Unless refinished down flush, wooden pins always stand slightly proud of the surface because the longitudinal grain of the pin shrinks less than the radial or tangential grain of the surrounding wood. The amount of protrusion will vary from so little as to be only detectable to the fingers, to ¹⁄₁₆" or more in old table legs that were turned green. A slight working of the pin in the joint may also account for some of this protrusion.
- Veneered surfaces often show some distortion due to the differential shrinkage between the primary and secondary woods, particularly if the grain runs in opposite directions. While we see this in drawer fronts and panels, the most striking example is the way in which the crest and base of Queen Anne and Chippendale mirrors curve to the rear when the pine or spruce backing shrinks more than the veneered front.

- Breadboard ends in table tops and desk lids will overlap because of the differential shrinkage between the cross grain of the center section and the longitudinal grain of the ends — unless the ends have been cut off to "even" things up. It is not uncommon for the lids on desks to shrink so much across the grain that there is a ½" gap between the slant lid and the top of the desk.
- Mitered joints in old picture and mirror frames will show a gap at the inside corners due to shrinkage across the grain of the frame.
- Wide panels of secondary woods, such as the bottoms of drawers, often exhibit considerable shrinkage, resulting in either splits or very noticeable gaps between the joints. Similarly, door panels shrink, particularly during dry winter months, sometimes enough to leave a gap between the panel edge and the door frame.
- The sides of chests and desks become significantly narrower over the years. If this shrinkage is resisted by the horizontal rails and moldings, the sides will then split or open up; and if the sides do not give, then the drawer rails will force out the drawer blades. Something has to give somewhere. Another common result is that the drawers will now be a little too deep for the case, and will not go quite all the way in.
- As cases shrink and get narrower, side moldings will protrude beyond the sides of the case. They will overlap at the back and may force out the front molding.
- When moldings are cross veneered, such as we see on Queen Anne mirrors, shrinkage across the grain will leave cracks of ¹⁄₁₆" or more between adjacent pieces of veneer.
- Wide table tops secured to rails tend to split lengthwise down the middle of the panel. An associated problem, popularly called bat-winging, is encountered in Pembroke tables when the top shrinks so much that the leaves bind on the side rails when folded down.
- Thin Hepplewhite legs will both twist and bend if the wood is not chosen carefully, with the result that sometimes we see one leg of a card table splaying out at a very different angle from the other three. This is less common in sideboards, perhaps because the legs are thicker and stiffened by the case.
- Shell and rosette inlays usually stand slightly proud of the surrounding surface, and if examined closely, will show small shrinkage cracks.
- Metal does not shrink, and where it is used as inlay, as was popular in Regency furniture, there are apt to be problems when the wood shrinks. The most common result is that the inlay will be buckled or forced out of the surrounding wood, a problem you often see in boxes and chair backs from this period. Similarly, the brass strapping found on cellarettes will often be loose because the wood has shrunk.
- Where the grain of side panels runs horizontally, and the panel is relatively deep, as we find in two drawer stands and sideboards, there will usually be a very noticeable gap between the top and the side.
- Wide boards often develop a considerable twist if not secured along the edges, which you will see in the leaves of card and dining tables.

## Smell

This last topic may sound obscure, but it is true, there is a characteristic smell associated with period furniture. Some old furniture, particularly case work, actually smells old. Open up a closed space, a drawer, a top, or a door, and you will often notice a musty, sweet scent. It is quite different from the cool, damp smell of mold. This scent is particularly common in American furniture, perhaps because of the frequent use of aromatic pines for secondary woods, and because these surfaces were left unfinished. Quite aside from economy, unfinished drawers would have imparted a sweet smell to stored clothing, not too unlike the effect of a modern cedar chest. Like patina, this scent may not much proof of any great age, but it is a nice final touch.

With this we come to the end of our topics. It has been a long chapter, but as we have seen, there is much to consider in identifying period furniture. However, before finishing up, something must be said about reproductions, for here we have furniture that has been designed and built to emulate the best of the past, and some of it emulates it very well indeed. With what we have learned, identifying a 1930s reproduction should give the reader no particular trouble. Nothing about it will be period. But how about an American Colonial Revival or English Victorian reproduction that was largely handmade in the old ways and styles, and is now more than a 100 years old? This is a more difficult problem for the beginner, but one that you will find becomes easier with time and experience.

Our problem starts in early Victorian England with a revival of interest in 18th century styles and workmanship. The 19th century was marked by all sorts of revivals, but the English in the 1840s and 50s were stepping back only a few years to make such familiar things as Hepplewhite chairs, and furthermore, they still did much handwork, so that not only the style, but also the construction was correct. Many of these reproductions are found in shops today, and they are very good furniture that is truly antique. This was followed by a similar revival in America in the 1870s following the Centennial of our nation, from which we now have much "Centennial" furniture. Generally, these Colonial Revival, or as some call them, second period, reproductions are not as successful as their English cousins, in part because the designers were less true to the original, and in part because far less handcraftsmanship remained in this country. You will find that American Colonial Revival furniture is usually much easier to spot than its English Victorian counterpart.

How do we identify one of these reproductions? Well, the first thing to keep in mind is that they are not fakes, that is, there was no intent to deceive the buyer. The purpose was simply to market a good quality reproduction, one that was faithful to the spirit of the original. Thus, you will not find period fastenings or hand planing except where the surfaces would show, and a handworked effect was sometimes desired. Normally the backboards are machine planed and fastened with common wire nails. Similarly, the insides of chair rails will not show handwork, and the corner blocks are likely to be fastened with long wood screws. Remember also, that on period work the back of Queen Anne and Chippendale chair splats will normally be beveled, and the shoe will be a separate piece. Also, most reproduction chairs will be fastened with dowels, a dead giveaway if there is enough play in one of the legs to spot the gap between the dowels.

By this time really big, thick boards were mostly a thing of the past, and the maker had to be satisfied with thinner and narrower stock. We particularly see this in chairs, which often look as though the maker skimped a little on the wood. In addition to fewer signs of handwork, the general high quality of reproductions resulted in a well finished product, and we see none of the charming, calculated haste that so characterizes period workmanship.

The producers of Colonial Revival furniture had an inherent obstacle in emulating the past, for not only did they see the world through Victorian eyes, but they saw it with the limited scholarship of the time. Thus we see regional styles mixed to produce impossible products, such as a Chippendale style chair with Philadelphia ball-and-claw feet and a Massachusetts splat. Proportions also had to suit modern taste, and chairs will usually be higher and narrower than they were in the 18th century. For this reason, and because thinner stock was used, Colonial Revival chairs tend to have a top-heavy look.

Another problem is that people naturally wanted a copy of the very best of the past, and much Colonial Revival furniture is grand all out of proportion to the relatively small amount of high style furniture that was actually produced. Thus when we see a magnificent secretary or a perfect set of a dozen or so claw-and-ball chairs at a small local auction, they almost have to be reproductions. With this comes a general lack of wear and none of the sort of small damage and repairs we see in most period furniture. More tellingly yet, what wear there is does not seem to be very old. Cracks and splits will not be filled with accumulated grime and wax. For the most part, reproductions just don't appear to be very old. In addition, they seem to be in remarkably good condition for their apparent age. Some period furniture also has this look — but it is very rare.

Although we have discussed the very common Colonial Revival side chairs, it should be noted that all the more successful forms were reproduced, and you will see good reproductions of Federal side chairs, Queen Anne bonnet-top secretaries, Chippendale mirrors, Philadelphia Chippendale dish top stands, New England snake-leg stands, and Federal card tables. In local auctions, they are often incorrectly identified.

For all this, the reader should be warned that the more faithful early reproductions can be difficult to identify, particularly when dealing with chairs and tables where there are fewer fastenings and little secondary wood. In spotting this sort of reproduction, there is no substitute for experience and critical judgment. Here we must trust the eye as much as the mind, for there may be few obvious clues. Perhaps the best indication of a reproduction is a curious lack of individuality, for having been designed for a mass market, the product had to please many, and the price of this is always character. Every proportion will be normal and correct, nothing will be in the least out of the ordinary. Nowhere will you see the overly generous top, the slightly too bold curve in a leg, the asymmetrical splat, and the exuberant use of inlay — all those little idiosyncrasies so beloved by the collector. It is not unlike the difference between an original work of art and a popular print. If you are patient, and take the time to look critically, the reproduction, however faithful, will almost always tell you that it is a reproduction.

Before leaving, there remain a few final remarks. The first concerns the Industrial Revolution. All collectors would like to believe that the revolution in manufacturing did not affect the furniture trades until well into the 19th century, but this is not really so, for as you may have sensed, the whole period of our subject has been one of continuous small innovation and change. When we consider the mass production of turned chairs, and the growth and specialization of shops, and read about mahogany yards, manufactories, and showrooms, and then note the improvements in construction, fastenings, and hardware, we realize that the furniture trades were anything but static. Quite aside from changes in style, we are aware that little was done in the old way if newer and better was available. Much as we might wish it, a great deal of our cherished old furniture was not made up to order in a small shop by a dedicated craftsman working in time honored ways. It was very possibly made to a standard design on speculation, or for consignment or wholesale to a larger establishment. Cabinetmakers were swept along by the same innovations in production and distribution that finally saw an end to all the crafts. They all swam in the same sea.

Although knowing period furniture when you see it may at first seem to be difficult, if you keep the topics we have discussed in mind, after a while you'll find that you can almost intuitively spot the old among the new. It will speak to you. The chapters on furniture types that follow provide some hints on origin, so you will also learn something about source. Perhaps in a little while you will be able to just glance at a chair across a room and say with conviction, "Boston area, perhaps 1780, or a little later."

# Chapter 6

# Fakes and Frauds

Fakes and frauds are ever popular topics, and you may already have skipped forward to look at this chapter. However, if your motive is anxiety over about unscrupulous dealers and rigged auctions, do not neglect the previous chapters, particularly those on understanding period and style and in identifying handworkmanship, for in collecting old furniture, as in all collecting, ignorance is the first cousin of fraud.

There are few markets in art that do not have some dishonesty here and there, and antique furniture is not the exception. In truth, it is notable for all sorts of fakery, if for no other reason in that old furniture is so easy to modify. Although continual misgiving would dampen our enthusiasm for collecting, a reasonable prudence is much in order, for while most dealers and auctioneers are both knowledgeable and honest, there are a significant number who are neither.

Trickery in antique furniture comes in a number of guises, but before we examine these, there are some general caveats that apply to all period furniture collecting. First off, there is no substitute for experience, and for the knowledge that comes with experience. It is quite your best inoculation against fraud. The more you know, the more obvious it is when something is not right. While professionals are sometimes taken in, it is the collector, and particularly the beginning collector, who is most at risk. As we'll discuss in the next chapter, when starting out you want to stick with reputable dealers. Later, as you gain experience, you may want to branch out to auctions, but when beginning, be very cautious, for you don't yet know how much you don't know. The old saying that a little knowledge is dangerous applies perfectly to antique furniture.

For the most part, period furniture was based on successful patterns that were emulated, with more or less success, by all those in the trade. While each piece of antique furniture is indeed unique, most follow established norms and are generally consistent in terms of design, construction, and proportion. From experience, the professional knows what things should look like. Just as a car buff can tell immediately that an old car has been customized, so professionals can often tell just at a glance that something is not right. Clear across a room they can spot the replaced top on a candlestand, the new feet on a chest of drawers, and the married highboy, for the overall design will not be consistent. The object will lack the balance and harmony found in all good period workmanship. However, at first you will not see these problems, and until you acquire a feel for the way old furniture should look, they will not be evident. This simple lack of experience will be your greatest handicap in dealing with fakes and frauds.

Antiques are bought and sold in an open market in which the price of each item rises, or falls, to its approximate market value. Good things do not sell for very little, nor poor things for very much. When something is offered for sale well below apparent market value, it usually means that there is a problem somewhere. However, when presented with a bargain, it is all too easy to see only the wonderful price, and not question the reason. As every swindler knows, greed blinds good judgment, and as collectors, we must always be aware of this very human failing. Low price should be a warning, not an inducement, to purchase.

The best way to avoid this simple trap is to never go looking for bargains, even if your funds are limited. Instead, shop for quality at a fair price, with the emphasis on quality, even if you sometimes pay a little more than you had intended. Good collections are built on quality, not on low price. You are far more likely to get in trouble over something that is too cheap than to get in trouble over something that is too expensive. Antiques are sold in an open market in which there are many potential buyers. If a piece is offered well below market value, it is almost always an indication that something is wrong.

All surfaces that come in to everyday contact with hands or feet should exhibit some measure of wear. While this is most obvious in the tops of tables and in the stretchers of chairs and tables, it is present everywhere in genuine period furniture. However, more significant and more subtle than this obvious wear, which is often illustrated, and not a little faked, is the gentle rounding of all exposed surfaces. Feel under the crest rail, under the arms, and under the side seat rails of an old chair and you will not find a single sharp edge. Legs will also be rounded, although here the wear will be from shoes, boots, brooms, and mops. A sharp edge in any of these areas is a sign of either some restoration or a reproduction.

In a similar way, drawer sides and drawer dividers should always show wear from the many thousands of openings and closings. Here the wear will be in proportion to use, the most handy drawer having the most wear. Thus the top drawer in a chest of drawers will typically show the most wear. Likewise, the middle drawers of a highboy, or chest on chest, will be most worn, while the small drawers at the top of the upper case will exhibit very little wear.

When examining old furniture, always watch for inconsistency. Unless furniture was to be painted, similar components would always be cut from the same board, or boards. Even after two centuries and more, they should exhibit just about the same color, grain, and figure. All drawer fronts should look the same, as should the case sides and the facing on the feet. Secondary woods will show a similar consistency; the bottoms of drawers, the sides and backs of drawers, and the back-boards, will all be alike. While the amount of oxidation and darkening will vary with location, it should still be logical and consistent. The backs of drawers will differ from the bottoms, and may be different woods, but the backs and all the bottoms should be about the same color, unless by chance the bottom drawer is exposed to the air. Even though the dovetail joints may look almost identical, if you spot a significant difference in the color, grain, or figure of the wood, you are almost certainly looking at some restoration. A good restorer can easily match dovetails, and can do quite a bit with stains, but it is very hard to match old quarter sawn wood.

In those places where a dovetail or a mortise-and-tenon joint would not do, cabinetmakers normally used glue blocks, for early screws were not only expensive, but were quite short. You will commonly find glue blocks used whenever there are two surfaces at right angles that need to be jointed: the tops and beds of tables, the tops and sides of case work, and the feet on desks and chests of drawers. Blocking was also used for reinforcement, to strengthen chair frames and to stiffen drawer bottoms. When examining furniture, always take a careful look at the glue blocks, for major repairs and restorations will usually result in new or refastened blocking. Glue blocks should all exhibit the same amount of patination and be about the same color as similar secondary woods. They should not appear to have been disturbed. Now and then a block will be missing, and there should always be an area of lighter color due to the less oxidized wood. Watch for blocks that appear to have been refastened, to be newer than the surrounding structure, or to be stained or inexplicably painted. Sometimes blocking is added to hide fakery, so also be on the lookout for blocking in illogical locations.

If furniture is modified, there will often remain some holes. Unlike the golf course divot, a hole once made in wood is there forever. Even if plugged very neatly, it is almost impossible to hide under a good light. Whenever you spot a hole, ask yourself, why is it there? The answer may be simple and obvious, perhaps a missing nail or replaced brasses. However, if neither simple nor obvious, you are probably looking at some sort of modification. Remember that while it is not hard to find old wood, obtaining old wide boards without nail holes is just about impossible. A replaced backboard is likely to show an odd nail hole or two, as will a country cupboard made up from old siding or flooring.

Should you see either stain or varnish on secondary surfaces, something also is wrong. You are almost certainly looking at either a repair, a modification, or a reproduction, for these areas were left bare in period work. Often there has been no dishonest intent; the makers of quality reproductions often varnished the insides of small desk drawers, and furniture repairers are apt to add some finish to the bottoms of tables, perhaps to keep them from warping. It is the stain in an out of the way place that should be questioned.

Like holes, stain on an unfinished surface is hard to hide in a good light. The faker has a real problem here, for the patina of old unfinished surfaces is much harder to match than the finish on primary surfaces. Careful staining will help get the color and shade right, but then the stain itself will generally show if we look for it. When examining old furniture, remember that altered secondary surfaces are easier to spot than altered primary surfaces. As in determining age, we always want to look in, under, and behind.

However, to spot a neatly plugged hole, or a little careful staining, we need both the room to look in and around, and good illumination, which may be a problem, for furniture is often displayed in poorly lit crowded rooms. When you are not comfortable with a dealer, insist on examination where you can get a good look where there is good light, even if it means moving things around a bit. Dealers often bring high intensity lights to auction previews, and do not hesitate to tip furniture on its back or even upside-down. Natural light, when you can find it, is by far the best.

Now let's take a look a the specific problems we are likely to encounter in old furniture. These are not covered in any particular order, although the first, misrepresentation, occurs everywhere, and the last, complete fake, is not very common among American furniture. The discussion will be kept fairly general so that we may concentrate on the principles. We'll cover more of the specific things to watch for when we get to the chapters on individual furniture types.

### Misrepresentation

Misrepresentation is the simplest and easiest of frauds, which probably does much to account for the continuing popularity of this simple dodge. In its two most common forms, English is passed off as American, and reproduction is passed off as period. You don't want to make either mistake, for whether paying American for English, or period for reproduction, you may be paying more than you should.

English furniture is the product of a very different environment, and while it may look similar, it is usually not difficult to identify. When examining a chest of drawers, a table, or a chair, keep in mind that:

- English cabinetmakers normally employed oak, or perhaps deal, for drawer sides and back boards; and beech for chair frames. Deal is a pine or fir, but differs from American pine in having more small knots, being obtained from much smaller trees. Beech is a strong, close grained wood, and while having little color or figure, its toughness and close grain make it ideal for chairs. It was commonly used not only for over upholstered rails, but for the entire frame if the chair was to be painted or gilded. Beech also takes a nice stain and was often employed as a budget mahogany in chairs — much the same way birch was employed in American tables and chests of drawers.
- Most really early furniture, such as the paneled chest (12-1), the joint stool (8-1), and the wainscot chair (8-2) will be English. There is very little surviving American 17th century furniture, and most of what does survive is now

held by museums and historical societies.
- Stools of all kinds are common among English furniture, but American examples are rare. Also, the back stool, an upholstered chair without arms, is almost always English.
- Small furniture such as Canterbury's, knife boxes and knife urns, barometers, tea caddies, and basin stands are generally English.
- Queen Anne and Chippendale sofas and settees will probably be English. Not until after the Revolution could more than a very few Americans afford such large upholstered furniture.
- Queen Anne and Chippendale period mirrors are usually English, although they may have been brought over to America long before the Revolution.
- American cabinetmakers almost never made flat top desks. Partner's desks (6-1) and Davenport desks (6-1) are English.
- Pillar form dining and breakfast tables that lack a bed or apron under the top are usually English (6-1).
- Sofa tables (6-1) are rare among American furniture.
- English desks and chests of drawers often have the upper drawer divided into two smaller drawers. Split drawers are far less common in American work, except of course, in the upper cases of highboys and chests-on-chests where it was desired to lift out the drawers.
- Chests of drawers having only three drawers will almost always be English. Some grand Newport furniture has only three drawers, as does some rural work, but for the most part American cabinetmakers did not make three drawer chests. Also, the backs on English chests of drawers and desks will be made up of a number of fairly narrow vertical boards. American cabinetmakers normally employ just one or two wide horizontal boards.
- Except in Philadelphia and New York, the square block under the top of tiptop tables will usually be maple or birch if the table is American, mahogany if the table is English.
- The hoof foot, the scroll foot, and the hairy paw foot will almost never be American. Also, the spade foot on Hepplewhite legs is normally a sign of English work, although it is also found on some of the better Philadelphia and New York furniture.
- English sideboards usually have arched center sections and spade feet; American sideboards rarely have arched center sections, and far less commonly, spade feet. In addition, English sideboards usually have a bowed front and seldom are given a central cupboard (6-1). Also, small sideboards are fairly rare among American furniture. Thus, the many little four and six leg sideboards you see in antique stores are almost certain to be English.
- English chairs are likely to be reinforced with a strut or brace fitted across each corner of the seat rails. This will then be nailed into notches cut into the rails. However, there are many exceptions, and some American chairs employ this same construction.
- English upholstered armchairs tend to have upholstered arms (6-1), while

American chairs tend to have bare arms. However, this is no more than a generalization, for there are many exceptions.

- English cabinetmakers did not like joints to show, and even on very average case work the joint between drawer dividers and case sides will be either stopped short of the front of the case, or be fitted with a covering strip to hide the joint. On slant top desks you will see either a mitered or a double-lap dovetail joint (5-1) employed where the sides meet the top.
- English Windsor chairs are very different from American Windsors, principally in the turnings, but also in the use of pierced central splat and a curved yoke stretcher (6-1). They have a solid feeling about them that is not found in any but the earliest American Windsors.
- English furniture tends to lack the lightness and verticality found in American work. Chests of drawers and desks often appear more heavy and massive, chairs more solid and low. This difference is very evident if you compare an English library armchair (6-1) with a Federal lolling chair (11-5).

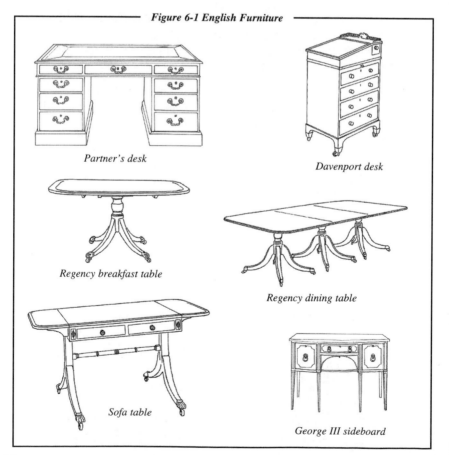

*Figure 6-1 English Furniture*

*Partner's desk*

*Davenport desk*

*Regency breakfast table*

*Regency dining table*

*Sofa table*

*George III sideboard*

*Figure 6-1 English Furniture*

Windsor chair

Library Armchair

Welsh dresser

In the previous chapter we discussed reproductions, and there is not much to add here except to note that you should be particularly careful when dealing with English furniture, for in England handcraftsmanship continued to be the norm in quality work right up through the 19th century; and during the Victorian period English cabinetmakers produced much fine Queen Anne, Chippendale, and Hepplewhite style furniture. For the most part this work is far truer to period than the somewhat later American Colonial Revival work, and here you would be well advised to rely on the judgment of a professional. However, in less faithful reproductions, remember that the splats on Queen Anne and Chippendale chairs should be beveled, that the shoe and the back rail should be separate pieces, and if there are stretchers, they should be flush with the outside of the legs.

When identifying old furniture, most of us instinctively look for handmade dovetails. However, we should remember that the introduction of power tools was a gradual process, and that initial mechanization was in the area of planing and cutting machines that saved the most labor and provided the best return on the investment. Far more important than an automatic dovetail cutter was power equipment that would size and level the rough mill stock. As a result, machine dovetailing, particularly in England, was not common until the end of the 19th century. This suggests that the handmade dovetails that we all associate with period furniture should be considered as no more than an indication of period workmanship.

The practice of doweling chair joints starts about the middle of the 19th century. If gauge marks were used to center the dowels, you will sometimes see a characteristic single scribe line used to center the joint. In contrast, laying out a mortise and tenon joint will leave two parallel scribe lines, one for each side of the mortise. Doweled chair joints will often be slightly loose, and if there is even a little bit of movement, with a good light you will be able to look through the joint and spot the gap between the dowels.

Another common form of misrepresentation are pairs and sets of furniture that did not start out as brothers and sisters. Because pairs and sets bring more than singles, there is a temptation to sell them this way. Most of this problem is found in side chairs where popular designs were emulated by everybody in the community, and it is not too difficult to locate almost identical examples. Look carefully at advertisements for assembled sets of chairs and you will see they are remarkably similar. To the casual observer, they appear to be a set. When examining a set of chairs, after satisfying yourself they are indeed period, your next question should always be "are they actually a set?" Because chairmakers employed patterns, and turners marking gauges, a set of old chairs will be dimensionally very similar, even after many years of wear and shrinkage. Don't let a dealer convince you that significant differences are due to "shrinkage" or to "handwork." Also, remember that while "identical" and "matched" sound nice, they do not mean a set.

Finally, it is not uncommon for sets of chairs to be expanded with the addition of one or two copies. Two armchairs added to four old side chairs makes a much more useable set. This is not in the least fraudulent, and indeed may be a good idea — provided you are aware of it. Buying a set of six chairs and only getting four that are period is better than ending up with six reproductions, but you don't much want to do either and not be aware of what you have done. The lesson here is that if you are seriously interested in a set of chairs, examine all of the set. Take your time at this, for after half a century or more a chair made up to match an existing set may be quite difficult to identify. Look closely at the splats to see if they all are of the same wood and exhibit the same amount of shrinkage. Run your hand lightly over the underside of the crest rail. Here there should be a gentle rounding from years of handling. An edge that is noticeably sharper than the others indicates a newer chair — or perhaps a replaced crest rail.

Carefully made up copies are most common in chairs, but we also see it done in chests, tables, and mirrors when it is desired to have a matching pair, perhaps to flank a doorway. However, these reproductions are generally limited to very fine furniture.

### Conversions

While many misrepresentations involve chairs, most conversions involve case work. Often the intention is only to convert an outmoded form into something more practical.

In the process, though, the subject comes out of the shop very different than when it went in — not unlike cosmetic surgery. Unfortunately, it is generally major surgery, not just a little tuck here and there. Thus we see tea caddys turned into note boxes, knife boxes to stationary boxes, butler's trays to coffee tables, toilet commodes to diminutive chests of drawers, and spinet pianos to desks and dressing tables.

Another, more subtle, and very fraudulent change is to convert things to more rare and valuable forms; to turn an ordinary pair of chairs into a double-chair-back settee, a pole screen or torchere to a candlestand, or a joint stool into the popular butterfly table. So common is this practice that a great many English stools seem to have started out life as chairs.

Some of these conversions start out innocently, the only intent being to make the piece more salable. Except for the serious collector, there is little demand for toilet commodes and spinet pianos, and a coffee table is about the only way to employ a handsome old mahogany butler's tray. However, the innocence ends when a conversion is passed off as complete and original 18th century workmanship. Here the collector is doubly cheated, not only in perhaps paying too much, but more importantly, in acquiring a piece that is no asset to a good collection.

When the upper and lower sections of a highboy or a chest on chest become separated, we get another class of conversions. The bottom acquires a new top and becomes a lowboy or a chest of drawers; the top a new base and becomes a chest of drawers. This sort of conversion, normally the product of simple necessity, is generally easy to spot. Lowboys are scaled about a fifth smaller than highboys, so a highboy base with a new top will be much larger than normal. Remember that lowboys were originally dressing tables, and should not be more than about 30" high. Conversely, the top of a highboy or chest on chest will appear too high and narrow for a chest of drawers, but unusually short for a tall chest of drawers. There will often be an oversize molding, and the top will be unfinished, for it was never intended to be seen from above. Remember also, that American chests of drawers normally have four graduated drawers, and the top drawer is seldom split into smaller drawers.

Lastly, there is one type of conversion, that for lack of a better term, might be called assembled pieces. Something that is difficult to sell, such as a large Victorian breakfront bookcase, will be taken apart and made into a number of smaller and more marketable items; in this case perhaps half a dozen or so small bookcases, each built around one of the glazed doors. A similar ploy is to fashion a table around an old drawer. The buyer, finding the drawer to be period workmanship, neglects to look further. The way to spot this reconstruction is to be suspicious of unusual size and proportions, for it is unlikely that assembled pieces will match the dimensions of genuine period work. Most such creations are made to a modern scale suitable for a small house or apartment.

In this same vein we also have furniture that did not even start out life as furniture. Earlier in this century in England there was thriving cottage industry in converting old oak paneling into high backed settees and wainscot chairs. The dealer could place his hand on such a piece and state, with complete and honest conviction, that "This is genuine 17th century workmanship."

Once we gain some experience, conversions should not give us much trouble, for normally they are easy to spot. After a little while we learn that low tables are modern, that tea caddys were not used for note paper, and that a desk or dressing table should not resemble a spinet piano. We also acquire a feel for what period furniture should look like, and when shown a highboy that has lost its upper case, we immediately realize that the proportions are all wrong. As a class of fakery, conversions are only a problem for beginners.

## Period Shift

What is the difference between relatively inexpensive Classical or Victorian furniture and much more expensive Federal or Georgian furniture? Well, only about 30 or 40 years. To convert one to the other, all that is required is a little shift back in time. As you would imagine, this sort of simple minded arithmetic is irresistible to the faker. As in conversions, case furniture is the principle victim of this sort of fakery, particularly if the drawers still retain the old hand cut dovetails.

The simplest technique in a chest of drawers is to just strip off the pretty Victorian mahogany pulls, or the late Federal brass rosette knobs, and replace them with Chippendale reproductions having solid back plates. These are preferred to bail pulls because the back plates hide the characteristic single holes of the original pulls. If a more thorough job is desired, the top can be given a molded edge and the French feet or turned legs replaced with bracket feet. Because Victorian and Empire chests are tall by 18th century standards, it may also be necessary to remove the top drawer. The result is generally quite handsome, for although the piece is not as early as it would appear, it is quite sufficiently old to have acquired a nice patina.

The best protection against this sort of fakery is a critical look at size and proportions, and a careful look at the secondary surfaces. Never forget to look in, under, and behind. For some reason, perhaps because better glues were available, later furniture tends to have rather delicate looking feet. In a subtle way, it lacks the boldness of period work. Also, if you lower a chest by removing a drawer, you will end up with only three drawers, which may be all right if the chest is English, but is rarely found in American work.

## Unwarranted Attribution

Unwarranted attribution, like pride, is a common sin. Here the value of an old piece is enhanced by the statement of suggestion that it is the product of the hand or the shop of a well known craftsman. So little period furniture is actually labeled or signed that any sort of attribution, however nebulous, will help increase value. Naturally, the more famous the cabinetmaker, the better the value.

When considering attribution, we should remember that popular and stylish designs were copied by everyone within the furniture community, and that the now famous cabinetmaker was, at best, no more than a preeminent artisan among many skilled peers; most of whom were not only working in the same styles, but purchasing their hardware and inlay from the same merchants and inlay makers. Samuel MacIntire, for instance, did not work alone in Salem. During the same period there were about 60 cabinetmakers working in the city, and supporting them, perhaps a dozen or so carvers and upholsterers.

Most attributions are no more than guesses as to authorship, and many are just plain wishful thinking, which is innocent so long as it does not affect price. To have any real merit, an attribution should meet one or more of the following criteria. The piece must either:

- Possess a valid label or signature.
- Carry documentation that clearly links its purchase to the maker. This means actual documentation, not anecdotal evidence. Hearsay does not count, any more than it counts in a court of law.
- Be identical, or very nearly identical, to a documented piece. Because much period furniture emulates successful designs, terms like "very similar to" and "just like" mean little. Similarly, attribution based on a comparison of inlay has merit only if the inlay appears to have been made up by the cabinetmaker, and is not just a product of the local inlay maker.
- Possess a truly unique design or construction feature that is directly attributable to only one shop in the region. Not only are there sometimes distinguishing characteristics among shops, but carving may reflect the hand of an individual carver.

As you see from this short list, legitimate attribution does not come easily, and will usually be limited to important pieces that have been the subject of much study. Aside from some lucky chance, perhaps the survival of a label or chalk signature, the average grade of work can never be firmly attributed to a particular shop or craftsman. In common with the cabinetmakers themselves, the provenance of most period furniture has faded into the twilight of history.

## Embellishment

Add a patriotic eagle to the top of a ordinary little candlestand and the price of the candlestand will double, or even triple. This is a typical example of a whole group of trickery in which relatively simple modifications are employed to enhance value. For want of a better word, we might call this embellishment. Because it is so common, we will cover only a few of the more popular forms, and then note some general guidelines to help you avoid this sort of thing.

A little inlay will do wonders to dress up an otherwise very ordinary piece, and while it is not hard to do, it is difficult to do well. Inlay making was a skilled trade in the 18th century, and the old shells and rosettes will be of uniformly high quality. Look closely at original work and you will see that it is beautifully done. It also will show some small signs of shrinkage. Later reproductions are seldom as good. If you see poor workmanship, and no signs of shrinkage, and it is obviously not the somewhat crude product of a rural craftsman, something is wrong. In many cases, shrinkage will cause the inlay to stand slightly proud of the surrounding surface, which you can detect by passing your fingers lightly over the surface. When examining old furniture, remember that in an age of handwork, both inlay and carving were always extra cost options, and the great majority of period furniture will exhibit no more decoration than perhaps a little inexpensive stringing.

Earlier in this century there was a thriving trade in faking cabinetmaker's labels, the labels being obtained from old bills and newspaper advertisements. This is not so common now because collectors are much more knowledgeable, but there must still be many of these old fakes around. If you look at illustrations of genuine labels, you will see they normally have a decorative border around all four sides, something not found on bill heads and advertisements. However, we need to say normally here because there are some genuine labels without borders. The simple labels used by John Townsend of Newport do not have borders, nor were they employed on some Late Federal furniture, and there are also English Regency labels without borders. In general, one might say that after about 1800 labels become simpler and are apt to lose their Rococo embellishments.

The surface under a label is protected from oxidation by the paper and glue, and will be somewhat lighter than the surrounding surface. You'll notice this where an old label has lifted at the edge or flaked off a little. However, this lightening will not be present under a later label — unless the faker has been unusually thorough. Most labels have lifted a little somewhere, and in a good light you should be able to spot the characteristic lighter background under the genuine old label.

Sometimes the return on embellishment justifies considerable rework, as would replacing the turned stretchers a Queen Anne chair with the flat sawn stretchers found on some Newport chairs. Similarly, we hear of adding Spanish feet to country chairs, recarving hairy paw feet to the more acceptable claw-and-ball form, jig sawing out some of the ever popular hearts, scalloping table tops and cupboard shelves, adding carving to cabriole legs, substituting ogee for bracket feet, reworking tea tables to provide a pie crust edge, and even adding a bonnet top to a highboy. There are a lot of things to keep in mind. When examining carving, remember that it should stand slightly proud of the surface because the cabinetmaker or chair maker always left the carver extra material to permit the carving to stand out from the surrounding surface. Look at the shell on a cabriole leg and you will see it is set out a little from the curve of the knee. Of necessity, later carving must be cut into the surface.

When a piece is deemed too large or too tall to sell, or is utterly lacking in charm, it is apt to be improved through a process of subtraction. The amount of subtraction will vary from the loss of a drawer to the complete rebuilding of large chests of drawers into smaller chests of drawers. Sideboards are particularly susceptible to this treatment because the originals are often too wide and deep for modern dining rooms. This sort of modification is not difficult to spot if you take out the drawers and have a look around with a good light. There should be all sorts of evidence of rework on the inside of the case. Often drawers must be shortened to fit the reduced case. Although you would think this would require taking all the drawers apart and cutting new dovetails, there is a far quicker way. With a fine saw the faker simply cuts off the fronts of the drawers just behind the dovetails, removes the desired amount of drawer, then carefully glues the fronts back on. The rework is not at all obvious, for the new joint is masked by what appears to be the scribe lines used to mark the depth of the dovetails. The best way to spot this is to not only be alert for signs rework, but to also check that the figure and grain of the wood carries through into the dovetails. You also want to keep in mind that drawers dovetailed in the front will normally also be dovetailed in the back, although here the dovetails are normally fewer and simpler. Except for some occasional rural workmanship, cabinetmakers did not dovetail the front and lap joint the back of a drawer. This is typical of the sort of inconsistency that we always need to watch out for in antique furniture. Unfortunately, many of these little clues are learned only with experience.

If you are not so swept away by enthusiasm that you do not take the time to think about what you are looking at, it is not all that difficult to spot furniture that has been embellished, for either something will be not quite right about the proportions, or the overall design will lack cohesiveness and consistency. Often the improvement will not harmonize with the rest of the design. Normally the attempt is to improve an otherwise average piece. Should you find rural work with high style inlay, or a piecrust top on an otherwise simple tea table, or a country desk signed by none other than Benjamin Frothingham, you have not found a wonderful bargain. Always remember that simple should be simple all over, and grand should be grand all over. If not, something is very wrong.

## Marriages

Whenever you contemplate furniture having both upper and lower cases, whether it be a highboy, a secretary, or a chest on chest, always ask yourself, "Did both sections start out life together?" If not, you are looking at what the trade calls a marriage. We might distinguish two types of marriages: the first when two old sections are combined, the second when a new section is made up to match an existing old section. Combining two old sections, and doing it quite well, is not as difficult as it sounds, for furniture from a given region can be remarkably similar. This sort of marriage is common among highboys, perhaps because Americans try to divide things equally, or at one time the highboy was too tall for a new home. The second type of marriage is normally found in desks that have been converted to secretaries with the addition of a later bookcase top. Many of these marriages probably start out innocently enough, and often they are a good idea. A married highboy in which the wood, the region, the style, and the proportions are a good match is much better than the alternative; a base with a new top and a top with a new base.

Where trouble arises is when the buyer is unaware of the marriage, for even the best marriages are nowhere nearly as desirable as the original. Such pieces should be honestly identified and offered at a considerable discount. Fortunately, detecting even good marriages is not difficult if you take the time to look. First off, stand back and see if the design is consistent. If the top is from a different region or a later date, the whole design may not hang together. There are likely to be differences in style, or perhaps the upper case will appear too small. The design will not seem consistent. Then ask yourself if both upper and lower cases are the same wood and appear to be from the same tree. If cut from the same board, or pair of boards, not only should the grain and figure of the wood be the same, but the sides should have the same thickness.

Then take a close look at the mid-molding where the upper and lower sections fit together. Here is where some artful fudging must be done to get a fit, because it is unlikely that the width and depth of the upper case will exactly match the original. The front and side moldings should be identical, and the back of the upper case should be flush with the back of the lower case. If the moldings seem to be new, or have been padded out a little, or the upper case overlaps or underlaps the lower, something is wrong. Now having said this, it should be mentioned that occasionally in rural work you will find that the upper case on a secretary is given an overlap to clear the chair rail.

Now pull out a couple of drawers in both sections and see if the dovetails appear identical and made by the same hand. Don't let a dealer kid you that cutting dovetails was a big job and one craftsman did the upper section and another the lower. An experienced apprentice could assemble a dozen or more drawers in a day.

Look at the brasses. If they are original and identical on both cases, you are probably safe, for it is very improbable that two marriageable sections would have identical brasses.

If not original, don't bother with the brasses, but instead check the history of the previous brasses in the history of the handle holes. If the drawers in the upper case show an extra hole or two where the brasses have been replaced, the drawers in the lower case should show an identical pattern. Finally, take a look at the backboards in a good light. Patina, construction, and fastenings should be the same on both cases, although the boards may run horizontally on the lower section and vertically on the upper. If your piece passes all these simple tests, you should have no worry.

Another variation on the two old sections theme is seen when a table has a top from another table. Again, this is not hard to spot if you look for screw holes in the underside which have no apparent reason (but do not appear to be the result of a reset top). Note that some of these marriages may be quite old, for in an age when working up a new top from scratch would have entailed much time and labor, use of an available top from another piece would have been an attractive economy.

Unlike conversions and embellishments, little or no damage is done in a marriage, and when two old sections are combined, the results are generally a great improvement over the previous unhappy state of affairs. However, it is still very wrong if you are not told of the marriage, and pay a premium for original condition.

### Major Restoration

There's nothing inherently fraudulent about restoration. When done, it is generally very necessary and is usually a good idea. Much lovely old furniture has been saved and put back into use through the restoration of shattered or missing parts. Our stock of period furniture would be far less but for the skilled work of a great many craftsmen over the past century. It was not their fault that some inspired handyman cut the legs off an old highboy so it would fit in a back bedroom. The problem arises when we are not told of the restoration, not told that the highboy has new legs.

Restoration is more common than you might think, particularly in the better furniture, in framed chairs, highboys, lowboys, and sideboards. As a general rule, the work is well done and the restoration is correct and true to period. Ironically, major restoration is often more difficult to spot than minor repairs. Such things as a little replaced veneer, or a patched drawer lip, are frequently much more obvious than a restored top on a lowboy or a set of new legs on a highboy, particularly if the restoration was done many years ago, for with time, the restored component tends to blend in with the original structure. To compound this very real problem, restorers are urged by dealers to make repairs and restorations as unobtrusive as possible, and a talented restorer can do wonders with carefully selected wood and some artful staining. When you examine a piece, always consider its inherent weaknesses, for what can be broken will be broken — and then often lost. Always look closely at lids on slant top desks, at tops of all kinds, at feet, and at any delicate or structurally weak legs. A whole set of new blocking is a pretty good indication of a replaced top. Sometimes a walnut lowboy will have a later mahogany top, mahogany being easier to obtain in wide boards. New feet on a chest of drawers or desk are not hard to spot if we are able to get a good look from the underside. To spot hidden leg splices on a highboy, locate a clear pattern of figure in the wood and follow it up through where you might expect a splice, such as where the leg joins the case. Another thing to watch for are new screws. A screw longer than an inch or so is in all probability a later addition and indicates a reinforcement or a repair. They are most commonly seen in the corner blocks on chairs.

When examining drawers, do not neglect to look carefully at all of them, for restored drawers are more common than you would think. Most often this will be the little drawers in desks, but you sometimes see a full size drawer that has been replaced. Another thing to watch for is a genuine old drawer that has a new front. Be suspicious of any drawer where the color and figure of the wood does not match the other drawers. Here we might also check for a consistent handle hole history.

Tables and chairs that are moved around a lot often loose several inches off the feet. The common solution is to splice on new sections to bring the piece back up to its original height. This sort of restoration is generally correct, for it is not difficult to estimate the appearance of the missing section. Unfortunately, it is also sometimes difficult to spot the splice line, particularly on turned legs where the join will usually be hidden in the groove of a turning. If the piece has a clear finish, see if the figure in the wood carries up through the turnings. If painted, a careful look from several different angles in a good light will generally show the splice. Another thing to watch for is the distinctive "X" mark of the modern lathe chuck on the bottom of a foot.

Generally the same primary woods will be used throughout a piece of furniture. A mahogany blockfront chest of drawers will be all mahogany; a walnut Queen Anne side chair all walnut. There are some exceptions among rural work. American highboys sometimes have case and legs of maple and drawer fronts of cherry; and candlestands occasionally have different woods used for the top and the pillar. However, even if different, the same wood will always be used for the same function. A stand with two legs of mahogany and one of birch is not right. The one, or perhaps the two, is a replacement. The same rule applies to secondary structure; for example, all drawer sides should be made from the same wood. I've read that Windsor chairs sometimes have legs of different woods, but if true, this is a special case. Perhaps there was more leeway in mass-produced painted furniture.

The older a piece the more likely there is to be a significant amount of restoration. This is not only due to the additional years of use, but also, being older and rarer, its value will have justified more restoration. Collectors accept far more repair and restoration on really early work, realizing that some restoration is inevitable, and in any event, is preferable to nothing. The turnip feet on William and Mary chests are very likely to be replacements, as are the structurally weak highboy and lowboy legs from the same period. If you spot replaced stretchers on these highboys and lowboys, the legs are also likely to be replaced, for when the stretchers go the unsupported legs will be soon to follow. Remember here that a turned leg that is not significantly out of round is probably not very old, for legs were much easier to turn on the old low speed lathes when the wood was somewhat green. Similarly, lift tops on early chests are very apt to be restored, having at some time either split down the middle or broken off at the snipe hinges.

Keep in mind that the amount of repair and restoration may be far more than you anticipate, and if you concentrate on nothing but details you may be missing the big picture. For instance, it is not unusual to see a highboy that has been completely taken apart and rebuilt, usually because the legs had to be restored. The highboy will look just about perfect, but no serious collector will touch it, for not only has a major element of the overall design been replaced, but it is impossible to know that the restoration is true to the original. Sometimes nothing remains but a fragment of the original structure. There are English library armchairs in which the entire beech frame has been restored. Nothing remains but the mahogany components that were resistant to worms; the front of the arms, the legs and the stretchers. However, until some upholstery is lifted and the frame is examined, such a chair might appear to be in almost original condition.

When the legs on a highboy are restored, or the lid on a desk is replaced, the simplest way to get the new wood to blend in with the old wood is to stain and refinish the whole piece. While at it, a few signs of wear are added to the new parts to help them blend in with the old. The final result is usually effective; everything looks both antique and in nice condition. There is a lesson here. Should you encounter period furniture that has been heavily refinished, always ask yourself why. Dealers and collectors do, and they generally don't like the answer one little bit.

**Missing Prices**

A surprising amount of old furniture is missing a significant portion of the original structure. Earlier we noted the many highboys that lack their upper cases, but this is only a more egregious example of a common problem, one that many dealers are loath to mention — any more than they wish to tell you of repairs and restorations. Unfortunately, missing pieces are not all that obvious unless we know what to expect in different forms of furniture. They do not stand out as would the missing lid on a desk or a missing foot on a chest of drawers. However, we need to be aware of this problem, for this sort of furniture adds nothing to the quality of your collection.

Here then are some of the things to watch for:

- Queen Anne mirrors normally had crests, usually with a gilt shell in the middle. These crests were made up as a separate component, and because they were normally just fastened with blocking, are now frequently missing.
- Chippendale tables and chairs with straight Marlborough legs often had little pierced brackets where the leg met the apron or rail; a nice little Rococo touch on otherwise somewhat linear furniture. These were normally just glued on, reinforced with a couple of small nails, and being fragile, tend to get lost. If you look closely on the inside of the legs, you usually will be able to spot a few of the original nail holes.
- Sheraton chests of drawers were often fitted with a splashboard across the back, or a small set of drawers on the top, or perhaps a small set of drawers supporting a dressing mirror. Always check the back of the top of these chests for holes where screws once fastened the splashboard; and the top for the holes of the screws than once kept the drawers in place.
- Sometimes you will come across a secretary that is now just a desk, having lost its bookcase top. There are a number of clues here to tell us that something is wrong. First off, the top of the desk may seem unusually wide, for it once had to support a bookcase. Because it did not show, the top may be made of a secondary wood, now stained up to match the rest of the case; and finally, if

we look closely, we should be able to see the filled in holes from the little nails that once secured the molding that held the top in position.

- Sideboards were often fitted with a brass gallery across the back and sides, which is now thought to have been hung with napkins to protect the wallpaper from splashed wine. If missing, you will be able to spot filled holes across the sides and back, provided they have not been hidden under later banding.
- When furniture is deemed too high, the simplest solution is to cut a few inches off the feet or legs. We see this frequently in large desks with high writing surfaces, and in Sheraton chests of drawers, but it can happen to any piece that seems too tall for modern use.
- Cornices, or lack of them, on any large case furniture should be regarded with suspicion, for not only are they prone to be cut down, but they were often made up as a separate section and have been lost. Original cornices are quite large and bold, as wide or wider than the feet. A small, weak cornice that does not complement the base is probably a replacement.

Lastly, there is some furniture of which has lost so much that it is nothing but a fragment of the original. If you come across a simple Hepplewhite or Sheraton side table that lacks the normal drawer and seems unusually large, you are probably looking at an end section of an old dining room table. More common yet are dressing mirrors that have been separated from the base and little drawers. These are easily to spot if you always remember to check for a pair of holes just above the midpoint on the sides of any smallish mirror that has straight sides. Although usefully small and frequently charming, such mirrors are now nothing but a fragment of the original.

## Complete Fake

Complete and outright fakes are the upper crust in fraud and fakery, for while their actual numbers are not all that great, they get the lion's share of attention in the media. This is not unreasonable, for a very clever fake that has been passed off as genuine period workmanship at a major auction is far more newsworthy than the small time trickery to which most of us are exposed.

The novice has little chance against a really well done fake. Here only the discerning eye which comes with experience offers reasonable protection. Fortunately, good fakes are not all that common among American furniture. Most consist of no more than a quality reproduction that has been artfully aged, which should not fool us if we take the time to look. Always inspect secondary woods carefully for evidence of staining, for it is very difficult to get these surfaces to appear old without using some stain.

The most common recent problem among American furniture lies in the ever popular country cupboards, which are easily made up from some old boards. Here you want to be on the lookout for inexplicable holes, for while old siding or flooring is not hard to come by, it will almost always carry a few holes associated with its previous occupation. Even if puttied over and painted, holes are difficult to hide in a good light if we just remember to take the time to look for them.

It might be noted that English furniture presents far more of a problem to the collector, for in England the apprenticeship system and the tradition of handwork continued right up into the 20th century. You want to be very careful here, for this convergence of skill and tradition led to a great many high quality fakes. A lot of Americans have returned from abroad with some very dubious antiques. They must be still turning up at estate sales.

In an earlier chapter it was noted that old furniture sometimes exhibits a very characteristic aroma of age. However, there is one aroma that you should never detect — the smell of paint. Even if a Windsor chair or a corner cupboard was given another coat of paint in Victorian times, the volatile oils will have long since evaporated, leaving a hard surface free of odor. New paint continues to slowly dry long after the surface has set up, which you can often detect if you bring your nose close to the surface. If you find sniffing around embarrassing, see if your thumbnail will leave a mark in the surface, for just as new paint is not really dry, it is not really hard.

While I've divided fakes and frauds into different problems, the reader should be warned that these are not mutually exclusive, for more than one problem may be present in an object; and although we have come to the end of this subject, we have by no means come to the end of fakery, for the lazy and the unscrupulous will always be looking for new ways to turn a quick profit. Also keep in mind, that as a collector, you will always be at a disadvantage because you handle relatively few pieces of old furniture. Auctioneers and dealers deal with fakes all the time and get to know instinctively when something is not right. From long experience, they also know just where to look. Probably the best protection is to stick to reputable dealers and to the better regional auctions. An honest dealer cannot afford deception, and the better auction houses will not include questionable pieces in their major auctions. If they handle a piece they feel has extensive rework or restoration, they will discreetly indicate as much in the catalog. Actually, if you deal with only reputable dealers you could have skipped this chapter. But then, the subject of fakery is always popular. Perhaps because we think that it only happens to others?

There has been a great deal of scholarship in period furniture since the turn of the century and a lot of pieces which misled both curators and collectors then are now very obviously fakes, not because we are more intelligent, but because we now know so much more. When you read accounts of some of the early notable frauds, the famous "nine shell" Newport chest and the Baltimore "griffin" gaming table, you find yourself wondering how the experts were fooled. The problem was twofold: they saw old furniture with an earlier vision of the past, and far less was known then about American period furniture. Now we know much more, and although we most certainly still have problems with vision, the increased knowledge is a great assistance in avoiding mistakes. The more recent books on major collections contain a wealth of detailed information not found in one of the classics by Nutting or Miller. These newer books do much to level the playing field, for while we will never see as much furniture as the professional, we can do just as much reading.

# Dealers, Shows, and Auctions

Perhaps half the pleasure in collecting old furniture lies in the search itself, which is fortunate, for with the limited amount of period furniture on the market, the limited size of our homes, and the even more limited size of our pocketbooks, it is likely to be a long search. However, in return for the time and effort, it is in collecting that we really find out about period furniture. If reading is our school, then collecting is the real world. Neither is complete without the other.

Before getting started, it is useful to have a feel for the relative amount of furniture from different periods. Just how common is period furniture? What can we actually expect to find in shops and at auctions? Nowhere is this better stated than by Morton Marsh, who suggests that "We might say, in a crude statistic, that for each 500 semi-antique pieces on the market we can expect 50 late Federal, 10 early Federal, 5 late Colonial, and only 1 Colonial." We see here that most old furniture is not period furniture at all, and of that which is actually period, the majority will be late Federal. This is also true of English furniture, most of which is either late Georgian or Regency. The antique shop which advertises 18th and 19th century period furniture, often, in fact, has very little of the former; somewhat like the can of mixed nuts, which however filled, always seems to come out mostly peanuts.

Quality was covered earlier, but now that we are looking at the market, it should be mentioned again. That something is 200 years old, by itself, does not mean very much. Not all old furniture is handsome or well made. At estate auctions you will often see a few pieces of period furniture, most of it not very attractive, in poor condition, and quite frequently modified. Its only virtue is age. Should low cost be the only criteria, it is possible to fill a house at minimal expense with such furniture, but it will be a sorry collection.

Always pass up old furniture that has been modified, even though the result is both practical and useful, and the price may be very tempting. As you gain experience, the modification will come to bother you, for you will realize that what you have acquired is little credit either to your judgment or to your collection. In a similar way, the more you collect, the more you will come to appreciate the original in period furniture. Unfortunately, others also feel this way, and an almost original piece commands a very considerable premium, often being double or more the cost of equal work that has no more than a few small repairs.

In this matter, you must decide on a level of quality, then try to stick with it. The siren song is always there to buy the lessor because it is cheaper, but if you do, the end result will inevitably be a lot of the lessor. More often than not, when you get something very cheaply, you will come to regret it. Never step below the level that you have set for yourself, even if at times there is a dry spell between purchases. You want to be proud of you collection — and pleased with yourself.

Here something might be said about country furniture and the simpler urban furniture, for although seldom represented in major collections, these comprise the great majority of period furniture. Much of the lower cost urban furniture, while lacking inlay, carving, and the best of woods, exhibits the same admirable proportions and superior construction found in most all high style work, which is what we might expect

**109**

from apprentice trained cabinetmakers with a lifetime of experience in their profession. In rural furniture we may also find good proportion and construction, as well as the spontaneity and exuberance found in all period furniture. The simplicity in execution and detail that characterizes country furniture is often combined with lovely woods and good workmanship. It can be a lot more charming than the more conventional urban furniture. Whatever you favor, remember that furniture, as a form of art, must stand on its own merit, not on the fashion of the moment or on an exulted provenance. The old saying that it is better to purchase a good painting by a minor artist than a poor effort of a major one is equally true for furniture.

Although it is a very considerable aid, no amount of reading and looking will make you an experienced collector, any more than it will make you a good sailor or a skilled auto mechanic. To be a collector you must go into the market and collect. In so doing it is inevitable that you will make some mistakes. Don't worry about this, for this is the way we all learn. There is not a dealer, nor a collector, great or small, that has not made some mistakes, and you are very unlikely to be the exception. Mistakes are an inevitable part of all collecting, and usually are no great a loss if you have the sense to learn from each.

The best way to start is to take a careful and realistic look at the market to determine at what level you can afford to buy quality. Visit a number of dealers and shows to learn what is available, and at what level you might be able to compete to build a good collection. Do not be discouraged if at first you see beautiful things that you could not begin to afford, or things you could afford but would not have in your home. You are just looking in the wrong places, you have not located the right dealers.

When beginning, start as near as you can aspire to the top of the market, for here you will find knowledgeable dealers and good auctions. Also try to get to the better antique shows. Even if you cannot afford most of the lovely things you see around you, it will immerse you in period furniture. This is where you acquire an understanding of quality and a feel for period workmanship. Small auctions and local shows, where there is a mixture of period, reproduction, and traditional furniture, with perhaps a fake or two thrown in, can be very confusing to the beginner. Keep in mind here that good collections are normally dispersed via the major auctions and the better dealers. You are not very likely to find something wonderful at a small local estate sale.

If contemplating a purchase, or a bid, consider the effects of scale. Shops may have high ceilings and most auctions are held in large halls or under tents. In such surroundings, it is easy to forget that period furniture can be quite large and tall. This sort of error may be no more than an embarrassment if something must be returned to a dealer, but it can be a real problem at an auction where there are no returns. When looking for something for a specific location, use your imagination and a tape measure to work up the maximum dimensions the location can handle, then keep note of this on a slip of paper. Don't overlook depth, for old chests of drawers and cellaret sideboards are often quite deep, perhaps too deep for an intended location.

Now there are three ways to acquire period furniture: we can purchase it from a dealer at a shop or at an antique show, bid successfully at an auction, or be patient and have it come to us through inheritance or gift. First off, we'll cover dealers, for this is by far the best place to start.

## Dealers

A dealer may not be the most economical source of period furniture, but he, or she, is the most safe and sure. This is where you should begin. Waving a paddle at auctions in pursuit of wonderful buys requires real knowledge and experience, and is no place for the novice unless one is an apostle of education in the school of hard knocks. Later, though, auctions can become a good source if you wish to forgo the services provided by dealers, and perhaps save some money besides.

Dealers in 18th and 19th century furniture provide four basic services to the collector. They are the primary source of period furniture; they provide knowledge and expertise; they have access to skilled repair and restoration; and most importantly, they cull out the reproduction, the junk, and the fake. Let's first look at these services, for they are the reason, and the justification, for their prices.

Most of the period furniture on the market is in the hands of dealers. This is the first place to look. Dealers spend endless hours and travel many miles in search of stock that will complement their shop and appeal to their regular customers. In addition to auctions, most buy and sell through a network of friends and acquaintances in the trade. They also get to know individuals who have collections of old furniture, and are able to buy from them, although they may have to wait years for the opportunity. In effect, they do all the searching for the collector. The other major market source of period furniture, auctions, are both infrequent and uncertain. Logically then, dealers are the first and best place to look.

An experienced dealer is very knowledgeable. From years of buying and selling they acquire a great deal of information, not only of period furniture, but of furniture local to their region. Many are scholars in their own right. They know just what to expect to find among the different forms of furniture, and which are the poor examples, the good examples, and the best examples. In addition, an experienced dealer has a knowledge of the market that even the most avid collector will probably never acquire.

Antique furniture purchased from a dealer will be in good condition and any repairs should be well done. You can use it the day it arrives home. It does not have to go into the workshop or out to a restorer for an indefinite period of cleanup or repair. Dealers know the furniture restorers that work in their area, and which can be trusted with something good. This is more important than it may sound, for it is not always easy to locate a restorer, and most who are good are also very busy.

A good shop not only provides you with many choices, but whatever your taste or interest, all the items for sale have merit. You do not have to worry about quality; and you should never have to worry about fakery. If good dealers seem to be expensive, it is mostly because they carry only the better things; they have filtered out the cheap.

While the major dealers are honest and knowledgeable, you want to be very careful with the smaller shops, for an unsettling number display furniture that has serious problems. There will be pieces that are incorrectly identified, or have been modified, or have had some major restoration. This may be due to ignorance or to dishonesty, or simply because the dealer has discovered that customers do not care about problems so long as the price is right. In any event, the result is the same. You can easily acquire something that does nothing but reduce the quality of your collection.

There is a considerable element of trust in the antique business, for even the experienced collector relies on the dealer's honesty and knowledge. Should you spot something in a shop that you feel is not right, make a tactful exit. Not only are there probably other funny things around, but you are unlikely to trust the dealer enough to buy anything. You are just wasting your time. Remember that while dealers may not be smarter than you, they have a great deal more experience. As many others have said — don't ever try to outsmart a dealer.

Dealers may tell you that they are finding it more and more difficult to find good stock, the inference being that you should buy now while there is still the chance. However, the supply of period furniture is not diminishing, at least to any significant extent. While the finer pieces gravitate toward museums, and there is some small annual loss to fire and accident, by and large the amount remains constant. Period furniture continually comes on the market as collectors upgrade their collections, as families move to smaller homes, as museums deaccession, or most commonly, as estates are settled. However, it is a random process. Some years there seem to be any number of good auctions, while in other years the supply does indeed seem to be less. Part of this is economic. More antiques come on the market in good times than in bad, for we all try to sell when prices are high. Also, an increase in demand from a change in fashion, and the resulting higher prices, brings pieces to the market, for there are times when one thing or another seems to be very common, but only at a high price. Here the rise in prices is as much due to demand as to any actual scarcity.

Rare is a much abused word in the antique business. There is hardly a dealer that can resist telling you that something is rare, and by implication, a buy you should not miss. Because period furniture was handmade and each piece is pretty much unique, it is not difficult to identify a rare feature. However, we want to distinguish between what is rare and what is just odd or unusual. Rare is an uncommon variation within the normal milieu. This is generally a variation in form, or in design, or in construction. A Boston bombé secretary is a rare form. Similarly, a New York card table with six legs rather than the five legs found in many New York tables is an uncommon design feature. A Philadelphia lowboy made of curly maple might be considered a rare construction. Rarity is normally attributed to variations in high style furniture where the norm is clearly defined. The work of rural craftsmen exhibits so many variations and idiosyncrasies that it is more difficult to define just what are legitimate rarities. Would you consider an unusual shape of an apron or an odd turning on a candlestand to be rare, or is this just the product of an inexperienced cabinetmaker? They may indeed be rare, and even possibly unique, but to the collector they are far less remarkable. Remember also, that while rarity may legitimately increase price, it should not be accepted as a substitute for quality. Some rarities, such as a lighthouse clock, or a ladder-back chair fitted with cabriole legs, are rare because they were unsuccessful designs that were only produced in very limited quantities.

There is also a lot of talk in the trade about original finishes, and again, we should be cautious. The dedicated collector so cherishes the original in period work that an apparently undisturbed finish is very appealing, but here there may be much wishful thinking. Not only do many pieces have later shellac over the original oil and wax, but it is doubtful if the early spirit varnishes were very durable. However well maintained, all finishes slowly dry out, and if not stripped and replaced, at least must be rubbed down and given further finish. After several hundred years, how much of the original finish really remains? Perhaps the most honest declaration is that an item has an "old finish."

Paints also dry out, get worn and chip off at the edges, and it is rare to find painted furniture that has not been repainted at least once. Although the surface may seem very old and dried out, you are probably not looking at the original paint. Shaker furniture is perhaps an even worse case, for the emphasis on neatness and cleanliness in the Shaker communities resulted in much stripping and repainting, and if this were not enough, publication of the Millennial Laws led to further stripping and repainting.

If the dealer does not volunteer the information, always inquire if there are any repairs or restorations. Generally the better the shop the fewer, for one of the things you pay for in a good shop is condition. If a piece is pretty much all original, the dealer will normally mention this, but if not, ask something to the effect "Are there any repairs or restoration you are aware of?" This is important, for repairs can be difficult to spot, particularly in the less than perfect light of a shop. When you get home and take a careful look at your new possession, you may find some additional small repairs that were either not mentioned, or you did not notice in the shop.

The word restored suggests that a part has been restored to its former state, and one would like to think this might consist of perhaps no more than a little patching, gluing, and refinishing. But this is not so. Restored means just what the dictionary says: "to bring back into existence." Restored feet on a chest of drawers are new feet; a restored lid on a desk lid is a new lid. If a dealer tells you that there has been "some restoration to the feet," he may be telling you tactfully that the feet are, in fact, just about all new. In a similar vein, inpainting is no more than an elegant word for touchup. A painted blanket chest that has had some inpainting has been touched up where the paint was worn or chipped off.

Good quality period furniture is sufficiently rare that a dealer's life is a constant scramble for new stock that will both compliment the shop and match the interests of regular customers. There are estimates that about three quarters of a dealer's business is with other dealers. While this is just an estimate, it is true that three quarters or more of the bidders at auctions are dealers, and that much of the business at antique shows is between dealers. Dealers often have a standing offer to buy back any item at cost. The piece you bought may not be the very best, but they can use it.

There is continual lateral movement of antiques among dealers to areas of greatest demand, which is one reason why you see so many out of state license plates at auctions. In general, Empire goes South, Victorian goes West, and English goes to the Texas Gulf coast where the mild climate is kind to old glues and veneers. Similarly, there is a vertical movement as pieces rise, or fall, to the level that can best handle them. A really good item that turns up in an out of the way place will rapidly pass through two or three hands before ending up in the shop of a major dealer. Should a small local dealer find himself with a very nice piece, much better than his normal stock, and well outside the price range of his regular customers, it will be passed on to another dealer that can put it to better use. Otherwise, it might sit unsold for years. Successful dealers make money by selling, not by maintaining small private museums. This suggests that unless you have a lot of time on your hands, do not haunt little out

**113**

of the way shops for that wonderful antique that others have missed. You are probably wasting your time. It is very unlikely to be there.

Although dealer markup varies widely with circumstances, the normal spread between wholesale and retail is typically about 100%. This sounds like a lot, but is similar to any business that must maintain a large stock that has a slow turnover. If you think this spread is a guarantee of instant riches, weigh the cost of a shop full of good period furniture, plus the expenses of cleanup and repair, rental, insurance, and advertising, against slow and intermittent sales. Selling period furniture is like selling art; the right person has to be matched with the right piece, and this may take quite a while. On repeat visits to dealers, you will often see the same piece sitting in the same place — sometimes for years. It is no way to get rich.

One advantage of this spread is that the dealer has a cushion to work with. While antique shops are not Oriental bazaars, it is possible to do a little dickering. However, this is not always necessary. To clinch sales, dealers will often offer to help out a bit if they sense you are a serious customer and really interested in a piece. If not, you can always hesitate a little, or ask "Is the price on this firm?"

Many dealers will date pieces as early as possible, and perhaps suggest a little provenance. If a style was popular from about 1790 to 1820, the label will often state "c.1790" or perhaps "18th century," for the last decade of the 18th century seems a lot earlier than the first decades of the 19th, although as was noted earlier, something is more likely to be later than earlier. You also will often hear comments like "this passed through my hands in the 80s," which adds a little provenance; or, "this would cost more now," which suggests the item would be a good investment. As a businessman the dealer will naturally put his stock in the best light, which is neither unethical nor dishonest. It is just good business.

However, do not let this small talk lead you to buy under pressure. Even if the dealer hovers around, the time to reconsider is before you reach for the checkbook. If not absolutely sure, come back later for a second and more objective look. Antiques move slowly and the odds are the piece will still be there. Buy under pressure and hardly will the ink be dry than doubts will rise around you like Ebenezer's ghosts. Buying in a market where every object is individual and unique requires careful judgment.

Many of the better dealers advertise they are open "by appointment only" or "by chance or appointment." Do not be intimidated. Their only purpose is to limit the casual visitor, not the serious collector. Also, don't ever feel that you must reciprocate an appointment with a purchase. Collecting is a long-term activity and the dealer knows there is a lot more looking than buying. They are happy to spend time with interested customers. Whether or not an appointment is indicated, you always want to call ahead if you are coming from any distance. Even well known dealers are small operations, and the shop may be closed while the owner is attending to a show or to family matters. Dealers often ask you what you are interested in, and you may wish to visit with a furniture period or a furniture type in mind. It provides an opening for talk and suggests to the long suffering dealer that you are a serious collector and are not just using his time for a little Saturday afternoon entertainment. Should the furniture be much more expensive than you had anticipated, be honest about this with the dealer. He will often direct you to other good shops that are less expensive. This is not just altruism. Successful dealers have a long-term view of their customers. If you have had a pleasant visit, there is a fair chance you will be back later when your finances improve, or when you realize that the quality you are seeking will not come cheaply.

With the advent of the Internet, some of the more active dealers now have both e-mail addresses and home pages or web sites. These are usually listed at the bottom of their advertisements. While period furniture most certainly needs to be seen and evaluated before purchase, a well planned web site that provides a summary of the major items in stock, with perhaps color images of a selected few, provides the collector with a picture of the shop and a feel for the quality and the general price range of the furniture.

## Shows

Quite the best way to meet a large number of dealers — and to obtain an overview of the market — is to attend a good regional antiques show. Such a show will not only introduce you to many dealers, but will save you innumerable needless visits to shops, for dealers in period furniture not only vary widely in their prices, but also in their focus, some favoring high style, some country, and some primitive. While you may only see a fraction of a dealer's stock at a show, you will obtain a very clear idea of what you might expect to find in his or her shop.

To meet the better dealers, go to the better shows. It is that simple. The better shows are normally the major regional events that take place once or twice a year. Not all dealers sell at shows, and there are some very good ones that never do, but at a first class show you can meet quite a number of well known dealers and see a lot of really beautiful furniture. The same principle that applies to dealers also applies to shows. It is much better to attend one good show than ten poor ones. You will save gas and time in the long run.

Shows are advertised in the Sunday papers, but to attend a really good show will probably require some advance planning. Fortunately, these are advertised well in advance in *Antiques Magazine* and in trade papers such as the *Maine Antique Digest*. In addition, some very nice things can be found at the smaller shows, and the prices may be more reasonable. Although it will take more time and looking, this is where you are apt to come across a good local dealer that does no more advertising than perhaps a line or two in the yellow pages. Also, some of the major dealers patronize the smaller shows if they are not far away and the cost is moderate.

Once you become familiar with some of the dealers in your price range you can look for them among the list of exhibitors that accompanies many of the advertisements. With experience, you can get a good feeling for the general quality of a show just by reviewing the dealers. Should the advertisement list nothing more appealing than Joe and Margie's Collectable Treasures, your visit will probably be a waste of time. The vertical movement in prices and in quality is just as true for shows.

There are different times to attend a show. Dealers and serious collectors go on the first day, preferably in the first few hours, even though there is usually a considerable premium for first day admission. Here they hope to find some wonderful things that have just come on the market, for antique dealers put aside special finds just for shows. This is when there is a lot of buying and selling between dealers.

You might wish to visit when things are quiet and you can have a good look around and chat with the dealers, who sometimes are just as interesting as their stock. Here you can do a little comparison shopping, and mull over a purchase without having to worry too much about it being gone when you come back. Some dealers will hold a piece for a little while, perhaps an hour or so, while you think it over, and they will be far happier to do this when things are slow. When there is time, try to have a good look around, then sit down with a snack and think about what you've seen, then go back for a second look. There are so many beautiful pieces at the better shows that you can miss some very nice things on the first pass.

Most people attend shows on a Saturday or Sunday afternoon, and here you can enjoy all the hustle and bustle of a good show, although it will be more difficult to take a really careful look at the dealers' booths. If going with friends, and there is the time, you might first visit the show by yourself, then return with them on the weekend when you can enjoy their company without having to worry about missing something.

And finally, there are sneaky people who go to a show on the last hour of the last day, sweet talk their way past the tired attendant without a buying a ticket, then try to dicker down some poor dealer who has had a bad week and doesn't want do drag everything back home again. Don't laugh. This sometimes works.

Unlike museums, shows provide a wonderful capsule view of the market. You get the same view at a shop, but the view is necessarily much more limited. You will find the better shows fascinating, not only for the number and variety of good quality antiques, but because you can rapidly get a feel for relative values. At first, you will tend to read the price tags to find out how old and where from, and sometimes to boggle over a price, but this will only serve to make you feel like a novice. Instead, you might first look at a piece and make your own guess of how old and where from, then look at the tag only if you are further interested. This will convey an impression of genteel erudition, even though at first you may not know a snuff box from a chamber pot. Many dealers now provide a thorough description on neat little cards, often with the price discreetly noted on the back. It is a big improvement over a tiny, unobtrusive tag.

There is a movement toward vetting shows. Before the opening, an independent group of professionals tours the booths looking for pieces that are incorrectly identified — or worse. The buyer then has a reasonable guarantee of authenticity. Unfortunately, vetting has been slow to spread. However, that it is felt to be necessary, even at major shows, suggests that one should not be carried away by bright lights and well known names into thinking that there cannot be a little fakery here and there. Some of this risk can be minimized by good documentation. When buying any antique, large or small, the dealer should always provide a bill of sale that clearly identifies the piece; for instance, "Federal mahogany inlaid candlestand, Massachusetts, c. 1810." If the receipt says nothing more than "Old mahogany table," you are probably getting just that — an old mahogany table.

When at a show, note the location of dealer's shop. This information is often included in the signs above the booths. It is useful to spot dealers that are no further away than a reasonable weekend drive. These are often the shops you will later visit. You will also meet some dealers that do not have shops. They only exhibit at shows. However, if you express an interest in their stock, they will be happy to tell you of the shows at which they regularly exhibit, and indeed, will contact you if they acquire something for which you have expressed a particular interest.

## Auctions

No method of collecting is more exciting, nor more filled with peril, than an auction. Within a matter of seconds you can make a great buy — or make a great mistake! Hopefully, this section will direct you to many more of the former, but never forget that the time honored injunction at auctions is, "fair room and fair warning."

The principle of beginning near the top of the market is also applicable to auctions. Don't get involved in the smaller auctions and estate sales until you can tell English from American, period from reproduction, and know a fake when you see one. However, this does not mean that you have to begin with Sotheby's or Christie's; any good regional auction house that publishes a catalog with a description of each lot, and perhaps the estimated bid range, is a good starting place. You will find that these catalogs are a wonderful learning tool. Cover the preview, catalog in hand, and you will quickly learn a lot about both period furniture and market prices. It is a very different world from museums, not only for the variety, but for being able to touch, pull out and look under. Even if you only buy from dealers, auction previews are a wonderful place to learn about old furniture.

Auctioneers put their best foot forward in their advertisements, and if the advertisement does not look promising, the lots will probably be no better. If a 1910 oak roll-top desk is illustrated, do not expect to find any period furniture. Often the advertisement will list, in very fine print, the more important lots, and here you can get a good feel for the auction. If no old furniture is mentioned, there will probably be none, for most auctioneers are quick to spot period workmanship.

At an auction, information on the items to be auctioned will range from nothing whatsoever, to simple fliers, to very complete catalogs that identify each lot in the order it will be brought up for sale. Generally, these catalogs describe each lot in some detail, providing information on source, period, an estimate of the date of manufacture, any known provenance, the dimensions, and perhaps a few short words on condition. There may also be an estimated price range. Often this is accompanied by a photograph. Particularly photogenic lots are likely to be shown in color. These color photos are works of art in their own right, for they are so flattering to their subject as to be not so much a picture of what the piece looks like now, but to how it will look when all cleaned up. In some measure, they provide the prospective owner with a feel for what to expect. This wonderful effect is achieved with high intensity lighting that brings out the color and figure of the wood under the dirt and old shellac. So flattering are these illustrations that it is easy to walk right past a lot without recognizing it from the photograph in the catalog.

When you pick up your catalog there will often be an additional sheet of information tucked inside or on lying on the counter. This typically contains amendments to the catalog entries, additional lots and corrections. Take the time to go over them carefully, for they can be important. Not only are some nice things added to the sale after the catalog is printed, but you do not want to overlook a correction that states "should read style rather than period and is probably 20th century."

In your eagerness to look through the catalog, do not ignore the printed information at the beginning. Here you will find the Conditions of Sale, bidding instructions, and perhaps even a limited warranty. The major auction houses have a great deal of expertise, and will generally warrant the description in their catalog. If they state that a lot is Connecticut, late 18th century, you can be pretty sure it is just that. Some firms, if they feel that a piece has some problems, perhaps having had major restoration, will indicate this discreetly by omitting the date and source from the description. Instead of stating "Chippendale Mahogany Armchair, New York, 1760 – 1780," they will just say "Chippendale Mahogany Armchair," and if probably a reproduction, then perhaps no more than "American Armchair." You will also find what legal redress you have if you feel there is a mistake. It is generally not much. The conditions of sale state very clearly that the lot goes to the highest bidder, and that the sale is legally complete at this time. You cannot change your mind.

While here, take a careful look at the date and time of the auction, and at the dates and times of the previews, for it is easier than you would think to arrive on the wrong day of the auction, or worse, to miss the preview and then be unable to bid. This is particularly important on auctions you attend frequently, for here you are likely to be casual about time and date. Occasionally a regular auction will be shifted to avoid a schedule conflict, or moved up by an hour or so if there is an unusual number of lots.

The most important thing to do at auctions, and far more important than the clever bidding strategies you read about, is to attend the preview. This is where you do your homework, and it is very necessary homework. Never, ever, bid on a lot you have not carefully examined beforehand. If you are unable to get to the preview, then don't go to the auction. Go, and you are just asking for trouble.

Fortunately, previews are a very pleasant homework, and indeed, are worth attending even if there is nothing you wish to bid on, or you cannot make the auction. Whenever possible, get to the preview a day or so before the auction, for this is when you can have an unhurried look. If you cannot get there a day or two day early, or if the auctioneer only previews on the day of the sale, then be sure to come early. The last hour before a sale is pretty much a madhouse.

The first thing to do at a preview is to stake out a chair with a reservation card or an old sweater. Auctions can run for four or five hours, and you don't want to have to stand for a couple of hours until a good seat finally opens up. When possible, try to find a seat at the end of a row so you can move around some without stepping on toes. Dealers often stand at the back and sides of the hall so that they can talk business with other dealers, watch the action, and perhaps bid unobtrusively, but I doubt this offers much advantage to a collector who does relatively little bidding. You want to sit where you have a good view of the lots as they are brought up — and where the auctioneer has a good view of you. This is important, for the only thing worse than bidding on the wrong lot is having your bid missed, and both are surprisingly easy to do.

It is at previews that dealers do most of their work, and here they will be busily pulling out drawers and turning things over, for this is when repairs and restorations are spotted. Dealers cannot afford to make errors, and they will really work over good pieces. Aside from perhaps an offhand remark, do not bother them, for they are hard at work. Anyhow, there is little use in asking an opinion, for they can hardly be expected to speak well of a lot they might later bid on. If you need some information, ask one of the staff. Should you find a lot on which you might bid, give it a thorough examination. Don't just give it a casual glance for fear others will see you are interested, for this will do nothing but get you in trouble. It is natural at first to feel that everyone is watching to see what you are interested in, but rest assured, the dealers have far more important concerns.

Concentrate on the pieces on which you might bid, not forgetting to check in the corners of the hall, for a nice item may be in an out of the way place. Normally, the better lots will be displayed in a row on either side of the auctioneer's podium. Should you see a good looking highboy or lowboy that is not out in front, it is probably an indication that it has some serious problems. Try to go over everything of interest, even if you think something might be over your budget. You do not want to have to pass on a lot because you did not take the time to examine it at the preview.

In a major auction there are so many lots that it is sometimes difficult to know just where to begin. After an initial survey to get a feel for things, you might follow these steps:

- Look for a lot that is attractive, would compliment your collection, and on which you could reasonably hope to bid, then
- Consider if there would be a place for it in your home, then
- Read exactly what the catalog says about it, then
- Go over it very, very carefully.

With this systematic editing, there will usually be no more than a few lots that you will really scrutinize, which is all right, because this is not the time to get hasty. When examining a lot, look for things that seem inconsistent or out of the ordinary. If you spot a problem, don't stop there. Should the inside of a drawer be varnished, ask yourself; "What else was done?" If a leg has been repaired, then; "Have other legs been broken?" Unless a finish has aged so much as to be almost black, it should be possible to see the figure of wood underneath the finish. If an area seems to be a different shade, or seems to have a very thick finish so that the figure of the wood does not show through, you are probably looking at a repair or a restoration. Take the time to look everywhere, for staining and inpainting can be remarkably good.

If you plan to bid on a major item such as a highboy, you may wish to have it examined by a restorer. From experience — and from years of artfully concealing repair and restoration — a good restorer knows just where to look for problems. Go over an old piece of furniture with one of these experts and you will be amazed at the problems they spot.

When you get back home, think about what you have seen, and check to see if things will actually fit where you thought. Don't neglect depth. On the day of the sale take a final honest look to see if your choices really look as good as they did at the preview. This homework is critical, for you don't know what will happen when bidding starts. Remember that the decision to bid is nine tenths made at the preview.

Aside from perhaps gluing a foot back on, furniture is always auctioned off as is, and condition will vary from almost perfect to a complete wreck. Now you would think that auctioneers could get better prices by fixing things up, but this is the last thing that dealers and collectors want. For them, the more original the better. At the preview you must look past missing veneer and deteriorated finish to see the real merit of a piece, to imagine what it will look like when all cleaned up. You will discover that minor damage and deteriorated finish does little to reduce the price of a good item. Dealers know just how easy this is to put to right. What you must learn is the difference between this sort of wear and that of restored legs and replaced tops. Keep in mind that there is a fundamental difference between repair and replacement. Pieces that are loose or separated may look terrible, but are seldom much of a problem to fix. That something is in pieces is not nearly so important as that all the pieces are there. Missing parts, however beautifully restored, can never be original, and it is the original you are paying for. Once the bidding starts, you will see what original does to price.

Don't let your enthusiasm for a piece keep you from carefully reading the two or three line description in the catalog. This sounds obvious, but if you get excited over something, it is easy to overlook. As noted earlier, the more vague the description, the more likely there is to be something wrong. The auctioneer will naturally be tactful about problems, and if it is noted, for example, that there is "some restoration to the top," you want to be sure that the top is not, in fact, completely restored.

Be careful when examining things. Even though the lots are normally covered by insurance, you'll really feel the fool if you damage something. Take care to pull out the slides before opening up a desk, for some of the old mahoganies are remarkably dense and heavy. Always look before you try to pull out a drawer. You will feel pretty silly if it is the dummy drawer on a blanket chest. If a drawer will not open, do not pull hard before some reflection. If it seems free in the case, but will not come out, you may have encountered one of the clever wood spring or Quaker locks we discussed earlier. Open the next drawer down and slide your hand under to see what is holding the upper drawer in place. If a box, then look for a locking pin that drops in from the top. It is always interesting to come across this old "budget" hardware.

Never, ever, pick up an old chair by the top, because the crest rail may be loose, and if it pulls free, you are very likely to either break out a mortise, or to break off a tenon, or to damage both. Similarly, never pick up a chest of drawers by the top. The safe way to do this is to open a top drawer and slide your hand under the drawer blade. These are tenoned into the sides of the case and should be reasonably solid. Then lift by placing the other hand firmly against the back. When dealers tip over a chest to look at the bottom, they are careful not to put a heavy crosswise load on the feet, which may be just about ready to fall off. Also be gentle when picking up tripod tables. Put one hand on the shaft and the other on the top. You don't know if the top is secure, or which way it may tilt. When picking up furniture with drawers, tilt the case slightly back so that the drawers don't slide out. Should you want to take a close look at a grandfather clock, particularly at the base where there is most likely to be some restoration, first slide the hood off forward, then lift out the works. Generally the pendulum and weights will already have been removed. At auctions the staff will be happy to help you move things. They don't want things broken any more than you do.

On the day of the sale you will find that auctioneers always put their lots in the best possible light, both figuratively and literally. The lighting where the items are displayed for bidding is always good, even if provided by nothing more elegant that a couple of large photo floodlights, for a bright concentrated light is flattering to even very ordinary lots. Like a catalog's color photographs, everything will look much better than it did at the preview.

Auctioneers always try for the best possible prices for the lots, as this determines not only their profit but also, to some extent, their future business. They will naturally speak well of each lot, and you should not expect otherwise. Rarely will they imply something is less than wonderful unless it is so poor as to be humorous. It is up to you, the buyer, to decide that the "nice old desk" does indeed look nice and is indeed old, but it has been over refinished, the feet are restored, and in fact, its only virtue is age.

Every book devotes a page or two to bidding strategies, the clever moves that gives one an edge over the other bidders. The purpose is to end up with the lowest possible winning bid; or perhaps more honestly, to induce all others to drop out before the price rises above your limit. These ploys are probably little use, for you will be bidding against dealers who have been to hundreds of auctions and have seen every trick in the book. The only person you may fool is another collector, another amateur like you. As a collector, you might prefer a simpler approach. First off, ignore the common advice to set an absolute upper bid limit. Instead, decide on a amount that you feel represents a fair market value, even though it may be above the published upper estimate. However, during the bidding, be prepared to exceed this amount a bit if others are starting to drop out and it appears that a few more bids might win. Here you have the advantage in that you do not have to sell later for a profit. Against a dealer, you should always be able to make the last and winning bid. In any event, you are after quality, and you know that this rarely comes cheaply.

Far more important than bidding strategy is what the pattern of bidding can tell you about the lot. If there is active bidding, the piece is probably fairly good. However, if nobody seems very interested, then something may be very wrong. If you are not sure about a lot, wait a little until a pattern has developed before deciding whether or not to get into the bidding. You will notice that no one likes to initiate the bidding on a major item, and after some difficulty, the auctioneer may have to start with a very low bid. However, you'll soon see that this doesn't indicate any lack of interest, and that the lot will then go for a song. At the other extreme, some lots start out well above the published estimate. This usually occurs on a very good item which has a number of left bids.

Don't ever follow the lead of a well known dealer, thinking that he will guide you to quality and to price. Not only do you not know why he is bidding, but if he spots this pattern he will cheerfully run you up to a ridiculous price on a good looking piece of junk. At an auction, you will generally be bidding against professionals, and you should do so with your own judgment of value and price. If the bidding rises above your limit, then stop. Every collector now and then weeps silently for the wonderful piece that got away, but these are misplaced tears, for the majority of us pursue fairly standard examples and common types. There are a lot of other things out there that are just as pretty if we are willing to be patient.

In addition to not having to sell at a profit, you have another, more subtle advantage over the dealer, in that you only have to please yourself, while the dealer must always please a customer. To use an earlier example, a single restored foot on a chest of drawers is not a big problem, but a dealer might have difficulty in selling such a chest of drawers to a serious collector. Another aspect is that at auction you are paying wholesale rather than retail, and the lower purchase price may justify some compromise. Perhaps this is why it has been noted that collectors at auctions are apt to be more flexible about repairs and restorations.

When selling at auction, the consignor may want to be protected from a very low winning bid. It would be more than a little disheartening to receive but $100 for a Philadelphia Queen Anne chair. To do this, the consignor and the auctioneer agree to a confidential reserve price below which the piece will not be sold. The reserve is usually about 80% of the low estimate in the catalog. By law, the reserve cannot exceed a published low estimate. Should there be little interest in the lot, the auctioneer will bid on behalf of the seller. If bidding does not reach the level of the reserve, the lot will then be bought in by the auction house, the auctioneer normally indicating this by saying that the lot is "passed." At this point the consignor has the choice of taking the item back home, or trying again later, perhaps with a lower reserve. Lots are usually bought in because the reserve is too high, or because the piece has serious problems. If the latter, you don't want it either; but if the former, keep in mind that the piece is still very much on the market. The owner doesn't really want it back, nor does he or she wish to pay a handling or "buy-in" charge, and a tactful approach to the auctioneer on the next business day may result in successfully negotiating a reduced price.

At an auction you may get something at a very fair price, but you are not likely to get it for a song if it is at all good, for even if none of the dealers present can use the lot, they will bid it for sale to another. This base price is sometimes known as the "dealers reserve." In such an environment it is very unlikely that anything good will sell for very little. Therefore, should something seem to be going for remarkably little, resist the temptation to jump in at the last minute for no better purpose than to grab at a bargain, for the odds are that it is no bargain. An auction is an open market. If something goes for very little, it is probably worth very little. A low price should be a warning, never an inducement to bid. A collection composed of the cheap will likely be just that. Cheap.

Contrary to many amusing stories, an auctioneer is careful not to assign bids, and absentmindedly scratching your ear will not find you the surprised new owner of a $60,000 clock. If not sure that you are bidding, the auctioneer will look at you and ask "Are you bidding?" If not, just shake your head. Actually, the real problem is just the reverse — the auctioneer may not spot your bid. This is no difficulty if there are still other bidders, another's bid here is just as good as yours, but it is very upsetting if yours was the last and winning bid. As the sale draws to a close, be sure that the auctioneer knows you are still in the bidding. Conversely, dropping out is no problem. Just shake you head when the auctioneer looks your way for the next bid.

There is a considerable similarity in period work, and in the excitement of an auction it is all too easy to bid on the wrong lot, particularly if you do not realize that there is a similar lot in the auction. At the preview, note down the lots of interest in your catalog, or if no catalog, on the flyer or on a scrap of paper. Auctioneers are generally careful to announce lot numbers where there may be some confusion, but if you are not sure, just call out "Number."

Pay very close attention as your lot comes up. You want to appear calm, but it is no time to be casual. If the lot number is stated, be sure that it agrees with your notes. Some lots, particularly sets of chairs, are sold "by the piece, for the lot," so pay close attention to any remarks. It would be quite a shock to bid $900 for a set of ten chairs, then to discover they were actually $900 each! When bidding, watch only the auctioneer. You can get a feel for the other bidders by seeing where the auctioneer looks and how fast other bids come in. Turning to look at another bidder breaks the link you have established with the auctioneer, and worse, gives an impression you are hesitant. Keep something white or light colored in hand so that you can catch the eye of the auctioneer if bidding is about to close and you are not sure that your bids are still being taken. You may find the bidding confusing at first, for the bid being asked is always one step ahead of the last bid. If a lot is being bid in $100 increments and the auctioneer says "Do I have $1000?," the last accepted bid was $900. Also, the auctioneer will not be looking at you when you are the high bidder, rather, he or she will be looking elsewhere in an effort to obtain another bid. When successful, you may not immediately realize that you are the winner. If you have won, the auctioneer will then request your bidder number. This will be the number on the paddle or the card obtained at the desk before the auction. Should this for some reason not be available, the auctioneer will request the "next number" from his staff. If you plan to bid on an early lot, register and pick up your paddle well in advance, for there is usually a long line at the registration desk during the few minutes between the end of the preview and the start of the auction.

The auctioneer must keep bid increments small to encourage continued bidding, but not so small as to slow the pace of the auction. No one would want to watch a $50,000 secretary auctioned in $100 increments! Bid increments are usually about 10% of the estimated price, although the auctioneer may increase the increment, typically going from $100 to $250, if the bidding has risen far above the estimate. During the bidding, to discourage competition, a bidder may "jump the bid" by calling out or signaling a much higher value, perhaps calling out "ten thousand" when the current bid level is about five thousand. This tactic is usually practiced by the major dealers who have a very good feel the real market value of an outstanding lot.

Auction houses normally charge a buyer's premium on the hammer or sale price and then a commission to the consignor. For example, if both the premium and the commission were 10%, and if the winning bid were $1000, the winning bidder would pay $1100 and the consignor would receive $900. Auction price, also called market price or fair market value, is about ⅔ of the dealer's retail price if we factor in the buyer's premium and remember that dealers often come down a bit to make a sale. However, price varies widely from lot to lot, and spirited bidding can bring a piece right up to a normal retail value. If the market has a real head of steam, the auction price may even be higher than what you would pay for the same quality in a shop. During these periods, auction prices are no bargain except to dealers who can sell while prices are still rising.

Try to arrange your schedule so that you are able to stay until the close of the auction if there is something there of legitimate interest. You may not get a bargain, but you may get a better price because many people leave early and interest seems to taper off toward the end. Most auctioneers bring up their best lots somewhere near the middle of the auction, and then fill in the end with minor lots. Among these there may be some nice items. Also, do not think for a minute that foul weather will present you with a poorly attended auction and a host of bargains. You will find that "Not snow, no, nor rain, nor heat, nor night" will deter collectors and dealers. Any thinning will be just among the casual.

If you cannot attend an auction, it is often possible to leave a bid. The bid will then be executed on your behalf either by the auctioneer or by a member of the staff. Should there be multiple left bids, the highest will win, if not exceeded by a telephone bid or by someone in the audience. In either event, your bid will be executed as cheaply as possible. Just as if it were made at the auction, a winning left bid will be the next bid increment above that of the under bidder. In the event that there are identical left bids, the first entered will take precedence.

The temptation here is to leave a few low bids in the hope of picking up something cheap. However, this is a not a great idea, for not only are you not likely to be successful, but if you do win, you are then left wondering why your winning bid was so low. Remember that you have had no opportunity observe the pattern of the bidding. What if the lot had so many problems that you were almost the only bidder?

The better approach is to leave a bid only on something that you have examined very carefully, that would be a real asset to your collection, and do this only if there is no way of attending the auction. Then leave an honest bid. Estimate a fair market price, then add a bit more, just as you might do as if actually bidding. This may be considerably in excess of the high estimate if you feel that the estimate has perhaps been set low to encourage bidding. Bidding this way has two advantages: it will provide the best chance of success, and perhaps more importantly, will leave you with no regrets if you are not successful. You have done all that you could do to win.

Many auction houses now permit telephone bids. These allow you to bid by telephone if for some reason you cannot, or perhaps do not wish, to attend the auction in person. Arrangements to bid by phone must be made before the auction, perhaps when attending the preview. During the auction you will be called a few bids before your lot is brought up, so don't stray far from the phone. While not the same as actually being present, telephone bidding is superior to a left bid in that you have feel for the action, and have the option of making a few additional bids if you feel that you are close to winning. Telephones permit anonymous bidding, which is at times is important to major dealers and collectors. Sometimes the bidder will be only a few yards distant.

When the last lot on which you planned to bid has come up, you should consider leaving, unless there is a particular reason for staying. Hanging around is just asking for trouble. Stories abound of amateurs who get carried away at auctions, but the biggest hazard at an auction is not that you pay too much, but rather that you end up with something that lowers the quality of your collection. This can easily happen when you have been outbid on an item you cherished, and then are sitting around feeling a little frustrated with money burning a hole in your pocket. Remember that good collections are built as much on patience as on money.

With experience, you will start to make your own estimates of what lots will bring, particularly when the catalog lists estimated price ranges. Then you can try to outguess the auction house. By and large you will find that the house estimates are fairly accurate, although many firms prefer to set estimates a bit low to encourage bidding. When something goes for a very high price, there is often applause at the end of bidding, either for the high bidder in winning — or perhaps for the runner-up in having avoided a very costly purchase. The real mark of the novice at this time is the comment, "Look at all the money they got for that beat up old wreck!" When something sells for a great deal more than you thought it would, there is always a lesson there for you.

When buying from a dealer, you can often bring the piece home to try it out without being committed to purchase. Now, to some measure, you can do the same thing at auctions, although it will take a bit longer to return. If you buy an item that is not as good as you thought, or for which you cannot find a good place in your home, it can always be auctioned off again. So long as your bidding was prudent, this may be done at little loss, and perhaps even at some gain. In effect, you will have both bought at fair market price and then sold at fair market price. When bidding, keep in mind that the true monetary value of anything is what you can sell it for on the day you bought it.

Auctions appear be a fair and open market, but this is not always so, for dealers are under constant pressure to acquire stock for as cheaply as possible, and sometimes this gets in the way of honesty. The result is called a pool, or a ring, or sometimes a bidding club. Here a group of dealers decide beforehand just who will bid on what, for there is no gain in bidding against each other. It will just drive up prices. Then, after the auction, another very private little auction is held out in the parking lot to decide just who gets what. This is very illegal, for it cheats both the consignor of a fair market price and the auction house of a portion of their commission. Unfortunately, pools are difficult to prevent and are even harder to prove, which is an excellent reason to set a reserve price when consigning anything really valuable.

An interesting subject for reflection is what happens when a dealer, a collector, or a museum realizes that it has a fake on its hands. Some of the more notable examples end up in museum study collections, but what of the others? Well, a great many are just quietly sold off through the anonymity of an auction where the published Conditions of Sale protects both the auctioneer and the consignor. The lesson here is that just because a piece carries a museum accession number does not mean that it may not have some serious problems.

When attending an estate auction, note if the lots are with or without "additions." In the past it was not uncommon for the lots from a well known estate to be seeded with lessor items and even outright fakes. This simple ruse is less common now that the public has become better educated. However, it is why an auctioneer will normally identify in the opening remarks at an estate auction if there are any additions.

There are a couple of other things to note before finishing up. Auctions are open to everybody, and some odd types attend for nothing but the thrill of bidding. After placing a winning bid, they just wander off. Auctioneers learn to spot these people, which is why you will sometimes notice that a bidder is being ignored. These people are an anathema to auctioneers, for when the lot has to be brought up again later, it seldom will do as well. Perhaps this is because there is now one less bidder?

The other thing you will sometimes see during previews is that a loose piece of molding or veneer will mysteriously vanish. It has been "borrowed." The original in period furniture is so greatly valued — and the cost of good restoration so high — that even a little missing piece will significantly reduce price. Sometimes the auction house will try to avoid this by locking up loose pieces. Should you see something small missing, it is worth inquiring to see if it has been put away for safekeeping.

### Inheritance

We should not leave a chapter that deals with the acquisition of period furniture without touching on inheritance, for much, and perhaps even the majority, old furniture is acquired this way. More importantly, these bequests often prove to be the seed for many fine collections. The new owners become interested in the things they have inherited, read up about them, and start to look around for others just as pretty. In a later chapter we again will visit this sometimes sad and difficult subject, but from the other end, from the viewpoint of passing on a collection to others.

While one would hope that scheming is usually the province of murder mysteries, it must be admitted that everyone now and then thinks about inheritance, and that household furnishings, particularly antique furniture, are inevitably among the thoughts. If the division may not be equal, or if there may be contending institutions, tactfully expressing an interest in the old furniture might improve your chances of success. More honest and impressive, though, would be to really learn about period furniture, perhaps doing some collecting on your own, even though what you could afford might be far less than what you might later inherit. Given the choice, we all try to leave cherished things to those who will also care for them. This is particularly true for old furniture, which requires both some understanding and attention to stay in good shape. Should there be a choice of beneficiaries, the more knowledgeable would seem to be the more likely to benefit.

Should you be so fortunate as to be left some old furniture, there are other things to consider. If the bequest arrives with little or no documentation, take the time to find out all about it, perhaps consulting an expert in period furniture. This sounds obvious, but among the lots at auction in recent years in New England has been a good Queen Anne table that had been simply left in the basement for the next owners, and more incredibly, a fine Chippendale claw-and-ball dining table that was left out beside a dumpster!

This leads to a final suggestion. If you come into some old furniture, and it is not in your taste, or cannot be used in the home, it is much better to pass it on to others than to have it sit unloved and neglected in a damp basement. We all carry some possessions through life, but they should be the ones that we have chosen.

# Chapter 8

## Cabinetmaker's Chairs

This chapter, and the sixteen that follow, provide an introduction to the period furniture the collector is most likely to encounter in the marketplace. Except where there is historical significance, we will avoid things seldom found in shops and at auctions. Understanding old furniture is difficult enough without the disorder of the unusual and the rare. For the most part, American furniture is illustrated in these chapters, although when appropriate, we will also see some English things that are common to the American market.

We will start our survey with chairs, not only because they are the most common surviving furniture, but also because they most clearly exhibit changes in style. While it is often difficult to tell Chippendale from Queen Anne in tables and chests of drawers, there is no such problem with chairs.

Almost all old chairs were made one of three different ways: they were either sawn and shaped, or turned on a lathe, or like Windsors were built around a thick plank seat. These forms are so different in history, construction, and style that each is allotted its own chapter. In addition, this first chapter will cover stools, as they are essentially just chairs without backs. They were made in much the same way, and by the same craftsmen, that made chairs.

The elements of the different styles are most evident in the chairs that were made by cabinetmakers and chairmakers, so these will be covered first. The defining characteristic of all these chairs is the use of sawn and shaped wood members that are fastened together by mortise-and-tenon joints. While some have turned stretchers with round tenons, the rectangular stretchers and seat rails of these chairs are always joined by rectangular tenons. Construction of sawn and shaped chairs requires considerable skill, for not only do chairs carry high loads, but also these chairs have compound curves and complex, non-square joints. In urban areas, particularly in England, chairmaking was a separate craft; cabinetmakers made tables and chests, chairmakers made chairs.

Chairs made by cabinetmakers have always been relatively expensive. In Colonial America sawn and shaped chairs cost between 2 and 3 pounds, while a Windsor chair cost 7 to 15 shillings (20 shillings to the pound), and a simple rush-bottomed turned chair only 3 to 5 shillings.

These chairs were generally made up to order, generally in sets of two armchairs and four to ten side chairs. Sometimes a corner chair would be part of the order. The customer could have a set made in up in mahogany, walnut, or maple, either with a claw-and-ball foot, or a less expensive pad or trifid foot, and with or without carving. There would also be the option of curved cabriole or straight Marlborough legs. Whatever the type of legs, the choice of wood, or the amount of embellishment, a good chairmaker provided uniform high quality, and you will find that the simpler chairs can be just as well made and proportioned as the grand examples we now see in museums.

Because of their initial cost and because they are not difficult to take apart, these chairs are often repaired. When you examine sets of old chairs, you will usually see a number of small repairs and very possibly, some restoration. These will normally be neatly done, and may in themselves be quite old. Look for such things as ended out feet, repaired or restored stretchers, replaced corner blocks, and glued up splits at the top of the front legs. Because English and American chairmakers joined the crest rail with a vertical tenon, it is not unusual for this joint to pull apart if the chair is picked up by the crest rail. When this goes, the splat will soon follow, so always be on the lookout for restored splats and crest rails. Sometimes this failure will twist off one of the vertical tenons. Now the correct way to repair this is to fit a loose tenon as described in Chapter 26, but this is not easy to do on a stile, and a simpler alternative is to cut a pair of new tenons into the top of the stiles, which reduces the height of the chair by an inch or so. Therefore, always check that the sides of the splat and the insides of the stiles transition smoothly into the crest rail. Because the backs of chairs were assembled before the final cutting was done, the curves we see here should be smooth and fair. Remove an inch or so of the stiles and there will almost always be a slight break in the curve.

The pierced and often somewhat delicate Chippendale splats may also become so broken up that they are replaced. If you are examining a pair or set of these chairs, check that all the splats appear to be cut from the same board and made by the same hand. You also want to check for repairs where the seat rails join the stiles. This is where a chair will fail when it is tilted back. To reduce labor and save wood, the upper ends of cabriole legs are generally formed with the addition of shaped blocking called knee brackets or returns. These were normally just glued on, perhaps reinforced with a nail. They tend to come off and get lost, so look here for signs that one or more have been restored.

Popular designs were imitated by just about everybody, and this gives rise to a couple of additional problems. One is that sets of chairs may not be sets at all. Not only may they have come from different shops, but a set may be augmented by later copies. The other problem is that chairs of the same style and period are frequently so similar that complete chairs can be assembled from bits and pieces of others, and worse, that these reconstructions can look fairly good. Here is where a really careful inspection pays off, for you want to look for such little inconsistencies as mysterious holes, illogical wear, and components that don't really seem to belong together. Should the chair have a drop seat, pop it out so you can get a good look at the framing. Drop seat chairs are usually numbered because the seats were not quite interchangeable, and here the style of the numbering should be identical on all the chairs in the set, although it may differ on the seat frames if some have been replaced. Needless to say, there should be no duplicate numbers. You also want to be aware of height loss. In addition to the cut down stiles we noted earlier, if the stretchers seem too close to the ground, the chair may have lost an inch or more in height from years of being pulled out from the wall.

Armchairs cost about half again more than side chairs, not only because of the extra labor in making up the arms, but because they had to be wider to provide adequate hip room. There is some talk that chairmakers, upon request, would finish off side chairs as armchairs, but this could only have been done on chairs that were already quite wide. Whether true or not, be suspicious of any armchair that seems a bit narrow, for converting a side chair to an arm chair is a common form of embellishment. While on this subject, it should be mentioned that arms are prone to work loose, and that the screw that fastens the arm to the seat rail may be a later replacement. Here we should not judge age by the fastenings.

Whenever examining an over upholstered chair, try to get a good look at the seat rails. These are very apt to be replaced in English chairs due to worm damage; and to be replaced everywhere due to accumulated nail damage. If a chair is recovered every 20 years or so, 200 years will see perhaps ten sets of upholstery tacks driven into the rails. This damage is compounded in Federal high style chairs when rows of brass tacks are used for decoration. At auctions, you will often find upholstery lifted off by dealers to check the rails. A really good chair or sofa is frequently stripped right down to the bare wood.

In the past many armchairs were fitted up with chamber pots. This is most commonly seen in corner chairs, but in fact, many large armchairs had chamber pots. The framing that carried the pot will usually have been removed, leaving only a mysterious set of nail holes on the inside of the rails. The missing framing is not a problem, but what is a problem is when the deep seat rails used to hide the pot are cut down to lighten the appearance of the chair and conceal its original function. Whenever examining a large armchair, be sure to turn it over and check the bottom of the seat rails for signs of rework. Although this change may improve appearance, it does nothing for quality.

Except for chairs in which the drop seats are rush covered, chairs made by cabinetmakers will be upholstered. This was done one of three ways: either by upholstering a frame or drop seat that rested within the seat rails, or by upholstering over unfinished seat rails, or sometimes by bringing the upholstery just half way down over the rails. In the past upholstery was very expensive, and with the exception of Philadelphia, where there was a penchant for drop seats, better chairs will often be those with

**Figure 8-1**

*Figure 8-1: Joint stool, 1600 – 1720. As perhaps the first mass-produced furniture, the joint or joined stool should be our first illustration. These sturdy stools were turned out by the thousands in a time when chairs were still rare. Most will be made of oak, and will be English. American joint stools, made of oak or maple with a pine top, are very rare, as are all American stools. Many of the joint stools on the market are Victorian reproductions, so look inside the seat rails for signs of handwork, which in period examples will often appear very rough and crude. Old stools have pinned mortise-and-tenon joints and will feel solid and heavy. For all their age, they are usually in fairly good condition but for the feet, which may be worn down, and for the seat, which has often been replaced.*

over upholstery. Now it is just the opposite, the wood is expensive and the upholstery is cheap. The other reversal is that all sorts of chairs were upholstered in leather, which was very durable and was much less expensive than fabric. So tough was this leather that a significant number of the original coverings still survive. In addition to leather, upholsterers employed a wide range of woven materials — silk damask, brocades, cotton prints, haircloth (the weft was horsehair), and a watered wool called morine or harateen — but only very rarely do any of these fabrics survive.

Old upholstery webbing is very similar to the modern material, but was used much more sparingly; often no more than two thin strips front to back and one across. If you see a webbing job that appears to have been done by the Grinch, look carefully at the nails that fasten it to the frame, for it may be original. If it appears to be original, but needs to be replaced or reinforced, leave it in place and carefully work in some additional strips on either side of the old webbing.

The best quality padding was curled horsehair, but this was expensive, and when anything remains, it will often be a cheaper substitute. Marsh grass was used in New England, wool and Spanish moss in the South. Finally, it might be mentioned that in the past expensive fabrics were protected in hot weather by summer or "washing" covers of linen, cotton, or chintz. These were fastened with ties and often given a decorative ruffle that extended below the seat. They are still a good idea for warm, sticky summer days.

**129**

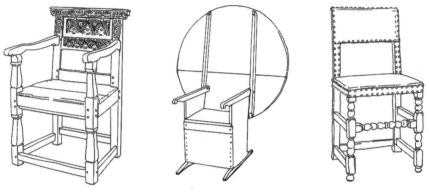

Figure 8-2          Figure 8-3          Figure 8-4

*Figure 8-2:* Wainscot chair, 1650 – 1700. The American wainscot chair, like the joint stool, is shown mostly for historical interest, for they are very rare and almost never come on the market. Like their somewhat more common English cousins, wainscot chairs will be made of rived quarter grain oak. In keeping with many early tables, these chairs have heavy mortised stretchers set low on the legs, perhaps as much to lift feet off cold floors as for strength. Wainscot chairs, with their characteristic paneled backs, seem to have been made by the same joyners that made room paneling. Many 19th century fakes are made up from just this same paneling.

*Figure 8-3:* Chair-table, 1680 – 1710, and later. These are perhaps the best known example of Colonial dual purpose furniture. With the top upright they resemble a simple sort of wainscot chair with a wide back to keep off the drafts; with the top down they form a small dining table. Some will have square tops rather than the round top shown here. Often there will be a storage compartment under the seat. They may not be as early as they look, for survival versions were made right up into the first decades of the 19th century. They are also called table-chairs, hutch tables, and monk's chairs, so in addition to the choice of function, we also have a choice of names. Like much Pilgrim century furniture, they were reproduced in Victorian times, and you want to be careful you are not looking at a nice 100 year old reproduction. Period versions should have tops of wide pine or maple boards, and oak or maple bottoms. They are fairly rare.

*Figure 8-4:* Cromwell chair, 1660 – 1700. This is the first American-made chair that we find with any sort of upholstery. While American examples are quite rare, such chairs are fairly common in England, where they may also be identified as farthingale or Charles II chairs. Armchairs will usually have thin padded arms outlined with brass upholstery nails. The legs, stiles, and stretchers are often decorated with the simple sausage turnings shown on the front legs and stretcher of this example. Better chairs may have twist turnings. Cromwell chairs are generally from New England and are made of oak and maple. They were upholstered in turkey work or leather. Turkey refers not to the fowl, but to the country, being a "needlework imitating the designs and texture of Oriental rugs made by knotting worsted yarn on canvas or coarse cloth."

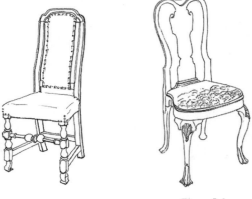

Figure 8-5

Figure 8-6

*Figure 8-5:* Queen Anne "Boston" chair, 1720 – 1750. With an almost endless supply of good cabinet woods, much falling water to power sawmills, and a ready market in the growing population, it was inevitable that Colonial Americans would turn to making furniture. These simple and sturdy maple Queen Anne chairs were one of the first products. Made in and around Boston, and shipped all up and down the coast, these "Boston" chairs dominated the middle quality chair market during the second quarter of the 18th century. Not until the 1750s did they find competition in the Philadelphia Windsor. While there are variations in the basic chair, all are similar in having box stretchers, turned or Spanish feet, and a curved Queen Anne back with an upholstered panel. Generally the maple frame was painted black or red. The seat and the back panel were normally upholstered in leather, which was then decorated with one or two rows of cast brass tacks. So indestructible was this upholstery that a significant number of these early chairs have survived with their original leather covering. Although these chairs would seem to be a transition between the William and Mary and Queen Anne styles, they are not the same sort of transition we sometimes find between Queen Anne and Chippendale. Rather, they present us with a unique and successful design that was produced for a quarter of a century before finally going out of fashion. When we get to the next chapter, we'll see a similar and equally popular Queen Anne design executed in a turned chair with a rush seat.

*Figure 8-6:* Philadelphia Queen Anne chair, 1730 – 1760. This handsome chair and the Boston example that follows are among the best of American chairs. All fully developed high style Philadelphia Queen Anne chairs will be similar to this illustration, having cabriole legs, a round or compass seat, and a boldly shaped solid splat. Some later examples have claw-and-ball feet, but the more normal treatment is the trifid foot shown here, often enhanced with a carved "stocking" at the ankle. Philadelphia had strong ties with the mother country, and these chairs are very similar in feeling to contemporary English work. Most are made of walnut and have the through tenoned side rails so often associated with Philadelphia work. The front and side rails follow the English practice of being joined with a large horizontal mortise-and-tenon joint, which is then locked into place by the cabriole leg being reduced at the top to form a stout dowel. You can spot this construction if you remember that, unlike New England Queen Anne chairs, the joints between the seat rails and the front legs will not be pinned. An interesting feature of the Queen Anne style is that the curve of the stiles and the shape of the splat usually combine to form, in the adjacent open area, the reverse silhouette of a pair of inward facing birds.

131

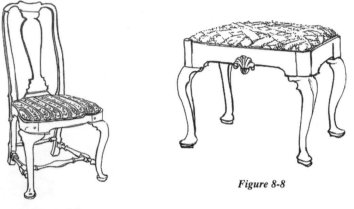

Figure 8-8

Figure 8-7

**Figure 8-7:** *Boston Queen Anne chair, 1730 – 1760. The simplest way to identify a New England Queen Anne chair is by the presence of stretchers, which are not usually found on contemporary Philadelphia high style chairs. In addition, New England chairs have a more vertical and less English look due to the higher back and the more restrained design of the stiles and the splat. Unlike the previous Philadelphia example, Boston chairmakers always tenoned the rails of a chair into the front legs, even when the front and side rails had to be given a fair amount of curve; and in a New England chair you can usually spot the pins used to lock these tenons. The other thing to look for is the use of a turned club foot with a distinct pad beneath the club. Philadelphia chairs of this period will usually have a pad or a trifid foot. In addition to walnut and mahogany, a great many New England Queen Anne chairs will be made of maple, and if from Connecticut, then often a hard cherry. The drop seat will either be rush covered or upholstered in a leather or a fabric. On all such chairs the stretchers and the front legs will almost always be joined with a narrow, vertical rectangular tenon. These chairs were such a successful design that it is not uncommon to find assembled sets so nearly identical that only careful inspection will show them to be of different parentage. In all areas, the general rule is that early Queen Anne chairs will have rectangular seats, then we see round or balloon seats in the fully developed form, and then a return to rectangular with the advent of Chippendale. However, there are so many Queen Anne chairs with rectangular seats that they may have always been available to the customer wishing to save a little money.*

**Figure 8-8:** *Queen Anne stool, 1750. Upholstered stools were made in all periods and styles from William and Mary right up through Sheraton. You will find them with trumpet turned, cabriole, Marlborough, Hepplewhite, and Sheraton legs; and with both drop seats and over upholstery. High quality reproductions have been popular since Victorian times, so always check the inside of the rails for signs of handwork. You also want to be careful that a stool is not the product of a pair of indifferent side chairs. Upholstered stools, like the George II example shown here, will almost always be English, or perhaps Continental. American examples are rare. While on stools, it should be mentioned that upholstered chairs without arms were called backed stools. Made in Queen Anne and Chippendale styles, they are also very rare among American furniture, perhaps because in a country where wood was abundant, an almost equally comfortable side chair could have been had for so much less.*

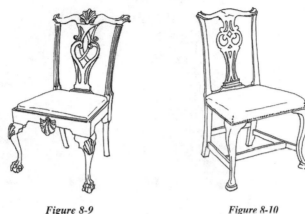

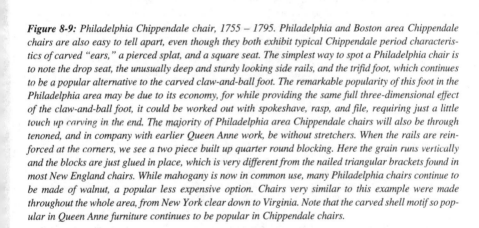

Figure 8-9                                    Figure 8-10

**Figure 8-9:** *Philadelphia Chippendale chair, 1755 – 1795. Philadelphia and Boston area Chippendale chairs are also easy to tell apart, even though they both exhibit typical Chippendale period characteristics of carved "ears," a pierced splat, and a square seat. The simplest way to spot a Philadelphia chair is to note the drop seat, the unusually deep and sturdy looking side rails, and the trifid foot, which continues to be a popular alternative to the carved claw-and-ball foot. The remarkable popularity of this foot in the Philadelphia area may be due to its economy, for while providing the same full three-dimensional effect of the claw-and-ball foot, it could be worked out with spokeshave, rasp, and file, requiring just a little touch up carving in the end. The majority of Philadelphia area Chippendale chairs will also be through tenoned, and in company with earlier Queen Anne work, be without stretchers. When the rails are reinforced at the corners, we see a two piece built up quarter round blocking. Here the grain runs vertically and the blocks are just glued in place, which is very different from the nailed triangular brackets found in most New England chairs. While mahogany is now in common use, many Philadelphia chairs continue to be made of walnut, a popular less expensive option. Chairs very similar to this example were made throughout the whole area, from New York clear down to Virginia. Note that the carved shell motif so popular in Queen Anne furniture continues to be popular in Chippendale chairs.*

**Figure 8-10:** *Boston Chippendale chair, 1755 – 1795. The easiest way to spot a Boston area Chippendale chair is to note the distinctive "owl's eye" splat. This pattern, borrowed from England, was so popular throughout eastern Massachusetts that it is almost a trademark of Boston work. Nowhere else is a splat pattern so indicative of a region. The owl's eye was used everywhere, on side chairs, armchairs, corner chairs, settees, and in all sorts of country work. In addition to this splat, Boston Chippendale chairs can be spotted by the simpler and less curved ears, the arrised (pointed) knees on the cabriole legs, and the curved back or "retracted" side claws on claw-and-ball feet. Even at this late date a considerable number of Boston cabriole leg chairs retain stretchers, perhaps due to an innate New England conservatism, or perhaps in response to hide glues made brittle by the bitter winters. However, this particular chair is unusual in that the stretchers are straight rather than being blocked and turned, a variation, and perhaps an economy, also found in some easy chairs. These chairs will usually be made of mahogany, for by now walnut has gone out of fashion in New England. By this time the Boston preference for over upholstered rails is apparent, for perhaps half these chairs will be treated this way. In common with Philadelphia work, many if these chairs are fitted with the less expensive club foot.*

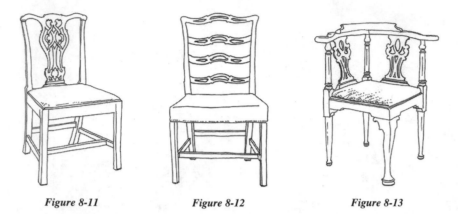

**Figure 8-11**    **Figure 8-12**    **Figure 8-13**

**Figure 8-11:** *Chippendale Marlborough leg chair, 1760 – 1790. Chippendale chairs having straight, square legs are more common than those having the cabriole leg and claw-and-ball feet which are popularly associated with this period. Marlborough legs were a less expensive option, requiring less wood and being easier to make than the cabriole leg. On better work they often will be molded, that is, curved in cross section by use of a molding plane. While these chairs were less expensive, not all such chairs are budget work. Some have finely carved backs and many were over upholstered. Unlike cabriole leg chairs, Marlborough leg chairs almost always have stretchers because there is not enough wood at the top of the front legs to provide for a strong joint. Note that in period work these stretchers will be flush, or almost flush, with the outside of the legs, although if the face of the leg is molded, the stretcher may be set in just a little to clear the molding.*

**Figure 8-12:** *Chippendale ladder-back chair, 1780 – 1800. Chippendale chairs also do not always have pierced vertical splats. There is a large subgroup of late Chippendale chairs which have two or three horizontal splats in lieu of a single vertical splat. Now known as ladder-backs, they were originally called "splatt back" or "slatt back." chairs. Except on very simple rural versions, the splats will be pierced, Chippendale fashion, and in all cases the shape of the crest rail will mimic the pattern of the crest splats, giving the impression of a chair with three or four identical horizontal splats. Most, but not all, of these chairs have Marlborough legs. Comfortable and popular, ladder-backs were made everywhere, usually in either mahogany or cherry. In period and in style, ladder-backs might be viewed as a transition between Chippendale and Hepplewhite, or between Colonial and Federal, for they arrived late in the Chippendale period, and later versions acquire tapered Hepplewhite legs.*

**Figure 8-13:** *Chippendale corner chair, 1755 – 1795. Corner or sword chairs were once called roundabout or writing chairs. These chairs were popular throughout most of the 18th century, but were expensive, and except for a rural chair which we'll see later, are not common. They were often used at desks. Except for a solid splat, there is little difference between Queen Anne and Chippendale in most chairs. In New England, these chairs may be fitted with X-form stretchers. Better quality chairs will have carved claw-and-ball feet. Actually, foot might be a better word, for frequently only the front foot will be carved. These chairs are an interesting design, for the diagonal plan of the legs allowed the buyer a wide range of embellishment. Starting at the top, one could have cabriole legs with carved claw-and-ball feet all around; or just cabriole legs with a claw-and-ball foot in the front; or just cabriole legs and pad or club feet all around; or just a cabriole leg on the front and straight legs elsewhere; or just straight legs everywhere. Whatever their relative grandeur, corner chairs will be usually large and robust, as though made not only for men, but for large men.*

**134**

Figure 8-14                    Figure 8-15                    Figure 8-16

*Figure 8-14:* Country Chippendale chair, 1760 – 1820. Simple Chippendale style chairs were made just about everywhere of local hardwoods. In company with similar turned chairs illustrated in the next chapter, they are quite the most common Chippendale chair. They are also found in ladder-back designs, usually with simplified solid splats. As a general rule, the pierced splats emulate designs found in high style Chippendale chairs. For all their rural charm, most of these chairs are now thought to be the work of city craftsmen. The dividing line between city and country is not always clear, for early chairs, like the "Boston" chair (8-5), have a very country feeling. When labeling a chair country, we should look for the use of local hardwoods and a general simplicity in design and construction. This chair shows most of the features associated with country work; the bottom of the splat is tendoned into a cross piece rather than into a shoe attached to the rear seat rail, the seat is rush covered, and the stretchers are of a box form rather than the more usual "H" pattern. When the seat is upholstered, we will find a simple drop seat that does not require the services of an upholsterer.

*Figure 8-15:* Philadelphia transitional chair, 1750 – 1790. The design of some period furniture exhibits a transition between one style and the next. This is most commonly seen in chairs, where the back will show the newer of the styles. For example, a chair with a Chippendale back might have a round Queen Anne compass seat. However, this rule has a lot of exceptions, as is shown by these popular Chippendale chairs that still retain the old fashioned Philadelphia Queen Anne splat. These handsome chairs are found with all the standard Philadelphia trifid, pad and claw-and-ball feet. Some of the earlier versions will have slipper feet. Most all will be made of walnut, as befits a conservative design. Here we might note that while the use of American black walnut is popularly associated with Philadelphia workmanship, it was used everywhere as a less expensive alternate to mahogany. It should also be noted that transitional does not imply inferiority. A transitional chair does not rest in a depression between two periods. It is just transitional in style. There is no reason for a such a chair to be deficient in either form or construction.

*Figure 8-16:* Southern Chippendale chair, 1760 – 1810. If you see a chair with box stretchers and an upward flaring splat pierced to four or five vertical ribs, you are probably looking at a Virginia chair. This splat design is very common in southern chairs, being to Virginia what the owl's eye pattern was to Boston. The use of a front stretcher rather than the usual medial stretcher, an arrangement known as box stretchers, is common to southern furniture, as it is to much country work, both here and in England. Many such chairs will be made of walnut rather than mahogany.

135

*Figure 8-17:* Hepplewhite arched-top chair, 1785 – 1810. These distinctive chairs with the classical urn in the middle of the ribbed splat were made of cherry and mahogany in both Connecticut and Rhode Island at the turn of the 18th century. They were known then as pedestal-back chairs. Unlike the ladder-backs we saw earlier, most seem to retain the by now rather out of fashion Marlborough leg.

*Figure 8-18:* Hepplewhite shield-back chair, 1785 – 1810. This is the chair most closely associated with the Hepplewhite style. In past times these chairs were called "vase-back" when the shield was pointed at the bottom, and "urn-back" when rounded at the bottom. Whatever the shape, they require very careful joinery to stand up to daily use, and represent a high point in the chairmaker's art. With the exception of New York, most of these chairs have stretchers. New York chairs, in addition to lacking stretchers, are also apt to follow English fashion and have spade feet. Similar chairs with round or oval backs, an Adam design, will generally be English. Note that by now most urban high style chairs are over upholstered.

*Figure 8-19:* Sheraton square-back chair, 1795 – 1815. Although these chairs often have tapered Hepplewhite legs, the flat stepped crest rail, the drapery swags, and the Prince-of-Wales feathers are taken directly from Sheraton's Drawing-Book. The spade feet would suggest that this is a New York chair. As befits the Sheraton style, there is more carving than in the previous Hepplewhite chair. A similar design, also borrowed from Sheraton, has a pierced splat that looks very much like a 1920s tennis racquet. They are popularly known as "racquet-backs." Many of these chairs will have swags of cast brass upholstery nails along the front and side rails, which while very Neoclassical, does nothing for their integrity, for the top of the unsupported front legs, in addition to having the mortises for the rail tenons, are further pierced by these decorative nails.

*Figure 8-20:* Sheraton scroll-back chair, 1800 – 1815. Here is a Sheraton chair with the turned and reeded legs most commonly associated with the Sheraton stlye. A back that curves over at the top is known as a scrolled back. The X-form splat may be either single, as in this example, doubled, or curved. The reeded legs and slightly swelled turned feet are typical of New York work. Similar New York chairs were also made with out swept sabre legs.

*Figure 8-21:* Empire sabre-leg chair, 1810 – 1825. This chapter has usually illustrated side chairs rather than armchairs, for they are far more common and more representative of the market, but here we'll show an armchair because the scrolled arms are so indicative of the Empire style. During this period scrolled arms were used everywhere, on armchairs, upholstered chairs, couches, and even on church pews. In keeping with an interest in things classical, the outward curve of the legs were taken from the klismos chairs found on Greek vases. These Empire chairs were very popular and survive by the thousands, and it is not difficult to find a nice set of four or six. However, you need to be careful of origin, for Regency chairs made of mahogany or beech can be very similar. Although they appear light and somewhat delicate, these handsome chairs are heavier and sturdier than you would think.

*Figure 8-22:* Classical gondola-back chair, 1815 – 1840. Although these solid and comfortable chairs would appear to be Empire because of their sabre legs, they follow a design that was reintroduced in France after Waterloo, and thus are Late Empire or Classical. However, they avoid the size and over decoration seen on much Classical case work, and are one of the most pleasing designs of this late last period.

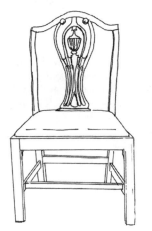

*Figure 8-18*

*Figure 8-17*

*Figure 8-19*

*Figure 8-21*

*Figure 8-20*

*Figure 8-22*

# Chapter 9

## Turner's Chairs

Turned chairs are notable in their longevity, for while they date back to at least the 16th century, they are still in production today. No other furniture in our survey has seen such a long life. The joint stool has come and gone, the wainscot chair is history, but turned chairs are still very much with us. The turner's simple rush-bottom chair is a classic example of a survival type, a popular form that continues in production long after going out of fashion. Benjamin Franklin would see nothing unusual in President Kennedy's well known rocker, although he might criticize the poor quality of the turnings and mention that rockers were a recent innovation. This long history, in conjunction with a propensity for style lag, does not make for easy or accurate dating, and we should be very conservative in assigning period to turned chairs. They often look a great deal older than they actually are.

There are two things to look for in all turned chairs: the proportions and the quality of the turnings. With the exception of some massive Pilgrim Century chairs, American turned chairs display a notable lightness and verticality. They do not have the solid look of their English or Continental counterparts. As one writer said, they almost seem ready to lift off the floor. Good proportion is somewhat difficult to describe, but you will find that not only are most American chairs easy to identify, but that the better quality chairs tend to be tall and elegant.

Good turnings are bold and crisp, which is just another way of saying they have a lot of curve and sharp edges. This is particularly important in the turnings seen when a chair is against a wall; the front stretcher, the front legs, and the back posts or stiles. On period chairs the front stretcher usually received the turner's best effort, and a good turning here is often the saving grace of an otherwise ordinary chair. Survival models have fewer decorative turnings, and what turnings there are will be executed in an uninspired and slapdash manner. Contrary to what you might think, a extremely simple and primitive chair is usually not very early, it is very late. This decline in the quality of the turnings is so pronounced that professionals will sometimes estimate the approximate date of a chair simply by the quality of the turnings.

Just as chairs made by cabinetmakers and chairmakers are defined by sawn and shaped legs joined by rectangular tenons, turned chairs are defined by turned legs joined by round tenons, although American chairs often exhibit a hybrid construction in which the back is sawn and shaped and the front legs and stretchers are turned. From early on turned chairs have been made in quantity, for turned furniture is well suited to mass production. Turner's shops were full of pieces seasoning and awaiting final assembly. Probate records, in addition to identifying the turner's tools, list hundreds of legs, stiles, and stretchers.

For the most part, these sturdy and inexpensive chairs have seen long and hard use. You will frequently encounter worn down legs, and also, ended out feet. Normally the latter is easy to spot, although the restorer will may try to hide the join in a turning. Always upend a turned chair to look at the bottom of the feet. Replaced feet usually look new on the bottom and may show either the characteristic "X" mark of the modern lathe, the bottom of a dowel, or a deep hole for a screw. Also check the seat rails. In old chairs the rails of splint and rush seat chairs were fashioned with a drawknife in the form of a thick blade to resist the inward pressure of the woven seat. In spite of this extra stiffening, rails tend to break, and then are often replaced with

**Figure 9-1**

**Figure 9-1:** *Pilgrim Century Carver chair, 1640 – 1720. These very early turned chairs are named after one owned by John Carver, governor of the Plymouth Colony. Similar chairs, but with additional rows of vertical spindles below the seat, are called Brewster chairs after William Brewster, the first minister of the colony. The most notable characteristic of these chairs are the massive and simply turned posts, which are often 2½" or more in diameter. One cannot but think that they would have been very handy to jamb against a door in event of an Indian attack. Note the mushroom caps on the front posts and the decorative finials on top of the stiles. Similar chairs were made in all regions from New Jersey to Massachusetts, first in ash and later in maple and sometimes in walnut. These "great chairs" were originally made as armchairs, but later were also made in side chairs. They are very rare, being only slightly more common than the American wainscot chair. Most have seen a lot of wear and survive in poor condition, frequently missing finials, mushrooms, and one or more of the stretchers.*

modern hardwood dowels. If you gently separate the rush, you should be able to discern if the rails are modern dowels.

Turned chairs are normally held together across the middle by the seat webbing, and then across the top by a single pin that locks in the crest rail or top most slat. Now if the chair must be taken apart to replace a broken slat, either the left or right pin must be drilled out. Therefore, it is always a good idea to see if both pins look untouched and are identical. If not, you can then start looking for the why.

In the following illustrations we will see that turned chairs can be divided into two general classes: those with slats that run horizontally, and those with slats that run vertically. Additionally, there is a major subtype in the painted and stenciled fancy chairs, but these we will only touch on, as most were made at the very end of the Federal period and are more the product of the factory than the shop. The Shakers also made a great many turned chairs, but these will be covered in a later chapter devoted the work of this remarkable sect.

**139**

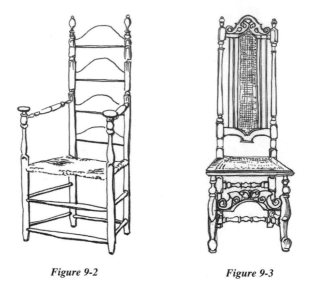

Figure 9-2                    Figure 9-3

*Figure 9-2:* Puritan slat-back chair, 1730. Carver type chairs were also made as slat-backs with three horizontal slats set between the same heavy posts. A somewhat later slat-back, one which you are more likely to find for sale, is this William and Mary chair. These turned chairs are associated with the William and Mary period because they predate the Queen Anne style in America, and because the high back is reminiscent of the high backs found in many chairs of this period. Aside from the high back and lighter posts, this chair is very similar in style and construction to the previous example. The arms continue to be turned, and the mushroom post top is retained to provide a hand rest. Because the posts are now much thinner, the mushroom tops have been developed into a separate design element and a proper handhold, and add much character to an otherwise very simple chair. Unfortunately, over the years these mushrooms tend to crack and chip, and many have now been cut off. Slat-back chairs are also called ladder-backs, even though they bear only a passing resemblance to the ladder-back cabinetmaker's chair illustrated in the previous chapter. While we think of this sort of chair as being very early, slat-backs with turned arms and mushroom caps seem to have been made right up into the early years of the 19th century, perhaps because the turner could avoid having to make sawn arms on what was by then a budget chair.

*Figure 9-3:* Restoration caned chair, 1690 – 1730. These high backed William and Mary side chairs are popularly known as Restoration chairs after the restoration of the monarchy in 1660. Then called cane chairs, they were made in London and exported to America by the thousands. Because carving and caning were labor intensive, very few were made in America. As with other chairs, there are variations in quality; the simpler having less carving and no turnings on the rear legs. Better examples were made of walnut, but most will be beech stained up to look like walnut, or painted black to imitate ebony. The seat should properly be fitted with a thick tasseled cushion; the wide opening between the back of the seat and the caned splat anticipated the use of a cushion filling this area. These chairs were produced by the thousands in large shops with many craftsmen doing nothing but turning, or carving, or assembling, and it is not unusual for the design of these chairs to lack consistency in that the carving on the crest rail and on the stretcher will be two different patterns.

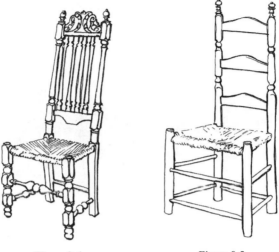

Figure 9-4                    Figure 9-5

*Figure 9-4:* Banister-back chair, 1700 – 1830. Caning and carving were expensive, and to meet the competition of London chairs, Americans substituted turning for carving, rush bottom seats and split balusters for caning. Baluster was corrupted to banister, and the result is an American original, the banister-back chair. Early banister-backs, like this example, have bold William and Mary style turnings and retain the carved crests of the Restoration chair. They are much prized by collectors. Later in the century both the turnings and the crest become much simpler. Some chairs will have rectangular molded splats in lieu of the turned balusters, and on a few the balusters are inexplicably reversed so as to have the curved side face the sitter's back. Balusters were made by gluing two pieces of stock together with a piece of paper or thin lath between, then turning the whole assembly, and then soaking the two halves apart. Look closely at one of these chairs and you will see the balusters are not quite full semicircles. As shown in this illustration, the turnings of the balusters will usually echo the turnings of the posts. Like slat-backs, banister-back chairs were popular over such a long period that they are difficult to date, and a simplified example may actually be Federal rather than Colonial.

*Figure 9-5:* New England slat-back chair, 1740 – 1840. Following their early start, slat-back chairs continued to be made, getting progressively simpler as the century draws to a close. Early versions will have high backs with five or six slats and turnings on all posts; later just three slats and turnings only on the stiles. However, even the simplest seem to retain pretty finials at the top of the stiles. The term "New England" is something of a misnomer, for simple slat-backs like this were made everywhere, and with so many little variations that most can only be identified as "American." In common with a great many Windsors, slat-backs were swept up by the 19th century craze for rocking chairs, and if not actually fitted with later rockers, will show evidence of the modification by plugged slots or filled cut outs in the feet.

141

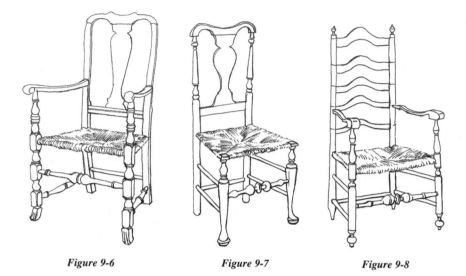

*Figure 9-6*          *Figure 9-7*          *Figure 9-8*

*Figure 9-6:* Queen Anne turned chair, 1730 – 1800. These handsome Queen Anne style chairs might be thought the country equivalent of the standard "Boston" chair shown in the previous chapter, but they seem to have been produced by the same urban chairmakers that made the popular Boston chairs. Except for seating of the bottom of the splat in a cross member rather than in the seat rail, the backs of both chairs are quite similar. Most of these chairs employ the very popular Spanish foot, although occasionally you will find one with a simpler turned foot. While not high style chairs, they still have the typical Queen Anne yoke shaped crest rail and reverse curved back, what is now called a fiddle or spoon back, but then was called a "crooked" back. Note that the handsome arms are sawn and shaped, providing a much more comfortable arm and hand rest than the turned arm and mush-room finial we saw earlier. This chair, and the Chippendale example to follow, illustrate a common feature of many American Queen Anne and Chippendale style turned chairs in having the back and rear legs sawn and shaped while the front legs and stretchers are turned. This hybrid construction is a help in visualizing the way in which sets and groups of chairs were normally made: first, all the backs would be assembled and trimmed; then the rails and front legs would be attached to the finished backs; and finally, the completed chairs would be painted or varnished.

*Figure 9-7:* Hudson River Valley yoke-back chair, 1740 – 1810. Chairs having these characteristic yoke backs were made on Long Island and all up and down the Hudson River Valley. They are a distinctive New York or Dutch version of the Queen Anne turned chair. Although retaining the round crest and vase shaped splat, there is no reverse curve to the back, and the front legs are very different, having straight tapering cabriole type legs with offset turned pad feet. On simpler versions the front legs do not taper and just end in ball feet, but in this example we see clearly that the turner's best effort has gone into the front of the chair. While most Queen Anne chairs have a yoke shaped crest rail, the flat rounded crest on turned posts gives the appearance of a yoke for a pair of oxen, and thus the popular name for these chairs.

*Figure 9-8:* Delaware Valley ladder-back chair, 1720 – 1830. These beautiful ladder-backs are perhaps the most elegant of all American turned chairs. Made in and around Philadelphia for well over a century, they are, without doubt, a high point in American chairs. Although made in differ-

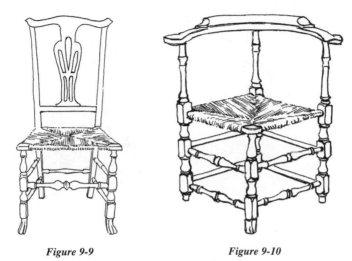

*Figure 9-9*                    *Figure 9-10*

ent grades from simple to quite grand, these fine chairs exhibit a remarkable consistency in design and proportion, as though their makers could think of no way to improve on perfection. The acorn finials, the arched slats, the William and Mary style front stretcher, the ball turned front feet, and the taper at the bottom of the back posts are found on all models. Note that the arms are notched out on the underside, perhaps to add lightness and spring to what is otherwise a simple sawn arm. The easiest way to spot a Delaware Valley chair is to look for the distinctive curved slats, which are arched at the top and generally also arched at the bottom. There will be four or five slats, always increasing in width toward the top.

*Figure 9-9:* Chippendale turned chair, 1760 – 1820. Chippendale style turned chairs were made everywhere of maple, walnut, and cherry. Although a turned chair, they are very similar in design and proportions to the country Chippendale chair we saw in the previous chapter (8-14). Most of these chairs follow the country Queen Anne practice of Spanish front feet, and indeed, would seem to be very much the same chair upgraded with a back in the newer Chippendale style. While this example has both a Chippendale crest rail and a Chippendale pierced splat, it is common to find these chairs with a Queen Anne vase splat below the Chippendale crest rail, thus neatly combining William and Mary, Queen Anne, and Chippendale elements in one small chair. Country work, which is frequently a mix of such stylistic elements, is not transitional in the manner that high style urban furniture may exhibit a transition between one major style and the next. Rural craftsmanship tends to hold on to features that are accepted by custom, and perhaps also, are easy to produce. This is particularly evident in these chairs, in which the William and Mary front legs continue to be used right into the 19th century.

*Figure 9-10:* Corner chair, 1720 – 1820. Simple turned corner chairs are much more common than their far grander cabriole leg urban relatives, largely because they continued to be produced in rural areas after going out of fashion in the years following the Revolution. This William and Mary example is above average quality; less sophisticated versions will lack the block and vase turnings. The double row of box stretchers is normal for these chairs. It makes for a very sturdy chair, which may be another reason why so many survive.

143

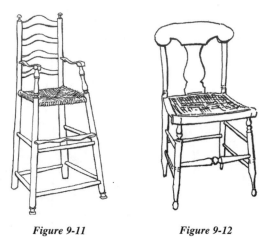

**Figure 9-11**          **Figure 9-12**

*Figure 9-11: High chair. Then as now, American high chairs are normally utilitarian furniture. Most all will be either turned chairs like this Delaware Valley example, or Windsors as we'll see in the next chapter. The legs are typically splayed out to provide additional stability, which improves both their proportions and their charm. Aside from the wear and tear you would expect from generations of family use, most are in good condition except for the footrests, which are often missing or restored.*

*Figure 9-12: Painted fancy chair, 1800 – 1840. Paint decorated chairs first appear in America after the Revolution, initially as expensive high style guilded and painted furniture. Somewhat later, Windsor chairs begin to be hand decorated, sometimes with delightful little country scenes painted on rectangular tablets in the crest rail. However, within a few years simpler versions are being produced, the skilled handwork replaced by the much quicker stenciling. By 1843 Lambert Hitchcock's factory has 100 employees and is turning out 1000 chairs a month. A great many of these painted fancy chairs survive, but it is not easy to find examples with the original paint in good condition.*

# Chapter 10

## Windsor Chairs

No book on American furniture would be complete without a section on the handsome and ubiquitous American Windsor. These wonderful chairs are well worth their own chapter. Indeed, they are worth a whole book, and should you be seriously interested in Windsors, you should look up Charles Santore's two excellent books on Windsor chairs. Mr. Santore sees Windsors as stick chairs, but an engineer would notice the thick seat that ties the legs and back together, and might think of them as plank chairs. Whatever the view, Windsors are yet another example of an earlier form so changed in the New World as to become uniquely American. This is to our advantage, for in the Windsor chair there is little chance of confusion between the English and the American product.

Chairs built around a thick plank seat were made all over Europe for many years prior to the development of a distinct Windsor type. Although the history of these simple rural chairs is unclear, what we would recognize as the modern Windsor was well known in England by the early 1700s. From here the design spread to Philadelphia where the first American Windsors are made sometime between 1730 and 1740. Almost immediately, these chairs become uniquely New World, for the earliest Philadelphia comb-backs and low-backs are very recognizably American products. At first, they competed with rush-bottom designs, and some chairmakers made both. These early Windsors had cylinder-and-ball turned feet and ornate stretchers, much in keeping with other turned chairs from this period, and were relatively expensive. However, in the 1760s Windsor chairmakers went to easily turned tapered legs and simpler stretchers, and production so increased that within a few years they became known simply as Philadelphia chairs. These sturdy and popular chairs were shipped all up and down the coast, and as far south as Grenada. As soon as Windsors started being shipped any distance, makers began to brand or label their products. This may have been done not so much for advertisement as to ensure that consignments did not become mixed up in transit.

Production remained centered in Philadelphia for about 20 years before spreading north to New York, then up to New England. With this expansion came new forms of Windsors. Even if a chair does not carry the chairmaker's brand or label, it is sometimes possible to suggest where it originated, for there were regional variations in production, some types being popular to just certain areas, others being made just about everywhere. Shortly after the Revolution, Philadelphia chairmakers introduced bamboo turnings, an Oriental motif whose simple form was ideal for mass production. Gradually this pattern replaced all others, although a few tapered leg Windsors continued to be made in the hinterlands until the 1820s. A number of early Federal Windsors are transitional, having tapered legs and bamboo turned stretchers. By this time Windsors were being produced everywhere by the thousands in small factories. Any late Windsor, unless a very obvious rural effort, will likely be the product of a factory, or manufactory as they were called then. The Windsor method of construction spread to other forms, and is also found in many stools, a few small tables, and even in some cradles.

In common with turned chairs, Windsor chairs have never gone out of production. However, it is not difficult to tell new from old. In an old chair the legs will frequently come up through the seat, the spindles up through the bow. Both will be wedged. For the most part, seats will be made from a single 2" thick pine or poplar plank, and will be very nicely shaped. Not until well into the 19th century do we see built up seats, and even here just two or three pieces of wood will be used. The modern factory product typically has a thin hardwood seat with little or no shaping that is made up of four or five pieces of wood. In addition, in old chairs signs of shrinkage will abound; spindles will not be flush with the top of the bow or the arm rests, and legs will no longer be flush with the surface the seat. Even when stripped or repainted, traces of the original paint will remain in out of the way places, particularly on the bottoms of seats. American Windsors were painted a leaf green before 1780, then a salmon red became popular, then finally black. The early green darkens with age, and now often looks like a dark brown with a green tint.

# Chapter 10 ───────────────────────────────

In Figure 6-1 there is an illustration of a typical English Windsor. Many sets of these strong, comfortable chairs have been brought over, and they often come on the market. English Windsors are most frequently characterized by a central splat set among the turned spindles, although this feature does not seem to have been present in early chairs, and in any event, was not used in the north of England. A surer way to spot the English product is by the generally heavier structure and by the turnings, which are unlike anything found in this country. English Windsors are also distinguished by a wide variation in quality. The normal garden variety will have beech legs and spindles, an elm seat, an ash bow, and an oak splat. Better will use fruit woods and employ yew for the bow — the same wood used in the famous longbow. The best quality are made of mahogany and have cabriole legs. These were certainly not garden or taproom furniture.

Windsors have long been popular with collectors, and this demand has led to a lot of restoration. But for the seat, there is not a part that may not have been replaced, particularly the spindles and bows which are highly stressed and tend to fail as the wood becomes brittle with age. Watch for spindles that are not all the same, or seem to zig a little when passing through a rail. If an armchair, check that the knuckle handholds have not been repaired, or perhaps cut off. Problems with worn feet are also found in Windsors, and you want to be careful that a new joint is not neatly tucked away in the groove of a turning.

Nor are Windsors exempt from a little improvement here and there. If the seat has an ornamental chisel line, it should neatly border all the posts and spindles, something you are not likely to see if the arms are a later addition. Except for the very young, potty seats have long gone out of fashion, but these were once common in Windsors where they were perhaps discreetly covered with a cushion. These openings are now plugged, which generally shows a bit, but has the merit that little of original seat is lost in fitting the plug. However, sometimes the whole chair is taken apart and all traces of the hole eliminated with a large splice of new wood extending clear across the seat, which is neater, but removes much of the original seat. Modified and restored Windsors may be repainted to cover up the changes and repairs, so remember that all pieces of a painted chair, if original, will have the same paint history. A leg lacking an earlier coat of paint will not be the original leg. However, this is easier to state than to check, for if a chair is not yours, you can hardly start poking around with a little sandpaper. In addition, it has been reported that the legs on Windsor chairs are sometimes made of different species of woods — an exception to the general rule that similar components should always be of the same woods. This might be true, for it would be possible to employ different woods having similar qualities in a product that was always painted.

Late in the 18th century America discovered the rocking chair, and many early Windsor chairs have been converted to rockers. Often these conversions are neatly done, and many appear to be early, perhaps dating from the 1820s when rocking chairs were very much in vogue. They are easy to identify, for the rocker will be fastened to a ledge cut in the side of the foot, the lower leg lacking the thickening needed to house the rocker blade (10-10). Original Windsor rockers are something of a rarity, and are mostly found in the late arrow-back designs. Another uncommon variation are Windsor chairs with padded seats. Although most of these have now lost the original pad, they can be spotted by an unusual lack of shaping in the seat and a row of tack holes that extends across the front and around to the sides.

*Figure 10-1*                                   *Figure 10-2*

*Figure 10-1:* Comb-back Windsor, 1740 – 1810. These handsome armchairs are the first uniquely American Windsors. The name comes from the shape of the back, which looks something like a comb. Most were made in and around Philadelphia, with a few from Connecticut and Rhode Island. Early comb-backs had cylinder turned legs with ball or blunt arrow feet like those shown in the next illustration, but most that you find on the market have this tapered leg which became popular in the 1760s. Note the carved volutes at the ends of crest rail. These are also commonly seen in fan-backs. Almost without exception, comb-backs will be armchairs.

*Figure 10-2:* Low-back Windsor, 1750 – 1790. Like the comb-back, most low-backs were made in Philadelphia. Early versions are similar to comb-backs, being just about identical from the seat rail down, which has led to some speculation that the comb-back was a later development. Actually, the comb-back seems to have appeared about a decade earlier. This illustration shows a low-back with the cylinder turned leg found on a great many of these chairs. The foot would then be either a round ball or the blunt arrow shown here. These early chairs are apt to be very large in scale with much wider seats than are found on later Windsors. Some low-backs were made elsewhere, particularly in Rhode Island. These differ from Philadelphia chairs in having thicker arms with spindles that do not come up through the arms. Sometimes they also employ the X-stretcher arrangement found in English Windsors.

Many of the characteristics that make for quality in turned chairs also apply to Windsors. Look for such things as lack of wear or damage, early or original paint, and the overall quality of the turnings. Here also consider the shape of seat, the shape of the back, the splay of the legs, and the general harmony of design. Many of the best chairs display a distinct verve and enthusiasm in their design. They almost seem to say — hey, look at me!

Lastly, it should be noted that in addition to such generic terms as brace-back, arrow-back, and thumb-back, there are variations in the basic words used to describe different types of Windsors, particularly between comb-backs and fan-backs, sack-backs and bow-backs. To be consistent, we will follow the terminology employed by Mr. Santore in *The Windsor Style in America.*

147

Figure 10-3          Figure 10-4          Figure 10-5


**Figure 10-3:** *Fan-back Windsor, 1765 – 1810. At first glance, a fan-back may look like a comb-back until we realize that there is no semicircular arm rail, the back instead being supported by a pair of turned posts. Even so, armchair fan-backs look a lot like comb-backs until one notes that the arm rail does not extend across the back. Fan-backs get their name from way the posts and spindles fan out-wards from the seat. These pretty chairs were popular in both Philadelphia and New England, but for some reason never caught on in New York. With the fan-back we come to the first American Windsor that lacks an arm rail to stiffen the back, and to compensate for this, many of these chairs have two diagonal spindles or braces to provide additional strength. Such chairs are often called brace-backs. Therefore, the chair shown here might correctly be called a brace-back, fan-back Windsor side chair.*

**Figure 10-4:** *Sack-back Windsor, 1760 – 1810. These very successful Windsors, introduced in Philadelphia in the 1760s, were soon being made just about everywhere. Called sack-backs by their makers because a cover or sack could be pulled over the back to keep off drafts, they are by far the most common surviving Windsor armchairs. As you'll note, they are basically just a comb-back Wind-sor with a steam-bent bow substituted for the comb. On a number of these chairs the middle spindles extend up through the bow to support a charming little comb set above the bow, giving the impres-sion of a double backed chair. Not only do large numbers of these sturdy chairs survive, but their great popularity seems to have led to a host of makers, for you will often encounter simple rural ver-sions for whom chairmaking would appear to have been no more than a part time avocation.*

**Figure 10-5:** *Bow-back Windsor, 1780 – 1810. The extremely common bow-back is yet another Wind-sor developed in Philadelphia. Later made almost everywhere, they are the most common of the 18th century Windsors. Philadelphia makers seem to have originated the idea of bamboo turned spindles on these chairs, for the great majority with this Oriental motif will be from the Delaware Valley. With the exception of those from Philadelphia, these chairs are very likely to have braced backs, probably for the same reason that we find them in fan-backs. However, bow-backs are far more likely to be found as armchairs. Often these armchairs will have mahogany arms, a nice touch on an otherwise utilitarian chair. The illustration shows a Connecticut chair with an upholstered seat, an unusual fea-ture that is also sometimes found in fan-backs.*

*Figure 10-6*          *Figure 10-7*          *Figure 10-8*

**Figure 10-6:** *Continuous-arm Windsor, 1790 – 1810. Now we come to a Windsor that is not only uniquely American, but whose design originated in New York rather than in Philadelphia. From here the production of these chairs spread north to New England, but never south to Philadelphia. The continuous-arm Windsor is unique in that both the back and arms are fashioned from a single piece of steam bent white oak or hickory. This elegant design is also the chair's downfall, for the wood tends to fail at the sharp bend between the arm and the back, and once broken, is difficult to repair. Indeed, this weakness seems to have had a deleterious effect on survival, for far fewer of these chairs survive than production would seem to warrant.*

**Figure 10-7:** *Rod-back Windsor, 1800 – 1830. This final contribution of Philadelphia Windsor chair-makers was introduced about 1800. Now the bamboo turnings, which we first saw in the spindles on bow-backs, have spread to the legs, giving the whole chair a somewhat Oriental motif. From here on, the crest rails of Windsors will be more or less flat, much in keeping with Sheraton chairs of this period. More significantly, the seats now have far less shaping, and the legs will almost always be supported with box rather than "H" stretchers. Compare this chair with the previous illustration and you will see the marked difference between 18th and 19th century Windsors. Although the early rod-backs had only a single crest rail, by far the most popular design is the double rail "birdcage" Windsor shown here. The back has seven spindles, of which only three continue to the top rail, giving an impression of a birdcage. In lieu of the middle spindle, there is often a pretty little painted or stenciled tablet set between two top rails. Rod-backs were made everywhere but in New York.*

**Figure 10-8:** *Step-down Windsor, 1810 – 1830. These somewhat different and slightly later rod-backs are so common that they are considered a separate type and have acquired their own name. Note that the stepped down crest rail that gives these chairs their name is similar to the crest rail of the Sheraton square-back chair shown in Figure 8-19. To keep up with the growing popularity of fancy chairs, Windsor chairmakers now often painted or stenciled this crest rail.*

*Figure 10-9*                *Figure 10-10*                *Figure 10-11*

*Figure 10-9:* Arrow-back Windsor, 1820 – 1840. The arrow-back Windsor is a late development of the rod-back form. The name comes from the use of one or more arrow shaped spindles across the back. Because of the flattened top of the back posts, such chairs are also called thumb-backs. Note that the seat now has very little shaping and the bamboo turnings have lost much of their form. Arrow-backs were also made with Sheraton style legs. From now on most Windsors will show some flattening on the front sides of the posts.

*Figure 10-10:* Windsor rocking chair, 1830. Windsor rocking chairs are not uncommon, but those that started out as rocking chairs are fairly rare. Most will have high backs like this bow-back example. Note here the thickening added to the lower leg to house the rocker blade. You will not see this if the chair was not planned as a rocker.

*Figure 10-11:* Writing arm Windsor, 1780 – 1800. These interesting chairs are another uncommon form, one that is never found among English Windsors. Most writing arm Windsors will be comb-backs, although you will also find low-back, rod-back, bow-back, and arrow-back versions. A rare few have the writing surface on the left rather than on the right. The best are not just conversions of standard chairs, but ground up designs with the shape of the seat modified to support the writing arm. Often there will be charming little drawers worked in under the arm or under the seat. For some reason, the great majority of writing arm Windsors were made in Connecticut, perhaps because the inhabitants of this state seemed to like their furniture a little bit different, and the writing arm Windsor is certainly that.

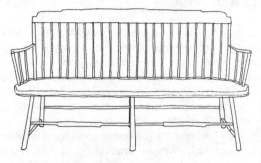

*Figure 10-13*

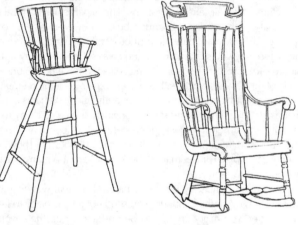

*Figure 10-12*                    *Figure 10-14*

*Figure 10-12:* Windsor high chair, 1810. Windsor high chairs are far less common than turned high chairs, but occasionally you will come across an example like this pretty little rod-back. High chairs were made in every major style except low-back, but in spite of this, they do not often come on the market. Perhaps they are too much of a family treasure to sell?

*Figure 10-13:* Windsor settee, 1810 – 1830. For all their size and additional cost, Windsor settees are surprisingly common. Most will be low-backs from the Philadelphia area, or rod-backs from New England like this handsome step-down example. They were frequently sold en suite with sets of matching chairs.

*Figure 10-14:* Boston rocker, 1835. The Boston rocker, and its first cousin, the Salem rocker, are a late development, but should be included because they often turn up in local auctions. Note that the flat seat on these chairs is given an exaggerated "S" curve, so much so that the spindles actually enter the back edge of the seat. For all their lateness, they are very comfortable chairs. The trick, as with fancy chairs, is finding one with the original paint and stenciling in good condition.

# Chapter 11

## Wing Chairs and Sofas

This will not be a long chapter, for there is relatively little upholstered furniture in America prior to the Federal period, upholstery fabric then being very expensive. Such furniture was only found in the grander homes, and even here, there was not much of it. Before the Revolution, a wing chair cost more than a highboy, and a sofa was more expensive yet. Only a fully dressed high post bed cost more than a sofa. Of the relatively few Colonial sofas that have survived, most all date from the latter half of the 18th century and are Chippendale in style. Not half a dozen are Queen Anne. However, by about 1800 rising prosperity and a reduction in the cost of textiles brings the comfort of upholstered furniture to within reach of many middle class families, which is why we now find a great many Federal lolling chairs and sofas. Even here, though, the upholstery on sofas is limited to just the seat, the side, and the back panels. The modern couch, with little or no wood showing, is still a thing of the future.

Upholstered furniture presents a unique problem to the collector, for it is difficult to examine the structure for repairs and restorations. This is particularly critical in English furniture where the usual beech framing is as much beloved by worms as by collectors. When dealers have pieces reupholstered, they often photograph the stripped frame as evidence of originality. This is also why you see armchairs and sofas sold bare of any upholstery.

The condition of the frame is important to the collector, for although unseen, it comprises the great majority of the original structure. Here a few repairs or reinforcements are not much of a problem, and may even contribute to a feel of authenticity. What is important is not the repairs, but that the framing is all, or mostly all, original. The easiest way to check this is to verify that the sequence of holes from the upholstery nails is logical and the same throughout the structure. Because the frame is generally simple and does not show, it is not uncommon for upholsterers to replace pieces that are broken or have too many nail holes to provide a good ground for the new fabric.

While surviving period upholstery is rare, remains of original webbing and padding are more common than you might think. Should you send out an old piece to be reupholstered, unless you know better, you might arrange to be on hand when the covering is removed. Another thing to keep in mind is that if you have a very good over upholstered chair, it is no longer necessary to further damage the rails with additional tacking, for the upholstery can be mounted on a separate frame that rests on and covers the old rails. Much the same sort of thing can be done with sofas, although here the treatment is more complicated.

Before going to the illustrations, something further might be said of wing chairs, which are by far the most common upholstered furniture. Originally called easy chairs, they first appeared in Restoration England in the 1660s, and then were popular during the William and Mary and Queen Anne periods before going out of fashion and becoming less common after the middle of the 18th century. In America, however, they did not appear until the 1720s, but then continued to be popular until about 1820, and many that you find for sale will be Federal rather than Colonial. For the most part, wing chairs seem to have been used in bedrooms and are sometimes being fitted with chamber pots. The frames were made by cabinetmakers and then sold to upholsterers for completion and sale, although evidence of the upholsterer's skill is now all but gone. If you wish to see a wing chair with its original padding and fabric, the Metropolitan Museum in New York has an example upholstered in embroidered needlework, the Brooklyn Museum in New York an example in a red worsted

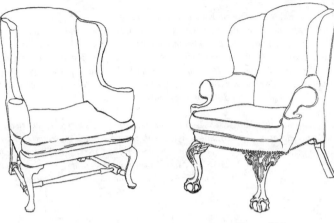

*Figure 11-1*                                    *Figure 11-2*

*Figure 11-1:* Massachusetts Queen Anne easy chair, 1730 – 1780. This is the basic form of wing chair made all over New England. Chippendale versions are very similar but for the use of ball-and-claw feet. Note that the upholstered arms scroll out rather than over. This vertical scroll is associated with New England chairs, rarely being used further south than New York. However, we need to be careful with this simple identifier, for early William and Mary chairs have the more common scrolled over arms, and then the scrolled over arm returns to New England in the Federal period. It is only Queen Anne and Chippendale wing chairs that scroll out. Also note that New England wing chairs, both Queen Anne and Chippendale, tend to retain the block-and-turned stretchers found in New England cabriole leg chairs. In common with other seating furniture, earlier chairs are apt to be made of walnut, later chairs of mahogany. For economy, the rear legs and stretcher on walnut chairs are typically maple with a walnut stain. When mahogany is used, the rear legs will normally also be of mahogany, and then be spliced into the stiles just above the fabric.

*Figure 11-2:* Philadelphia Chippendale easy chair, 1760 – 1790. Philadelphia wing chairs are most easily identified by their scrolled over arms, a feature not found north of New York City during this period. The other easy identifier is the lack of stretchers, for in common with Philadelphia side chairs, Philadelphia wing chairs very seldom have stretchers. This is a very grand chair, for carving on the legs of wing chairs is rare. Less expensive wing chairs will have the same pad or trifid foot we saw earlier in chairs from this area, and will frequently be made of walnut. In some measure wing chairs compensated for the rather sparse padding normal to this time by being given thick down cushions. Wing chairs as grand as this are identified in probate records as being used in parlors.

wool, the Winterthur Museum in Delaware another example in embroidered needlework, and the Museum of Fine Arts in Boston an example in a blue worsted material. One of this select group was actually sent out for recovering, for so rare is surviving upholstery in wing chairs that it did not occur to the museum staff that the upholstery might indeed be original. The upholsterer, to his lasting credit, had the wit, and the honesty, to inquire if the museum really wanted the original upholstery stripped off!

153

*Figure 11-3:* Chippendale Marlborough leg easy chair, 1770 – 1810. Chippendale style wing chairs were often made with square, molded legs like this fine Rhode Island chair. In addition to the normal H-stretcher arrangement, there will always be another stretcher connecting the rear legs. In the Federal period these chairs were also made with a tapered Hepplewhite leg, although the old fashioned Chippendale leg continued in popularity right up into the 19th century, perhaps because the heavier leg looked better under a large chair. By now the scrolled over arm is coming north and there is less distinction between Philadelphia and Boston area work.

*Figure 11-4:* Sheraton easy chair, 1815. Because of their long popularity in America, wing chairs were also made in Sheraton and in Empire styles with turned front legs. Empire chairs will have somewhat thicker legs than the Sheraton example shown here, but are still well proportioned because the size of the chair can afford a heavier leg. After the turn of the century, the wings tend to become deeper, and may be attached, as shown in Figure 11-3, to the outside of the horizontal rolls which form the arms.

*Figure 11-5:* Federal lolling chair, 1780 – 1820. Now popularly named after a similar chair once owned by Martha Washington, these graceful upholstered armchairs were originally called lolling chairs. Most examples are Hepplewhite in style and originate in eastern Massachusetts. To a lessor extent, the collector will also see Sheraton and Empire models. The stretchers shown here become less common after the turn of the century. Lolling chairs are both higher and narrower than comparable English armchairs, exhibiting a lighter and more vertical appearance very much in keeping with the Neoclassical taste of the Federal period. With few exceptions, the arms will not be upholstered, perhaps a frugal American response to the area of greatest wear. These handsome chairs are a unique American form, and indeed, are our only significant contribution to this period. Probate records indicate that unlike wing chairs, they were used in parlors rather than in bedrooms.

*Figure 11-6:* Empire armchair, 1820 – 1840. Classical armchairs will usually have the upholstery set within a mahogany frame. Many have a round back that curves around the sitter, similar in feeling to the Classical gondola-back side chair we saw earlier. The front legs are either cylindrical, tapering, or a heavy sabre form. Although not a rare form, these sturdy and comfortable armchairs do not often come on the market.

*Figure 11-7:* Chippendale settee, 1760 – 1780. Double chair-back settees were seldom made in America. The few that you see for sale will generally be English or perhaps Continental. Although most popular during the Chippendale period, there are both earlier Queen Anne styles and later Hepplewhite shield-back forms. A few will be triple-chair-backs. Settees are now quite expensive, so we need to be careful that they have not been faked up from a pair of ordinary armchairs. Note that a settee is given extra width to provide sufficient elbow room, and should be considerably wider than just two armchairs placed side by side. Settees were commonly made up in pairs and sold en suite with a set of side chairs. Although we see them now as grand high style furniture, they require much less fabric than a sofa, and may have been seen then as a less expensive substitute.

*Figure 11-8:* Chippendale camel-back sofa, 1760 – 1800. Camel-backs are by far the common form of Chippendale sofa. Not many of these large and expensive sofas were made in America, and like settees, most of those on the market will be English. Philadelphia sofas, in emulation of English designs, usually have these blocked feet, a feature we will see again in a Philadelphia Chippendale Pembroke table. Some of these sofas were made in New York and Newport, but most will be from Philadelphia. In common with a number of other Chippendale forms, these handsome sofas continued to be made during the early Federal period, and there are some with tapered Hepplewhite legs.

*Figure 11-3*          *Figure 11-4*          *Figure 11-5*

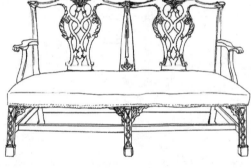

*Figure 11-7*

*Figure 11-6*

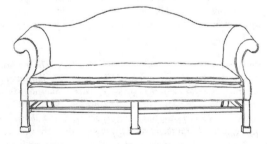

*Figure 11-8*

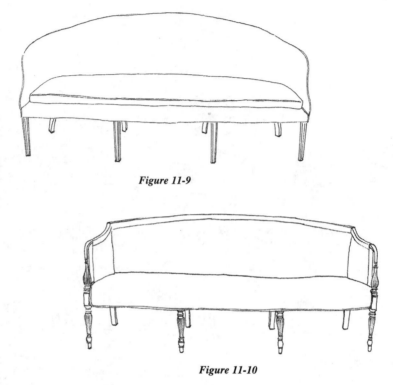

*Figure 11-9*

*Figure 11-10*

**Figure 11-9:** *Federal cabriole sofa, 1790 – 1800. Sofas with round or cabriole backs are a Hepple-white form. They are far less common than the following Sheraton square back design, perhaps because they were not as comfortable, or perhaps because they were more difficult to frame and upholster. In either event, they soon were replaced in popularity by sofas having square backs, and curved back sofas do not become popular again until the Victorian period. While we normally place sofas against walls, in Colonial and Federal America they were set out in the room so as to be near the fireplace.*

**Figure 11-10:** *Federal square sofa, 1790 – 1820. The majority of Federal sofas will be similar to this illustration, with turned or reeded Sheraton legs and a square or slightly arched back. The free stand-ing arms that flow down into the legs are a Sheraton innovation. Similar sofas were made with tapered Hepplewhite legs or curved sabre legs. Many will have the exposed crest rail shown here, giv-ing the same impression of upholstery set within a mahogany frame that we saw in Empire armchairs. In conjunction with the bare arms, this not only gives the sofa a crisp, framed look, but also avoids having fabric in the areas of greatest wear. Better models will have a birch or a maple inlay in the squared section at the top of the front legs, and then perhaps a carved tablet in the crest rail.*

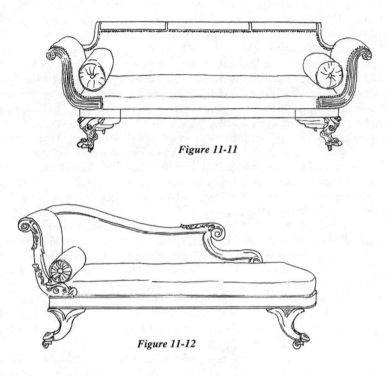

*Figure 11-11*

*Figure 11-12*

**Figure 11-11:** *Classical sofa, 1810 – 1830. The best of these large handsome sofas are the earlier models where the scrolled arms are not too thick and the carved legs exhibit some restraint. Later the arms thicken and the legs acquire very large paw feet. A few are caned and fitted with loose cushions.*

**Figure 11-12:** *Classical Récamier couch, 1820 – 1830. These asymmetrical couches borrow their popular name from a well known painting by Jacques-Louis David of the famous society beauty and wit, Juliette Récamier. The painting actually shows Madame Récamier seated on a somewhat different couch, but nevertheless, these asymmetrical couches are now popularly known as Récamiers, even though they were then called Grecian couches. Later, when we get to beds, we'll see that similar couches, known as daybeds, are actually a very old form.*

# Chapter 12

## Chests and Blanket Chests

This chapter and the next four cover case work, which is furniture built around a box or case. We'll start off with the simplest and the earliest, lift-top chests, then proceed to the more sophisticated, chests of drawers, desks, highboys, lowboys, and sideboards.

For the most part, chests are nothing more than a large rectangular box with a hinged top. There are three ways to make this box. The simplest, and most certainly the oldest, is to simply nail together four wide boards, with a fifth for the bottom and a sixth for the top. To avoid nailing into end grain, the two end boards have the grain running vertically. These usually extend below the bottom to provide feet. If wide stock is available, this makes a very serviceable chest, and these six-board chests are common among American furniture. You will see a few at most every auction.

If wide stock is not available, or a larger and stronger chest is required than edge nailed boards will allow, the case can be made up of panels mounted between grooved vertical stiles and horizontal rails. The stiles and rails are then fastened together with mortise and tenon joints. The stiles will extend below the case to provide feet. This construction was the providence of the joiner, and indeed, much of the joiner's work involved the large chests of the sort we'll see in this chapter.

The third method is to avoid the cross grain ends of the six-board chest by running the grain of all the boards horizontally, then joining the corners with dovetail joints. The key here is the use of a dovetail joint, for nails will not hold in end grain. The feet now become a separate element, for they can no longer be provided by a simple extension of the stiles or the end boards. Lift-top chests are more interesting than this simple construction would suggest, for not only are they among the earliest of furniture, but within this one form we see the complete history of furniture development — the carpenter's simple nailing in the six-board chest, the joiner's mortise and tenon construction in the paneled chest, and the cabinetmaker's sophisticated joinery in the dovetailed chest.

You will find that a great many chests have a little inner compartment, or till, in the upper left hand corner. Why the left hand corner? Well, if you are right handed, it would be natural to lift the top with your right hand and reach in the till with the left. Not only do right-handed people instinctively use the right hand first, but the right hand and arm are normally somewhat stronger than the left. Sometimes you will find the till on the right. Presumably this was to suit a left-handed customer.

It is popular now to call lift-top chests blanket chests, and indeed they are useful for storing bulky fabrics. However, the general presence of tills in these early chests tells us something very different. Setting aside a separate place for small items suggests that chests were normally used, not for blankets, but for clothing, much the way we now employ chests of drawers and closets. In the past the average person had no more than a few changes of clothing; perhaps two sets of everyday work clothes (one for the Monday wash), and a better suit or dress for church and social events. For this, a simple chest was more than adequate, provided there was a handy place for small items. Only the better off would need more, which may explain the relative scarcity of chests of drawers prior to the Revolution, and why those that survive are generally of good quality. Six-board chests, sometimes with the addition of one or two drawers under the bin, were probably the most common American case furniture right up into the early 19th century.

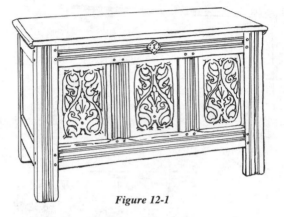

*Figure 12-1*

*Figure 12-1:* Pilgrim Century paneled chest, 1640 – 1700. American paneled chests are rare, perhaps not just because of their age, but because once sawmills were established, a six-board chest would have been far more economical. While the panels on most of these chests are carved, some have no more decoration than a little molding worked into the stiles and rails. These very early chests have been the subject of much study, and it is sometimes possible to identify the maker from the carving. Although made of oak, these "joyned" chests are not as heavy as they seem, for the panels themselves are quite thin. English chests from this period have paneled tops, but here we see the use of a single wide pine board. Even at this early date the abundance of wood in the New World is starting to separate English and American furniture.

When considering any lift-top chest, look carefully at the top. The main structure is pretty much indestructible, but not so the top, particularly if once fastened with snipe or cotter-pin hinges. It is not uncommon to find the snipe hinges have worn through and have been replaced by later strap hinges. If so, check the top to be sure that the holes for the snipe hinges are also there, and that they match the holes in the case. If not, you are looking at a later top. Also, the till was usually given its own top, hinged on simple wood pintles that pivoted in holes bored in the front and back of the case. Should there not be a top, the presence or absence of these holes will tell you if it is missing.

The tops of most chests will be stiffened with a pair of cleats nailed under each end. Any warping or bowing of the top will tend to pull out the nails, so check to be sure that the cleats match each other and that both appear to be original. Also, the very early paneled chests, being rare and expensive, may have considerable restoration. They should be carefully examined. It is not unusual to see these grand old chests with restoration both above and below — a new top and ended out feet.

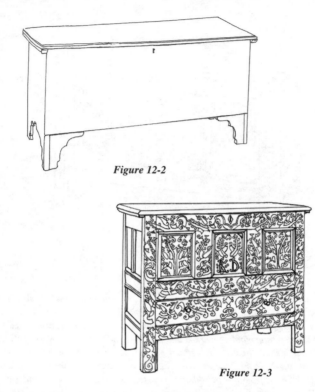

Figure 12-2

Figure 12-3

*Figure 12-2: Six-board chest, 1680 – 1840. America's answer to the demand for inexpensive case furniture was the six-board chest. To this ancient form we contributed the use of wide softwood boards, resulting in a design at once so practical and economical that it continues to be produced well up into the 19th century. A few of these simple chests survive from the Pilgrim Century. They differ from later work in being rather long and narrow, and in usually having some decorative molding or carving worked into the front. These chests were always painted, either with a single overall color, or with a variety of fanciful decoration, or with grain painting. Of all furniture forms, chests and blanket chests are the most likely to exhibit grain painting. Collectors are most interested in the shape of the legs and the quality and condition of the painting.*

*Figure 12-3: Hadley type chest, 1680 – 1740. These carved and paneled chests were made in and around the small town or Hadley in Western Massachusetts, and are today known as Hadley chests. They will have either one or two side hung drawers under the bin. About 150 survive, enough so that they sometimes come on the market. Similar paneled chests were made in Connecticut and in eastern Massachusetts. They often carry the initials of the owner, but seem to have been hope chests rather than dower chests, for the initials that have been identified are those of young women. The shallow allover carving is typical of this type of chest. This was then highlighted with red, black, or green paint applied to the raised surfaces. You will find that a number of these very early chests are but fragments of the original, not only in having replaced lids, but also in missing the drawer and a portion of the legs.*

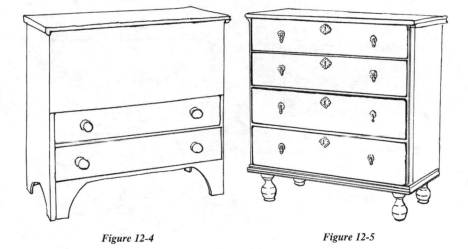

Figure 12-4                    Figure 12-5

*Figure 12-4:* Chest with drawers, 1740 – 1840. This sort of simple chest with one or two drawers under the bin was made just about everywhere. Most all are made of pine or poplar and were originally painted, sometimes with a colorful grain painting in imitation of walnut or mahogany. There are two types of chests with drawers: those like this in which one or two drawers are worked in under the bin, and those shown in the two following illustrations in which additional drawers are simulated on the front of the bin to provide the illusion of a chest of drawers. The former are often identified as chests with drawers, and the latter as blanket chests, although technically, they are all just chests with drawers. They seem very different, but are not. While similar in form to the previous Hadley type chest, in design and construction they are just the basic six-board chest with drawers added below the bin.

*Figure 12-5:* William and Mary blanket chest, 1720 – 1760, and later. This early blanket chest appears to be a four drawer chest of drawers, but it is not, for the two upper drawers are simulated. Although William and Mary in style, these chests are more common than you might think — in part because many of them are later than the style itself would suggest. As such, they illustrate the style lag so often found in rural work. In this and in the following New England chest, the false drawer fronts are so neatly integrated into the design that it is easy to find oneself foolishly tugging at a dummy drawer.

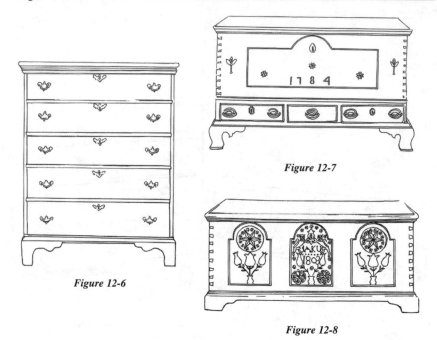

Figure 12-7

Figure 12-6

Figure 12-8

*Figure 12-6*: *New England blanket chest, 1740 – 1820. This is the standard form of blanket chest found at auctions throughout New England. They are invariably rural work, sometimes made of maple, but more often just painted up pine. Most will have two actual and two or three simulated drawers. Many, like this five drawer example, are quite high, and look like a rather short tall chest of drawers. Country work of this sort doesn't fit very neatly into furniture periods, although we would consider the molding under the top and the simple bracket feet to be more Queen Anne than Chippendale, even though such chests are as likely to date from the 19th century as the 18th century.*

*Figure 12-7*: *Pennsylvania dower chest, 1784. There are two basic types of Delaware Valley chests: those made of hardwoods and given a clear finish as in this example, and those made of softwoods and given a polychrome paint finish as in the next. Unlike the Hadley chests, these large, dovetailed chests are dower or dowry chests, and often have the bride's married initials, or marriage date, or both, inlayed on the front. Although neither high style nor rare, they are much in demand by collectors, not only for their better than average quality, but for the charming family data inlaid on the front. Much in keeping with other Delaware Valley work, these chests have a broad, solid English or German look about them that is quite unlike New England furniture. They are noticeably larger than New England six-board chests, and some are very large indeed.*

*Figure 12-8*: *Pennsylvania painted dower chest, 1803. Here is the other common form of Delaware Valley chest. This chest does not have drawers underneath the bin, but they are found on both types. Although constructed of softwood, either pine or poplar, these chests are also very different from a six-board chest, being dovetailed at the corners and given a bracket-foot base. It is common to find the polychrome design placed within the arched "tombstone" panels shown here, a shape normally associated with the earlier Queen Anne period. There has been much research into the craftsmen that painted these delightful dower chests, and it is often possible to associate a chest with an artist. This one is attributed to Daniel Otto, the "Flat Tulip" artist.*

# Chapter 13

## Chests of Drawers

This chapter will survey chests of drawers and their first cousins, the tall chest, the chest-on-chest, and the chest-on-frame. There is also a chest-on-chest-on-frame, but these are fairly rare and seldom come on the market. Before getting started, it might be noted that the word drawer comes from the method of use, for they were "drawn out" through the front of the case.

The deeper lift-top chests become, the more difficult it is to get at things near the bottom of the bin. As we saw in the last chapter, this problem was solved by adding drawers under the bin. Another solution was to do away with the bin and to fashion the chest entirely of drawers. In addition to making the storage space more accessible, chests of drawers allowed a fixed top for setting out boxes and other small objects. While we might think this would have been a later development, chests with drawers and chests of drawers seem to have been developed concurrently, or almost so, for both date from the same period.

The early Jacobean chest of drawers shown in this chapter has the same paneled construction and side hung drawers found in Hadley chests. In chests of drawers, however, these thick, heavy drawers are a drawback, for there is no way to have a lighter, more vertical case until the bulk and weight of the drawers are reduced. As we have seen, this problem was solved by the development of the lightweight dovetailed drawer, and with it, the relatively light dovetailed case. By the time of William and Mary, the chest of drawers attains its modern form, and thereafter, little changes but for the style of the feet and the case.

Chests of drawers receive much use, and in addition to everyday wear, there may be a considerable repair and modification. This gives us a number of things to watch for. Because the drawers are so accessible, we tend to look just at them. However, this is a mistake, for it is in the case that we are most likely to find modifications — and perhaps a little fraud. After taking out the drawers, put a good light on the underside of the top to check that it is undisturbed. Then look at the inside of the bottom to be sure there are not a couple mysterious holes from the turned Empire feet that were removed because someone felt the chest would sell better if it were 18th century workmanship. If you see these holes, but the case seems to be very old, you may be looking at the reverse, a William and Mary chest of drawers that has been given more stylish Queen Anne bracket feet. Should the case be unusually large and have just three deep drawers, you are probably looking at the lower section of a chest-on-chest. American chests of drawers almost always have four drawers.

Bring the chest forward to have a look at the back, which should appear undisturbed and have an overall even patina. Look for replaced backboards, perhaps stained up to match the originals. Should you find all of them replaced by a large piece of plywood, look for another chest of drawers. Then gently tip the chest on its back to have a look at the feet, for here you are most likely to find some restoration. Gently, because one or more of the feet may be loose. Dealers often flip chests of drawers upside down to get a really good look, but you may not want to do this unless there is a pad for the top. Here you are likely to find a replaced block or two. This is not a problem. What you are looking for is a replaced foot, or worse yet, two replaced feet,

**Figure 13-1**

**Figure 13-1:** *Jacobean chest of drawers, 1675. American examples of these early paneled chests of drawers rarely come on the market. The drawer fronts are typically decorated with applied geometric moldings, sometimes flanked with turned and split spindles. The drawers will be quite heavy and hung from rails. Sometimes the case is made in two sections, each section being given a pair drawers. At this early date drawers are not yet graduated in depth, and the deepest drawer will often be in the middle. Most of these great, heavy old oak or walnut chests are from New England. In England, they are called Charles II chests. Many have the ball feet found in the following William and Mary period.*

or possibly an entirely new base. Watch out for screws and any signs of stain. The feet on old chests should be fastened with nothing but glue blocks.

Sheraton chests of drawers have their own class of problems. They should be roughly square across the front, perhaps 40" wide and 40" high. If not, the legs may have been cut down. By this time it was fashionable to attach a splashboard to the back, or add little drawers and a then perhaps a mirror to the top (13-17). If lacking these embellishments, check to see if they are missing. The splashboard was normally screwed to the back of the top; the drawers were kept in place with screws passing from the inside the front and back of the little drawer case into the top of the chest. Watch out for a pattern of little plugged holes near the back of the top.

When looking at chests-on-chests, be alert for a marriage between the upper and lower sections, even though this is far more common in highboys. If examining a chest-on-frame, check that the frame appears original to the case, for a neatly made up frame is a good way to improve on an undistinguished tall chest of drawers.

Drawers get a lot of use, so it is not unusual to find repairs to either the sides where they ride on the rails, or to the rails themselves. Normally this wear is corrected by leveling out the worn section and adding a slip of wood to bring the drawer back to true again. Such wear is inevitable, and should not detract from value if the repairs are neatly done.

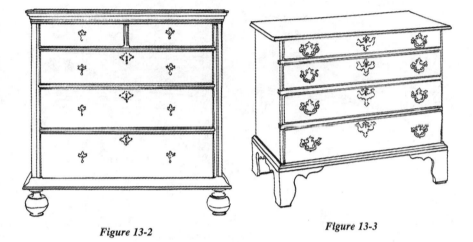

Figure 13-2

Figure 13-3

**Figure 13-2:** *William and Mary chest of drawers, 1710 – 1760. William and Mary chests of draw-ers are more numerous, and with a little patience you should be able to find one, although it will not come cheaply if the feet are original. While they were made everywhere, most will be from the Delaware Valley where they were made of walnut with the two over three drawer arrangement shown here. English William and Mary chests of drawers, which lack the verticality of this exam-ple, are made differently, being walnut veneered over pine, often with marquetry drawer fronts. The ball feet are also different, tending to be more flattened, frequently looking more like a large bun than this oversized turnip.*

**Figure 13-3:** *New England Queen Anne chest of drawers, 1760 – 1800. These simple straight-front chests of drawers were made of local woods all over New England. They are sometimes identified as Queen Anne if made with the simple Queen Anne bracket foot. However, they not only lack a Queen Anne style top, but are much later, most being identified in auction catalogs as either Chip-pendale or Federal. The example shown here with a molded top and Chippendale brasses would date between 1760 and 1780.*

Figure 13-4                                    Figure 13-5

**Figure 13-4:** *Boston Chippendale block-front chest of drawers, 1740 – 1790. American block-front furniture first appears in Boston in the late 1730s; the earliest documented example being a block-front secretary signed by Job Coit in 1738. Thereafter, it remains a popular and fashionable form until almost the end of the century when Rococo finally gives way to Neoclassicism. While we associate block-front furniture with Boston, it was produced all up and down New England from Portsmouth in the North to Connecticut in the South. There were even a few pieces made in New York City. With the exception of Connecticut and the Connecticut River valley, block-front furniture will almost always be made of mahogany. So many of these handsome chests survive that it is easy to forget that they were then expensive high style furniture, costing about half again more than a straight-front mahogany chest of drawers. There are two forms of blocking: a rounded blocking which was generally employed for smaller case work such as dressing tables and this small chest of drawers, and the flattened blocking shown in the large desk in the next chapter. Note that in chests of drawers the blocking is terminated at the top by bringing it up under a conforming top; and at the bottom the shape is carried down into the apron and legs. In block-front furniture we see the preference in Colonial America for obtaining additional decoration by shaping rather than by carving. When an American cabinetmaker received a commission for something out of the ordinary, this was often provided not by carving, but by additional work with saw, plane, and scraper; thus the popularity of quarter columns in mid-Atlantic furniture and the block-front in New England.*

**Figure 13-5:** *Boston Chippendale bombe chest of drawers, 1760 – 1790. These magnificent chests of drawers are without doubt a high point in New England Rococo furniture. Made in limited numbers in both Boston and Salem, they must have been very expensive, for the curved sides are worked out from a single thick mahogany plank. In common with the block-front, the form is not unique to America, although in England the curved sides are simply veneered over pine. To a lessor extent, this rare form is also found in chests-on-chests, in desks, and in secretaries. As grand as this chest seems, it is not actually the very top of the line, for some examples will have claw-and-ball feet, and some of the chests of drawers have serpentine fronts. Bombe furniture might be seen as the ultimate expression of the American preference for shaping rather than carving.*

*Figure 13-6*                                    *Figure 13-7*

*Figure 13-6:* Philadelphia Chippendale chest of drawers, 1760 – 1800. Here is a typical Delaware Valley chest of drawers. The bail handles, quarter columns, and ogee bracket feet are characteristic of furniture from this region. Although the use of molding under a slightly overhanging top is regarded as a Queen Anne feature, the ogee feet place this handsome chest of drawers within the Chippendale style. In the 18th century such feet were called "swelled brackets." Large numbers of these sturdy chests were made in mahogany, walnut, cherry, and sometimes, tiger maple. Aside from a loyalty to walnut and a generally solid English feeling, Philadelphia furniture is most distinguished by the use of quarter columns, which are common on all case furniture. Alternatively we also see either fluted or inlayed chamfered corners. Like walnut, quarter-columns are found elsewhere, but it is in Philadelphia that they were so popular as to be used on even average grade work.

*Figure 13-7:* Philadelphia Chippendale serpentine-front chest of drawers, 1770 – 1790. What the bombe was to Boston these grand big serpentine-front chests were to Philadelphia. The best known makers of these large English pattern chests are Jonathan Gostelowe and Thomas Jones. Note that the canted corners are a logical and elegant method of terminating a serpentine front that sweeps out towards the ends. Similar chests were made in New England, but to a smaller scale and often with somewhat thinner corners. These chests of drawers are not common and seldom come on the market.

*Figure 13-8:* New England Chippendale reverse-serpentine-front chest of drawers, 1760 – 1800. Chests of drawers having serpentine fronts were so popular throughout New England that any such case furniture is likely to be from this area. This is a better than average example of a common type, having blocked drawer ends and a conforming molded top. These chests are found with either serpentine or reverse-serpentine fronts, and bracket, ogee, and claw-and-ball feet. Most have the reverse-serpentine or oxbow front shown here, perhaps because the outward sweep at the ends of a serpentine front normally involves the additional labor of canted corners or claw-and-ball feet. In the past all chests with shaped fronts, whether blocked or serpentine, were called "swelled" chests.

*Figure 13-9:* New England Chippendale serpentine-front chest of drawers, 1760 – 1780. Swelled chests were also given claw-and-ball feet, although what makes this handsome chest of drawers unusual is not so much the feet as the uncommon serpentine front of the case. As we have seen with other American furniture, there is a style lag here, for most all of these Chippendale style serpentine chests of drawers are now thought to be Federal rather than Colonial. Here we might note that you will sometimes also see bow-front chests of drawers with claw-and ball feet. These will probably date a bit later, perhaps 1780 – 1810.

*Figure 13-10:* Federal bow-front chest of drawers with molded base, 1780 – 1810. After the Revolution, the Rococo block-front chest of drawers gives way to the simpler, more Neoclassical bow-front chest of drawers. With this change there is a return to the veneered drawer fronts that had gone out of fashion early in the century, but this time with large flinches of mahogany rather than with small pieces of walnut. These very popular bow-front chests of drawers were made in two general styles: those with a molded base supporting bracket, ogee, or French feet; and those in which the sides of the case transition directly into French feet. This is a good quality chest with a molded top and ogee feet. Most will have the simpler bracket foot and may lack the molding around the top.

*Figure 13-11:* Federal bow-front chest of drawers with French feet, 1790 – 1820. This is the other form of bow-front chest of drawers in which the French foot is simply an extension of the front and sides of the case. These chests of drawers are somewhat later, are far more common, and seem to have been made everywhere. By this time most chests of drawers no longer have the molded top we saw in the previous illustration. Instead, they will be given a square edge with perhaps a little stringing or inlay along the edge. After the Revolution, chests of drawers started to be called bureaus, and you will sometimes find them identified this way in auction catalogs.

Figure 13-8

Figure 13-9

Figure 13-10

Figure 13-11

*Figure 13-12*

**Figure 13-12**: *Federal straight-front chest of drawers, 1800 – 1820. Simple chests of drawers with straight fronts provided an economical alternative to the more fashionable bow-front models. Most have a veneered top and French feet. Often the drawers are edged with a little stringing and the apron given a line of inlay. A number were made of birch and given a mahogany stain. These will usually be from northern New England where birch was often employed as a budget mahogany.*

**Figure 13-13**: *Portsmouth Federal chest of drawers, 1790 – 1810. Chests with rectangular panels across the drawer faces and a dropped panel below are usually associated with Portsmouth, New Hampshire, although they were also made up along the north shore of Massachusetts. Better work may, in addition, have ellipses in the center panels. The panels themselves are usually inlayed in a light wood such as birch or maple, which makes for a very colorful chest. Although these appear to be mahogany chests of drawers, often the only mahogany is found in the trim around the drawer fronts. The case may be no more than inexpensive birch stained up to look like mahogany.*

**Figure 13-14**: *New York Federal chest of drawers, 1800 – 1810. These unusual chests with a deep drawer at the top were made in New York and Northern New Jersey. The two diamond inlays flanking an oval inlay in the upper drawer are often associated with the work of the New York cabinetmaker Michael Allison. The deep top drawer may have been used for storing the large hats and bonnets that were popular during this period. In some chests this top drawer is fitted with a butler's desk.*

**Figure 13-15**: *Country chest of drawers, 1800. While most Federal work employs mahogany or mahogany veneers, simpler chests of drawers were made of maple, birch, pine, and cherry. Devoid of inlay and generally painted, many are little more than a six board chest with the drawers carried right up to the top.*

**Figure 13-16**: *Sheraton straight-front chest of drawers, 1800 – 1830. Sheraton chests of drawers with turret or cookie corners are so numerous that we might illustrate both the straight-front and the swelled-front forms. The three-quarter columns attached to each corner will be either turned or reeded. Later Empire and Classical versions have thicker columns with ring and spiral turnings. Note that these chests are roughly square across the front, that is, if we include the legs, they are just about as high as they are wide. We need to keep this in mind, for a great many of these fine chests of drawers have had their legs shortened in an effort to make them more "modern."*

**170**

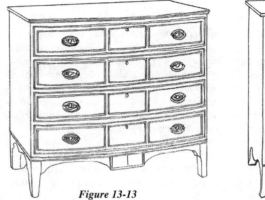

*Figure 13-13*

*Figure 13-14*

*Figure 13-15*

*Figure 13-16*

**Chapter 13**

*Figure 13-17:* Sheraton swelled-front chest of drawers, 1800 – 18303. Many Sheraton chests of drawers were made with swelled or bowed fronts. Unlike the bow-front, these will be flattened in the middle to avoid appearing top-heavy on the rather thin legs. This chest of drawers illustrates another feature of the Sheraton style; the row of small drawers and dressing mirror that are attached to the top of the case. It also illustrates what might be missing if you find some mysterious plugged holes in the top of one of these chests. Similiar chests of drawers may have just the small drawers and a splashboard, or alternatively, just a splashboard. Not all of these chests are American, for the turret corner form was also popular in Regency England.

*Figure 13-18:* Classical chest of drawers, 1825. With the advent Empire or Classical, the rear columns are discarded and the front columns separate from the case and are brought up under a deep overhanging drawer. Better models will have gilt-stenciling, carving, and perhaps a mirror above the row of small drawers on the top of the case. By this time veneer is being cut in large sheets, and the entire case will be of veneered construction. This example has the turned feet commonly associated with the Classical style, but often you will see carved paw feet.

*Figure 13-19:* New England tall chest of drawers, 1780 – 1810. Tall chests of drawers are rare among English furniture, so those you see are almost sure to be American. Where raw materials are inexpensive they provide much extra storage at little extra cost, which probably accounts for their popularity in America. In the past they may have been only slightly more expensive than a chest of drawers, for in lieu of a carefully leveled top they require only a simple cornice molding. Generally they will have five to seven drawers, six being the most common. In New England tall chests of drawers are for the most part country furniture, made of either maple or birch and given inexpensive pulls. Better examples are often made of tiger maple.

*Figure 13-20:* Pennsylvania tall chest of drawers, 1760 – 1810. Not until we get down to the Delaware Valley do we find really elegant tall chests of drawers. Here they are usually made of walnut and given a handsome molded cornice, ogee bracket feet, and often, the quarter columns so common to this region. There will normally be three short drawers over five or six long, or three short drawers over two short drawers over four or five long. In common with chests from this area, a date and the initials of the owner will sometimes be inlayed in the top drawers, suggesting that they were also treated as dower chests. These grand tall chests of drawers continue to be popular after the Revolution and up into the 19th century, acquiring Hepplewhite French feet and string inlay in the process.

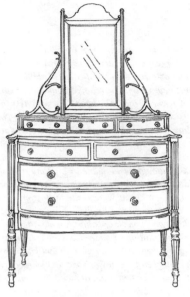

*Figure 13-17*

*Figure 13-18*

*Figure 13-19*

*Figure 13-20*

**Figure 13-21:** *New England chest-on-chest, 1780. Although they were never as popular in America as in England, chests-on-chests are not uncommon, and a large number survive, many from New England. The majority of these are rural work made of maple or birch with the drawer blade dovetails left exposed, and usually painted or stained up to resemble mahogany. The relative frequency of rural examples suggests that, like the New England tall chest of drawers, they may have been seen as a simpler and less expensive alternative to the highboy with its shaped cabriole legs and special case construction, for any country cabinetmaker that could produce a serviceable chest of drawers could also turn out a chest-on-chest.*

**Figure 13-22:** *Philadelphia chest-on-chest, 1760 – 1800. Although fashionable in England from the early years of the 18th century, the chest-on-chest was late in reaching America, and American examples are rare before the 1760s. While some high style chests-on-chests were made in Boston and in Connecticut, most will be from New York and Philadelphia, the two most English of American Colonial cities. Quite a number are very grand indeed, with a swan's neck cresting, a bonnet-top, or a pitched pediment like the Philadelphia chest shown here. In addition to quarter columns, high style chests-on-chests are likely to have a row of dentil molding and fretwork under the cornice. Those from New England tend to have bonnet tops, sometimes with a blocked front lower case. In common with tall chests of drawers, Delaware Valley chests-on-chests tend to be better quality than those made in New England. In common with highboys, the upper drawer, or drawers, of chests-on-chests were split so that they could be easily lifted out to get at the contents.*

**Figure 13-23:** *New Hampshire chest-on-chest, 1770 – 1800. These tall maple chests-on-chests were a standard form in New Hampshire, and you will often see them in New England auctions. The use of maple is so common in this region that the great majority of rural New Hampshire furniture will be made of this wood. Often these large chests-of-drawers will have a scrolled apron and short, bandy cabriole legs. Not all will be maple, for birch in board widths was used from Boston north into New Hampshire and Maine. A charming feature of this rural case work is way in which drawers were sometimes made to serve double duty. Frequently the three small drawers in the upper case and the bottom two drawers in the lower case will each be but a single large drawer, the fronts being molded to simulate the presence of additional drawers. A number of these large chests-on-chests have been attributed to members of the extended Dunlap family of cabinetmakers.*

**Figure 13-24:** *Chest-on-frame, 1740 – 1800. Chests-on-frame are not common, even though they were made everywhere from New Hampshire down to Virginia. While there are some very handsome examples like this Delaware Valley chest-on-frame, they do not seem to have been considered high style furniture, for they are normally made of local woods. Most will have six drawers, and perhaps should more properly be considered tall chests of drawers on frames. Typically somewhat grander than tall chests, they may also have been seen as a lower cost alternative to a highboy. The frame will usually be fairly low and without drawers, but some are higher and will have one or more drawers worked into the frame. There are a few with so many drawers that the deliniation between chest-on-frame and highboy is not all that clear.*

*Figure 13-21*

*Figure 13-22*

*Figure 13-23*

*Figure 13-24*

# Chapter 14

## Desks and Secretaries

Although desks were in use in England by the 1670s, they are fairly rare in America until the middle of the next century. Nevertheless, there was a high level of literacy in America, particularly in New England, where the Puritans encouraged education so that everyone could read the bible. This emphasis on education may be the reason for the remarkable number of surviving New England desks.

The first desks appear to have been nothing more complicated than a slant top box set on a table or stool. The box was hinged at the top and often had a little ledge at the lower side to keep the paper from sliding off. Inside there was storage for paper, pen, and ink. This basic form, with the addition of legs, is found much later in simple counting house or schoolmaster's desks. However, within a few years the nuisance of having to lift the top whenever anything was needed, and the difficulty in sitting up to a box, led to designs in which the writing surface folded out to provide comfortable seating with easy access to ink and paper. By 1700, the desk had achieved its modern form, and in common with so many other furniture types, has seen little real change since then.

Early desks developed in two ways. One type had a large square writing surface hinged at the bottom that folded up vertically when closed (14-16). When open, it was held level by a pair of brass chains. These fall-front desks, somewhat rare in America, are now known as secrétaire à abattant, which is French for "writing desk with flap." The other type is the classic slant-front design in which a fold out writing surface is supported by two slides or lopers that pull out from the case. Originally these desks were made up as a separate section that rested on a case of drawers, and long after the drawers and the desk became one unit, English cabinetmakers continued to simulate this effect with a mid-molding on the front and sides of the case. In America, we see the same general idea expressed in the lovely little Queen Anne desk-on-frame (14-2). The other interesting feature of these early desks is the presence of a sliding door at the back of the writing surface which gives access to a shallow storage well between the slides. At this time the slides are thick and just about square in cross section. However, within a few years the slides are thinned and deepened so that an additional drawer can be worked into the case between the slides. Now the bin is obsolete and the sliding door is replaced by a flush writing surface.

Toward the end of the 18th century in England a new type of desk is developed. Here a deep drawer is fitted out as a desk with little drawers and pigeonholes. When unlocked, the front folds down to form the writing surface and the drawer pulls out about half way to provide leg room (14-9 and 14-19). These secretary drawers are far more common among English furniture, where by 1800 they were considered newer and more fashionable than the earlier slant front design. In America, they are called butler's desks. After the Revolution during the Federal period we see a number of other designs, the most common having a rather narrow writing flap that folds out and is supported by two short slides (14-11). Paper and ink were then kept behind a pair of doors. In New England sliding tambour doors were used on some of the better work, from which we get the term tambour desk.

The names attached to all these different designs can be confusing. In the 18th century slant-front desks were called fall fronts, probably to distinguish them from the earlier designs which were hinged at the top. They were also called "scrutiors" or "scriptors" after the French escritoire or writing desk. In the 1780s in England, the terms "secretary" and "secretary bookcase" were introduced to describe the new type with the secretary drawer. Now we call slant-fronts simply desks and secretaries, while the English use the terms bureau and bureau bookcase, retaining the terms secretary and secretary bookcase for those fitted with secretary drawers.

Better quality desks are often fitted with little secret drawers to conceal valuables. In addition to the usual pair of document drawers behind the columns on either side of the prospect door, there are sometimes little hidden compartments behind the inside drawers or at the rear of the prospect locker. These are normally reached by removing one of the inside drawers and releasing a latch which allows a block of partitions to slide forward. Also, should the pigeonholes have arched tops, there may be flat little drawers worked in behind them.

The problems with back boards and feet that were noted in the previous chapter on chests of drawers also apply to desks. In addition, you want to take a very careful look at slant lids, for these are easily broken off when an inquisitive child fails to pull out the slides before opening the desk. The difficulty is not so much repairs in the area of the hinge, and perhaps replacement of the hinges, which are all too common, but rather, that the whole lid has been replaced. If the case shows the marks of shifted or replaced hinges, but the lid does not show corresponding marks, the lid is not original to the desk. Remember also that the cabinetmaker would try to use the same stock on both the drawer fronts and the lid, the board with the best figure being reserved for the lid. If the color and figure of the drawer fronts and the lid are not similar, something is probably wrong. Also, you should expect to see shrinkage across the grain of the lid. Even very dense mahogany should show a little shrinkage. While here, check to see if the two slides that support the lid appear to be original and match each other. In addition, don't forget to check for replacements among the little inside drawers, for it is not uncommon for one or more to get lost. The easiest way is to compare one with the other. Often they will have been numbered in pencil during the final fitting up. If they are all alike, and the numbering appears consistent, then you know they were all made by the same hand. Ah, but you are not home free yet, for you must also check to see that they appear to be the same age as the desk, for sometimes all the drawers, or even the entire interior of a desk, will have been restored.

When examining any secretary, the first and major concern should be that the bookcase top is original to the desk. All secretaries will have one of four bookcases: the original bookcase, a bookcase that has been added later, a bookcase from another secretary, or a missing bookcase. First off, examine the sides of the desk and the sides of the bookcase to see if they are the same wood and seem to have been taken from the same board. Then look at the back. All the backboards should be made of the same secondary wood and have similar patination, although the boards of the bookcase may run vertically and the boards of the desk may run horizontally. The top should fit the bottom. Typically, it will be about two inches narrower and an inch less in depth. It should be flush with the back, and there should be no sign that a new molding has been worked up to make the top and bottom fit.

# Chapter 14

English cabinetmakers usually employed mitered dovetails to finish off the top of a desk so that the joint used to fasten the sides and top of the case would not show. In America, the normal practice was to leave the dovetails showing, but to make them very fine and neat. Should you come across a secretary where the dovetails are mitered, or where the top of the desk section has been inexplicably finished, you are looking at a desk with a later bookcase top. If you see a desk whose top is a secondary wood, or seems unusually deep, you are probably looking at a secretary that has lost its bookcase. Examine the top and you may spot some filled holes where small nails were once used to fasten the molding.

Prior to about 1780, most secretaries have paneled doors. Large sheets of glass were expensive and only very good work justified the additional cost of mirrored doors. This was particularly true in America where glass was imported and where there were lots of wide boards available for paneling. The modern form of secretary, with glazed bookcase doors made up of small panes of glass set in muntins, does not appear until Hepplewhite in England and Federal in America. However, the absence of glass doors is no particular sign of early workmanship, for many American secretaries, particularly those from rural areas, retain paneled doors right up into the 19th century. Sometimes you will come across a secretary that has been modernized at some time, the paneled doors replaced with Hepplewhite style glazing. Now that it is popular to display china in secretaries, you will also find panels replaced by single sheets of glass. All too often the removed panels are put away — and then lost. When examining a glazed door, in addition to checking for old glass, keep in mind that unless the glazing is in a remarkable state of preservation, we should expect to see some differences in the putty as panes have broken and been replaced over the years.

This chapter has more than the usual number of illustrations, for among case furniture desks exhibit the greatest variation in form and design. Some seldom come on the market and others are very common. Perhaps 19 out of 20 will be either a simple slant-front (14-4) or have a folding writing flap (14-11). Among the illustrations you will not find a kneehole desk, for in America these seem to have been used more as a dressing table than a desk. They are in the next chapter with the other bedroom furniture, the highboys and lowboys.

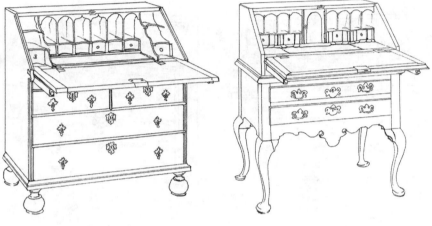

Figure 14-1

Figure 14-2

**Figure 14-1:** William and Mary slant-front desk, 1710 – 1740. Like their counterparts among chests of drawers, William and Mary slant-front desks can be found with a little patience. Most are simply constructed of pine, maple, or walnut, although there are a few grand Boston examples where the lid and drawer fronts are veneered in burled walnut. This is a fine example with a beautifully fitted interior. Note that the slides are almost square, and that the drawers and pigeonholes are recessed in the center to leave room for the sliding cover over the well. A rare few of these early slant-front desks have bookcase tops.

**Figure 14-2:** Queen Anne slant-front desk-on-frame, 1720 – 1810. These charming small Queen Anne desks were made everywhere of local woods, often of cherry in Connecticut and walnut farther south. They usually come with one, two, or three drawers in either the desk section or in the frame. In common with many early desks, this example has a sliding door at the back of the writing surface. Although Queen Anne in style, simple versions of these desks continued to be made right up into the 19th century.

179

Figure 14-3                    Figure 14-4

**Figure 14-3:** *Queen Anne slant-front desk, 1740 – 1770. Desks with these "bandy" cabriole legs appear to be an exclusive product of New England. In style, they are more Queen Anne than Chippendale because of the lack of ornamentation and the use of cabriole legs. Note that the upper tier of inside drawers is set back an inch or two from the lower. These "stepped" interiors are popularly regarded as a sign of early work. The large opening between the bottom tier of drawers was probably intended for ledgers.*

**Figure 14-4:** *Chippendale slant-front desk, 1760 – 1800. Here is a better than average example of the basic slant-front, bracket-foot desk that was made by the thousands all over New England. This desk shows the modern interior arrangement of small drawers across the bottom, pigeonholes across the top, and a prospect door in the middle, but you will find almost every combination in old desks. Frequently a deep drawer will substitute for the prospect door; and for some reason, after 1800, you will often find the pigeonholes on the bottom and the drawers on the top. Note that with the advent of Chippendale the simple Queen Anne bracket foot has acquired Rococo embellishments.*

Figure 14-6

*Figure 14-5*

*Figure 14-5:* Newport slant-front desk, 1760 – 1790. This is the standard Newport desk with a plain front opening to a lovely carved and molded three shell interior. The very well known Newport block-and-shell treatment that we see in dressing tables (15-19) was employed on secretaries, but not on desks. Should you see a desk with a block-and-shell front, it will be from Connecticut, not Rhode Island. The ogee bracket feet shown here become much more the norm on Chippendale style desks as one goes further south. Unlike much Boston production work of this period, these desks are carefully made with the very best mahogany.

*Figure 14-6:* Massachusetts block-front desk, 1760 – 1790. In common with block-front chests of drawers, there are a great many surviving block-front desks. These large, handsome desks are found with either bracket, ogee, or ball-and-claw feet. The blocking terminates on the top drawer, usually by being rounded off at the corners. Notice that the interior layout is very similar to the previous Newport desk, although the shape of the shells will be very different. This layout is also found in the following Delaware Valley desk. It seems to have been a standard arrangement on top quality desks during this period, perhaps because the stacked drawers in the corners permit additional interior carving.

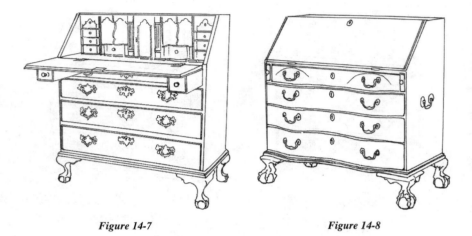

Figure 14-7                                    Figure 14-8

*Figure 14-7:* Pennsylvania Chippendale slant-front desk, 1780. In addition to a preference for walnut, desks from the Philadelphia area may employ a pair of candle drawers in lieu of slides to support the lid. This charming feature was used in other areas, but is most common to desks from the Delaware Valley. As a general rule, Philadelphia area case work will employ thicker stock than Boston area case work, which we can see in desks where the sides of the case are exposed under the slant lid.

*Figure 14-8:* Massachusetts reverse-serpentine-front desk, 1760 – 1800. These big oxbow-front desks were very popular in their time, and they often come on the market. Although Chippendale in style, most are Federal, many being originally fitted with Hepplewhite style oval brasses. Together with the serpentine-front chests of drawers we saw earlier, they are perhaps the most notable Chippendale carryover among American furniture. Interestingly, for all their exterior grandeur, which often includes a pair of carrying handles, these handsome desks usually have very simple interiors consisting of no more than a line of pigeonholes over a double row of small drawers. On later desk the drawers are sometimes decorated with a little Neoclassical inlay.

Figure 14-9

Figure 14-10

**Figure 14-9:** *Butler's desk, 1790. When you see an unusually deep top drawer, there will often be a desk behind it, for you are looking at a secretary drawer. This Chippendale model is unusual, most of these desks have French feet and resemble the New York Federal chest of drawers shown in the previous chapter (13-14). To give the appearance of graduated drawers, the face of the secretary drawer will sometimes be made to resemble two drawers. Although common in England by the turn of the century, this form of desk never seems to have been very popular in America.*

**Figure 14-10:** *Federal slant-front desk, 1785 – 1815. Hepplewhite slant-front desks with French feet were made everywhere, testimony to the enduring popularity of the slant-front, even when not in the latest fashion. Better models will be given some inlay like the charming little fans that border the lid and drawers of this Connecticut cherrywood desk.*

Figure 14-11

Figure 14-12

*Figure 14-11:* *Federal writing-flap desk, 1790 – 1820. This is the standard, and by far the most common, New England desk of the Federal period. Here we have a relatively narrow writing flap that folds over to rest on two short, deep pulls. The upper part with the two hinged doors is usually a separate section that is kept in position by a molding around the front and sides. Although there is no glazed door bookcase, these desks are sometimes identified as secretaries because of the separate upper section. Occasionally, these desks will be in the form of a true secretary with a third bookcase section on top. These desks will have two, three, or four long drawers; the fewer the better, for they have a tendency to look square and blocky. Four drawer versions will have French feet, and are not unlike a Federal chest of drawers with an attached desk section. This desk, and the two that follow, are often called lady's desks. Sheraton versions with turned legs will be a little later, perhaps 1805 – 1830.*

*Figure 14-12:* *Federal tambour desk, 1800 – 1820. This desk is similar to the previous example but for the use of sliding tambour doors in the upper section. Tambour doors are complex and require additional labor, and these uncommon desks, much prized by collectors, are associated with quality work. Some very fine examples by John and Thomas Seymour have inlay set directly into the tambour shutters. Most have no more than two long drawers in the case, which ensures a light and graceful desk. Tambour desks were made in and around Boston. They are uniquely American, for in England the tambour action is only found in cylinder-top desks.*

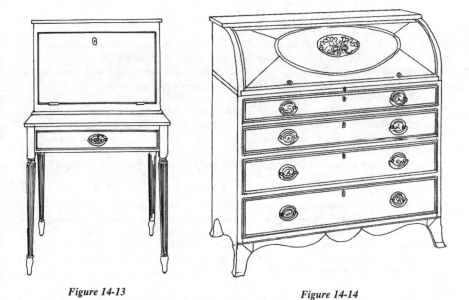

Figure 14-13

Figure 14-14

**Figure 14-13:** *Lady's writing desk, 1810. These delicate little desks, rare in America, are known as bonheur du jours. The "happiness of the day" alludes to their tremendous popularity when first introduced in France, although the name might equally well apply to dashing off invitations for a get-together with old friends. Whatever the source, these charming, diminutive, and very feminine desks speak to a time before the telephone when much communication must have involved quick little notes.*

**Figure 14-14:** *Federal cylinder-fall desk, 1790 – 1810. Cylinder-top, or perhaps more correctly, cylinder-fall, desks are not common in America. The few that you see will probably be from either New York or Baltimore. After the top is opened a writing surface slides out, sometimes in conjunction with opening. The focus of the design is the cylindrical top, and here we often see the dramatic Neoclassical oval inlay shown here.*

*Figure 14-15:* Massachusetts fold-top desk, 1790 – 1820. For lack of a better name we might call these fold-top desks, for the front of the top folds up and over to form the writing surface. When closed, these uncommon little Federal desks appear to be a large box on legs. They are sometimes called a lady's desk, and if mounted on a separate frame, then a captain's desk.

*Figure 14-16:* William and Mary fall-front secretary, 1680 – 1720. These large William and Mary secretaries are rare among American furniture, and not very common even in England. Here the front swings down to form a writing surface that is supported by a pair of brass chains. In common with other large case work of this period, there will usually be a blind drawer fitted in the cornice. Although similar in form and operation, their size and two part construction is very different from the later secrétaire à abattant (14-21).

*Figure 14-17:* Chippendale flat-top secretary, 1750 – 1800. Simple secretaries with a flat molded cornice were made everywhere, more often than not of local woods. Many are of a charming small scale and fit nicely into a small house. They are the most common form of Chippendale secretary, although there is little in them that is Chippendale in style aside from the pulls, and in any event, many are Federal rather than Colonial. As with all secretaries, you want to be careful that the desk and the bookcase started out life together.

*Figure 14-18:* Chippendale block-front secretary, 1760 – 1790. At the high end of the price scale we see these grand mahogany Boston block-front secretaries, with either a bonnet top or the molded swan's neck cresting shown here. Many have carved or turned finials, and most will be fitted with a pair of candleslides above the desk section. The bookcase section will often be partitioned to hold ledgers, bespeaking of a time in which these imposing secretaries were very much the center of a gentleman's business activity. Similar secretaries were made in Connecticut and in all the major urban centers, sometimes with the pitched pediment we saw earlier in a Philadelphia chest-on-chest.

*Figure 14-19:* Butler's secretary, 1800. Although secretaries fitted with secretary drawers were more fashionable than slant front secretaries by the turn of the century, this form of desk and bookcase was never very popular in America, and those you come across are likely to be English. Most American examples will be a product of the major urban centers: Boston or Salem, New York, Philadelphia, and Charleston. The glazed bookcase doors were usually fitted with pleated silk panels to provide a neat appearance and protect the contents from the sun. Open the doors and you will often see little holes at the corners where curtain rods were once mounted.

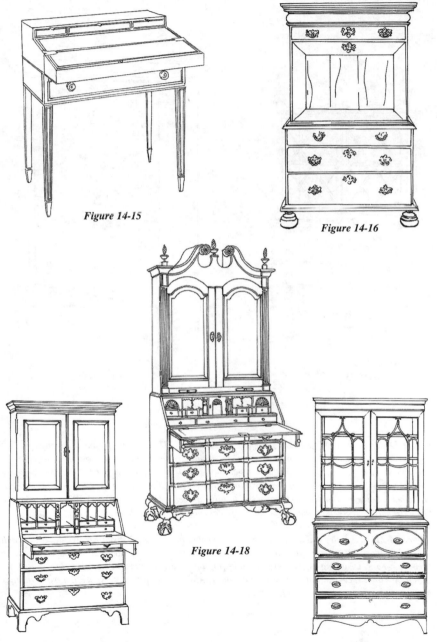

Figure 14-15

Figure 14-16

Figure 14-18

Figure 14-17

Figure 14-19

Figure 14-20                                    Figure 14-21

**Figure 14-20:** *Federal writing-flap secretary, 1790 – 1820. This is quite the most common type of Federal secretary, a secretary bookcase version of the writing flap desk we saw in Figure 14-11. Often these simple secretaries will have pigeonholes and small drawers set behind the bookcase doors. By now finials will be brass rather than wood, very similar to those we will see later on Federal clocks. Somewhat better models are apt to have arched or Gothic doors. Small secretaries like this were made everywhere, but are particularly common to New England.*

**Figure 14-21:** *Secrétaire à abattant, 1815 – 1825. These one piece fall-front Empire desks are high style urban work. They were made in Boston, New York, and Philadelphia, with the majority coming from New York. Dropping the veneered writing flap often reveals a magnificent interior, sometimes with a mirrored recess in lieu of the prospect door. Although useful where space is restricted, they are not common among American furniture.*

Figure 14-22

Figure 14-23

**Figure 14-22:** *Classical secretary, 1825 – 1835. This is the standard Late Federal secretary. Note the same columns and deep overhanging top drawer seen earlier in Classical bureaus (13-18). Many have paw feet. By this time the light Neoclassical look of Hepplewhite and Sheraton has given way to the heavier, more ornate look of Greco-Roman Revival. The bookcase behind the glazed doors will be unfinished, for the inside would have been hidden by pleated curtains.*

**Figure 14-23:** *Gentleman's secretary, 1795 – 1800. Breakfront bookcases and breakfront secretaries are fairly rare among American furniture. These relatively small gentleman's secretaries are perhaps the most notable example. In form they are a small breakfront secretary, for the deep center drawer is a secretary drawer. They were made in Salem, some as venture cargo. A few years ago one of them turned up in South Africa.*

# Chapter 15

## Highboys, Lowboys, Presses, and Dressing Tables

What Windsors are to chairs, highboys and lowboys are to case furniture. Both forms were borrowed from England, then much enhanced in America. In the New World the abundance of fine cabinet woods: maple, cherry, walnut, and mahogany; combined with an affection for lightness and verticality, led to beautiful highboys and lowboys, the likes of which are seen nowhere else. The American highboy is, without question, one of the great achievements of the American cabinetmaker.

In addition to highboys and lowboys, this chapter will include other case furniture that was used in the bedroom: the kas or scrank, the clothes or linen press, and several types of chamber or dressing tables. It also covers the kneehole desk, which in America was employed more as a dressing table than a desk, the small drawers being used for powder, combs, brushes, kerchiefs, and gloves.

Like many other names in this book, highboy and lowboy are modern terms. In the past a highboy was called a high chest of drawers or a chest of drawers on frame, a lowboy a dressing or chamber table. In England highboys have always been called chests on stands. There is a trend to return to the original names, and most books on museum collections, as well as some auction catalogs, now use the terms high chest of drawers and dressing table.

In England, the highboy did not have the long and successful career enjoyed by its American cousin. Highboys first appear in England about 1680 in the form of a chest on a one drawer stand, and then are fashionable only during the rather short reigns of William and Mary, Queen Anne, and George I, what in England is now called the Walnut Period. Then they lost favor to the more commodious chest-on-chest — just about the time highboys and lowboys become common in America. With few exceptions, English highboys never achieve the harmony and grace of the American product. Viewing them, one has the impression that they were never able to outgrow their inception as a chest on a stand.

Aside from the ever present possibility of an illicit marriage, the biggest concern with highboys is just what you would expect — the rather delicate legs. What lids are to desks, legs are to highboys. To start off, both the legs and the stretchers on William and Mary pieces are very likely to be restored. The way in which the top of the leg is simply doweled into a glue block is just about a guarantee of eventual failure. Here you might try checking diameter with a pair of calipers, for legs were turned when the wood was fairly green, and three centuries of shrinkage should result in considerable out of round. Also, the amount of out of round should be about the same on all legs. If not, one or more may be a later replacement. Although somewhat stronger, cabriole legs are also prone to fail, and if the case is not taken apart to fit a whole new leg, then a new leg may be spliced in just below the apron. When examining cabriole legs, be sure that there is not a splice in this area, and that the figure of the wood carries up past the turn of the cabriole to the corners of the case, for except for Newport work, these legs were always one piece right up to the top of the lower case.

Another thing to be careful of is the addition of a bonnet top, for at one time bonnet-top highboys were much in demand, and this led to a number of unfortunate conversions. This enhancement is usually not difficult to spot, for the modification is so extensive that it cannot be done without giving rise to some peculiar framing. Remember also that bonnet tops were employed on better than average quality furniture, and if there is carving in the upper case, we should expect similar carving in the lower case.

Because of their enduring popularity, there are a great many rebuilt highboys. These were probably found in sad condition with the legs broken or cut off short, and to correct this damage the lower case may be completely taken apart to tenon in new legs. Then some drawer fronts might be replaced to correct broken lipping, and finally, the whole piece given a complete refinish using stain and modern varnish. Should you come across a highboy in almost perfect condition, and with a recent finish, you may be looking at one of these products.

Aside from lowboys that are not lowboys at all, but are instead the lower case of a highboy, the most common problem among lowboys is the top, which were fastened with glue blocks, and are prone to come loose when the top shrinks across the grain of the sides. Consider first if the top is of the same wood as the case. A walnut lowboy will sometimes have a later mahogany top, it being much easier to obtain wide boards of mahogany. Then pull out the drawers and take a close look at the blocking on the underside of the top. Often you will find that the top has been refastened. This is no great problem so long as the top appears to be original. Ask yourself if the design is consistent. The top should always be in harmony with the case. One would expect to find a simple top on a simple case, a grand top on a grand case. Something is wrong if a grand case has a much simpler top. If, for example, the front is veneered in burl walnut, then you should expect to find the same treatment on the top. Similarly, any top without molded edges will probably be a replacement.

Before going on to the illustrations, it should be noted that production of highboys did not end with Chippendale and the Revolution. Although very much out of style by Federal times, they continued to be made, particularly in rural areas, perhaps as late as 1820. If examining a simple flat-top highboy, check to see if the backboards are not fastened with cut nails.

Except for Newport, where lowboys were not popular, highboys and lowboys were usually made up in pairs, or en suite, the highboy being set against a bedroom wall and the matching lowboy being placed between two windows where there was plenty of light. Usually the lowboy would have a dressing mirror (21-16) on the top, or perhaps a mirror would be hung behind on the wall. In the following illustrations we will discuss first lowboys and then highboys, even though they are stylistically very similar. Now that pairs are usually separated, it is more logical to compare lowboy with lowboy, highboy with highboy.

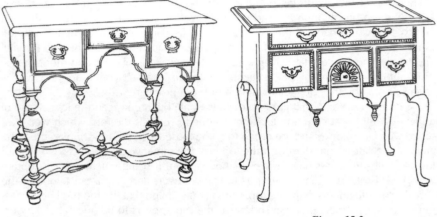

Figure 15-1                                        Figure 15-2

**Figure 15-1:** *William and Mary lowboy, c.1720. These early lowboys were made in all the urban centers, but most commonly will be from either Boston or Philadelphia. They are fairly rare, and those that retain their original top and legs are even more rare. New England William and Mary lowboys, if not made of maple and then painted or japanned, will usually have a top and front of white pine veneered in burl walnut; whereas Delaware Valley lowboys will normally be solid walnut, for Virginia black walnut was abundant in the Middle Atlantic colonies. Note in this and in the following illustrations that the top often extends well beyond the sides of the case. These bold overhangs are a common feature of period work.*

**Figure 15-2:** *Queen Anne walnut veneered lowboy, 1740 – 1760. The cabriole leg first comes into use on American highboys and lowboys in the 1730s. This early lowboy is also veneered, for in New England the practice of veneering the front and top of high style furniture with a crotch or burl walnut veneer continues up into the middle of the 18th century. We will see the same treatment later in a New England Queen Anne highboy (15-10). This dressing table illustrates another feature of early Queen Anne work — the use of an inlaid or carved and gilded shell centered in the lower drawer. Furniture from this period will also be decorated with inlaid stars of contrasting woods, normally on the sides of the case and on the lids of desks.*

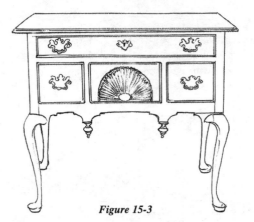

*Figure 15-3*

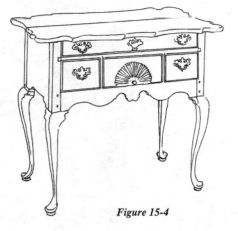

*Figure 15-4*

**Figure 15-3:** *Massachusetts Queen Anne lowboy, 1730 – 1780. The standard New England Queen Anne lowboy will have one long drawer over three short drawers with a fan carving in the center drawer. A slightly simpler version has a shallow center drawer with a shaped skirt curving up between the left and right drawers. Most will be made of maple, cherry, or walnut, most often cherry if from the Connecticut River Valley, and walnut elsewhere. While most lowboys have the one long drawer over three short drawer arrangement shown here, there are also lowboys with as little as one and as many as five drawers.*

**Figure 15-4:** *Connecticut Queen Anne lowboy, c.1750. In addition to a devotion to cherry, furniture made in the Connecticut River Valley is marked by a number of charming idiosyncrasies. Perhaps best known are the scalloped tops found on lowboys, chests of drawers, and all sorts of tables. Connecticut lowboys are also apt to be somewhat larger and higher than is normal for lowboys, and we will find some 32" high rather than the 28" to 30" height found in most other dressing tables.*

193

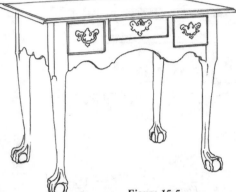

*Figure 15-5*

*Figure 15-6*

**Figure 15-5:** *New York Chippendale lowboy, c.1750. The unusual shallow three drawer arrangement and blocky claw-and-ball feet identify this as a New York lowboy. These lowboys are uncommon, but are included in this survey because they illustrate something else uncommon in American furniture, the use of tapered legs with claw-and-ball feet. New York Colonial furniture is very English, and the single level of drawers and tapered legs are found in many English lowboys.*

**Figure 15-6:** *Philadelphia Chippendale carved lowboy, 1750 – 1780. Lowboys from the Philadelphia area have a solid, substantial look that is very different from New England work. They come in a wide variety of grades from the very best shown here to the far less costly model that follows. Note how the center drawer has been deepened to provide an area for the elegant shell and acanthus carving. While most of these high style claw-and-ball foot lowboys have fluted quarter columns, the less expensive dispense with the carving on the drawer front and legs. Although by this time mahogany is the fashionable wood, many of these grand big dressing tables are made of walnut.*

194

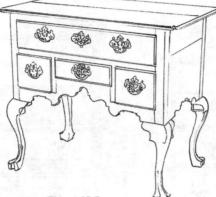

*Figure 15-7*

*Figure 15-8*

**Figure 15-7:** *Philadelphia Queen Anne lowboy, 1740 – 1780. Simpler Delaware Valley lowboys from the same period are often identified as being Queen Anne in style, perhaps due to the use of walnut and the trifid feet. This illustrates a very basic model; better work will have canted corners and perhaps shells carved on the knees of the cabriole legs. Although less massive than the previous example, these lowboys are still a very recognizable product of the Delaware Valley, being deeper across the front and sides than a New England lowboy from the same period (15-3). Similarly proportioned lowboys — in cherry — are sometimes found in Connecticut*

**Figure 15-8:** *Delaware Valley Spanish-foot lowboy, 1730 – 1760. Another less common design from the Delaware Valley are these somewhat eccentric Spanish-foot lowboys. They are characterized by a four square drawer arrangement and frequently are given the charming heart pierced apron shown here. Similar highboys commonly have extravagantly curved cabriole legs. The Spanish foot associated with the William and Mary period is by this time long out of style, and in any event, is not often employed in case furniture. Perhaps, like the trifid foot, it was just easy to carve.*

**195**

**Figure 15-9**                                            **Figure 15-10**

**Figure 15-9:** *William and Mary highboy, 1700 – 1730. William and Mary highboys do not often come on the market, although they are significantly more common than their companion lowboys. Better New England work will have walnut veneer on the drawers fronts and apron. As we saw earlier in the William and Mary secretary (14-16), these highboys will often have a blind frieze drawer worked into the cornice molding. With a few rural exceptions, the shape of the stretchers will always echo the shape of the apron. They are no more structurally sound than William and Mary lowboys, and more often than not, the stretchers and legs will have been restored. Note that to provide a finished effect and a graceful termination, the apron is given a cock beaded molding.*

**Figure 15-10:** *Queen Anne walnut veneered highboy, 1730 – 1750. Walnut veneered highboys and lowboys were high style furniture in early Colonial New England. As we saw earlier, only the front of the case is veneered, the sides will be solid. In common with the dressing table from the same period (15-2), the veneered drawer fronts will be crossbanded to provide a framed effect and to minimize the effects of shrinkage. Although this highboy is as well proportioned as any that follow, the American cabriole leg highboy did not start out perfect, for there are a number of early highboys that lack the long drawer, or drawers, in the lower case, and exhibit an unfortunate leggy look.*

*Figure 15-11*                           *Figure 15-12*

**Figure 15-11:** *New England Queen Anne flat-top highboy, 1740 – 1790. New England flat-top high-boys are so common that it is not easy to select a truly representative example. However, most will be similar to this illustration with two rows of lipped drawers in the lower case and four or five in the upper case. Usually the top row will be split into two short drawers. The fan-carved lower drawer is very common. Sometimes there will be a matching fan-carved drawer in the upper case. Construction will be of local woods, cherry or maple, or perhaps maple and pine if stained or painted, or maple and walnut if given a clear finish. Brasses that are both early and original will be quite small. Then as now, the tops of highboys were often used to show off valuable articles, which were sometimes displayed in tiers by the use of detachable wood steps, and a rare few flat-top highboys still retain these original "China steps."*

**Figure 15-12:** *New England Queen Anne bonnet-top highboy, 1740 – 1790. In a general way, New England bonnet-tops can be considered high style urban furniture and flat-tops country furniture, so long as we keep in mind that much country furniture was actually less expensive urban work. Bonnet-top highboys usually have a shell in the upper case to complement the shell in the lower case. Note how the deep top drawer provides room for the upper shell and helps fill in the tympanum, the space enclosed by the arch. Although Queen Anne in stlye, some bonnet-tops have Chippendale claw-and-ball feet. In common with much Chippendale furniture, they also saw limited production in the early years following the Revolution.*

**Figure 15-13**

**Figure 15-14**

**Figure 15-13:** *Newport Queen Anne flat-top highboy, 1750 – 1760. Although Rhode Island is very much a part of New England, the Newport highboy is so different in scale and construction from other New England work that we might illustrate the two most common examples. These early Newport flat-top highboys are often attributed to Christopher Townsend from one that is inscribed and dated by him in 1748. They illustrate the characteristic slipper foot found in much early Newport work. Although it would appear that the legs on this highboy are made in the normal manner, and extend to form the corners of the case, they are actually detachable, passing inside the bottom of the case where they are held in position by glue blocks. What appears to be upper section of the leg is just a thin covering board. The lower case is then fastened at the corners with dovetail joints, rather than being tenoned into the legs. Look at the back of case on a Newport highboy and you will see the dovetails that join the lower case. The other construction anomaly is that the midmolding is attached to the upper rather than the lower case. The upper section is then kept in position by cleats on the bottom of the case.*

**Figure 15-14:** *Newport Queen Anne bonnet-top highboy, c.1750. Newport bonnet-top highboys are easily identified by the treatment of the tympanum, for Newport cabinetmakers employed a pair of applied panels rather than a deep drawer to fill this area. Note also that the carving is simpler, there is only a single large shell, and that it is cut into the apron rather than into the face of the middle drawer as we saw in the previous bonnet-top highboy. Although not evident in this illustration, Newport highboys are significantly smaller than other New England highboys. All Newport highboys, as well as the much less common lowboys, will have detachable legs.*

Figure 15-15

Figure 15-16

**Figure 15-15:** *New Hampshire Dunlap type highboy, c.1785. Before leaving New England we should look at a highboy made by the extended Dunlap family in the area around the present city of Manchester. The maple case, the rather deep lower case supported by bandy Queen Anne legs, and the scrolled apron are very typical of their work. This large highboy illustrates the false drawer facades often found in country work, and in New Hampshire work in particular. There appears to be thirteen drawers in this highboy, but there are actually only seven, for the top five drawers and the bottom three are actually just two large drawers with false fronts.*

**Figure 15-16:** *Philadelphia Chippendale carved highboy, 1750 – 1780. This is the senior partner of the high style Philadelphia dressing table shown in Figure 15-6. These magnificent highboys are generally considered to be the grandest of American furniture, which might be expected, for Philadelphia at this time was by far the largest and most wealthy American city. Note that the deep acanthus and shell carved drawer in the lower case is repeated in the upper case. To save labor and material, the shells in these drawers were first carved into the drawer face, then the acanthus carved separately and glued on, what is known as applied carving. The deep lower case and the very solid legs are typical of Philadelphia highboys. Delicate, almost fragile looking highboy legs will not be found south of Connecticut.*

199

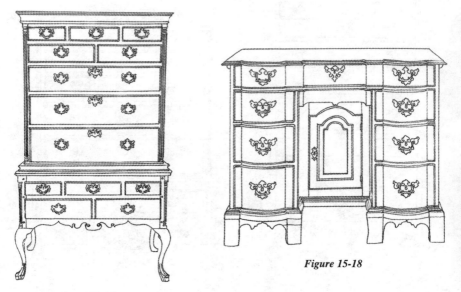

*Figure 15-18*

*Figure 15-17*

*Figure 15-17: Philadelphia Chippendale highboy, 1740 – 1780. Here is the less expensive and far more typical Delaware Valley highboy. The quarter columns and the trifid feet are found throughout the Delaware Valley. Almost all these highboys will be made of walnut. Although far less massive than the previous example. They are still far more solid and heavier looking than what we would expect to find in New England. Note that the upper two rows of drawers on this highboy lack escutcheons and do not appear to be fitted with locks. They are probably secured with wooden spring clips or "Quaker locks" that are accessed from the drawers below.*

*Figure 15-18: Boston block-front dressing table, 1750 – 1790. Originally known as bureau tables, and now often called kneehole desks, dressing tables are most likely to be Boston work, although similar dressing tables, both with and without the blocked front, were also made in New York and Philadelphia. They are far more common among English furniture, where they also seem to have been used as desks, as many English models are fitted with writing slides.*

*Figure 15-19*               *Figure 15-20*

*Figure 15-19:* *Newport block-and-shell dressing table, 1765 – 1790. These small dressing tables are the most common of the wonderful Newport block-and-shell furniture, even though there are no more than about 50 of them. The same magnificent shell design is also found in chests of drawers, in chests-on-chests, and in secretaries. Similar case work is also found to the west of Newport in Connecticut's New London County, but here they lack the small scale and sophistication of Newport furniture. Stylistically these lovely little dressing tables present something of an anomaly, for although the ogee bracket feet and the period of production would suggest Chippendale, the carved shells and the conforming molding under the top are very much Queen Anne features.*

*Figure 15-20:* *Massachusetts Federal dressing table, 1790 – 1815. After the Revolution, the lowboy goes out of style and is replaced by a more Neoclassical dressing table. These charming little Massachusetts chamber tables are nothing more complicated than a side table with a small set of drawers added to the top. In lieu of these fixed drawers, you will sometimes see the use of a separate little set of drawers or a dressing mirror, the case fashioned to conform to the shape of the top of the table. Some have square tapering Hepplewhite legs.*

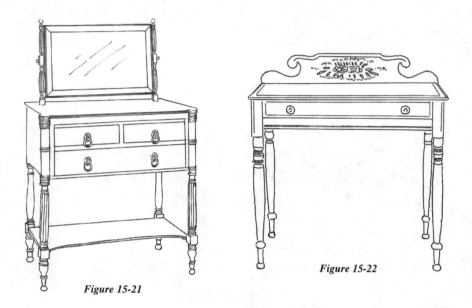

**Figure 15-22**

**Figure 15-21**

**Figure 15-21:** *New York Federal dressing table, 1800 – 1815. These Sheraton mahogany dressing or chamber tables are usually New York City workmanship. Sometimes there will be a row of small drawers below the mirror. The low shelf is very characteristic of New York City work. In the next chapter we will see an almost identical form employed as a serving table.*

**Figure 15-22:** *Painted dressing table, 1820 – 1840. Not all dressing tables are high style urban furniture. In the early years of the 19th century dressing tables become very popular, and these charming little painted dressers are the happy result. In addition to the scrolled splashboard, many will have one or two tiers of small drawers on the back of the top. They were made in all regions, sometimes of hardwoods but more generally of popular or pine which was then either grain painted or painted and stenciled. While they are fairly common, the problem, as in all painted furniture, is finding one with the original paint in good condition.*

**Figure 15-23:** *Kas and shrank, 1730 – 1790. These large Baroque wardrobes are called kas or kasten when made by descendants of the Dutch settlers in New York and northern New Jersey, and schranks when made by the Palatinate Germans who settled Lancaster County in Pennsylvania. The form is common in Northern Europe, which is probably why these two very different groups of immigrants produced such similar furniture. Both kas and shrank will have the two door, two drawer arrangement shown here. Most have this large and ornate molded cornice, the rectangular panels flanking the doors, and the diamonds set between the lower drawers. Some later kasten will have bracket rather than ball feet. In common with other period furniture, these wardrobes can be taken apart to be moved, but unlike other furniture, they don't simply unstack. Instead, they are held together with pins and wedges, and can be taken completely apart; the doors, the top, the ends, and the base are all separate components.*

*Figure 15-23*

*Figure 15-24*  *Figure 15-25*

*Figure 15-24: Clothes press, 1780 – 1810. The clothes or linen press was never very popular in America, but every so often one of these large two section pieces will come on the market. Behind the doors you will find either drawers or pull out shelves for clothing or linens. Most examples are Federal rather than Colonial, and will be from the mid-Atlantic states, Pennsylvania, New York, or New Jersey.*

*Figure 15-25: Classical wardrobe, 1825. Large two door mahogany veneered wardrobes were big city furniture, and are often from New York. Although the French armoire was never made in America, to some extent these wardrobes represent the final development of this form among period furniture. Note that in common with other Classical work, this wardrobe has a pair of columns that terminate in paw feet.*

**203**

# Chapter 16

## Sideboards and Cupboards

Sideboards and cupboards are covered last, for they are the most recent case furniture. The modern cellaret sideboard does not appear until the 1770s, and the great majority of cupboards are 19th century. Cupboards were common in the 18th century, but most were simple kitchen or keeping room furniture, and very few have survived. While we will take a look at an earlier cupboard, much of what you see on the market will date from 1790 to 1840, and perhaps even later.

The cellaret sideboard is named for a deep drawer that was used to hold wine bottles, a cellaret being just a small storage place. This drawer is normally located in the lower right of the case, provided that the sideboard is not fitted with a pair of separate bottle drawers. In England, the cellaret drawer was sometimes lined with lead to hold water to cool the wine. Due to the Revolution, cellaret sideboards are not made in America until early in the Federal period, perhaps two decades after they first became popular in England. Then, almost as if to make up for lost time, they are made in large numbers everywhere. In general, Hepplewhite style sideboards are somewhat more common than Sheraton, perhaps because the tapered Hepplewhite leg was a little stronger and did not require the services of a turner.

Like everything else, sideboards and cupboards are not immune from a little fraud here and there. To meet the demand for early cupboards, a number of later pieces have had doors removed and sides scalloped to give them a suitably Colonial appearance. Conversely, glazed doors are sometimes added to open cupboards to make them more useful. When looking at glazed doors, remember that the cabinetmaker would normally line up the horizontal muntins with the shelves so that the edges of the shelves would not show. If they don't line up, you may be looking at later doors.

Simple country cupboards are probably the most faked of all American furniture, not only because they go so well in family rooms, but because they are so easy to make. All you need is some weathered boarding, an old paneled door, and a handful of cut nails, and you are in business. You don't even have to worry about moldings and feet, for you can pass your creation off as a built-in from an old farm house. Needless to say, we want to be very careful with such country work. Whenever examining a cupboard, remember that while finding old boards is not difficult, finding them without some nail holes is almost impossible. If you spot one hole, look for another in parallel across the grain, for this is where it will be when the board was once fastened to the side of a barn.

Aside from repairs to the rather thin legs, the most common problem with sideboards is that the original was too wide, or too high, or too deep, for modern taste. Even the very common small bow-front English sideboards are quite deep by modern standards. To correct this problem, the whole case must be taken apart and rebuilt. Therefore, when examining a sideboard, pull out the drawers and take a careful look at the inside of the case for signs of rework. Check the drawers, particularly the backs, to see if the dovetails appear original. The last inch or so at the end of the drawer slides should not show much wear. If they do, you may be looking at a sideboard that has been reduced in depth. Here also, you may find the whole top is a replacement, for the wide tops on sideboards are subject to serious splitting.

Later sideboards tend to get deeper and heavier, losing the lightness and grace of earlier work. To correct this problem, the lower central drawer or cupboard will be removed and replaced by a curved apron. Therefore, we always want to check the inside of the middle pair of legs for signs of rework, perhaps neatly plugged mortise holes. In period sideboards the legs always extend to the top of the case, drawers and cupboards being set between the legs. If not so, you are very probably looking at a modified or a reproduction sideboard.

Normally, the entire front of a sideboard will be veneered and decorated with inlay, stringing, or banding. Take the time to go over this area carefully, for there may be a lot more restoration than meets the eye. Also, there may be a lot more damaged and missing inlay than meets the eye. Keep in mind that restoring inlay correctly is both time consuming and very expensive. Remember also that much of the character and the quality of a sideboard lies in the front of the case. If it is in poor shape, look for another sideboard. There are many to choose from.

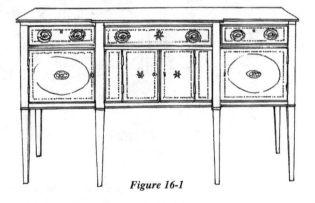

*Figure 16-1*

*Figure 16-1:* Straight-front sideboard, 1790 – 1810. Sideboards with flat fronts are not as common as the simpler construction would suggest. Most will be from New England, although by the Federal period there are fewer regional differences among American furniture, and it is not always easy to determine the source of a sideboard. To minimize the box like look, the middle section will sometimes be swelled, or the middle doors will be recessed, or the center section will project out a little as shown here. On some the center cupboard is fitted with tambour doors.

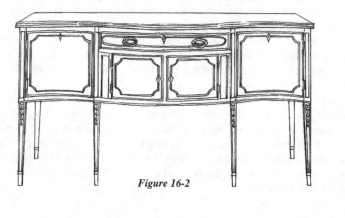

**Figure 16-2**

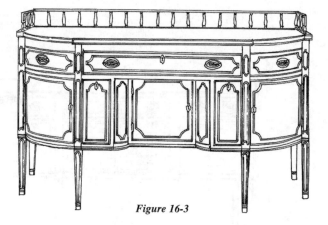

**Figure 16-3**

*Figure 16-2:* Serpentine-front sideboard, 1790 – 1810. While the serpentine front is fairly rare in chests of drawers, it is very common in sideboards. Serpentine-front sideboards were made everywhere, but are most likely to be from one of the Middle Atlantic states, somewhere between New York and Baltimore. This New York sideboard employs a cupboard in lieu of the deep bottle drawer. The serpentine curve is so effective in reducing the apparent mass of the case that these sideboards often do not have a recessed center section.

*Figure 16-3:* Swelled-front sideboard, 1790 – 1810. There are only a few true bow-front sideboards; most will have a convex curve at the ends and then be flat across the middle, not too unlike the Sheraton swelled-front chest of drawers we saw earlier (13-17). They are often referred to as D-front sideboards. When the center cupboard is recessed, the sideboard is likely to be from New York. Otherwise, it will probably be from Massachusetts. This is a better than average sideboard with a brass gallery and a pair of narrow bottle drawers flanking the center cupboard. If you see some plugged holes around the top of a sideboard, it probably once had such a gallery.

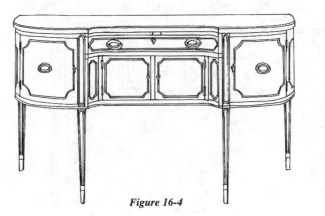

*Figure 16-4*

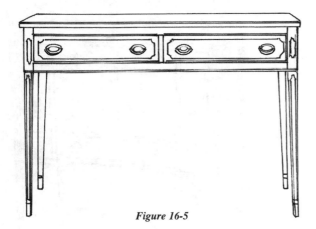

*Figure 16-5*

**Figure 16-4:** *Four-leg sideboard, 1790 – 1810. Full-size sideboards normally have two legs in the back and four across the front, but some with convex ends omit the front corner legs, instead curving the sides around to meet the two middle legs. There are also a few grand eight leg designs in which the middle pair of legs are doubled. On very fine work you will also see the middle legs canted to follow the curve of the case. Sideboards having the center section recessed were popular in the mid-Atlantic states. Later we will see a Philadelphia card table with a similar shape.*

**Figure 16-5:** *Southern hunt board, c.1800. In the south we see the use of a high, narrow one drawer deep buffet or hunt board like this fine Baltimore example. There are no bottle drawers, for in the south, wine was normally kept in a separate cellaret (24-3). Huntboards are unusually high, purportedly to keep the hounds away from the food. Many simpler examples are made of walnut or hard pine, and are so unsophisticated that there is some thought that they were not actually used as dining room furniture.*

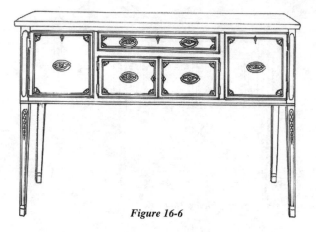

*Figure 16-6*

*Figure 16-7*

**Figure 16-6:** *Small Hepplewhite sideboard, c.1800. Small sideboards are fairly rare among American furniture. The reduced size was apparently not dictated by economy, for many are finely made. With the smaller size there is less need to curve the facade to reduce the bulk of the case, and most will have straight fronts, although there are some with serpentine or swelled fronts.*

**Figure 16-7:** *Massachusetts Sheraton sideboard, c.1810. These rather stocky little New England sideboards were made in Boston and Salem. Note how the case has been made quite deep and given three tiers of drawers in order to obtain adequate storage within the reduced width. In common with Sheraton chests of drawers, these small sideboards are almost square across the front, being about 40" wide and 40" high.*

*Figure 16-8*

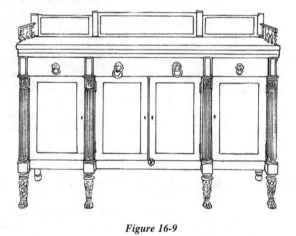

*Figure 16-9*

*Figure 16-8:* Late Sheraton sideboard, c.1815. Almost no furniture in America avoided the cookie corner treatment, and sideboards are not an exception. The solid legs and rather large fluting identify this example as late Sheraton. These sideboards are still graceful, for the facade is not too deep and the mass of the case permits these heavier legs. Later we will see that the same sort of legs are not as successful on a much smaller card table.

*Figure 16-9:* Classical sideboard, c.1825. With Empire, sideboards become deeper and acquire paw feet, neither of which is an improvement, for in the process they lose the light Neoclassic look of earlier work. Here we see the same columns and overhanging top drawer that we saw in a Classical secretary and a Classical chests of drawers. Most of these sideboards will be from New York, which by this time was America's largest city.

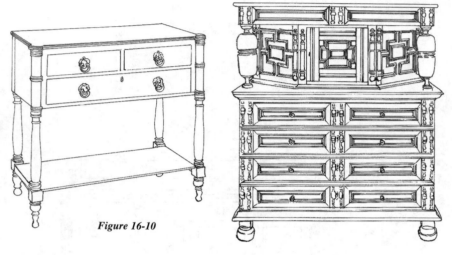

Figure 16-10

Figure 16-11

**Figure 16-10:** *Sheraton serving table, 1810 – 1820. Serving tables were made everywhere, but are not nearly as common as sideboards. They seem to have been used in conjunction with sideboards to provide additional serving area. These New York tables are perhaps the most common. If you return to the previous chapter, you'll see a very similar design with a low shelf employed as a dressing table. So popular was this form in New York City that there are even small secretaries that are fitted with this very characteristic shelf.*

**Figure 16-11:** *Court cupboard, c.1670. These very early cupboards or sideboards were made in limited numbers during the last third of the 17th century. They are the very grandest of Pilgrim Century furniture. Although the form predates the 1670s, the paneled construction and the use of side hung drawers with applied geometric moldings are similar to other work of this period. Court has nothing to do with kings and queens. Rather, it is the French word for short, so this might be considered a "short" cupboard. Some of these cupboards are open at the bottom with an additional shelf for displaying silver. Cupboards with drawers or doors in the lower case are often called press cupboards on the theory that they were once used for storing table linens.*

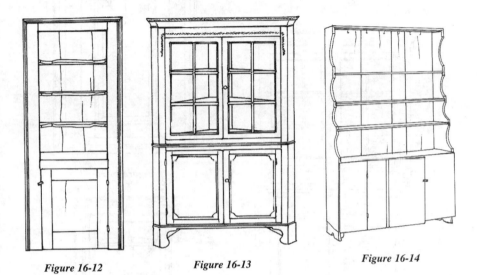

Figure 16-12

Figure 16-13

Figure 16-14

*Figure 16-12:* Open corner cupboard, c.1750. Simple cupboards with scalloped shelves are about the earliest you will find for sale. Most will be painted pine. Many were once built in, and lack both feet and cornice molding. Early corner cupboards generally have a beveled or flattened back. This was probably done to allow room for the exposed corner posts found in old post and beam houses.

*Figure 16-13:* Pennsylvania corner cupboard, 1770 – 1830. These handsome cupboards with glazed upper doors and reverse fielded lower doors are usually from the Delaware Valley. They were made of walnut, cherry, and sometimes painted up poplar. When determining origin, remember that built in cupboards are more likely to be from New England. Further south, cupboards were generally made as separate pieces of furniture. Because they were treated as furniture, they will normally be much better quality.

*Figure 16-14:* Pewter cupboard, c.1810. This sort of simple country work often looks much earlier than it is. When looking at cupboards, remember what we learned about paint and hardware. The popular copper blue-green paints and cast-iron butt hinges both appear right at the very end of the 18th century, and the milk based red, white, and gray paints are perhaps 1830. This is the sort of primitive cupboard that is so easily assembled from old pine boards and a handful of cut nails. While finding boards free of nail holes may be a problem, finding old hardware is not, for cigar boxes full of old nails, screws, and hinges regularly turn up at auctions.

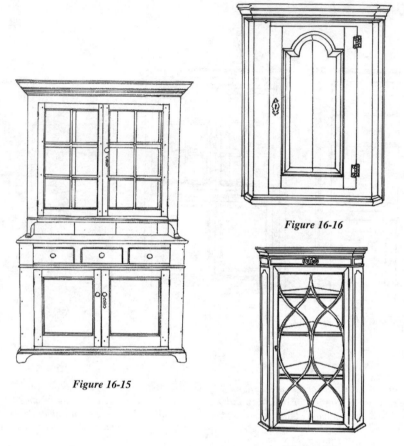

Figure 16-16

Figure 16-15

Figure 16-17

*Figure 16-15:* *Step-back cupboard, 1760 – 1840. Two part step-back cupboards with paneled or glazed doors were made in all areas, but are most often from Pennsylvania. Note that the glazed doors in the upper case and the paneled doors in the lower case are very similar in feeling to the Pennsylvania corner cupboard we saw earlier.*

*Figure 16-16:* *Hanging paneled door cupboard, c.1750. Before leaving, we should take a brief look at cupboards designed to hang from walls. Hanging wall and corner cupboards are common, what you might expect from a time in which houses were filled with small children — and also with small rodents. The great majority are simple painted pine kitchen furniture, but every so often you will come across better walnut or cherry examples like this handsome Queen Anne cupboard. In common with other cupboards, the best work is likely to be from the mid-Atlantic states.*

*Figure 16-17:* *Hanging glazed door corner cupboard, c.1790. Perhaps due to the cost of glass, hanging cabinets with glazed doors are much less common, and will generally date from the 19th century. Many are more formal furniture, and will be English like this mahogany veneered and inlayed Neoclassical cupboard.*

# Chapter 17
## Dining and Side Tables

Having first covered seating furniture, and then case work, we finally come to tables, the last in the trinity of major furniture types. There are so many ways to make a table, which then find so many uses, that the following three chapters will forgo some uncommon forms in favor of those you are most likely to encounter in shops and at auctions. Even with this editing, though, we will cover dozens of designs.

Before getting started, it might be useful to talk about tables in general. With the exception of tables in which the top rests on a pillar or column, most all will have a top, a bed, and four or more legs. The bed is the box section that supports the legs and forms the junction between them and the top. In period work this is usually comprised of four rails which are tenoned into the tops of the legs. The top is then fastened to the rails. Often a drawer or two will be fitted into the bed. An alternative construction is found in the rare Windsor table (17-21), in which the legs are doweled into a pair of cleats and then braced with stretchers at the top and bottom of the legs.

In terms of numbers if not in precedent, tables may well predate chairs, for in Elizabethan times tables were mostly served by simple benches and stools. The earliest dining table you'll see in any number is the common gate-leg table (17-1), which first appears about 1670 during the reign of Charles II. Largely a product of the turner, these tables were very popular in America, continuing to be produced right up through the middle of the 18th century. Made of local woods, gate-legs usually have a single swing leg on either side and a top that is fastened down with hardwood pins. The edges of the top will be flat or slightly rounded and there may be either a butt joint, a shallow bead-and-groove joint, or a rule joint where the leaves meet the top. Although complicated looking, they were not difficult to make.

The next step in the evolution of the dining table was the product of the cabinetmaker. This was the development, about 1730, of the cabriole leg table (17-2). These new tables were a revolution in both design and construction. Here the use of a finely cut wood hinge and a deep swinging rail allowed the cabinetmaker to dispense with the additional pair of legs to support the leaves. On most of these tables there are only four legs, the pair at the opposite corners swinging out to support the leaves. The result is a folding table of elegant simplicity. In keeping with the general sophistication of these handsome tables, the edges of the top were given an curved ovolo molding, and a rule joint is used where the leaves meet the top. This new joint proved so successful, that thereafter, it is almost universally found on table leaves, even on later gate-leg tables. Only on very simple country work do we still find the use of a butt joint, perhaps because the rule joint requires an extra pair of molding planes and special off-set hinges. Another significant improvement is that the top is now fastened from the underside with glue blocks or screws. With the exception of some rural work, you will not find the tops on cabriole leg tables fastened with hardwood pins.

The cabriole leg table dominated the Colonial period, being produced by the thousands in maple, cherry, walnut, and mahogany, and in both Queen Anne and

Chippendale styles. Many were made with square tops and sold in pairs so that they could be put together to provide a single large dining table. They are among the most common of the surviving Colonial furniture.

The next major advance was to shift the legs to the corners of the table where they would be out of the way of knees, then to build the table in two sections, each with a single large folding leaf (17-6). To provide a banquet sized table, a third section with additional leaves might be added in the center. This type of table appears about the middle of the 18th century in England, but does not reach America until after the Revolution.

The last major innovation was the pillar dining table. Here each section of the top is mounted on a heavy center pillar, not too unlike an overgrown tea table (17-9). To provide extra length, additional leaves, or one or more center sections, would be inserted between the two ends. Although we think of these as modern dining room tables, they came into use at the turn of the 18th century — about 200 years ago. These were probably the first dining tables that were not brought out and set up for dinner. Until this time dining tables were always designed to be folded and set against walls when not in use so that the room could be used for other purposes. Although pillar dining tables are fitted with casters and tilting mechanisms, this may have been just for sweeping up, or to provide room for dancing, for they seem too large to be always placed against a wall when not in use.

The most common problem with dining tables are the tops, and more specifically, the leaves. At auction previews, if you are seriously interested in a table, do not hesitate to get under to take a good look. You may feel a little foolish, but not half so foolish as bringing home an old table and then discovering that one or both of the leaves is a replacement. A better approach is to turn the whole table upside down on a pad, but this may not be possible if space is limited or if the table is being used to display a number of small lots. In any event, always try to get a good look at the leaf hinges, the overall patina of the underside, and the curved marks left by the swinging rails. The hinges should appear undisturbed, and the patination should be the same where the leaves butt against the top. If there is much less rail wear on one end, or there are two arcs, or the arc does not match the swing of the rail, something is wrong. Also, the bottom of a table inside the frame formed by the bed should have an almost untouched patina, while the outside edges will show paint, finger oils, and match scratches.

It is not uncommon for an old dining table to have the top reset, or to have inherited a top from another table. The former is not much of a problem, but the latter you don't want to overlook, for such tables are really no different than married highboys. When looking at the underside of a table, in addition to an even patina, check that the glue blocks or screws seem old and undisturbed. Above all, be wary of mysterious holes. Mismatched tops are particularly common in pillar tables where it is easy to obtain a reasonable fit.

While peering at the underside of a dining table, don't neglect the legs, particularly if they appear somewhat delicate. The most likely point of failure on Sheraton style tables is the first turning below the skirt, and here you might check for a neat little splice line. Among cabriole leg tables, it is the swing legs that are most likely to be worn, repaired, or replaced. Often the hinges will show some repairs. In the old days these legs might very well have been swung every single day.

Finally, never buy a drop leaf table without setting up both leaves and then standing back to see how things look. Unlike the top, there is no frame to keep the leaves flat, and there can be a remarkable amount of twist, particularly if the table is made of local woods. This is far less a problem with mahogany tables because mahogany is such a stable wood.

For convenience, the following illustrations are arranged in four general groups: first dining tables, then breakfast tables, then tavern tables, and finally, a miscellany of side, library, sofa, and center tables. Where there seems to be some disagreement as to the primary function of a table, I've indicated possible alternate uses. Although separated by less than a dozen generations from the original owners, it is surprising how little detail is left to us of their day to day habits. Of famous battles we have reports by the dozen, but where breakfast was taken on a sultry summer morning is a complete mystery.

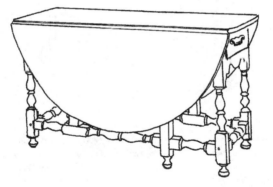

*Figure 17-1*

*Figure 17-1:* William and Mary gate-leg table, 1710 – 1760. These early tables were originally called "turned" or "drop-leave" tables. The term gate-leg, for all its clarity, is modern. Gate-leg tables are found in a wide range of sizes from diminutive breakfast or tea tables to large double-gated dining tables with two swing legs under each leaf. American examples will be either maple or walnut; maple or perhaps walnut if from New England, walnut if from Pennsylvania. A rare few have Spanish feet. Early tables can be identified by the bead-and-groove joint at the juncture of the leaves and top. Gate-leg tables with square rather than turned stretchers will be English, or perhaps southern. Go over these tables with care, for they frequently have replaced leaves or replaced tops, or both. Always bring up the leaves and sight along the top. You should expect to see a series of shallow curves, for local woods are not as stable as mahogany. Also, oak reproductions were made in the early 1900s when Pilgrim Century furniture was very much in vogue.

**215**

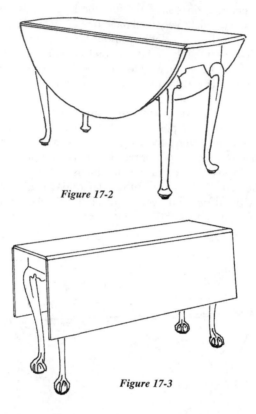

Figure 17-2

Figure 17-3

*Figure 17-2:* Queen Anne cabriole leg dining table, 1740 – 1790. This is the standard Queen Anne table with cabriole legs, pad feet, a straight skirt or apron and an oval top. The top will usually be fastened from the underside with screws or cleats, although some simpler, or perhaps earlier, versions will be pinned from the top. More often than not they are made of maple, but you will also find the use of tiger maple, cherry, walnut, and mahogany. Philadelphia area tables may be fitted with trifid feet. Because these tables were made right up through the Colonial period in parallel with Chippendale, many have rectangular tops and curved aprons. Just as there is no clear demarcation between Queen Anne and Chippendale in chests of drawers, there is no clear division in these handsome and very successful tables. Note that when tables go to two fixed legs and two swing legs, there will no longer be a deep drawer built into the bed.

*Figure 17-3:* Chippendale cabriole leg dining table, 1750 – 1790. Aside from a generally larger size and the frequent use of claw-and-ball feet, there is little to distinguish Chippendale from Queen Anne in a cabriole leg table. Either may have a scrolled apron and an oval top, although later tables tend to be square so a pair of tables could be butted together to provide a single large table. Occasionally you will see a table with just a single leaf. Unlike Queen Anne tables, most will be made of mahogany. Original tables are apt to have very deep leaves, and you want to be careful that they have not been cut down or rounded at some time to give the table a more modern appearance. The production of both Queen Anne and Chippendale tables was quite standardized, so much so that they were made and priced in 6" increments of bed length from 3' to 5' – 6".

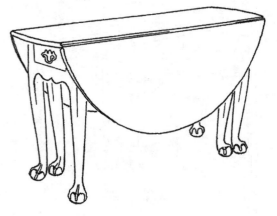

*Figure 17-4*

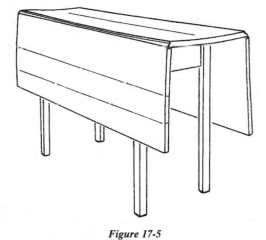

*Figure 17-5*

**Figure 17-4:** *Chippendale six leg dining table, c.1750. Both Queen Anne and Chippendale tables were sometimes made with four fixed corner legs and two swing legs. Many of these are from New York where fixed legs seem to have been preferred on both dining and card tables. New York dining tables are also apt to be larger than normal. Some very large oval tables even have eight legs — two swing legs on each side. Note that the deep drawer is retained when there are four fixed legs.*

**Figure 17-5:** *Chippendale Marlborough leg dining table, 1770 – 1800. In common with chairs, Chippendale dining tables were often made with the less expensive Marlborough leg. However, this is also not a sign of inferior quality, for while many were made with local woods, some are well made with very dense mahogany. If you see one of these tables with molded stop-fluted legs, you are probably looking at Rhode Island work.*

**217**

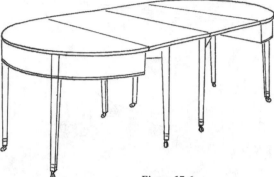

*Figure 17-6*

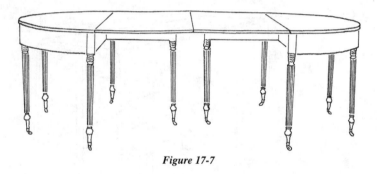

*Figure 17-7*

**Figure 17-6:** *Federal Hepplewhite dining table, 1790 – 1815. This table, and the Sheraton example that follows, are the most common formal dining tables you will find on the market. Normally made of mahogany, but sometimes cherry, they come in a wide range of quality and decoration from no inlay at all, to a little stringing in the apron, to stringing in the apron and inlay down the sides of the legs. Each end section has a single wide leaf supported by a swinging leg. A number were made with a center section that carried the leaves, so if you come across an oversized console table at an auction, it may be the end section from one of these tables. A few very large tables have leaves on both the center and end sections, providing a banquet table 12' or 13' long.*

**Figure 17-7:** *Federal Sheraton dining table, 1790 – 1830. This is the Sheraton version of the standard two part Federal dining table. The ends of these tables may be either round, canted, D-shaped, or square; the circular legs either with or without reeding. In common with the Sheraton style, there may be carving in the apron and at the tops of the legs. Sheraton legs tend to be delicate, so always check here for repairs. As we saw earlier in sideboards, later work tends to have thicker legs.*

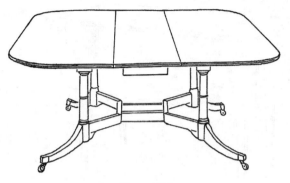

*Figure 17-8*

*Figure 17-9*

**Figure 17-8:** *Accordian-action dining table, 1800 – 1820. Accordian-action dining tables of any type are fairly rare among American period furniture, but you will occasionally see one of these expansion tables. In England, this elegant design in which the stretchers pivot on a floating rectangular frame is called a Cumberland-action table.*

**Figure 17-9:** *Federal Empire dining table, c.1815. The pillar form dining table appears in England at the end of the 18th century, but most American tables of this type are Empire and date from the first quarter of the next century. American tables, like this fine New York City example, usually retain an apron under the top, perhaps because it was felt necessary to hide the leaf supports. More often than not these large tables have four legs supporting each column, something almost never seen in smaller period tea tables and candlestands. As a general rule, the simpler the column and legs, the earlier the table.*

**219**

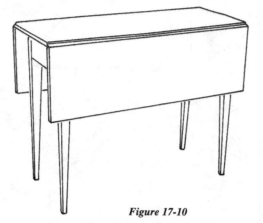

*Figure 17-10*

*Figure 17-11*

**Figure 17-10:** *Federal drop-leaf table, 1800 – 1820 and later. Before leaving dining tables, we should note a simple swing leg table which seldom rates an illustration in auction catalogs. In spite of this neglect, these simple drop-leaf tables are a very common Federal period dining table. Some even dispense with the complication of swinging the legs, and are just overgrown Pembroke tables with one or two brackets supporting each leaf. Usually made of local woods, simple country Shera-ton examples continued to be made well into the middle of the 19th century.*

**Figure 17-11:** *Queen Anne breakfast table, 1740 – 1780. We will turn to breakfast tables with per-haps the most delightful of all, these diminutive little Queen Anne cabriole leg designs. In form and operation, they are just a scaled down version of the Queen Anne dining table we saw earlier in this chapter. Usually made of walnut or mahogany, and generally in Massachusetts, they would have been equally suitable for tea or cards.*

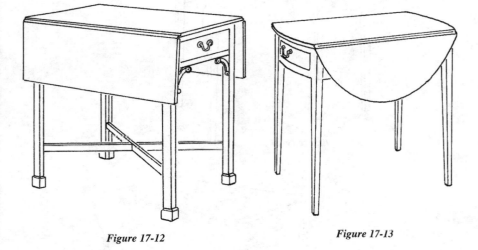

*Figure 17-12*                                                    *Figure 17-13*

**Figure 17-12:** *Chippendale Pembroke table, 1760 – 1810. With Chippendale we come to a new form of drop-leaf table. Rather than swinging a leg to support the leaf on a small table, we now have a hinged bracket or fly that is mounted on the bed. The first of these tables is reputed to have been made for the Countess of Pembroke in 1750, and unlike many other words for old furniture, Pembroke is not a modern term. Chippendale models will have square molded legs, and are usually fitted with X-stretchers like this handsome Philadelphia example. Look back to the chapter on upholstered furniture and you will see the same block foot on a Philadelphia sofa (11-8). These popular Chippendale style tables continued to be produced well up into the 19th century.*

**Figure 17-13:** *Federal oval-top Pembroke table, 1790 – 1810. The design we most often associate with Pembroke tables are these Hepplewhite style tables in which the bed and drawer face echo the curve of the oval top. In addition to stringing on the top and drawer face, these lovely little high style tables often have beautifully inlayed legs; paterae, tablets, or "bookends" worked in at the top, then bellflowers down the outside faces, and then crossbanded cuffs at the bottom. Almost identical tables were made in all the urban centers, being so similar that they are usually identified as to source by the secondary woods and the pattern of the inlay.*

Figure 17-14

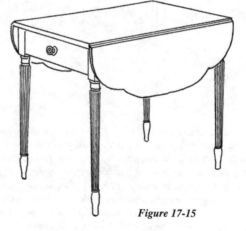

Figure 17-15

**Figure 17-14:** *Federal serpentine-top Pembroke table, 1790 – 1810. The square bed on these Hepplewhite tables allowed the cabinetmaker more latitude in the shape of the leaves, and these pretty butterfly leaf tables are a happy result. You will find that simpler Pembroke tables sometimes employ pivot supports rather than hinged brackets, and are without pulls; the drawer being opened with just the key or by reaching under and lifting the bottom forward. In others, the face of the drawer is given a deep lip that is beveled on the inside to provide purchase for the fingers — a feature often found in modern furniture.*

**Figure 17-15:** *Federal Sheraton Pembroke table, 1790 – 1830. Sheraton Pembroke tables tend to be larger, more the size we would now consider to be a breakfast table. They often measure about 3' by 4' with the leaves extended, and many have two hinged brackets supporting each leaf. These tables are good illustrators of the differences between Sheraton and Hepplewhite styles, not only in the turned and reeded legs, and in the use of simple rosette pulls, but in the more monocromatic feeling due to a general absence of inlay.*

222

*Figure 17-16*

*Figure 17-17*

**Figure 17-16:** *Federal breakfast or library table, 1800 – 1820. These Empire style tables are variously identified as either breakfast or library tables, and could have been used for either function, for by this time grander houses had separate rooms set aside as studies or libraries. In form, they are a cross between a pillar form dining room table and a large Pembroke table. High style urban work, they were made in Boston, New York, Philadelphia, and Baltimore.*

**Figure 17-17:** *William and Mary center table, 1700 – 1780. These square top tables were made in New England of maple and pine, and in Pennsylvania of walnut or tulip poplar. They are the sort of all purpose table one would find in the kitchen area of a farm house. As a general rule, the larger and bolder the top, the earlier the table. Softwood tops will often be stiffened with breadboard ends. Simple tables like this see a lot of heavy wear and you want to check that the top has not been replaced or reversed. In addition to the choice of woods, it is possible to determine the source of a table by the baluster turnings on the legs. This table would be identified as coming from New England because the central elements of the turnings tend to mirror each other. Pennsylvania and southern tables are more likely to have a single large baluster. Pennsylvania tables are also apt to have two drawers, one smaller than the other.*

223

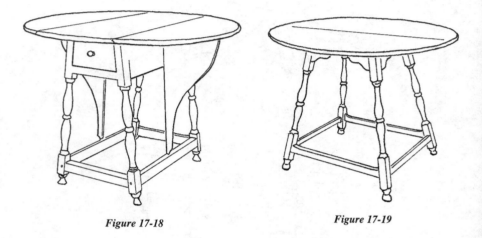

*Figure 17-18*                    *Figure 17-19*

**Figure 17-18:** *William and Mary butterfly table, 1700 – 1750. Butterfly tables appear to be a unique-ly American invention. Made of local woods throughout New England, they are quite rare and sel-dom come on the market. To some extent the design is a simple version of a Pembroke table, the butterfly shaped brackets pivoting on the stretcher rather than on the rails. You need to be careful with these tables, for in being both very early and very much American, they have been so popular with collectors that a number have been created from other furniture. There are also early repro-ductions made in tiger maple.*

**Figure 17-19:** *William and Mary tavern table, 1720 – 1770. This small table, and the following Queen Anne model, are popularly called tavern tables. The turned legs and stretchers identify this table as William and Mary style, although most such tables will postdate the William and Mary peri-od. The idea that these small occasional tables once served as tavern tables seems to be a romantic invention, for there is no mention of such tables in old documents.*

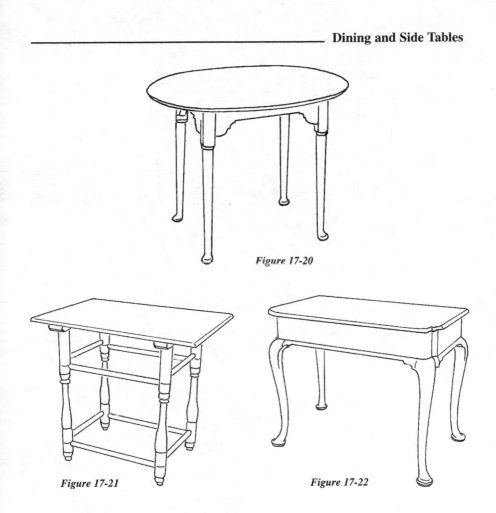

*Figure 17-20*

*Figure 17-21*

*Figure 17-22*

**Figure 17-20:** *Queen Anne tavern table, 1740 – 1780. Here is the more common Queen Anne tavern table with turned legs and pad feet. They are frequently identified as tea tables, and we will see a very similar Queen Anne tea table in the next chapter. These charming little tables are generally a product of New England and are usually made of maple, tiger maple, or a combination of both. Although there are a few with rectangular tops, most will have a circular or oval top stiffened with a single transverse cleat that is notched into the rails.*

**Figure 17-21:** *Windsor tavern table, c.1780. Although an easy and inexpensive way for a chairmaker to make a small table, Windsor tables are rare, perhaps because they are not particularly handsome, and perhaps also because there is no easy way to give them a drawer. Note that the table has two sets of stretchers to provide the legs adequate support.*

**Figure 17-22:** *Mixing table, c.1750. Because alcohol damaged spirit varnishes, marble top tables were used in grand homes for setting out bottles and mixing up drinks. Although popular from Queen Anne right up through Sheraton, they are rare among American furniture. As a general rule, the top will overlap the back by three or four inches so as to fit flush against the wall.*

*Figure 17-23*

*Figure 17-24*

**Figure 17-23:** *Classical pier table, 1810 – 1835. Pier tables are named for their intended location, for they were set against the pier between two windows. Although made in all the major urban centers, the majority of these very formal Empire or Classical tables will be from New York. While there are variations, they typically have two front columns, turned or paw feet, and a mirrored backboard flanked by a pair of pilasters. Most have white marble tops, for by now machinery has been developed to inexpensively cut and polish marble.*

**Figure 17-24:** *Classical center table, c.1815. With the increase in the number and size of rooms, tables can now placed in the middle of the best parlor, and these large circular tables are the result. This is a Philadelphia table, but similar tables were produced in all the major cities. In lieu of the center column, you will also see designs with marble tops and pillars at each corner. Note that these center tables have feet rather than legs, although some models have short scrolled legs that are attached to a circular base. A good way to spot Empire or Classic style is to watch for tables in which the column rises from a circular or triangular base.*

## Tea and Card Tables

We will cover tea and card tables together, for both were used for pleasure and both are somewhat intermediate in size between the large dining tables of the previous chapter and the small candlestands and sewing tables in the next. Because we are covering only two forms, we will be able to take a closer look at the products of different areas. Drinking tea and playing cards became popular about the start of the 18th century, spreading with the growth of the middle classes who had the time and the money for such things. Both tea and card tables appeared about the same time, card tables during the reign of William and Mary, tea tables a few years later during the reign of Queen Anne.

Card tables are nothing if not consistent, for once developed, the basic idea of a small gaming table with a fold over leaf that rested swing out leg did not change for over 150 years. From the time of William and Mary, these small tables marched right up through Queen Anne, Chippendale, Hepplewhite, Sheraton, and Empire with hardly a pause. Over the years the style of the table and the method of bringing out the leg varied, but the general design did not alter in the least. Not until after the first decade of the 19th century, when card tables went to pedestal bases and swiveling tops, did the swinging leg fall into disuse.

Card tables are extraordinary plentiful. With the exception of chairs, they are the most common Federal furniture. In addition to being fashionable during a time of growing population and wealth, their light weight and small size made them a perfect occasional table, useful not only for playing cards, but for eating breakfast and writing letters. They often appear in paintings from this period. By this time much furniture was being made up for sale by others, or for stock, and most of these handsome little tables seem to have been sold ready made. They were usually sold in pairs, a few in double pairs or sets of four.

The great majority of American card tables are Federal, and most are in fairly good condition, for they are not really all that old. However, this should not be an inducement to carelessness. Card tables, particularly those from New England, are lightly made, and many have seen some repairs and restoration. In addition to checking for missing veneer, broken out legs, and damage in the area of the hinges, we want to be careful that the swinging leg has not been restored, and that the top is not from another table. Federal cards tables are so standardized that it is not all that difficult to locate a reasonable match for a badly split or warped top. Always turn a card table over to get a good look at the bottom. Also watch for warp or twist in the leaves. If not constrained by a top with a felt insert, the simplest solution for a warped top is simply to display the table with the folding leaf open against the wall. Should the top have pretty figuring, this may be the best way to display it anyway.

The problems with tops are worse with circular tea tables, for it is far easier to marry a top and a base on a table where the dimensions are not dictated by the width and depth of the bed. Here you not only want to check the underside of the top for staining and mysterious holes, but also to step back and examine the overall design for consistency. Is the size of the top in harmony with the spread of the legs,

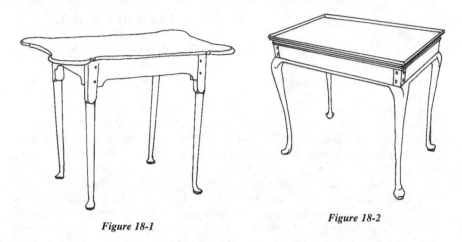

Figure 18-2

Figure 18-1

**Figure 18-1:** *Queen Anne porringer-top tea table, 1740 – 1780. These charming little New England tea tables are quite similar to the oval top tavern tables we saw in the previous chapter. However, they are a step grander, for the top will usually have these outset rounded "porringer" corners, and they are often given cabriole rather than turned legs. Most will be made of maple or walnut, although there are a few mahogany examples.*

**Figure 18-2:** *Queen Anne tray-top tea table, 1740 – 1780. Based on Chinese and English designs, rectangular tray-top tea tables are the height of Queen Anne elegance, particularly when combined with the New England penchant for lightness and verticality. Many are fitted with candleslides at either end. Newport versions are apt to have delicate slipper feet. Not common, and perhaps never very common, they are rare south of New England. Many of these rather delicate tables have been repaired at one time or another, and even if the legs are sound there may be some restoration to the top or the gallery.*

**Figure 18-3:** *Massachusetts Chippendale tea table, 1760 – 1800. Round tea tables are far more common. We will start first with a Massachusetts table, then work down the coast for a look at some others. Boston area tables often exhibit a spiral-turned urn at the base of the column, a feature also found*

or does one look too large or too small for the other? Also, a simple top should rest on a simple base, a grand top on a grand base. If you see finely carved legs and column, then just a simple top, you are probably looking at a marriage.

In common with candlestands, the legs on circular tea tables are usually reinforced with a triangular iron brace to keep the blind dovetails (5-1) from splitting out. If there is no brace, and you can see from a pattern of holes that there once was one, see if the foot of the column has not had some repairs, or perhaps one of the legs has been restored. Should the brace still be in place, then check the legs for repairs. A leg may break anywhere, but most usually the failure will be where it thins and curves up toward the foot.

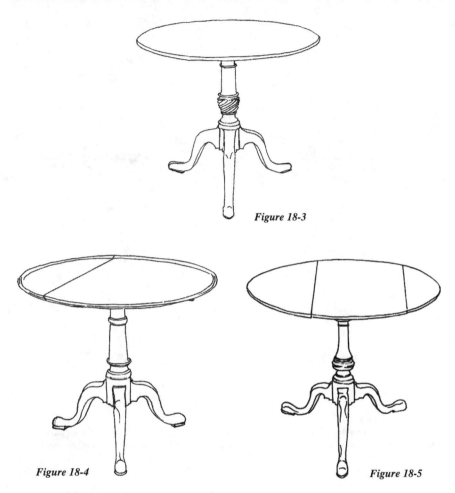

Figure 18-3

Figure 18-4

Figure 18-5

in many English tables. Similar tables were also made with square or serpentine tops, the cleats set diagonally so the top forms a diamond shape when tilted.

*Figure 18-4:* Rhode Island Chippendale tea table, 1750 – 1790. Rhode Island pillar form tea tables are not common. They typically have simple, sturdy "gun barrel" columns like this walnut example. Note that a walnut top will usually be made up of two boards, with perhaps an additional narrow filler in the middle, for only mahogany could routinely provide boards 30 or more inches wide.

*Figure 18-5:* Connecticut Chippendale tea table, c.1785. Tables with this modified compressed ball standard are often attributed to the Chapin family of cabinetmakers. In common with much other Connecticut work, they are made of cherry. Except for some of these Connecticut tables, New England tea tables rarely are given the birdcage mechanism that allows the top to both turn and tilt.

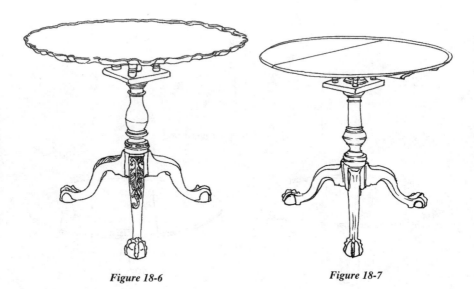

*Figure 18-6*                                         *Figure 18-7*

**Figure 18-6:** *Philadelphia Chippendale piecrust tea table, 1750 – 1780. Philadelphia tea tables come in such a range of embellishment that we will look at two, the first this grand mahogany table with claw-and-ball feet, acanthus-carved cabriole legs, and a scalloped or "piecrust" top. The vase-form column, while typical of Philadelphia work, is not as common as the compressed ball shown in the next illustration. In the past such tables were called pillar-and-claw or claw tables.*

**Figure 18-7:** *Philadelphia Chippendale dished top tea table, 1750 – 1780. Here is a middle grade walnut tea table with claw-and-ball feet, a turned dished top, and the immensely popular compressed ball standard so often found on Philadelphia tables. Simpler tables will have just a plane top, or just pad feet, or both. In the next chapter we'll see the same compressed ball used in candlestands. Dished tops are found everywhere, but are particularly common on tables from the Philadelphia area. They were made on a lathe, and provided tables with an edge stop at a fraction the cost of a carved scalloped top.*

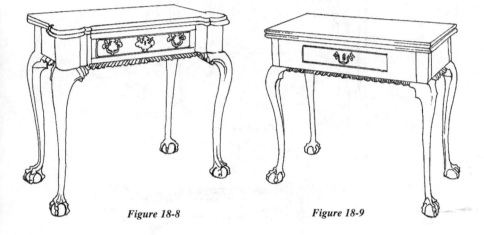

*Figure 18-8*                    *Figure 18-9*

*Figure 18-8:* *Chippendale turret-top card table, c.1760. Although gaming tables date from the reign of William and Mary, very few were made in America until the 1750s. Among the earliest, and the grandest, are these turret-top tables. Similar tables were made in New England, but most of the very few that come on the market will be from Philadelphia. While fairly rare in America, turret-top gaming tables are common among English furniture. In New York and New England similar Chippendale tables will have square projecting corners reminiscent of the blocking so popular in New England. Whatever the form, the top will open to a lined playing surface fitted with shallow dished out candle holders in the corners and counter wells along the sides. Because the inside is protected from sunlight and wear when closed, a few even survive with their original lining.*

*Figure 18-9:* *Philadelphia Chippendale cabriole leg card table, c.1770. This is the more common Philadelphia cabriole leg card table. Again we see the rectangular playing surface, the center drawer, and the applied gadrooned molding that was popular in Philadelphia. Unlike lowboys, most of these high style tables are made of mahogany.*

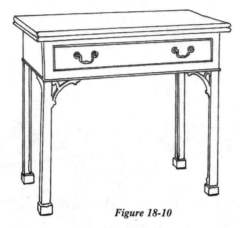

*Figure 18-10*

*Figure 18-11*

**Figure 18-10:** *Philadelphia Chippendale Marlborough leg card table, 1760 – 1790. These are the most common Colonial period card tables, for by this time Philadelphia was the largest city in America. Although a budget model in comparison to the two previous examples, they are still very handsome tables. With a few exceptions, a simple rectangular Chippendale card table will always be from somewhere in the Philadelphia area. We have already seen these blocked feet in a Philadelphia Chippendale camel-back sofa (11-8). This is the last card table we will see with a wide, shallow drawer across the front. Federal period price books list such a drawer as an option, but they are very rare in Federal card tables.*

**Figure 18-11:** *Rhode Island Chippendale card table, c.1780. Not all square Chippendale style card tables are from the Delaware Valley, for they were made elsewhere, perhaps most commonly in Rhode Island. These small molded leg serpentine-front card tables are an American original, nothing like them exists among English furniture. Later Sheraton versions of these tables will have reeded legs.*

*Figure 18-12*

*Figure 18-13*

**Figure 18-12:** *Federal demi-lune card table, 1790 – 1810. Circular half-round or demi-lune Hepplewhite card tables were made everywhere, and like much Federal furniture, can best be identified as to source by an analysis of the secondary woods, the turnings, and the inlay. However, if you come across one with a medial brace running from front to back under the top, it will probably be from Baltimore. In all but the simplest budget models the bowed front and tapered legs will be given some inlay.*

**Figure 18-13:** *Federal Massachusetts card table, 1790 – 1810. These elliptical tables with serpentine sides and a bowed front are unique to New England. Most were made in Boston and up along the North Shore in Salem or Newburyport. More often than not they will have these double tapered legs. Just short of the floor the leg is given a little cuff of inlay, and then below the cuff the leg tapers sharply inwards so that the bottom of the foot is less than an inch across.*

**233**

*Figure 18-14*

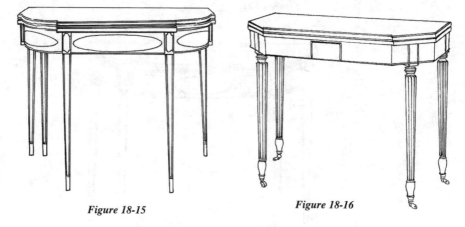

*Figure 18-15*

*Figure 18-16*

**Figure 18-14:** *Federal swell-front card table, c.1800. Swell-front card tables are also typically a product of New England. They are often country work, for the simple swelled front was more within the capability of the rural cabinetmaker. Some fine tables of this type were made by John Dunlap II in New Hampshire.*

**Figure 18-15:** *Federal D-front card table, 1790 – 1810. The shape of these D-front card tables is very similar to the shape of D-front sideboards. This is a five leg New York table with four fixed legs and one swinging leg. Although five leg card tables were made elsewhere, the majority will be from New York City where it was the most common form of card table. A rare few tables will even have six legs, four fixed and two swinging. As you face the table, the fifth leg will almost invariably be on the left, the same side as the swing leg on four leg card tables. New York tables will sometimes have a small drawer fitted into the inner rail behind the swing leg.*

**Figure 18-16:** *Federal canted-corner card table, c.1810. Card tables with canted corners will usually be from New York City, although this unusual form was also made in New England. Similar corners are also found in work tables and dining room tables.*

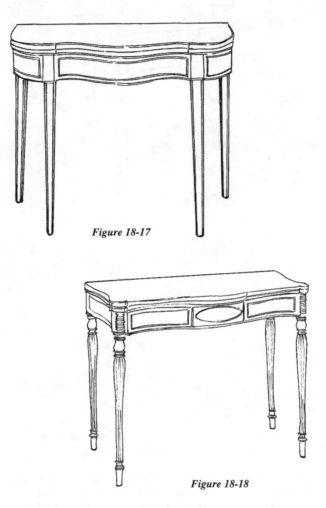

Figure 18-17

Figure 18-18

**Figure 18-17:** *Federal serpentine-front card table, 1800 – 1810. Kidney-shaped card tables are usually from the mid-Atlantic states, Philadelphia or perhaps Baltimore. Note that even at this late date Philadelphia work still exhibits a somewhat solid English look. As a rule, card tables from the mid-Atlantic states are heavier and more solidly constructed than those from New England.*

**Figure 18-18:** *Federal cookie-corner card table, 1790 – 1820. Sheraton cookie-corner card tables are generally from New England, usually from Boston or the North Shore. Many are decorated with a center oval and flanking rectangular panels of contrasting bird's-eye maple or flame birch, similar in feeling to the Portsmouth chest of drawers we saw in an earlier chapter.*

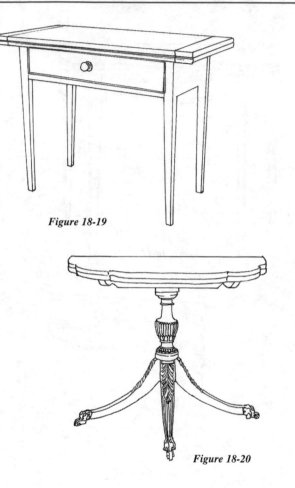

Figure 18-19

Figure 18-20

**Figure 18-19:** *Federal country card table, 1770 – 1830. Cards were a universal avocation and not all players were well off. The results are these simple country card tables. Most are Federal and have Hepplewhite legs. Often the legs are fixed and the top just swivels on an offset wooden pivot. While simple rural tables are very common, there are far fewer country card tables than their simplified form and low cost would indicate, suggesting perhaps that there was much less time for cards in rural areas.*

**Figure 18-20:** *Federal trick-leg card table, 1805 – 1815. These high style carved New York tables are commonly attributed to the shop of Duncan Phyfe, but were also made by other cabinetmakers, both in New York and in Philadelphia. This example, however, is most likely to be from New York, for the waterleaf carving on the face of the legs was very popular in New York. These card tables are unique in that they incorporate swinging legs in a pillar form table, which permits them to be kept against walls when not in use. The two rear legs are connected by iron rods and hinged iron braces to two hinged flys so that the legs swing out when the corresponding flys are pulled out. The whole mechanism is hidden in the column and under the top — hence the "trick" leg. They are unique to America, and were, as you might suspect, much more expensive than the average card table.*

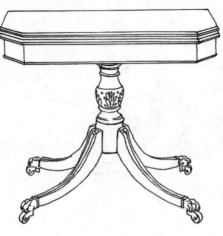

*Figure 18-21*

*Figure 18-22*

*Figure 18-21:* *Federal pedestal-base card table, 1810 – 1830. Gaming tables went to pedestal bases about the same time as dining tables. Since they are quite common and there are a number of variations, we'll look at three styles. Earlier tables usually have this urn-shaped carved column and then molded or carved downswept legs. Later Classical versions have a heavier pedestal, a platform base, and more carving. This table, and the two that follow, swivels to open.*

*Figure 18-22:* *Federal lyre-base card table, 1800 – 1820. By the second decade of the 19th century, the interest in things classical becomes less restrained, and we see both lyre-back chairs and these lyre-base card tables. As a general rule, a solid carved lyre indicates Boston work, a cut out lyre Philadelphia. This then would be a Philadelphia table.*

**237**

*Figure 18-23*

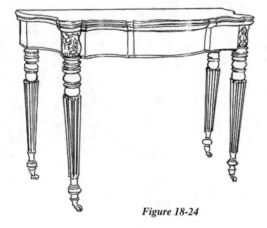

*Figure 18-24*

**Figure 18-23:** *Federal colonette card table, c.1810. These uncommon tables are among the most elegant of late Federal work. Even more grand are the rare few in which the front colonettes are replaced by a winged caryatid or a pair of winged griffins. This table with the canted corner top is from New York, but similar tables were also made in Philadelphia. The use of four small columns or colonettes to support the top was also employed in the accordion-action dining table we saw in the last chapter.*

**Figure 18-24:** *Late Sheraton card table, c.1820. Cookie-corner swing-leg card tables continued to be made right up through the Classical period, the legs getting thicker and the reeding heavier as time passes. Often the legs will be spiral carved rather than reeded. Although somewhat heavy looking, these tables are usually well made.*

# Chapter 19
## Candlestands and Sewing Tables

Lastly, we have the small tables: candlestands, sewing tables, light stands, kettle stands, and night tables. Because dealers and auctioneers so often refer to candlestands and sewing tables by their old names of "stands" and "work tables," we'll do things a little differently this time and also use these names. Like tea tables, candlestands are so common that we will again look at typical examples from different regions.

While we'll see a few earlier examples, most surviving stands will be either Late Colonial or Federal. Charming little William and Mary walnut stands with twist turned columns are found among English furniture, but American stands from this period are both simpler and very rare. The problem in distinguishing Queen Anne from Chippendale among American case work also afflicts stands, for unless covered with Rococo embellishments, there is little to differentiate one from the other. Also, as we saw earlier, much American Chippendale actually dates from the Federal period. It is Chippendale only in style.

As you gain experience, you will notice that the turnings cabinetmakers employed in the columns of tea tables often carry over into stands, which is what we might expect from furniture made in the same area for the same customers. Tea tables and stands are often very similar, one just a smaller version of the other. Once you acquire a feeling for the turnings common to different regions, you'll be able to tell where a stand is likely to have come from.

When we get to Philadelphia work, we'll see that the affection for table tops that rotate carries over into stands, so much so that even some Federal stands with rectangular tops were fitted with little birdcage mechanisms. This propensity for tops that could be turned, even on a small table where it would have been just as easy to reach across, suggests that rotation by itself was important. Why? Well, if you have ever tried to turn a candle that was burning unevenly in a draft, you'll find how easy it is to spill hot wax on your hand or on the table top. Might it not be better just to smoothly rotate the whole table top?

The majority of American stands have tilting tops, perhaps not so much for setting against a wall as to allow them to double as pole screens in front of fires. There are even a few stands that are a combination of both pole screen and candlestand. Look under the top and you will generally find that a small brass spring lock is used to secure the top. Except for some wood cleats and iron blacksmith latches found in rural work, tilt-top tables are almost always latched down with these round or hourglass-shaped cast brass locks (5-10). Like much American hardware, they were imported from Birmingham. Because these latch down with a snap, candlestands were often called "snap stands" or "snaps." Unlike the far more visible pulls on case work, these obscure little brasses are more likely than not to be original.

Work tables, in the old sense of a small table specifically designed for sewing, are a Hepplewhite period development, first appearing in Federal America after the Revolution. This relatively late arrival did not in the least diminish their popularity, for thousands were made from about 1790 right up into Victorian times before handwork gave way to the treadle sewing machine. You will see in the illustrations that the development of work tables parallels the development of Federal card tables; first raised on four Hepplewhite or Sheraton legs, then on a pedestal with downswept molded legs, and finally on a heavy pedestal on a platform base.

The problems we saw in the last chapter with the tops and legs of tea tables now appear in spades, for the legs of stands are easily broken, and the tops are easily swapped. I suspect that some of the many married tops may be quite early, for in a time when everything had to be planed and scraped down from rough mill stock, borrowing a top from a broken up table would have been a sensible economy. Because it is easy for even an amateur to make a new top, you will sometimes come across some very inept restorations. Except for very simple rural work, the tops of early stands should be either made of thin stock or chamfered on the underside to give the appearance of thinness. Almost never will a period top be made of two boards. Later stands will have thicker tops, some of which are veneered. Remember here that the top should be in keeping with the base; a light, delicate stand should have a light, delicate top, a heavier stand a thicker top.

If a stand has a tilting top, there are other ways to confirm that the top is original. First, look to see if the area protected by the plate is somewhat less darkened by less exposure to the air. In addition, because the plate will have shrunk a little over the years, the square tenon that joins it to the pedestal may project slightly and have left a corresponding mark on the underside of the table. This mark should match the size and position of the tenon.

You want to be careful that you do not purchase a stand that has been cut down to look better with modern furniture. Although there are quite a number of exceptions, most period stands are about 27" to 29" high, much higher than modern reproductions. This extra height may have been felt necessary for reading, it would bring the light from a candle past the shoulder and down on the print. Fortunately, cut down stands are usually not hard to spot, for not only will the column seem too short, but there are likely to be signs of rework around the plate.

Because of their inherent fragility, we need to be especially careful with stands, for one way or another, a great number — perhaps even the majority — have at some time been repaired or modified.

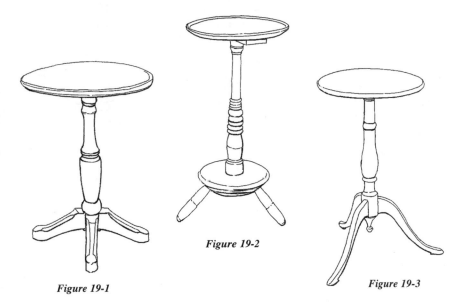

*Figure 19-2*

*Figure 19-1*

*Figure 19-3*

**Figure 19-1:** *Pilgrim Century stand, 1690 – 1720. Very early stands usually have some form of the X-base shown in this Connecticut table. The woods will be local and often are a mixture, oak and maple, or perhaps walnut and maple. Most of these small stands are now found in the Pilgrim Century rooms of museums, which is perhaps no great loss to the collector, for in spite of their historical interest, they seldom are as handsome as this New England example.*

**Figure 19-2:** *Turner's stand, 18th century. Another early and uncommon form are these three leg stands. Like the Windsor table we saw earlier, they seem to be the product of the turner rather than the cabinetmaker. In common with much simple rural furniture, they may not all be as early as they look.*

**Figure 19-3:** *Early Queen Anne stand, 1740 – 1760. With Queen Anne the cabriole leg comes into use, and with it the modern form of candlestand. These legs are a great improvement, for they lift the column off the floor and do much to provide the feeling of lightness and grace that we associate with these small tables. The rather high, bold stance is typical of early stands — and of the enthusiasm and naiveté of early work. Note that the legs on this stand are tenoned into the column, a feature which we will see again later when we get to a New Hampshire table.*

241

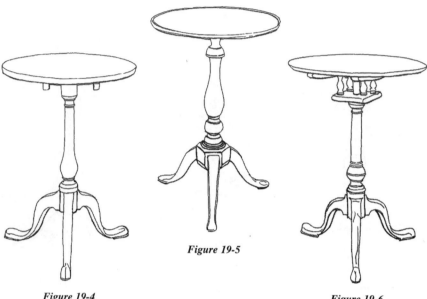

Figure 19-5

Figure 19-4

Figure 19-6

*Figure 19-4:* New York Queen Anne stand, 1760 – 1790. Furniture from Colonial New York is not common, and we will not often see one of these handsome little tables. This Queen Anne tilt-top stand with the simple baluster-and-ring column is typical of New York work. The presence of cabriole legs and the general simplicity of form would identify it as Queen Anne in style.

*Figure 19-5:* Newport Queen Anne stand, c.1750. Newport stands are somewhat more common than New York stands. The handsome and unusual plinth at the base of the column is a characteristic of early Newport work. Some very grand models will have a cluster of three columns rising from the plinth. We will also find stands with the "gun barrel" turning that we saw earlier (18-4) in a Rhode Island tea table.

*Figure 19-6:* Philadelphia Chippendale birdcage stand, 1760 – 1790. Here is the standard Philadelphia stand with the same birdcage and compressed ball standard we saw earlier in tea tables (18-7). The majority of these tables will also have a dished top, and the very best work a piecrust top. Somewhat later tables will have vase-form (18-6) or urn shaped columns. Note how the turning mechanism, inconspicuous on a larger tea table, becomes a dominant feature in this much smaller table. It can lead to a very strange looking table when the top is unusually small.

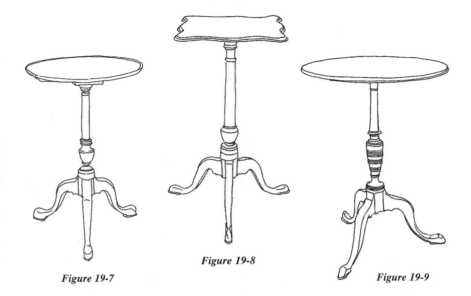

Figure 19-8

Figure 19-7

Figure 19-9

*Figure 19-7:* Philadelphia Chippendale stand, 1780 – 1790. The birdcage added about half to the cost of a stand, and not all Philadelphia stands are fitted with this device. However, the use of walnut and the dished top are good indications of Philadelphia workmanship. Even more simple Delaware Valley stands omit the dished top, as this large turning would itself almost double the cost of a candlestand. As a general rule, Philadelphia stands are significantly larger than New England stands. While this stand is Chippendale in style, the presence of a Neoclassical urn in the column suggests that it is more likely to be a product of the Federal rather than the Colonial period. It is a good example of the way in which newer features creep into earlier styles. With the advent of the Federal period, the urn becomes a common motif. We will see some form of urn in the column of almost every stand that follows.

*Figure 19-8:* Massachusetts Federal serpentine-top stand, 1770 – 1810. There are so many surviving Massachusetts stands that we'll look at two of the more common, the first this elegant little serpentine-top model. Similar stands are also found with square and octagonal tops. Although sometimes identified as Chippendale, these little stands exhibit a lightness that is very much Neoclassical. They tend to become even more slender and vertical as the century draws to a close.

*Figure 19-9:* Massachusetts Federal oval-top stand, 1790 – 1810. The other fashionable Massachusetts stand has an oval or circular top. This is a somewhat later model with the ring-and-urn pedestal often found in these tables. Because the bulbous foot is popularly called a snake foot, these are sometimes described as snake-foot stands. While better stands were made of mahogany, you will often come across Massachusetts and New Hampshire examples made of birch, then either painted black or red, or stained up to look like mahogany.

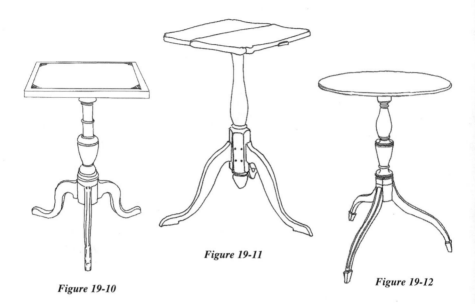

*Figure 19-11*

*Figure 19-10*

*Figure 19-12*

*Figure 19-10:* Connecticut Federal square-top stand, 1790 – 1800. But for the use of cherry, many Connecticut stands resemble Massachusetts work. However, these rather short stands with the square top and the prominent urn shape in the column are a Connecticut original. Often there will be a little molding or railing around the top. You will find that stands with a heavy lower shaft often dispense with the triangular iron reinforcement used to support the blind dovetails at the base of the column.

*Figure 19-11:* New Hampshire Federal stand, c.1780. If you see a simple maple or maple and birch stand with the legs mortise-and-tenoned into a hexagonal base, you are probably looking at New Hampshire work. Because this joint does not lock in place as does a blind dovetail joint, it will normally be pinned at the top and bottom of the tenon. This construction is easy to spot, not only by the pinning, but also, in that the column will extended well below the bottom of the legs to provide adequate stock at the bottom of the mortise. The column is then terminated with a turned ball or an acorn pendant.

*Figure 19-12:* Federal spider-leg stand, 1790 – 1810. These stands are properly described as having "arched tapering legs," but most dealers and collectors simply refer to them as spider-leg stands. As a general rule, spider-leg stands are a bit later than cabriole leg stands, most of them dating from the 19th century. Sometimes the legs will be so delicate that you wonder how they ever survived. Unlike other American work, the legs on these stands often terminate in spade feet, although in many tables the spade is much simplified. If you see one of these tables with a rectangular top and canted corners, it is probably from Portsmouth, New Hampshire.

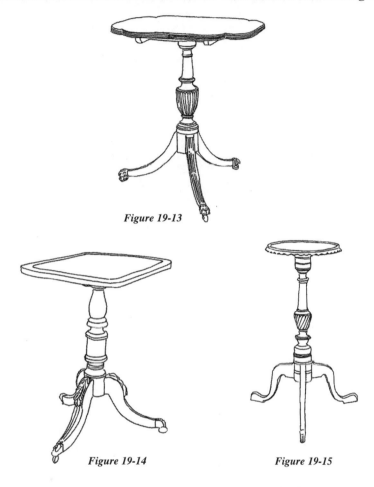

*Figure 19-13*

*Figure 19-14*                    *Figure 19-15*

**Figure 19-13:** *Late Federal stand, c.1810. With Empire, stands get generally heavier and acquire the downswept legs we saw earlier in card tables. In better work they are fitted with brass paw feet and casters. Note that the somewhat thick top with the reeded edges is very much in harmony with the rest of this handsome and solid table.*

**Figure 19-14:** *Classical stand, c.1815. With this Classical table we come to the final development of three-leg stands. Note the stout column with the vase-and-drum turning and the acanthus-carved legs. Fine stands in this pattern were made by both Duncan Phyfe and Charles-Honoré Lannuier in New York City.*

**Figure 19-15:** *Kettle stand, c.1795. Stands with small dished tops for kettles or wine bottles are quite rare among American furniture, but we might show one in event that you come across a candlestand with a dished top that appears is original but seems to be unusually small. Another form of three-leg stand, one not made in America, is the tall, slender torchere or candle stand. These will normally also have a dished top or gallery to help keep the candlestick in place.*

245

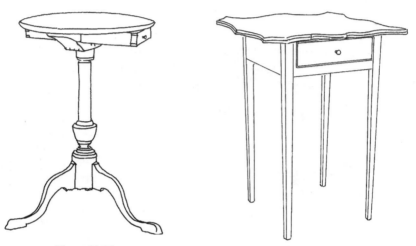

*Figure 19-16*

*Figure 19-17*

*Figure 19-16: Candle drawer stand, c.1780. Another uncommon but charming variation among stands has a small candle drawer worked in under the top. As you might expect, these delightful little stands, whatever their quality or condition, do not come cheaply.*

*Figure 19-17: Federal light stand, 1800 – 1830. With the advent of oil lamps, the instability of the three-leg stand becomes a liability. It is one thing to splatter a little hot wax on the floor, quite another to break a glass lamp full of flammable oil. The solution was a stand with four legs. Such stands, rare before the Revolution, now become very common, so much so that there is hardly an antique shop that does not have a few around. Made in both Hepplewhite and Sheraton styles, they vary from the charming country table shown here to the more formal table in the next illustration. Note that the cabinetmaker has used a little cast brass screw knob in lieu of a drawer pull, a little economy often found in country work.*

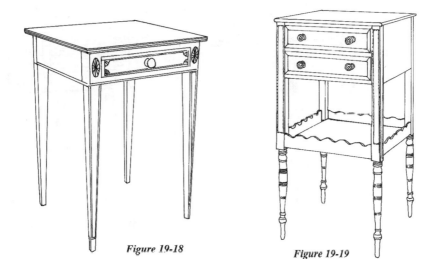

*Figure 19-18*                    *Figure 19-19*

***Figure 19-18:*** *Federal inlaid light stand, c.1810. Here is a larger and better quality light stand with the top, drawer, and legs outlined with stringing, quarter fan inlays at the corners of the drawer, oval patera at the tops of the legs, and a proper drawer pull, in this case one of pressed glass. This amount of decoration is unusual, most four leg stands will be devoid of any more ornamentation than perhaps a little stringing.*

***Figure 19-19:*** *Federal night table, 1810 – 1820. These unusual New England stands are often identified as night tables because the galleried shelf might once have been used to hold a chamber pot. Although not common, they are often reproduced, the shelf being very handy for books and magazines. Any small four leg stand with a hinged opening top or a single deep drawer will most certainly be a night table.*

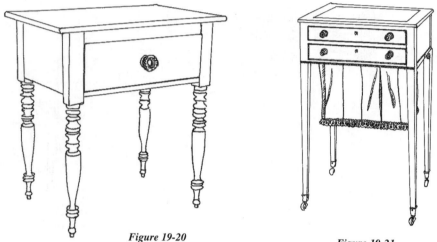

*Figure 19-20*

*Figure 19-21*

**Figure 19-20:** *Classical light stand, c.1830. Light stands continued to be made everywhere well up into the 19th century. In style, most will be country Sheraton like this tiger maple example from Western Pennsylvania or Ohio. Although identified in the auction catalog as a light stand, the deep drawer of this rather heavy table suggests that it may have been intended as a night stand.*

**Figure 19-21:** *Federal Hepplewhite work table, 1790 – 1810. We'll start on work tables with this early Hepplewhite model. The sewing bag will be attached to either the bottom of a simulated lower drawer, or to a separate slide mounted just below the lower drawer. Here the slide moves to the side, so that when pulled out, there is room for one's legs. English work tables are similar in design, but are apt to have a thin platform or delicate X-form stretchers between the legs.*

*Figure 19-22*                                    *Figure 19-23*

*Figure 19-22: Federal Sheraton work table, c.1815. Sheraton tables with fluted legs appear by 1800. Later models, like this Philadelphia table, are apt to be have a pair of small leaves to provide extra work area. Work tables likely this that were fitted with a sewing bag were often called "pouch" tables.*

*Figure 19-23: Federal Sheraton astragal-end work table, 1795 – 1815. Work tables with curved or astragal ends were made from New York south to Maryland. The curved ends open at the top to form bins for scraps and yarn. Because Martha Washington owned one, they are often called Martha Washington tables. In general, New England sewing tables will be either square or have canted corners, New York tables will have canted corners or astragal ends, Philadelphia tables will have astragal ends or be oval, and Baltimore tables will be either oval or square.*

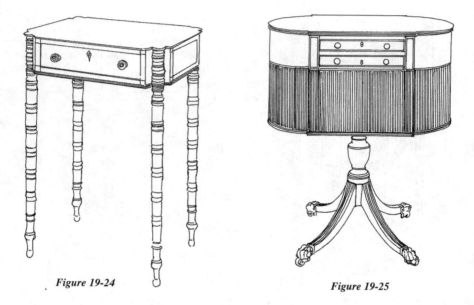

Figure 19-24                                                      Figure 19-25

**Figure 19-24:** *Federal Sheraton cookie-corner work table, c.1810. Sewing tables were also subject to the popular cookie-corner treatment. Note in this fine little one drawer Boston table that the turned legs are set in canted corners so as to not project beyond the sides of the case. Many work tables are missing the sewing pouch, and if there is not a simulated drawer, look under the table to see if there is not a missing slide.*

**Figure 19-25:** *Federal pedestal-base work table, 1800 – 1830. In common with breakfast and card tables, sewing tables also go to pedestal bases at the turn of the century. Fine work tables were also made with lyre and colonette bases. They often have bins on either side, for there is no longer room between the legs for a sewing bag. Note that aside from having four legs, the base of this table is almost identical to the Federal stand we saw earlier (19-13).*

*Figure 19-26*                                   *Figure 19-27*

*Figure 19-26:* New York Federal work table, 1810 – 1830. If this New York sewing table gives you a certain feeling of deja vu, it is for good reason, for we have seen much the same design used in both a New York dressing table (15-21) and in a New York serving table (16-10). Here the lower shelf, so popular in federal New York, was probably intended for a sewing basket.

*Figure 19-27:* Classical work table, 1810 – 1830. As time passes the design of work tables becomes more standardized. This table is typical of the period; a square case flanked by carved or turned columns. These are the last of the period sewing tables. In a sense they also represent the end of another era of handcraftsmanship, for in only a few years Elias Howe will develop the first successful sewing machine.

# Chapter 20

## Beds

In collecting period furniture, you will find that while antique beds are quite common, really early beds are surprisingly rare. While some Pilgrim Century furniture survives, and Colonial chests, tables, and chairs are found everywhere, not many beds predate the Revolution. To keep things in order, we'll start off with a few 18th century examples, but you are not likely to see anything at dealers' shops and auction previews that dates much before the 1790s.

This suggests that the great majority of early beds were so simple that they were discarded as soon as better was available. Probate records indicate that a fully dressed high post bed was the most expensive piece of furniture in the Colonial home. However, most all the cost was in the mattress feathers and in the many yards of hand woven fabric. With a few notable exceptions, the frame seems to have been a simple structure of local woods either painted or stained up to match the other bedroom furniture. After all, it hardly showed. When the hangings became too faded and worn for further use, they went into the rag bag and the inexpensive frame went into the wood box.

The earliest beds you are likely to come across are the elegant pencil-post bed (20-4) used by the master and mistress of the house, and the simple low post bed (20-3) used by everybody else who was fortunate enough not to be sleeping on a straw filled pallet on the floor. Although both designs date from early in the 18th century, most examples postdate the Revolution. When looking at beds, remember that while the old red paint may be 18th century, milk base paints and grain painting are 19th century. In common with other early beds, there are usually no bolts to keep these beds together, the mortise-and-tenon joints of the frame are kept tight by the roping that supports the mattress. This hemp roping was prone to stretch and sag, and had to be periodically tightened with a bed key, which looks very much like an overgrown wooden clothespin with a cross arm at the top to provide leverage. Loose roping did not make for a comfortable bed or a restful night, hence the old admonition, "sleep tight."

About 1790 we first see the modern high post bed with turned, reeded, and carved posts. The foot posts, which are exposed when the bed is stripped to its summer hangings, are made of mahogany and finished in keeping with the rest of the bedroom. Here though, the charming economy of effort in period work is very evident, for the head posts and headboard, which do not show, are left uncarved and continue to be made of local woods. Sometimes the head posts will be just tapered rather than turned. After 1800 we find beds with all the posts finished, but even here the practice seems to have been confined to finer work in the larger cities, for many Classical bedsteads will have unfinished head posts.

By this time beds are fastened with an iron bolt that passes through the post to a nut set into the rail. The head of the bolt is then hidden behind a little swinging brass cover. These bolts were kept tight with an iron bed wrench. Both these wrenches and the old wooden bed keys sometimes turn up at auctions. In 1820 John Hewitt, a New York cabinetmaker, developed a cast iron catch hook to replace the bolts and the mortise-and-tenon joints. The hook was tapered so that weight of the occupants served to force down and tighten the joint. Modern beds are still fastened much this same way.

An old bed is not difficult to assemble from pieces, so we want to be careful that we are buying one bed, and not the leftovers from several others. In the past it was normal

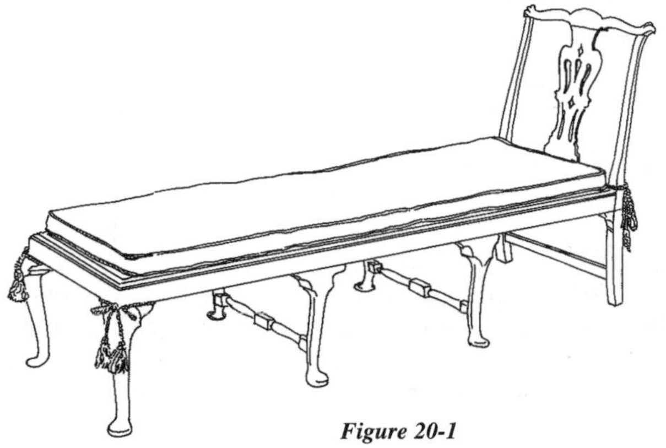

**Figure 20-1**

*Figure 20-1: Chippendale daybed, c.1770. Daybeds were made from the time of Charles II right up through the 18th century before finally going out of style. For all this long history, they are not common among American furniture. They are more comfortable than you might think, for over the cane or canvas bottom was a long feather cushion and at the back several large pillows. On many the back is set between the stiles, and may be lowered on a pair of chains. You can identify the period and estimate the age of a daybed by the back and the legs, for these followed the current styles in chairs. Daybeds seem to have been employed more as couches than as beds, for probate records list them in the parlors of houses.*

practice to number the rails just inside the tenons, and the posts just under the mortises, with pairs of Roman numerals so that the bed would go together the same way each time. On early beds that disassemble into separate posts and rails there will be a sequence of number pairs from I to VIII (that is I - I, II - II, etc.) beside the mortise and the matching tenon. If these numbers do not form a logical sequence, or do not seem to have been made by the same hand, and with the same chisel, something has been changed.

Old beds have often been reworked to keep them up to date, and we want to be careful that the rework is not so extensive as to compromise the quality of the bed. You will frequently see angle irons added to the rails to carry a modern box spring. This is no problem, but then the headboard may have been raised to a more modern height so as to clear the box spring and mattress. Sometimes it will also have been replaced with a finer headboard that will look well behind the pillows. Fortunately, this sort of modification is easy to spot, for there will be a pattern of filled mortise holes on the inside of the head posts. Keep in mind here that the headboard should not be finished if the headposts are not finished.

Often you will see that the rails have been lengthened a bit to provide a longer bed. This should not affect the value of a bed so long as the rails are original. Here you might check that the knobs or holes that carried the roping are the same all the way around, and that they show equal wear. Remember also that the roping exerted an inward force on the rails, and to keep the rails from bowing in, they were made the same width as the posts, either square or perhaps a little thinner in cross section. Only modern rails are deep and thin.

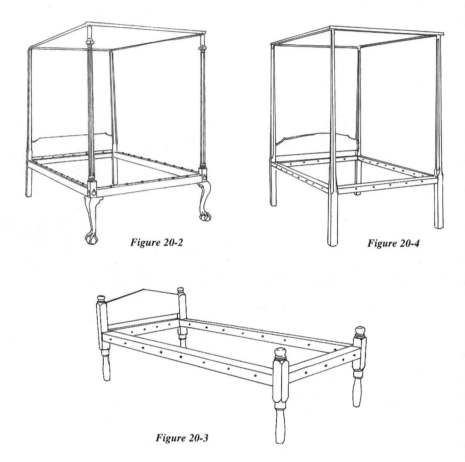

Figure 20-2

Figure 20-4

Figure 20-3

**Figure 20-2:** *Chippendale tester bedstead, c.1770. Chippendale and Queen Anne style mahogany beds with carved posts and cabriole legs are even more rare than daybeds. This fine Boston four-poster is typical of early bedsteads in that while the foot posts are turned, fluted, and given cabriole legs, the headboard is unfinished and head posts are simply tapered and sided.*

**Figure 20-3:** *Low-post bedstead, 18th century. This sort of simple bedstead was made everywhere. The general simplicity of this example suggests that it may be an early bed. Often called hired man's beds, it is thought that the very low posts allowed them to be tucked up under the eaves. More often than not, the roping that carries the mattress is simply passed through holes drilled in the rails. Unlike modern beds, the head and foot of this bed are not units. Remove the roping and the whole bed disassembles into nine separate pieces: four posts, four rails, and the headboard.*

**Figure 20-4:** *Pencil-post bedstead, c.1800. Here is the classic pencil-post design so beloved of collectors. They are a good example of the American preference for lightness and verticality in furniture. Such bedsteads were normally hung with cotton prints or wools that matched the curtains.*

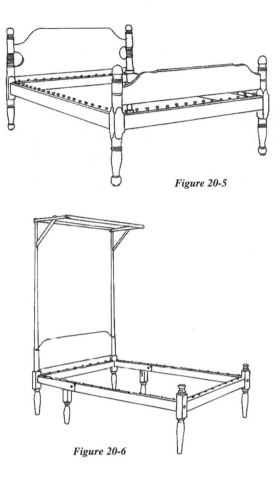

Figure 20-5

Figure 20-6

**Figure 20-5:** *Federal low-post bedstead, c.1820. Later low-post beds become somewhat higher and often acquire footboards. However, they continue to be made of local woods and are invariably painted or perhaps grain painted. This New England bed is better than average quality, for the maker has taken the time and trouble to provide knobs to carry the roping. Here the closeness of the knobs suggests that the roping was used to support a canvas stretcher.*

**Figure 20-6:** *Fold-up bedstead, c.1810. These unusual beds were once far more common than the few surviving examples would indicate. They were known as slaw beds; slaw being a corruption of the 16th century word "slough," which meant clothed. When folded up they were stowed behind curtains hung from the overhead frame, and were, in effect, clothed. The presence of such beds is a reminder to us of how crowded houses once were.*

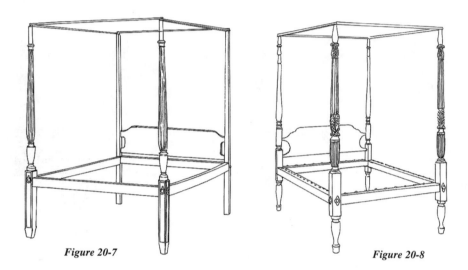

*Figure 20-7*                                          *Figure 20-8*

**Figure 20-7:** *Federal Hepplewhite tester bedstead, 1790 – 1815. Hepplewhite style tall post beds with square or tapering legs are far less common than the Sheraton models which follow within just a few years. You can tell this is a Massachusetts bed by the second taper just below the cuff of the foot posts. Note that by now better quality beds are kept together with bolts, the heads being hidden by neat little swinging brass covers.*

**Figure 20-8:** *Federal Sheraton tester bedstead, 1800 – 1820. The most common tester bed will have these turned Sheraton legs. The head posts will be either squared and tapered, or turned in imitation of the foot posts. In lieu of simple frames to carry the hangings, these beds were sometimes given very fine carved and painted testers.*

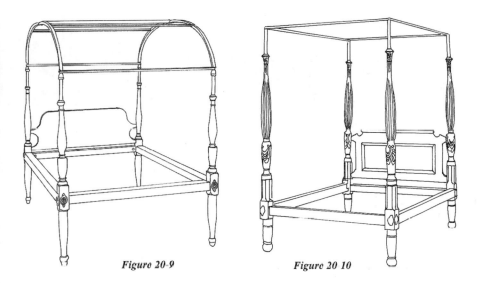

*Figure 20-9*                                    *Figure 20 10*

***Figure 20-9:*** *Federal Sheraton field bedstead, 1800 – 1820. Here is the romantic field or tent bedstead found in thousands of bed and breakfasts. In the past they were considered to be less formal beds for use by children or guests, and were not used in the master bedroom. Original curved testers will be hinged in the middle and may be either the continuous curve shown here, two matching cyma curves, or a low serpentine curve. Should the testers be missing on a four post bed, you can tell something of the original by noting the height of the posts. Beds with arched or serpentine canopies will naturally have shorter posts, while those with straight canopies will have posts six feet or more high.*

***Figure 20-10:*** *Federal mahogany tester bedstead, 1800 – 1820. Fine tester beds, particularly those from Philadelphia, will sometimes have all four posts carved and finished. When this is done the headboard will also be finished.*

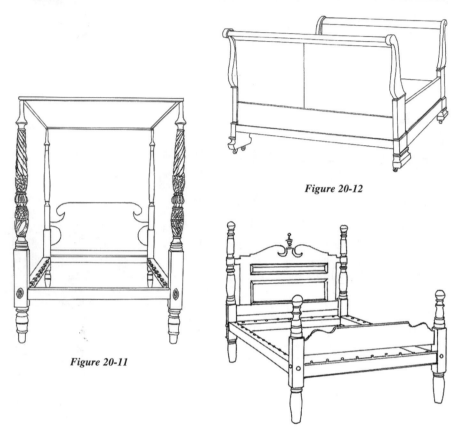

**Figure 20-12**

**Figure 20-11**

**Figure 20-13**

**Figure 20-11:** *Classical tester beadstead, c.1820. With the advent of Classical the posts get heavier and more ornate, the same trend we saw earlier in sideboards and card tables. The spiral carving and the roll-over scroll in the headboard are also very characteristic of this period. Note that although by this time the head posts are likely to be turned, they still may not be carved.*

**Figure 20-12:** *Classical mahogany sleigh bedstead, 1820 – 1840. Sleigh beds, inspired by the Napoleon bed, used to be called French or Grecian beds. Most are typical of later Empire or Classical furniture in being made of great wide sheets of thin mahogany veneer over slabs of pine or poplar. The deep rails have iron hooks that lock into the symmetrical headboard and footboard. These beds will be finished all around, being designed to stand with the side rather than the head against the wall.*

**Figure 20-13:** *Classical low-post bedstead, c.1830. As time passes, the low-post bed gets higher and acquires turned balls or carved pineapples at the top of the posts. Sometimes in lieu of a footboard there will be a raised turned blanket rail. They are by far the most common antique beds.*

**258**

## Mirrors

Although sold by every dealer in American furniture, and found among the lots at every Americana auction, mirrors are the least American of period furniture. A mirror is little more than a decorative frame supporting a piece of reflecting glass, and until the 1790s, the majority of the frames, and all of the glass, is imported. When a Queen Anne or Chippendale mirror is described as "American or English," you can be fairly sure that all or part of it is the latter. Actually, mirrors are not even all that English, for in the past they came from Venice. It was not until 1673, half a century after the Pilgrims landed on Cape Cod, that the first English plate glassworks was set up at Lambeth, just across the Thames from London. Lambeth is close by Vauxhall Gardens, and this glass came to be called Vauxhall glass.

For the next century and a half, most mirror glass, and a great many of the frames, were imported from London. In addition, a large number of inexpensive small mirrors arrived from Northern Europe, particularly from Holland and Denmark. Not until about 1800 do American craftsmen come to dominate the domestic market in mirrors, but even at this time, the glass is imported, for it was not until late in the 19th century that good quality mirror glass was produced in America.

After you have seen a number of mirrors, you will notice that there is a certain commonality in the dimensions. This is because mirror plates were made in standard sizes, 8" x 10", 10" x 14", 12" x 20", 20" x 34", et cetera. Also, the word mirror was not used to describe a mirror that hung on a wall until about the time of the Civil War. Before this time they were called a "looking glass" or a "glass." The word first seems to have been used in connection with the newly fashionable circular girandole mirrors (21-11).

Mirrors are perhaps the easiest period furniture to identify, for not only is the back open to examination, but construction, shrinkage, and patina, both front and back, will tell us of age. First, look at the front. It is common on Queen Anne and Chippendale mirrors to have the glass bordered with a molded cross banding of walnut or mahogany. Shrinkage across the grain of this banding will leave cracks between the individual pieces of veneer. In a similar way, shrinkage of the softwood backing against the hardwood veneered front almost inevitably curves back the crest and the base of the frame. Often the curve is quite pronounced. If the glass is original, in addition to flaws in the mirror, it will not be truly flat, and if you move a bit you will see that your image is distorted. On better mirrors, particularly those of the Queen Anne period, it was customary to bevel the edges of the mirror. Because old glass is fairly thin, these bevels will be narrow and shallow, and if you run your finger along the bevel you will feel the irregularities of the hand grinding.

In the past, gilding was always done on a base of gessoed wood. The part to be gilded, perhaps a phoenix or a shell, would first be carved out of soft wood, then covered with thin layers of a plaster and glue mix called gesso until there was an absolutely smooth surface on which to lay the wafer thin gold leaf. The last coat of gesso would be given some color to help the gilding, for gold leaf is so thin as to be almost transparent.

About 1790, mirror makers began to replace gessoed wood with a molded composition of hide glue and whiting. Only the crest, such as the urn shown on the mirror in Figure 21-7, continued to be carved and gilded. When you see a little gilded bird on a late Chippendale mirror, it will usually be done on this inexpensive molded base. This later gave way to plaster of Paris, and if you see gilding done this way, you are looking a relatively modern product.

Look at the back and you will see rough, unfinished backboards and two centuries and more of dust, dirt, and smoke from fires. Sometimes the back will be almost black, particularly if the mirror is from England where soft coal has been used in fireplaces since the 17th century. Except on the smallest mirrors, the crest and the base are likely to be stiffened with short pieces of wood. When there is a gilded carving in the crest, you will often see that it has been worked out of a separate block of soft wood and then inserted into the crest. Usually this carving will extend beyond the face of the crest, providing a three-dimensional effect not seen in Colonial Revival reproductions. On many mirrors the cord or wire that supported the mirror was passed through small holes drilled through the frame of the mirror. Even if now fitted with modern steel eyes and picture wire, there will still be the old holes in the frame. If you can see under the backboard, note that the mirror is held in place, well clear of the backboard, by small glue blocks around the edge of the frame.

While looking at the back, see if there is a label, or perhaps the remains of a label. Mirrors were sold everywhere, and often carry the name and address of the maker, the distributor, or the importer. Aside from clocks, which might be considered a special case, mirrors are by far the most commonly labeled period furniture. By use of these labels and associated newspaper advertisements, researchers have identified well over a hundred firms that sold mirrors up and down the Eastern seaboard. (See *Antiques Magazine*, May 1981, "Check List of Looking-glass and Frame Makers and Merchants Known by Their Labels" by Betty Ring). Perhaps the best known are the Elliott family of Philadelphia, of whom three generations sold drugs, artists supplies, and looking-glasses between 1753 and 1809. Those engaged in the manufacture of mirrors often advertised themselves as "carvers, gilders, and frame makers" in addition to looking-glass makers, and their labels are also found on the backs of framed samplers and framed mourning embroidery. This suggests a business environment not too unlike a modern frame shop, which may be why so many inexpensive Chippendale mirrors appear to be little more than a picture frame that has been given a crest, a skirt, and some ears.

Old mirrors have a variety of problems, not the least of which is the very real likelihood of having been dropped at some time. Fortunately, it is not hard to spot repairs. All we need to do is to look carefully at the back. This should always be done — no matter how good a mirror looks from the front. A good veneer patch can be difficult to detect, but a new ear on a Chippendale mirror will usually show if we take a careful look at the back; usually, because a really good restorer can do wonders to disguise a new ear. Here you will often see differences in patination that indicate some of the little pieces of wood used to stiffen the crest and base are missing. Sometimes you will also find that the old backboards have been replaced with a piece of plywood.

With the advent of inexpensive mirror glass in the 1880s, many old mirrors began to get new glass. However, even at this time mirroring did not hold up very well, and today many of these early replacements look far older than they actually are.

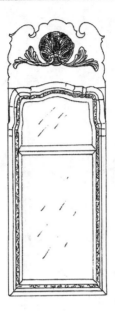

*Figure 21-1*

*Figure 21-1: Queen Anne mirror, 1720 – 1780. Mirrors from the William and Mary period are so seldom found on the market that we will start instead with Queen Anne. The typical Queen Anne mirror is tall and narrow with a scalloped crest, often with a gilded shell or leaf centered in the crest. The crest is a separate piece, and because it was just butted to the top of the frame and secured with glue blocks, it is all too common to find these old mirrors with the crest missing. Early Queen Anne mirrors will be walnut veneered, and the mirror will be divided into two beveled panels, because at this time it was difficult to make large sheets of glass. Sometimes there will be a design cut into the upper panel. Later Queen Anne style mirrors are likely to employ mahogany veneer and have a single piece of glass, similar to the Chippendale designs that follow.*

Because they had a limited life, mirrors from this period often carry a stamped date, apparently to deter customers from demanding replacement of a somewhat deteriorated mirror that had actually been installed many years before.

It was not until about the middle of this century that dealers and collectors realized that the price they were paying in replacing the glass was far more than just the small cost of new glass, for they were losing much that was original in an old mirror. Although many now belittle replaced glass, resilvering an old mirror is very difficult, and I suspect that many were in such poor shape that replacing the glass was felt to be a justified improvement. Sometimes the old mirror is saved. Should you come across a mirror that seems to be very heavy, and it is not because the mirror has been incorrectly restored with a piece of heavy plate glass, the original mirror may be resting behind the new glass.

*Figure 21-2*          *Figure 21-3*

**Figure 21-2:** *Chippendale parcel gilt mirror, 1750 – 1770. These grand big architectural mirrors used to be called Constitution mirrors, even though they antedate our Constitution by at least two decades. Most American examples were made in Philadelphia, where this sort of Georgian formality was very much in style. The skinny bird at the top is a phoenix, a motif that may have been more significant in a time when cities were subject to major fires and not infrequently "rising from the ashes." If you are able to identifying the woods used in the frame, you can determine where such mirror was made, for if the frame and backboard are spruce, or spruce and pine, then the mirror is probably English, and if entirely pine, or perhaps pine and poplar, then probably American. Although predating the Revolution, these handsome mirrors were a popular Colonial Revival reproduction, often being given a patriotic eagle in lieu of a phoenix, even though the eagle was not adopted as our national bird until 1782.*

**Figure 21-3:** *Chippendale mahogany and gilt mirror, 1760 – 1780. This is the standard form of English Chippendale mirror. These mirrors were immensely popular in the 18th century, and can be found in most antique shops. The pierced splats on Chippendale chairs and the scrolled crest, base, and ears of these handsome mirrors are the most common examples of Rococo style among the average grade of furniture. As you would expect, the ears are somewhat fragile, and here we should always check for repairs. While some early versions of these mirrors are veneered in walnut, the great majority will be mahogany veneered over pine or spruce. This example has a gilt shell in the crest, but you will often see a leaf or a phoenix used instead. Note that the mirror is surrounded by a gilt border and molded crossbanding, and that the upper corners of the border are curved.*

Figure 21-5

Figure 21-6

Figure 21-4

**Figure 21-4:** *Northern European gilt mirror, 1770 – 1800. Not all mirrors sold in America were English. In addition to some from Spain, a great many were brought over from Northern Europe, particularly from Sweden and Holland. Although Rococo in style, most seem to have been imported in the years following the Revolution. While they vary somewhat in size and decoration, almost all are similar to this example, being of walnut veneer and having square frames, tall crests, short bases, and some applied gilt Rococo ornamentation on both the crest and the base.*

**Figure 21-5:** *Chippendale mahogany mirror, c.1805. Later and less expensive versions of the popular Chippendale mirror continued to be made right up into the 19th century. Although still Chippendale in style, the rectangular frame with mitered corners is more Neoclassical than Rococo. A number of these mirrors carry the label of John Elliott & Sons of Philadelphia. By this time the gilt border is gone and the crest will be devoid of any ornamentation except perhaps an inlayed shell or a rather sad little composition bird.*

**Figure 21-6:** *Chippendale mahogany and giltwood mirror, c.1770. Before leaving Chippendale and Rococo, we might see what could be done for the customer who wished to spend some extra money for a better mirror. If you look back a few figures, you'll see that this majestic mirror is little more than the standard Chippendale mirror that has been enhanced with a raised giltwood phoenix, giltwood acanthus leaves on the crest, and then giltwood leaf filets down the sides.*

Figure 21-8

Figure 21-9

Figure 21-7

**Figure 21-7:** *Federal mahogany and parcel gilt mirror, 1790 – 1810. These large high style Federal mirrors would seem at first glance to be just another Chippendale form, but they have acquired Classical features and are lighter in feeling — far more Hepplewhite than Chippendale. Note the square gilt border, the inlayed shell in the tympanium, and the urn and wheat stalks above — all Neoclassical features. Occasionally there will be an eglomise panel above the mirror. Only the scrolled skirt and lower pair of ears survive to remind us of the now vanished Rococo. These mirrors were made in all the larger cities, especially in New York. As one of the first American-made mirrors, they were reproduced during the Colonial Revival that followed the American Centennial. Although by now such reproductions may look quite old, they should exhibit a lack of patination, wear, and repairs. Also, the upper corners of the frame will employ a miter joint reinforced with a spline rather than the lap joint used on the larger period mirrors.*

**Figure 21-8:** *Federal gilded filigree mirror, 1800 – 1825. Hepplewhite gilt filigree mirrors are about as close as we get to the Adam style in American furniture. Never common, very few of these light, delicate they have survived with their flowers and leaves intact. By this time molded composition is used as a base for much of the gilded decoration. The same type of mirror is also found in an oval shape.*

**Figure 21-9:** *Federal giltwood and églomisé mirror, 1800 – 1825. These gilt "tabernacle" mirrors are the most numerous of the many surviving Federal mirrors. They are also called "pediment" or*

*Figure 21-10*

"pillar" mirrors. The pillars on each side are actually gilded hollow colonnettes inset with a twist. A single pillar with a single twist is most common, but sometimes you will see a pair of pillars. Although these mirrors are very common, you will find that it takes some looking to find one with the original gilding and an unrestored tablet. It is not too difficult to tell a restored tablet, for not only will inpainting show, but the original is characterized by very fine brushwork that restorers seldom seem to get just right. Églomisé is a French term for a reverse painted glass tablet that is set into a piece of furniture. There are a wonderful variety of charming subjects on these tablets: landscapes, children or family groups, baskets of flowers, a naval engagement, an eagle, or some other patriotic symbol. The naval engagement will either commemorate the short naval war with France, or the following War of 1812 with England. If the ships have three masts, it may be the encounter between the Constitution and the Guerriere, or maybe the Constellation and the L'Insurgente; and if two masts, perhaps the Enterprise and the Boxer. Although a very Federal design, not all these mirrors are American, for similar mirrors we made in England.

*Figure 21-10:* Federal giltwood overmantel mirror, 1790 – 1830. Overmantel mirrors or "chimney glasses" date to Queen Anne, but are not found in America in any quantity until after the Revolution. They were made in a variety of styles, the most common being the three panel, four column configuration shown here. Fine Federal examples are often decorated with eglomise tablets. Overmantel mirrors continued in popularity through the 19th century, and you will find many Classical or Empire models with the split baluster turnings so common to this period.

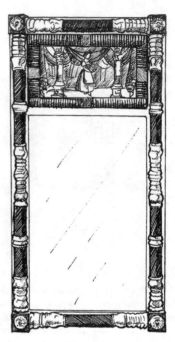

*Figure 21-11*

*Figure 21-12*

***Figure 21-11:*** *Girandole giltwood mirror, 1800 – 1830. English glass makers discovered the technique of making convex glass about 1790, and within a few years these circular convex mirrors were being made everywhere. Similar mirrors were made in Boston, New York, and Philadelphia. In spite of the very patriotic eagle, a great many, perhaps most, are English or French rather than American. They are usually called girandole mirrors, although this French term actually refers just to mirrors with attached candlearms.*

***Figure 21-12:*** *Classical mirror, 1820 – 1840. These Classical or Empire mirrors are frequently found in smaller antique shops. This is a nice example with a painted eglomise tablet at the top. The split baluster turnings and the corner rosettes are very characteristic of this period. In the next chapter we will see the same decoration on an Empire pillar and scroll clock. When the half round pilasters are gilded, the vase or cylinder sections will usually be painted black.*

Figure 21-13                                    Figure 21-14

**Figure 21-13:** *Country Queen Anne mirror. Unlike most period furniture, mirrors of the same style could be had in all sizes from grand big pier glasses to the charming little country Queen Anne and Chippendale mirrors shown in this and the next illustration. These two are not dated, for this sort of simple mirror was made for such an extended period that it would be difficult to say if a given example was 18th century or 19th century. If the original brads fastening the backboard still remain in place, see if they are the early hand wrought nails, or the cut nails which came into use about the turn of the century.*

**Figure 21-14:** *Country Chippendale mirror. Like their Queen Anne counterparts, these popular little Chippendale mirrors were made well up into the 19th century. Some examples carry the label of James Todd of Portland, Maine, the label itself illustrating a Classical mirror from the 1820s. Note that both these small mirrors lack the integrated design found in earlier Chippendale designs. They are just simple frames with a crest, a base, and some ears tacked on.*

Figure 21-15                                        Figure 21-16

**Figure 21-15:** *Courting mirror, 1790 – 1830. These charming little boxed mirrors were given to young women by their suitors. For some reason, both mirror and box were then hung on the wall, perhaps because this would protect the rather fragile mirror until it was moved to a new home. Whatever the reason, they are often found still mounted in their original boxes; and if you are very lucky, still with the original cover. While made everywhere, the majority appear to have been imported from Holland. Like tabernacle mirrors, they are common, but fragile and difficult to find in good condition.*

**Figure 21-16:** *Federal dressing mirror, 1790 – 1810. While dressing or shaving mirrors date to the early years of the 18th century, Colonial examples are not common. After the Revolution, though, they became popular, and it is not hard to find a Federal example. Most have just a rectangular mirror above a simple, square mahogany veneered case; better will have bowfront or serpentine cases, figured maple or satinwood veneer, and oval or shield-shaped mirrors. In the past these charming little mirrors were often called "swingers."*

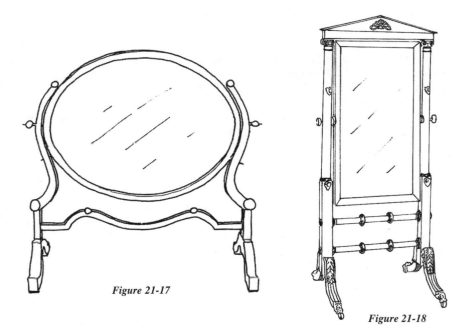

*Figure 21-17*

*Figure 21-18*

**Figure 21-17:** *Federal shaving mirror, c.1810. Far less common are these elegant little shaving mirrors, perhaps because not as many have survived intact. If you come across a small mirror with a pair of mysterious holes just above the midpoint of the sides, you may be looking at a shaving or a dressing mirror that has become separated from its stand. A larger mirror with the same pair of holes will likely be from the back of a chest of drawers.*

**Figure 21-18:** *Federal cheval mirror, 1820 – 1850. Screen dressing glasses or cheval mirrors first appear in the 1820s, but are rare in America until the middle of the century. The supporting frame resembles a sawhorse, and hence cheval — the French word for horse.*

# Chapter 22

## Clocks and Barometers

### Clocks

Because our collecting is likely to result in acquiring an old clock, and perhaps also a barometer, these two forms deserve more than just a passing mention. Actually, clocks and barometers deserve far more than just this short chapter, for quite apart from their significant presence among the decorative arts, they have a long and interesting scientific and technological history of their own. Of necessity, this chapter must cover a lot of ground rather briefly, concentrating on the more common American clocks found in shops and at auctions. It is a light treatment of a complex subject, and if you are planning to add a clock or barometer to your collection, you would do well to learn more before entering the market.

Clocks have a mechanical aspect not often encountered in furniture, and as this has a major bearing on their design, we might discuss this first. The first mechanical clocks were developed in Europe at the close of the 13th century, and within a hundred years all the larger cities had clock towers. These early clocks kept very poor time, and but for the strike, were little better than a sundial. However, once the basic mechanism of a slowly released gear train had been developed, attention turned to improving accuracy. For a clock to be accurate there must be an even motive force throughout the period of operation and a precise escapement to release the gear train at a constant rate. The first is not difficult, simply a weight attached to a rope wrapped around a drum. So long as the drum is of constant diameter, the force on the gear train will be exactly the same whether the clock has just been wound up or is almost run down. The second was not resolved until Galileo noticed that a pendulum of a given length swung at a constant rate whatever the arc of the swing. Christiaan Huygens, a Dutch mathematician and physicist, realized that this would provide the perfect escapement, and developed the first pendulum clock on or about 1656. These early pendulum clocks had a verge escapement that swung a 10" half second pendulum. They were not all that accurate, for the short bob pendulum swung through an arc of about 50 degrees, which introduces a slight change in the period known as circular error. In spite of this deviation, these early clocks were accurate to within several minutes a day, quite good enough to justify the addition of a minute hand. Then, in 1671, Dr. Robert Hooke devised the anchor escapement which allowed the use of a 39" one second pendulum that swung through a small precise arc. This gave us the first really accurate clock. Within 15 years the accuracy of clocks went from a few minutes per day to a few seconds per month. It was a remarkable development.

The long pendulum then led to a tall case that would protect it and hide the weights. All that remained was some means of assuring that the strike always stayed in sync with the time (i.e., that the clock did not strike two when the hour hand said three), and this was solved five years later by Dr. Edward Barlow's invention of the rack strike. Within a few years English craftsmen not only developed the first accurate clock, they devised clocks that chimed tunes, that ran for a month or for a year on one wind, and even a few that employed a 61" one and a quarter second pendulum.

English clockmakers also turned their attention to improving the bracket or table clock. Here the 10" half second bob pendulum and verge escapement were retained, the latter because the far more accurate anchor escapement is very sensitive to level. However, the major problem with bracket clocks is not the escapement but the motive power, for the steel springs of this period could not provide even power. As they unwound, their power steadily diminished, and the clock went slower. This problem was solved, or at least greatly mitigated, by the introduction of the fusee, a spirally grooved, conical pulley with a tiny chain that wound around the drum that holds the spring. As the spring winds down, the chain slowly spirals down the increasing diameter of the conical pulley, increasing leverage on the drive train to compensate for the decreasing power of the spring. The fusee did much to improve the accuracy of spring powered clocks, but at the price of much additional cost and complication, and American bracket clocks are a great rarity. For all this trouble the fusee had a long history, not being discarded in England until high quality steel springs were finally developed in the 1850s.

These early years of intensive development, from about 1660 to 1700, were the golden age of English clockmaking; the time of Daniel Quare, Thomas Tompion, and Joseph Knibb. If you have the money you can own one of these beautiful little William and Mary period clocks. America was also to have a golden age of clockmaking, but as we shall see, not for another 100 years.

Before going further, we should note that a grandfather clock is properly called a long-case or a tall-case clock; long-case when in England, tall-case when in America. They came to be called grandfather clocks after Henry Clay Work wrote a popular sentimental song about "Grandfather's Clock" in 1876. Although not very descriptive, the name is now so universally used to describe these clocks that dealers should not scorn you if you use the term.

Relatively few tall-case clocks were produced in America until after the Revolution. While thousands were being made in England, not many seem to have been made in America; perhaps not so much because of the mercantile system as because there was less demand for accurate time in a largely agrarian society. Although the Colonies had a population of about 4 million by the time of the Revolution, there are only 67 known clockmakers prior to 1775, and many of these appear to have made only a handful of movements. To add to the uncertainties of this period, there is one of identification, for clock making was a specialized industry, and in addition to obtaining gears, pulleys, dials, and hands from suppliers, the clockmaker could purchase complete works and just add his name to the dial. Although not common, and sometimes of questionable ancestry, American pre-Revolutionary clocks are generally of good quality, as though purchased by people who could afford the best.

Not until after the return of peace did American clockmakers really set to work. Production initially centered on tall-case clocks with eight-day brass works. The best known makers from this period are the famous Willard family in Massachusetts, although equally fine clocks were made all over the country. This is when we see the introduction of the elegant narrow-waisted Roxbury type cases so typical of Boston area clocks (22-8). These clocks first had the engraved and silvered brass

271

dials that American clockmakers started to use in the 1760s, then starting about 1785, less costly and easier to read painted iron dials. Prior to this time, clock dials employed a built up construction in which a silvered chapter ring and brass corner spandrels were pinned to a brass dial. Chapter is an old name for Roman numerals, so a chapter ring is just a Roman numeral ring. Some English makers turned to high quality enameled dials in the 1780s, but Americans, even on good work, preferred painted iron, probably because they were easier to make. A great many, perhaps the majority, of these painted dials were imported, and you will sometimes find the name of a Birmingham manufacturer on the back. If not a part of the order, the clockmaker might then add his name to the dial, which is why you will see dials in which the clockmaker's name is obviously a later addition.

About the same time that painted iron dials were introduced, we begin to see budget dials that are either just painted on a thin board, or are printed on paper which is then glued to a thin board. These are usually found on American clocks with inexpensive 30 hour wooden works.

The design and construction of the dial tell us a lot about the source and age of a tall-case clock. We know that:

• While clocks with built up dials continued to be made into the 1790s, most predate the Revolution, and thus, are very likely to be English.
• A tall-case clock with an enameled dial will not be earlier than 1780, and will almost certainly be English.
• A clock with a brass dial, or perhaps a silvered brass dial, in which both the chapter ring and the corner spandrels are engraved directly on the plate, will be American, and will date between 1760 and 1790.
• A clock with a painted dial will not be earlier than about 1785, and may be either English or American.
• A clock with a wood or paper dial will probably date from the early 19th century, will probably have 30 hour wooden works, and will almost certainly be American.

The other features of tall-case clocks are not as helpful in determining source and age, for as we will see in the illustrations, case styles tend to lag furniture styles, and there is much similarity between English and American cases. Also, the basic design of the eight-day brass movement hardly changed at all between 1720 and 1840.

Coincident with these improvements and economies in tall-case design, Massachusetts clockmakers developed an entirely new form of shelf or bracket clock, one that required only one third the amount of brass and avoided the use of a steel spring and the attendant fusee (22-12). This was done by reducing the size and thickness of the works, then giving the clock a deep base that would house the pendulum and the drive weight. At first these clocks only ran for one to three days, but soon the design was refined and clockmakers were turning out eight-day models. Look at these handsome little clocks and you will notice they resemble an English bracket clock sitting on a box, which is logical, for they were basically just an inexpensive substitute.

Then, in 1802, Simon Willard applied for a patent on a new form of clock housed in what we call a banjo case (22-13). Many people think that Simon Willard invented the banjo clock, but this is not true, banjo case clocks were already being made in England. What the patent covered were a number of mechanical improvements, the most notable being an accurate pendulum that hung in front of the weight where it could easily be started by opening the tablet door at the bottom of the case. Normally there will be a little window in the églomisé painting so that the movement of pendulum is visible behind the glass tablet. These fine little eight-day clocks were an instant success, and in spite of the patent, were not only copied by other clockmakers in Boston, but were also made in New York, Philadelphia, and Baltimore. Not all this activity was illegal, for Mr. Willard licensed the manufacture of his wonderful clock. In common with the shelf clock, most banjos are technically timepieces rather than clocks, for they have no striking movement. Only a few of the later models have what is correctly termed a time and strike movement.

Clocks with wooden works had been made in America since the 1750s, but now the demand for less expensive timepieces, and the embargoes that preceded the War of 1812, turned clockmakers again to wood, for here was a raw material that America had in abundance. Quite the best known and most successful of these clockmakers was Eli Terry, who started his remarkable career as a maker of conventional tall-case clocks before turning to wood — and to mass production. His principle innovation was to employ water powered machinery to mass produce clock parts. After a couple of pilot runs, in 1807 he contracted to supply four thousand 30 hour tall-case movements with dials and hands. The first thousand were produced within a year and the rest soon followed. These movements were shipped all over the country, and used either as uncased "wag on the wall" clocks, or had simple cases made by a local cabinetmaker.

Mr. Terry then turned to the design of smaller wooden movements which could be used in a shelf or mantle clock, and in 1814 invented the famous pillar and scroll clock (22-18). These handsome mahogany cased clocks had 30 hour wooden time and strike movements. Just as we saw in Windsor chairs, different kinds of woods were used for different components; cherry for the wheels, laurel for the pinions, and oak for the plates. To avoid a high case, the winding chords were passed over pulleys set in the top of the case, allowing the time and strike weights to fall the full length of the case. The pillar and scroll clock, like the banjo before it, was a complete and perfect design from the very start, and although made for the next two decades, it was never significantly improved. They also were made by everyone and sold just about everywhere. Most of those you come across were not made by Eli Terry, although they may very well have a Terry movement.

With this change from brass to wood came a shift in manufacturing from Massachusetts to Connecticut. Massachusetts would continue making quality clocks, but Connecticut would turn out a great many more inexpensive ones. However, the wooden movement which initiated this shift proved to have a short life, for no amount of Yankee ingenuity could overcome the inherent limitations of the material. Even with good upkeep, a spell of damp weather was apt to give trouble. The solution was a return to brass, but this time in a new way. By happy coincidence, Connecticut was also the center of the brass industry, and by the 1830s improvements in manufacturing permitted plates and gears to be stamped out of rolled sheet brass. The final cam fell into place when Joseph Shaylor Ives developed the brass clock spring in 1836. Now it was possible to mass produce a reliable spring driven clock that could be shipped anywhere. Within a few years these inexpensive 30 hour brass clocks were being turned out by the thousands. They could be shipped anywhere — to the ruin of English clockmakers.

With this background, let's now consider what we need to watch for and be careful about, for in common with old furniture, many years of use and a considerable measure of standardization has led to a lot of modified and married clocks. When examining a tall-case clock, always ask yourself two questions: has the case been shortened, and are the works original to the case? When a clock is too tall for a room, the simplest solution is to remove the center finial, and if this is not enough, then perhaps the fretwork crest, or perhaps the feet. A more subtle and far more damaging solution is to take the whole case apart and shorten the waist. Fortunately, later restoration of the feet and the crest is not that hard to spot, and a shortened waist will show if you can get a good light on the inside of the case. Here also is where a lot of looking will help, for a case that has been shortened will be out of proportion. Something should not seem quite right.

Before lifting off the hood to examine the movement, see if the door frame matches the dial. If the outline of the dial does not quite match the outline of the door opening, or the dial seems to be set back a little, you may be looking at a dial from another clock. Then slide off the hood and take a close look at the seat or saddle board. This is the piece of wood that rests on the top of the case and supports the clock movement. It is the interface between the movement and the case. If other works have been fitted into the case, the seat board will almost surely be modified to some extent. If it looks new, or has been cut down, or has a couple of mysterious extra holes, the works may be from another clock. Unlike furniture, marriages are not just limited to clocks from the same area, for by the 1720s both the mechanism itself and the size and general shape of dials were pretty much standardized, so much so that even period need not match. There is no reason why English clockworks of 1760 could not find themselves in a much later Federal case. This may not be in the least fraudulent, the case may have been made in the early 19th century to replace a very tired and out of fashion English case.

When looking at the works, take a look at the bearings visible on the back plate. Some may have been rebushed, which is to be expected. What you want to watch for, though, is the unfortunate practice of correcting wear by use of a steel punch to mash the worn bearing holes back into round. While here, also check the plate that supports the dial. If the dial has been exchanged, this plate may show the extra or elongated holes that were required to match the feet of the new dial. It is quite possible to have a tall-case clock in which the case, the works, and the dial all come from different sources.

Banjo clocks have their own set of problems, principally due to a rather delicate case and their long popularity as one of the first truly American clocks. The net result has been a half century and more of careful repair, restoration, and reconstruction, in addition to other less honest improvements. With time this work has gently melded into the original so that it is not all that easy to spot a rebuilt or modified banjo. When scenes on the glass tablet from the War of 1812 became popular, an amazing number of naval battles and single ship actions appeared on the market. Another popular improvement was to add "S. Willard, Patent" to dials, even though many such signatures had already been used by Mr. Willard's apprentices.

The reverse painted tablets and door panels on banjo and pillar and scroll clocks are inherently fragile, for if the thin glass does not get broken, the painting will tend flake off. Probably the majority of doors and tablets, if not replaced outright, have acquired some inpainting over the years. Therefore, we always want to take a close look at the tablets. Even if they look right, be sure to examine the back for signs of inpainting. Original églomisé was done by professionals, and in common with old inlay, will be of high quality. Do not be dismayed if some of the painting has flaked off, so long as enough remains to provide a clear picture of the original, for églomisé restoration has become a trade, and if you decide restoration is appropriate, there are specialists who can do very fine inpainting.

Adding the maker's name to a clock was an additional cost, particularly if the work had to contracted out to an engraver or painter. As a result, there are many unsigned clocks. Now while a signed clock is more desirable than an unsigned clock, and one with a matching label on the inside of the case is far better yet, do not scorn the lack of a signature. There are many good quality unsigned clocks, so consider first the condition of the works and the quality of the case. In a market with precious few bargains, a well made but unsigned clock can be a very good buy.

Of necessity, the following survey is very much incomplete in that it must stop about 1830 with the introduction of factory production and before the virtual explosion of types and forms following the introduction of stamped brass works. Thus the reader will see none of the wagon spring, ogee, steeple, and acorn clocks so beloved by the collector of American clocks. This whole fascinating period is best left to other books on the subject.

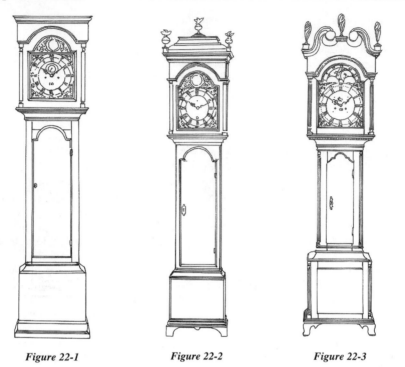

Figure 22-1          Figure 22-2          Figure 22-3

**Figure 22-1:** *Flat top tall-case clock, c.1750. These simple tall-case clocks are about the earliest American clocks you will find on the market. They are a holdover from the William and Mary style of the 1680s, but with the break arch that appeared at the turn of the 17th century. This feature, common by 1720, allowed the clockmaker a semicircle in which to display the phases of the moon, rocking boats, Father Time, and a host of other clever and inventive objects. The arched or tombstone door in the waist is associated with the Queen Anne style, and this clock would probably be identified this way in an auction catalog. While a flat top case may seem very old, it is no more than an indication of early work, for this simple form continues to be used in rural work right up into the 19th century.*

**Figure 22-2:** *Bell top tall-case clock, 1740 – 1780. Bell top cases are another stylistic holdover, but this time from Queen Anne, as this form of hood was popular in England in the early years of the 18th century. These grand and rare clocks are not typical of any one region, but were made just about everywhere, in the Boston area, in Connecticut, and in and around Philadelphia. The large extended hood, while imposing, makes for a very tall clock, which perhaps has contributed to their rarity.*

**Figure 22-3:** *Pennsylvania tall-case clock, 1770 – 1820. Clocks with a bold swan's-neck pediment are typical of Philadelphia and Eastern Pennsylvania. The further from Philadelphia, the more extravagant the pediment. As you might expect, many of these large, handsome clocks have quarter columns flanking the waist section. Similar clocks were made in all the middle Atlantic states, usually of walnut, cherry, or figured maple. Note that although this clock has a painted iron dial and is very probably Federal rather than Colonial, the case with its double arch door and ogee bracket feet would be considered Chippendale or Rococo in style.*

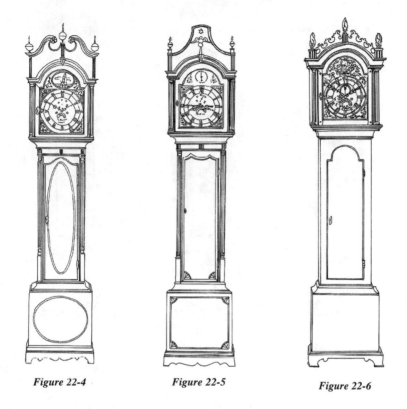

*Figure 22-4*       *Figure 22-5*       *Figure 22-6*

**Figure 22-4:** *New Jersey tall-case clock, 1800 – 1820. New Jersey Federal tall-case clocks are characterized by the use of fine mahogany veeners, often with an ellipse in the door and a circle in the box base. Note that the swan's-neck pediment is more restrained than in the previous Philadelphia example. Almost identical clocks were made just across the Hudson in New York City. Although this clock is superficially similar to the previous illustration, the slender case, the square door, and the inlayed ellipse and circle tell us that the case is Neoclassical rather than Rococo. In many ways it is similar to the transition we saw earlier between the Chippendale parcel gilt mirror and the Neoclassical parcel gilt mirror.*

**Figure 22-5:** *New York tall-case clock, 1790 – 1810. Another type popular in the New York City area is this rather formal clock with hollowed pediment hood. As you might expect of New York City work, the hollowed pediment is also common among English clocks. Note that with the advent of Neoclassicism, the waist door no longer has a Queen Anne arch.*

**Figure 22-6:** *Connecticut tall-case clock, c.1780. The idiosyncratic character of Connecticut cabinetmaking carries over into clock cases, and here we are apt to see this charming "whale's tail" fretwork on the hood. Because Connecticut was situated between the two major style centers of Boston and Philadelphia, we will also see Philadelphia swan's-neck and Boston fretwork hoods in Connecticut clocks. However, most all the cases will be made of cherry.*

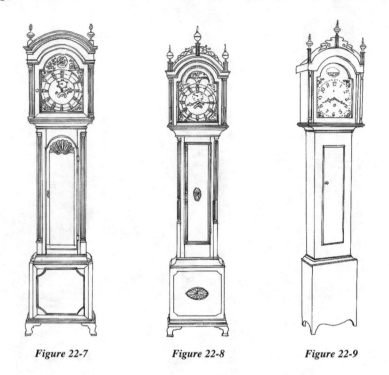

Figure 22-7            Figure 22-8            Figure 22-9

*Figure 22-7:* Rhode Island tall-case clock, c.1780. If you see a fine mahogany clock with a conserv-ative arched hood, and then an arched waist door with perhaps a carved shell at the top of the door, you will be looking at Rhode Island work. Not all Rhode Island clocks exhibit this Newport penchant for the Queen Anne style; other Rhode Island cases have more conventional swan's-neck or fretwork hoods, but unlike Connecticut, will be made of mahogany.

*Figure 22-8:* Massachusetts tall-case clock, 1790 – 1810. This is the well known tall-case clock made by Simon Willard, his brothers, his son, and many others throughout New England. In addition to generally fine workmanship, they are most distinguished by the beautiful tall, slender "Roxbury" type cases. If you compare this with the previous illustration, you will see the case is actually a Neoclassic interpretation of the basic Queen Anne design, being lighter and slimmer, having a square inlayed rather than an arched door, and then with some fretwork and a central finial on the hood to add a touch of lightness and verti-cality. Better work will see the quarter columns stop fluted with strips of brass. Simon Willard, and many others, had their cases made by a group of clock case makers in the town of Roxbury, now a part Boston. As much as the clockmakers themselves, they should have credit for these lovely New England clocks.

*Figure 22-9:* Country tall-case clock, c.1820. Many of the 30 hour wooden works made by Eli Terry ended up in this sort of simple country clock. Open the door and you will see the small weights and the chain pull up wind used by 30 hour clocks. The cases are usually grain painted to resemble mahogany, and to complete the happy illusion, there will often be a couple of fake winding holes on the dial. Sometimes the case will postdate the works by a few years, the clock having started out as

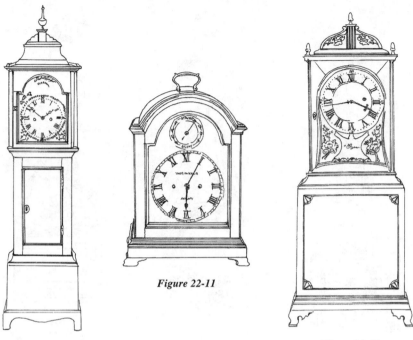

Figure 22-11

Figure 22-10

Figure 22-12

an even more simple wag on the wall clock. Although this is the last full size tall-case clock in our survey, it should be noted that the production of tall-case clocks with brass works continued in rural areas right up into the 1840s. The 8-day movements will be housed in a simple case of local woods. These were usually painted, although a great many have now been stripped and given a clear finish.

**Figure 22-10:** Dwarf tall-case clock, c.1815. Dwarf tall-case clocks that actually started life as dwarf tall-case clocks are rare and far more expensive than their often simple cases would suggest. In spite of their charm, they are difficult to case and are rarely well proportioned. A great many were made by Joshua Wilder of Hingham, Massachusetts, who seems to have specialized in these diminutive tall-case clocks.

**Figure 22-11:** Bracket clock, c.1815. American bracket clocks, like this example from Philadelphia, are very rare, and to this day it is not clear if these few were actually made in this country or simply imported with the name of the American distributor on the dial.

**Figure 22-12:** Massachusetts shelf clock, 1800 – 1820. Here is the New England answer to the complicated and expensive bracket clock, a simple weight driven shelf clock. Many of these fine little clocks have the round dial and kidney shaped door shown here. Another type has a square dial set in a domed top with a charming little painted scene in the break arch. Note that all these clocks are just timepieces; there is just a single winding hole between 2 and 3 o'clock. Although perhaps intended as an inexpensive substitute for the bracket clock, not many of these lovely little clocks were produced, and they are very expensive now.

**Figure 22-13**

**Figure 22-14**

**Figure 22-15**

*Figure 22-13:* Banjo clock, 1800 – 1835. At last we come to Simon Willard's famous banjo clock. These wall clocks used to be called "patent timepieces" because a great many have the inscription "S. Willard, Patent" on the dials. In addition to Simon Willard, they were made by his brother Aaron, Aaron Junior, and a host of others from as far north as Vermont to as far south as Baltimore. Simon Willard made 400 movements himself. If you look past the églomisé tablet and throat panel you'll notice that these well known clocks are basically just a simple eight-day weight driven timepieces in an ornate case. The serious collector looks for examples in unusually good condition, the gilded and carved 'presentation' models, and the rare few that are real clocks with both a time and strike train. Although this example has an eagle finial, it is more common to find a simple gilded lemon form above the dial.

*Figure 22-14:* Girandole banjo clock, c.1820. Among the variations prized by collectors are these "girandole" banjos, invented by Lemuel Curtis about 1815. The circular lower case with its convex glass is similar to the girandole mirrors we saw in the last chapter. Note that this rather ornate clock has two winding holes, and thus is a clock rather than a timepiece. The throats of such banjos will be a little thicker to allow room for the additional weight required to drive the strike mechanism.

*Figure 22-15:* Lyre banjo clock, c.1835. Here is another somewhat later form of banjo clock. In common with later banjos, these clocks have very little gilding and usually lack the delicacy of earlier work. The lyre was a popular classical motif, and we also see it in chairs, card tables, and sewing tables.

Figure 22-16

*Figure 22-17*

*Figure 22-18*

*Figure 22-16: Howard type banjo clock, c.1880. Although not regarded as really antique by many collectors, these handsome mahogany and rosewood banjos often turn up at auctions. They were first made about 1840 by the firm of Howard & Davis in Boston, which was then reorganized as E. Howard & Company in 1857, and later as the Howard Clock and Watch Company in 1861. Edward Howard had a good background for this type of clock, for he served five years as an apprentice to Aaron Willard, Jr. Unlike early banjos, these popular clocks were made in a range of sizes to suit every need, very large versions being used as office regulators.*

*Figure 22-17: Lighthouse clock, c.1825. In 1822, at age 67, Simon Willard turned his attention to the design of a new type of weight driven shelf clock and came up with this unique solution, purportedly based on the Eddystone lighthouse off the south coast of England. Most of these timepieces are also alarm clocks. Alarm or not, they were not a success, and only about 30 were ever made. However, success did come later, for the combination of great rarity and a famous name have made them among the most expensive antique clocks in America.*

*Figure 22-18: Pillar and scroll clock, 1815 – 1830. Here is Eli Terry's remarkable clock. One would never guess that behind the mahogany veneered case, the delicate hands, and the two winding holes of a striking clock, there is only an inexpensive 30 hour wooden movement. Look at the top behind the swan's-neck crest and you will see the two pulleys that carry the chords from the winding drums to the weights. The feet on these clocks are somewhat delicate, and in addition to the glass tablet, you want to check here for restoration. In common with the banjo, these handsome mantle clocks were made everywhere, many with Terry movements.*

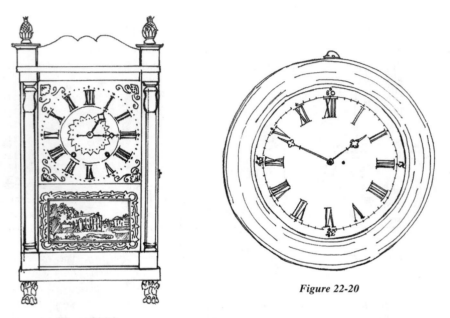

Figure 22-20

Figure 22-19

*Figure 22-19: Empire pillar and scroll clock, c.1830. Within a few years the popular pillar and scroll clock acquires Classical features, in this example half round pilasters and little paw feet. With this these handsome clocks loose much of their lightness and delicacy — and much of their appeal to the collector.*

*Figure 22-20: Gallery clock, c.1810. Before leaving Federal clocks, we should note these large giltwood timepieces which seem to have been intended for use in public buildings, perhaps in the back of a gallery. As you might guess from the close in position of the winding hole, behind the imposing dial are quite small brass works, not too unlike the diminutive electric motors that drive modern office clocks.*

## Barometers

Once we know a little about the history of clocks, barometers should not be a problem, for to a considerable degree their development parallels that of clocks. Just as the clock measures time, so the barometer measures the weight of air, what we commonly think of as air pressure. The barometer was invented by Evangelista Torricelli in 1643, just a few years before Christiaan Huygens developed the pendulum escapement that gave us the first accurate clock. After some years as scientific instruments, domestic barometers began to be made for wealthy clients in the last two decades of the 17th century, about the same time as we see the first tall-case clocks. In fact, many early English clockmakers also produced these mercurial barometers, or to use the delightful old term, quicksilver weather-glasses.

Because there is only a modest variation in air pressure, efforts were soon made to make the small changes more readable. About 1662, Dr. Robert Hooke, father of the anchor escapement, devised a wheel barometer in which the small changes in the height of the mercury column were translated to a pointer on a dial. This was done with a little weight that floated on the top of the mercury, to which was attached a length of thread that in turn looped around a small drum attached to the back of a pointer. The pointer turned as the mercury level rose and fell. The other solution was to angle the top of the glass column so that the rise and fall of the mercury was magnified (22-21), an idea credited to Sir Samuel Moreland, Charles II's "Master Mechanic." Neither did much to improve accuracy, and the scientific community continued to employ finely made stick barometers like that shown in Figure 22-22.

In common with the tall-case clock, the 18th century saw few changes in the barometer other than to improve the quality of the glass tube and to add a venier to stick barometers so that the level of the mercury could be accurately read to hundredths of an inch. Just as the mechanism of pendulum clocks hardly changed between 1720 and 1840, so also there was little change in barometers. Like the clock, a barometer in one's house seems to have been a symbol of affluence and education. Neither was found in many homes until the last few decades of the 18th century.

The most common barometer, the banjo (22-23), is a relative newcomer. This new form of wheel barometer was introduced from France about 1780, but it did not become common in England until around 1800, and not until after 1820 does it equal the popularity of the stick barometer. Thereafter, banjo barometers continue to be produced in large numbers well up through the middle of the century, and many that you see for sale are more Victorian than Regency. Associating 1800 with the introduction of the banjo barometer should be easy to remember, for this is when Simon Willard patented his banjo clock.

About this same time we also find the first Italian surnames on the dials of English barometers. Italians seem to have followed the banjo barometer across from France, perhaps starting out much earlier as glassblowers in Venice. So successful were they that by 1840 they come to dominate the business, which is why the majority of English barometers have Italian surnames on the dials. The manufacture of barometers, like the manufacture of clocks, was a specialized trade, with different craftsmen making the dials, the brass bezel, the hands, and the cases. In this environment it would be natural for the glassblower to be the prime contractor, for the glass tube is not only

**283**

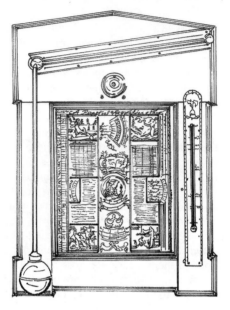

*Figure 22-21*

***Figure 22-21*** *Angle barometer, c. 1770. The most common way to handle the rather awkward shape of the mercury column on an angle or elbow barometer is to mount the whole instrument within an architectural frame. To provide balance, the maker has added a large thermometer on the right. In the center is a hydrometer, and below that a perpetual calendar with printed instructions, making this grand Georgian barometer a complete little self-contained weather station.*

at the heart of the barometer, but was probably the most difficult part to make. It was to the barometer what the clockworks were to the clock.

The great majority of barometers on the American market are English, either imported after the Revolution, or brought over by dealers and tourists. Unlike clocks, American craftsmen never made very many barometers. Probably they could not compete on a product that was relatively inexpensive and easily shipped. The few American examples that come on the market date from the first half of the 19th century. They generally bring far more at auctions than their quality would warrant.

The first thing most of us do when examining a barometer is to open the narrow little door in the back of the case to see if the glass mercury tube has been replaced. Although this may have some effect on price, it does not mean much, for mercury's noteworthy affinity for foreign substances just about guarantees that the tube will have been replaced at some time, particularly if a stick barometer where the mercury level must be visible. Other restoration is also not hard to spot. Check the case for patched veneer and missing edge beading, keeping in mind that good repairs may not come cheap. Many barometers are topped off with a delicate little classical broken pediment, and you want to be careful that some, or perhaps all, of this small structure has not been restored.

**284**

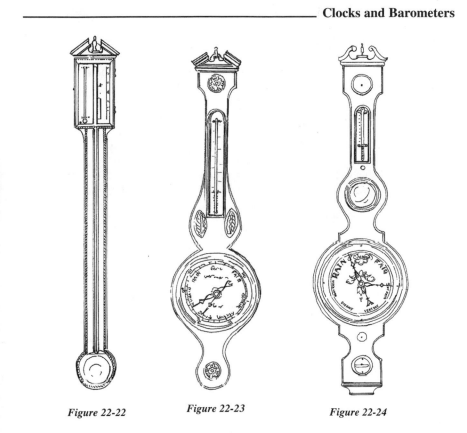

*Figure 22-22*     *Figure 22-23*     *Figure 22-24*

***Figure 22-22:*** *Stick barometer, c.1790. The stick barometer is perhaps the most elegant and the most Neoclassical of all the barometers. The top will be either this Classical broken pediment, a curved scroll, or a round hood. Within the dial area there is usually a small thermometer on one side and the vernier slide on the other. Similar barometers were mounted on brass gimbals for shipboard use.*

***Figure 22-23:*** *Banjo barometer, c.1800. This is the standard good quality banjo barometer, the mahogany veneered case decorated with rosettes at top and bottom and a pair of shells neatly filling the swell just above the dial, a nicely balanced design so successful that it remained almost unchanged for 40 years. There will often be a small ivory knob below the dial for setting the reference hand, and sometimes the thermometer will be given its own little case so that it may be removed and used elsewhere. Satinwood was much favored as a veneer in Regency England, and sometimes you will see satinwood veneered barometers.*

***Figure 22-24:*** *Victorian banjo barometer, c.1850. With time, dials get larger and cases more ornate. A handy reference to age is the little convex 'girandole' mirror above the dial, which dates from about 1840. You will also see mother of pearl inlay on these later barometers. At the top of the case is a hydrometer and at the bottom a spirit level to add a touch of the scientific to this very domestic product.*

**285**

# Chapter 23

## Shaker Furniture

Sooner or later, and probably sooner than later, you are going to come across some Shaker furniture. Auctions of Americana frequently include one or two pieces of Shaker furniture. These are usually some of the later production chairs, but sometimes an early chair, a work table, or a cupboard will be among the lots. Here we need to know what to expect, for in style, Shaker is no more than a refined country Sheraton, and we don't want to mistake one for the other. To paraphrase an earlier caveat, you don't want to pay for Shaker and bring home Sheraton.

The remarkable story of Mother Ann and the Shakers is so well known that we might pass over this unique chapter in American history and go directly to their furniture. First, though, we should consider the Shaker cabinetmaker, for understanding the environment in which they worked goes a long way toward an understanding of the furniture. The Shaker way of life always seems to have attracted skilled craftsmen, for from their very beginnings in the last few years of the 18th century, Shaker communities were noted for their "skilled mechanics" and the high quality of their work. Much of this might be ascribed to the backgrounds of the converts, for unlike some communal societies, membership was largely drawn from the working people of the surrounding countryside. For the most part, they were not the product of colleges and not utopian dreamers. After dinner the talk was not of things philosophical. It was about what they had done that day and how their work might be improved on the next. If this sounds very average, remember that the Shakers' daily round of tasks were an integral part of their religious belief. They did their best in a neat, orderly, and efficient manner, because every day they were literally at God's work. A well known admonition was, "Put your hands to work, and your hearts to God."

In the search for simplicity and purity in keeping with Shaker beliefs, furniture was carefully made, avoided ostentatious, dirt catching carving, and shunned fancy cabinet woods, veneering, and brass pulls as being too worldly. Everything was removed that did not contribute to neatness and utility. This union of monastic piety and skilled craftsmanship led to beautifully constructed, wonderfully simplified furniture that is much prized by collectors. The effort to avoid worldly beauty simply led the Shakers to it by another path.

However simple their furniture may seem to us now, the Shakers were not in the least conservative when it came to industrial progress. Although they withdrew from the everyday world, they did not withdraw from the advances going on all around them. While their furniture soon came to be very old fashioned in a Victorian America, they had no use for tradition just for tradition's sake, and turned to labor saving woodworking machinery just as soon as it was available. By the 1860s they were employing mortising and planing machines. When they turned their talents to the mass production of chairs in the 1880s, it was with the aid of steam power, boring machines, mechanical shapers, and duplicating lathes. In Shaker furniture we first see the basis of much of our contemporary furniture, the juxtaposition of traditional design with modern construction methods.

Although they continually looked for improvements, the Shakers had no use for change just for the sake of change. Once they got something right, that was the way it stayed. Never were they slaves to changes in fashion or the dictates of style. Country Hepplewhite and Sheraton were quite good enough for them, even on things made after the Civil War. First Directoire and Empire, then Renaissance Revival and Rococo Revival swept by them with hardly a nudge. They would not improve upon perfection.

Shaker furniture, particularly among the eastern settlements, is notably homogeneous, for stylistic harmony was encouraged and successful designs were exchanged among the communities, and this, in combination with a prohibition against signatures, makes their furniture difficult to place or to date unless, as is frequently the case, the origin is known. Chairs are not as big a problem as case work, for as we will see, here there was some evolution in design. Also, the source may be gleaned from the design of the turned pommels on the top of the posts, which varied slightly between the communities.

For the most part tables and case work will date from the first half of the 19th century when the communities were most successful and membership was growing. Very little furniture other than chairs and some sewing desks was made after the middle of the century when membership started to decline. There was no need, for what they had was so nicely made, and so well cared for, that like "the wonderful one horse open shay," it just lasted forever.

Before we go to the illustrations, something more should be said of the famous Shaker chairs, for much of the Shaker reputation for craftsmanship rests on this one product. In form, these delightful little chairs are nothing more than an elegantly refined version of the standard New England slat-back that we first saw in the chapter on turned chairs. The principle innovations were to omit all the "worldly" ornamental turnings, and to lighten up the frame. Actually, the one change probably led to the other. If you look at the traditional slat-back (9-5), you'll notice that the diameter of the back posts or stiles is governed by the depth of the turnings, for this will be the weakest point. Eliminate the turnings and the stiles need not be any thicker than was the deepest turning. In practice, they can be lighter yet, for grooves tend to focus loads. However, this is not all, for reducing the diameter of the stiles and legs disproportionately reduces the weight of the chair because cross-sectional area is a function of the square of the radius. If you reduce the diameter of a stile by 25%, you will reduce its weight by over 40%. This is why Shaker chairs are so wonderfully light. Light weight was important, for when not in use, chairs were hung upside down by the rear stretchers on the peg boards that circled each room. This made rooms easy to sweep.

There are two restrictions in straight back chairs: one must sit upright to be comfortable, and at times, there is an almost irresistible urge to tilt back. Even if the feet don't slip and deposit the unfortunate sitter on the floor, the hard maple legs will leave marks in the softer pine floors. The Shaker solution to these two problems is a story in itself.

Until the 1840s, Shaker chairs had no rake to the back. Although long proponents of comfortable rockers, their delicate little side chairs were straight up and down. Now you would think the logical solution to more comfort would have been to steam bend a curve in the back, but no, the Shakers took a different tack. What they did was to tilt back all the vertical members in the chair so that while the legs remained parallel, and the seat horizontal, the whole chair tilted to the rear. The amount of tilt was considerable, the pommels overhanging the bottom of the rear legs by about four inches, giving the impression of a tired and sagging chair that is just about to fall apart. As you would imagine, these are very strange looking chairs.

The problem of brethren who could not resist in tilting back their chairs was also solved in typical Shaker fashion. Realizing that tilting was inevitable, they simply designed chairs to be tilted. This was done by hollowing out the base of the rear legs to accept a semicircular hardwood ball joint that allowed the chair to be tilted back while the flat of the ball remained flush on the floor. These ingenious "tilters" were held in place by a rawhide thong that passed up through the middle of the ball joint, then out through a small hole drilled in the side of the leg. Here it was pinned to hold the tilter in place. Unfortunately, tilters tend to come loose and get lost, and you will come across old chairs that have been cut down after the tilters were lost.

Shaker furniture is so well made and was given such good care that you should not have to worry about unobtrusive repairs and restorations, although as we will see in one of the illustrations, they would not hesitate to modify existing furniture to suit another purpose. However, we want to be careful that what we are buying is actually Shaker. Leaf through any of the illustrated books on Shaker furniture and you'll notice that in style, their furniture is in many ways just an austere country Sheraton, not all that different from work being done by hundreds of rural cabinetmakers in the first half of the 19th century. The difficulty lies not so much with chairs and tables, which have very distinctive Shaker features, as it does in case work, which much resembles other country furniture. A simple pine chest or cupboard with an old painted surface can look very Shaker. It doesn't even have to be particularly pretty, for in truth, once we get away from the forms that the Shakers really had a chance to refine, much Shaker work is not all that handsome.

Perhaps the best indication of Shaker workmanship is the care put into construction, for Shaker cabinetmakers were not only engaged in building a heaven on earth, but they also seem to have had the time to get everything just right. Thus, their furniture quite lacks the small evidences of careless haste that are so characteristic of period work. For the most part, everything, from the largest built-in cupboard to the smallest oval box, is most beautifully made. It is a pleasure to examine.

I would suggest to the reader, that if you plan to collect some Shaker furniture, that you first do a lot of looking and reading. With the exception of chairs, and perhaps a few stands, Shakers did not manufacture furniture for the "world," and as a result, there is not a great deal of it around. What remains outside of museums and the existing communities is very expensive. The high price, and the similarity to other rural furniture, is a constant inducement to imaginative attribution. There is probably more "Shaker" furniture on the market than ever existed. Fortunately, studying the real thing is not difficult, for not only are there quite a number of beautifully illustrated books on the subject, but many of the communities are open to the public, and here you can see genuine Shaker furniture in its original setting.

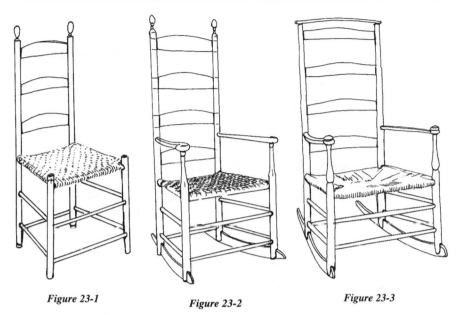

Figure 23-1

Figure 23-2

Figure 23-3

*Figure 23-1:* Side chair, c.1830. Here is the standard Shaker side chair, and while an early example, already a refined design. For over a hundred years, until the last production ends in the 1940s, there will be little change in these fine little chairs. The little ridge at the bottom of the rear legs indicates that this is a "tilter." There are two stretchers across the front and sides, but only a single stretcher across the back. This made it easy to swing the chair up onto a couple of wall pegs. So concerned were the Shakers with cleanliness that chairs were hung upside down to keep dust off the seat. Note that aside from the pommels, there are no decorative turnings. This utter lack of ornamentation is the most notable characteristic of Shaker chairs, and indeed, of all Shaker work. In the other chairs that follow, we will see a similar austerity. Only in armchairs are the front stiles given a little additional decoration.

*Figure 23-2:* Armed rocker, c.1830. Although they worked hard, the Shakers never saw any virtue in discomfort, and turned to rocking chairs as enthusiastically as other Americans in the first half of the 19th century. In common with other early rocking chairs, the rockers do not extend far beyond the rear posts, making it all too easy to tip over backward. These are known in the trade as "suicide rockers." These early rocking chairs are among the most handsome, and expensive, Shaker chairs. Note that the slats increase slightly in width between the bottom and the top; and that, in common with other turned chairs, there will be pairs of scribe lines on the back posts to indicate the mortise cuts for the slats.

*Figure 23-3:* Production armed rocker, 1880 – 1920. From quite early on some communities sold chairs to the public. The success of this business came to the attention of Brother Robert Wagan, and he turned the South Family at Mount Lebanon to the mass production of chairs. In 1872 a steam powered factory was built that could turn out about two dozen chairs a day. These strong, light, and handsome chairs enjoyed wide popularity, many thousands being made before production finally tapered off in 1920. This model is fitted with a shawl-bar, perhaps something of a misnomer, as this somewhat delicate crest rail was actually intended as an anchor for very Victorian looking cushions that were sold with these chairs. The largest chairs sold for $8.00, the back and seat cushions for another $8.50. Many of these fine chairs have since lost their shawl-bars.

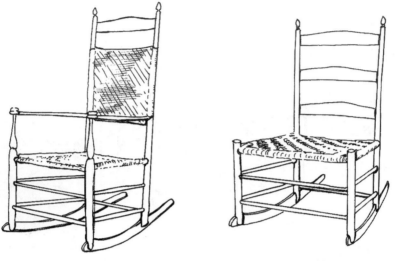

Figure 23-4

Figure 23-5

*Figure 23-4:* Production armed rocker, 1880 – 1920. Here is another form of the basic rocker, this time with a padded back in lieu of curved slats. Production chairs were made in eight standard sizes from diminutive little children's chairs (Size 0) to large masculine chairs (Size 7). Those at or near the ends of the spectrum are the most prized by collectors. Early Shaker chairs had seats of wood splint, rush, and sometimes cane, but by the middle of the 19th century, most chairs were seated with a woven cloth tape called listing, which was more comfortable and easier to install. The listing was woven over a thin cushion which made for a very soft seat. Chairs could be ordered with black, navy blue, peacock blue, light blue, maroon, pomegranate, brown, grass green, dark olive, light olive, old gold, drab, scarlet, or orange listing, or any two colors in combination. Pomegranate is a rather pretty orange-red, and drab is just as it sounds — a dull brownish or yellowish gray.

*Figure 23-5:* Production armless rocker, 1880 – 1920. These are the most common production rockers, perhaps because 50 cents could be saved by omitting the armrests. Production chairs were always identified by a size number (0 – 7) stamped in the back of the top slat, and then later by a trademark decal after others began to copy the style. The decals were normally applied either to the back of the bottom slat or to the inside of a rocker blade. Although now mostly worn off, you can often spot the outline of the decal if you take a careful look. It might be noted that the presence of a stamped number does not always indicate a production chair, for early chairs made for use in the communities sometimes also have a number stamped on the top slat, perhaps to indicate the room to which a chair was assigned.

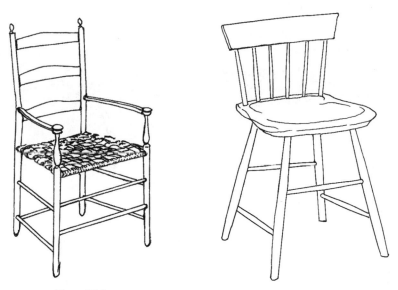

*Figure 23-6*  *Figure 23-7*

*Figure 23-6:* Production armchair, c.1890. Side chairs seem to have been less popular than rockers, for while no less elegant, they are less common. In keeping with Victorian taste, these chairs were usually finished with a dark stain followed by a couple coats of varnish. The Shakers themselves preferred either clear finishes, or thinned paints that let the figure of the wood show through. By now the Shakers had solved the problem of a comfortable back in a more conventional manner, they steam bent a gentle curve into the stiles. Although not at present as popular as rockers, these are singularly handsome chairs.

*Figure 23-7:* Low-back dining chair, c.1830. Dining chairs having low backs were employed in most communities. The Shakers initially used long benches that could be tucked under the communal dining tables when not in use, but found them so inconvenient that they went to chairs, but with low backs so that they could also be tucked under the tables. This dining chair is unusual in that it is a Windsor. Most communities employed turned chairs similar to that shown in Figure 23-1, but with just two low slats. If you look back to Chapter 10, you will see that but for the low back and the lack of worldly turnings, this chair is similar to any of the late Windsor chairs.

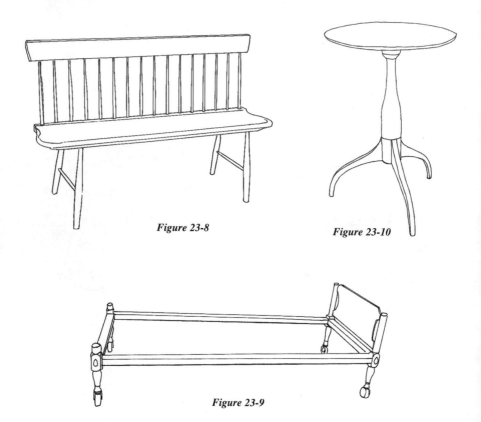

Figure 23-8

Figure 23-10

Figure 23-9

**Figure 23-8:** *Settee, 1820 – 1840. These elegantly simple meeting-house benches were developed by either the Canterbury or the Harvard communities as a comfortable alternative to benches. Although relatively uncommon, they were made in many of the communities in sizes from four to twelve feet in length. Careful shaping of the seat and the back provides a far more comfortable settee than the simple form would suggest.*

**Figure 23-9:** *Bed, 1840 – 1860. Shaker beds are utterly plain and simple, for in a hard working, celibate, and somewhat monastic society there was nothing to do after retiring but to sleep. They are typically rather short and narrow, what we would now identify as a cot; and are almost invariably fitted with 3" wooden wheels set crosswise to the frame so that they could easily be rolled away from the wall when made up or swept behind. Among all Shaker furniture, they seem to have received the least attention as to design.*

**Figure 23-10:** *Spider-leg stand, c.1830. Perhaps nowhere is the Shaker pursuit of "true simplicity" more evident than in the design of these grand little stands. The same distinctive swelled column was also used in many small sewing and writing tables. As a general rule, stands were made of cherry. In common with slat-back chairs, this stand and the following snake-leg example were somewhat old-fashioned by the time they were being made in the 1830s.*

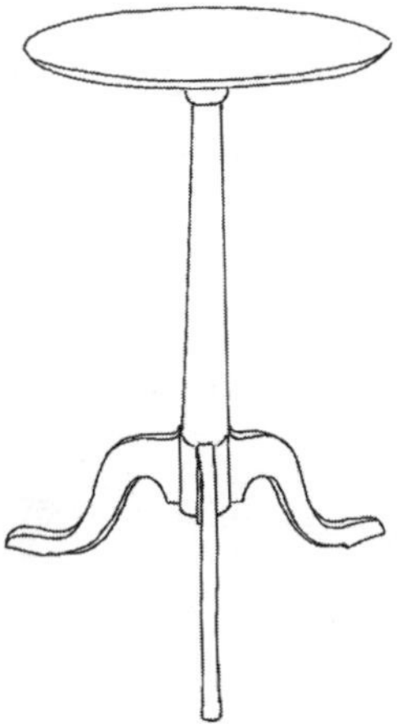

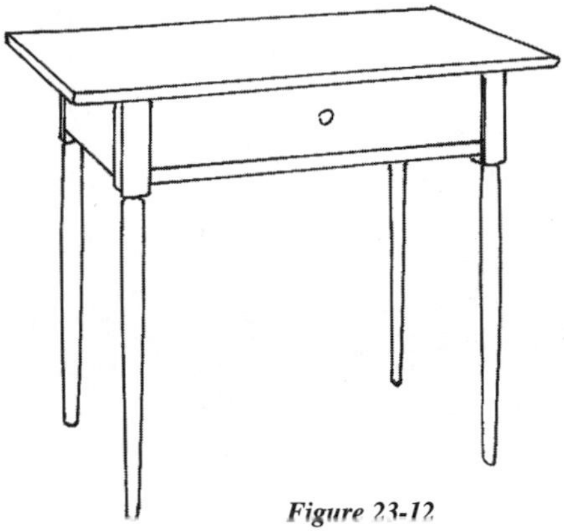

*Figure 23-12*

*Figure 23-11*

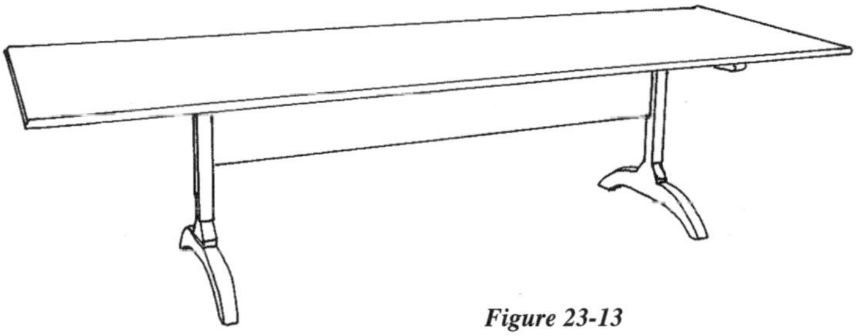

*Figure 23-13*

*Figure 23-11:* Snake-leg stand, c.1830. Snake-leg stands could be equally simple, although not all are this plain. Many of the columns have more complex turnings than the simple taper shown here. Two methods were employed to join the top to the column. The first method was conventional, the top of the column was just mortised into a rectangular support running across the grain of the top. The second method is far more interesting, and far more typically Shaker. Here screw threads were cut into the top of the column which was then screwed into a beveled circular pad that supported the top. These unique solutions to simple problems are one of the great charms of Shaker work.

*Figure 23-12:* Work table, late 19th century. This small work table with a breadboard top illustrates the distinctive leg turnings employed by many of the communities. They consist of nothing more than a slightly swelled column with the greatest diameter near the top of the leg. In common with Shaker chairs, this small work table exhibits no ornamentation whatsoever other than the very simple leg turnings.

*Figure 23-13:* Communal dining table, c.1840. Except for the ministry, Shakers all ate together at these large dining tables. The design is typical Shaker, an elegant refinement of the basic trestle table with the cross bracing tucked up under the top so as to clear the legs of the diners. The length varied with the needs of the community. Most are 9 to 11 feet in length, a few over 21 feet. The ministry, two elders and two eldresses, dined apart at similar, but much smaller "ministry" tables.

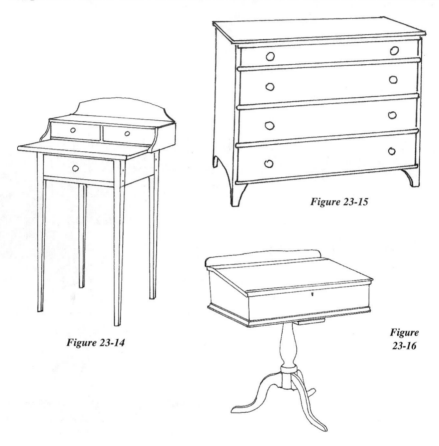

Figure 23-15

Figure 23-14

Figure 23-16

**Figure 23-14:** *Sewing stand. As we saw in chairs, Shaker inventiveness is often best illustrated in the small furniture. Here the cabinetmaker has modified a Hepplewhite one-drawer stand to serve as a little sewing table by adding an overhanging gallery with a backboard and a couple of additional drawers for needles and thread. Often these stands have a low raised molding around the top to keep needles and thread from rolling off.*

**Figure 23-15:** *Chest of drawers. The Shakers were exponents of built-in furniture, and as a result, blanket chests and chests of drawers are not all that common. In style, chests of drawers vary from this simple derivative of a six-board chest, to equally plain models with bracket bases, to a considerable number with turned legs and paneled ends which are, in style, nothing more than late country Sheraton. Case furniture will be usually made of pine or butternut in the east, walnut in the west.*

**Figure 23-16:** *Eldresses' desk, c.1830. Desks are not common among Shaker furniture, probably because the leadership did not encourage personal letters. Even among of the ministry there may not have been a lot of correspondence, for with all their talents, the Shakers never developed the desk much beyond some rather simple writing tables with slant tops. This eldresses' writing desk is no exception, for while a unique form, it is not the most graceful or practical of desks.*

Figure 23-17

Figure 23-18

Figure 23-19

*Figure 23-17: Sewing desk, c.1860. Toward the latter half of the 19th century, the increasingly female communities turned to sewing projects to augment their income. These handsome and practical sewing desks are the happy result. Placing one set of deep drawers on the side provides access without having to close the sewing slide.*

*Figure 23-18: Chest of drawers and cupboard, c.1850. Furniture planned for just one particular spot tends to be somewhat individualistic. Here we have a tall chest of drawers with a small cupboard added to the top. Why was this done? Well, the Shakers were not only against dirt, but also saw no point in useless dusting, so they ran most case furniture right up to the ceiling. Shaker communities were primarily large farms, and there would have been a lot of dust around. We can see that is was once a built-in case of drawers, for the base is unfinished and has lost its molding. As the communities shrank, unused buildings were torn down and the contents sold by the thrifty Shakers, which is why so much of this once built-in furniture survives today.*

*Figure 23-19: Chimney cupboard, c.1850. Here is another piece that is a curious mix of chest and cupboard, in this case a narrow cupboard with a couple of small drawers in between. Although strange looking now, this cupboard once served a particular location and function, for which it was probably ideally suited.*

# Chapter 24

## Miscellaneous Small Furniture

Every grouping of associated objects includes a few, like the duck-billed platypus, that don't seem to fit anywhere. Period furniture is no exception. This last chapter on furniture types covers a variety of small pieces that regularly appear on the market, but could not be included elsewhere without being placed in an obscure location. It also discusses the pianoforte, not because it is particularly common, or is even, strictly speaking, furniture, but because it is often found in the guise of a desk or a dressing table. As these last few types in themselves defy logical grouping, they are simply presented in alphabetical order.

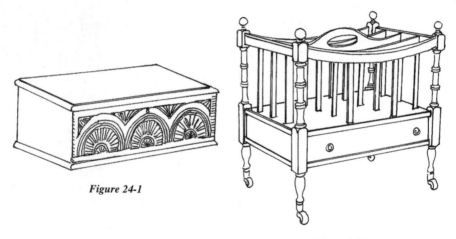

*Figure 24-1*

*Figure 24-2*

*Figure 24-1: Bible box, 1680 – 1710. These Pilgrim Century lift-top boxes are often called Bible boxes in the belief that they once held the family Bible. Actually, they seem to have been used as a handy and easily moved container for all sorts of valuables at a time when house fires were all too common. Those with slanting tops may also have been used as desks, the case holding quill pens, ink, and paper. At the end of this chapter we'll see how this form may have evolved into a specialized writing box. In common with early American lift-top chests, usually only the front face is carved; and while the sides may be of oak, the top and bottom will be of lighter pine. American examples are quite rare, most of these early boxes will be either English or Continental.*

*Figure 24-2: Canterbury, c.1810. In the last years of the 18th century an Archbishop of Canterbury commissioned one of these music racks, and Canterburies they have been ever since. Although planned for sheet music, they are so useful for oversize books and magazines that far more survive now than the pianos they once served. Most of the Canterburies on the market will be English. Here again we need to be careful about age, for the Victorian love of the piano kept them in production right up through the 19th century.*

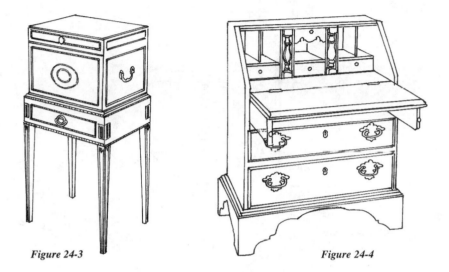

*Figure 24-3*                                    *Figure 24-4*

**Figure 24-3:** *Cellarette, c.1800. Cellarettes are popularly associated with southern furniture, although in fact, they were made everywhere, and are often from New York. This is the standard American type, a partitioned lift-top chest raised on a Hepplewhite style stand. English cellarettes are more likely to take the form of a large brass-bound circular or octagonal bucket raised on four short legs. Sometimes you will also come across a lead lined container with an open top and no bottle partitions. This is a wine cooler, which was filled with water to keep the wine cool on a hot summer day.*

**Figure 24-4:** *Child's desk, c.1760. The great majority of children's furniture consists of diminutive chairs, lift-top chests, and chests of drawers. As you would expect, inexpensive turned side chairs are by far the most common. However, quite the most charming of the lot are these delightful little slant-lid desks, complete with little drawers and cubbyholes just like their full-scale brethren. For the most part children's furniture is both simple and strong, lacking the veneer, inlay, and carving found in other period work. High style examples are very rare.*

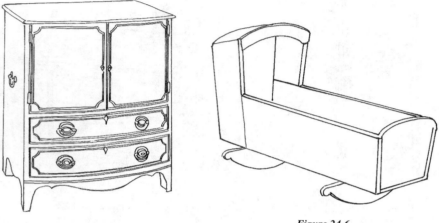

Figure 24-5

Figure 24-6

**Figure 24-5:** *Commode, c.1800. The word commode is confusing, for it has two very different meanings. In England, it is any large, ornate chest of drawers suitable for use in a drawing room. However, in Victorian times the term also came to be used as a more discreet name for a small chest or stand designed to enclose a seat and a chamber pot; an early toilet, but without the inestimable convenience of running water. Because of their small size among the general run of period furniture, commodes are more popular among collectors than you might think. Sadly, many have been converted into little chests of drawers.*

**Figure 24-6:** *Cradle, 1750 – 1820. This is the standard hooded cradle that was made all up and down the east coast for at least a century. The basic design saw few changes, and aside from small differences in the paint and the fastenings, there is very little to tell Colonial from Federal. Like the modern crib, old cradles tend to be utilitarian furniture. While there are some dovetailed mahogany examples, most you will find are simply nailed up painted pine.*

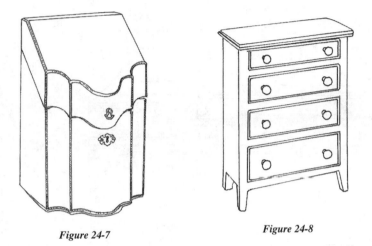

*Figure 24-7*

*Figure 24-8*

***Figure 24-7:*** *Knife box, c.1800. By the end of the 18th century flatware was being made up in large sets, and it became fashionable to keep this silver in a pair of mahogany veneered knife boxes on either end of the sideboard. Open one up and you will often see a handsome star inlayed in the underside of the top. Much less common, but even more grand, are the mahogany knife urns from this same period. However, within a few years it was realized that a felt-lined drawer in the sideboard would better slow tarnishing, and these elegant indicators of good taste and wealth went out of fashion. Like tea caddys, many of these boxes have had their interiors replaced with neat little stationary bins. Also like tea caddys, the great majority are English.*

***Figure 24-8:*** *Miniature chest of drawers, c.1810. No period furniture is so little understood and so awash in myth as are miniatures, perhaps because there is so little to tell us why so much time and effort was put into these charming little examples of the cabinetmaker's art. There are any number of explanations: they are examples of the conceits that were popular in the 18th century; they were made by apprentices as proof of their competence to be journeymen; they were used by salesmen as samples; they were employed as advertisements in a cabinetmaker's storefront window. In truth, most miniatures are nothing more or less than children's toys. This is apparent when we realize that the great majority are rather simply made little chairs, beds, and chests of drawers, then note that they generally come in two sizes: a larger size that would compliment a 12" or 15" doll, and a smaller size that would fit nicely in a doll house. Unlike children's furniture, miniatures cover the complete range of furniture and accessories popular to each period, and are remarkably faithful to each style. From as early as William and Mary, and continuing right up through Empire, there is everything the child would find at home. Of all these types, simple chests of drawers are by far the most common, followed by beds and chairs — just the sort of thing a young lady would use with her dolls.*

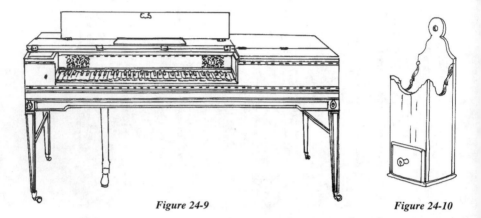

Figure 24-9                                        Figure 24-10

*Figure 24-9:* Pianoforte, c.1810. Nothing is more inimical to survival than to go out of fashion — and then to have no other use. Such was the fate of these spinet pianos which were popular in the early years of the 19th century before being replaced by the modern piano with its iron frame. Only a very few remain with both keys and pedals intact. The others that survive have usually been converted into desks and dressing tables, which is unfortunate, but perhaps not too bad if there is no alternative. It is better to save something than nothing. While this piano from the first decade of the 19th century is Hepplewhite in style, the majority of surviving examples will be a little later, perhaps 1820 – 1830, and will be fitted with rather heavy late Sheraton style legs.

*Figure 24-10:* Pipe box, 1740 – 1820. Pipe boxes are perhaps the most charming members of a whole group of wall-mounted boxes designed to keep salt, candles, and tobacco out of the reach of rodents and small children. The small size and simplicity of these little boxes belies their cost, for they are much in demand by collectors. If you wonder at the design, the deep bin held long-stem clay pipes, and the little drawer, perhaps tobacco, or a striker and a flint. While there are some mahogany examples, most are cherry or painted pine. The rather shallow drawer is easily lost, so be careful that it has not been replaced.

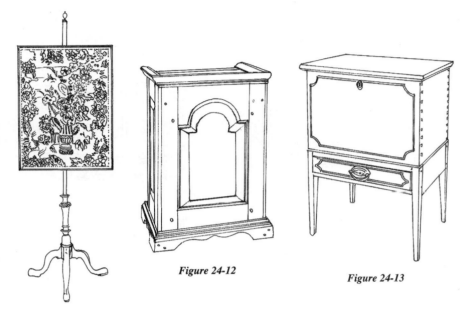

Figure 24-12

Figure 24-13

Figure 24-11

*Figure 24-11:* Pole screen, c.1780. Spend any time in front of a fireplace and you'll soon discover that for all of the pleasure of the warmth, you need to shield your face from the heat and the glare of the fire. The 18th century solution to this problem were these pretty little adjustable pole screens. The screen itself will be either a framed needlework or a thin mahogany panel. Some are fitted with a little shelf to serve double duty as a candlestand; which suggests that tilt-top candlestands may also have served double duty as fire screens. Although no longer necessary, pole screens still survive in considerable numbers, perhaps because of the cherished family embroidery. However, like other delicate furniture, it is difficult to find one in good condition.

*Figure 24-12:* Spice cabinet, c.1750. Small chests for spices are not unique to America, nor to the Delaware Valley, but it is here that they achieved their greatest success. While we will find some William and Mary examples with bun feet, most will be Queen Anne and have bracket feet. Usually they are made of walnut and have this Queen Anne style paneled arched door. Open the door and you will generally find a nest of small drawers grouped around a somewhat larger center drawer. Like pipe boxes, they are much sought by collectors, and the few that come on the market bring very high prices.

*Figure 24-13:* Sugar chest, c.1810. South of the Mason-Dixon line, sugar, coffee, and tea were often stored in a compartmented lift-top chest. This inlaid cherry chest is an unusually fine example. Most are much simpler rural products made of walnut or other local hardwoods.

Figure 24-14                                    Figure 24-15

**Figure 24-14:** Wall shelf, c.1820. Wall shelves are fairly common, but are such a utilitarian product that it is not always easy to find a good example. Sometimes made of mahogany, more commonly of pine, walnut, or butternut, the sides often show the profile of a whale. A few are fitted with drawers across the bottom like this charming little New England shelf.

**Figure 24-15:** Washstand, 1790 – 1825. Prior to the advent of bathrooms, most bedrooms would have had one of these washstands tucked into a corner. The large opening in the top once held a wash basin, the lower shelf a pitcher of water. Often there is a smaller circular hole or a little shelf for the soap dish. Very similar, but less common, are square washstands. Some urban models are larger and fully enclosed, with a lift top over the basin and then folding or tambour doors to conceal the pitcher and perhaps a chamber pot. Wash stands date to at least the middle of the 18th century, from when we see the charming little circular three leg basin stands. Federal washstands survive in large numbers, for while they have lost their original function, there is always room for a pretty little mahogany occasional table. If you lack a basin to fill the large opening in the top, it can be neatly covered by a thin piece of varnished mahogany that conforms to the shape of the top. The splash boards will keep it in place so there is no need for nails or screws to mar the top.

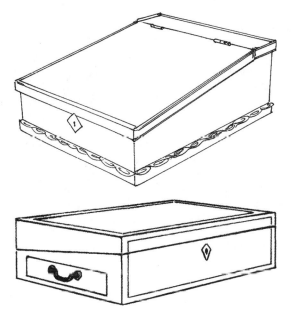

*Figure 24-16*

*Figure 24-16:* Writing boxes. Writing boxes are so common that we will illustrate two different forms, the first a simple lift-top box with a slanting lid, the second the more usual type which opens to provide a sloping felt covered writing surface. Inside both examples there will be storage for paper and correspondence, and compartments for the pens, a bottle of ink, and a sand shaker. Most of these boxes date from the 19th century, although lift-top writing boxes were in use much earlier. Better models will have a small drawer worked into the side or the end of the case. The drawer is then locked with a long pin that drops in from above. Writing boxes may once have been largely the province of junior family members who did not have a desk of their own. They were also used as traveling desks. While meeting with the Continental Congress in the early summer of 1776, Thomas Jefferson drafted the Declaration of Independence on a writing box brought up from Monticello.

# Chapter 25

## Care and Conservation

Having brought home your first piece of old furniture, you may wonder how to care for this attractive object that has just cost you so much. Well, it's not very difficult. The routine maintenance of cleaning, waxing, and polishing we will cover in a little bit, but first we should discuss the major hazards to old furniture: humidity, sunlight, and beetles, for they are the immediate problem.

If your home is north of the Mason-Dixon line or west of the Mississippi, your first concern should be humidity, particularly the very low humidity that arrives with a winter cold snap. One of the many virtues of the old hide glues is that given a chance, they will creep a little to accommodate the expansion and contraction of wood with changes in humidity, but something is very likely to fail when there is a rapid change. The difficulty with winter is that cold air carries very little moisture. Now if we lived in a barn this would not be a major problem because the air, although supporting less moisture, would still be relatively humid. However, in a house the relative humidity decreases in proportion to the difference between the inside and outside temperatures. This was not so much of a concern in the past when houses were not all that much warmer than barns, but it is a serious problem in modern houses where central heating and effective insulation allow the inside air to be much warmer, and relatively, much dryer, than the outside air. For example, if on a winter day it is 30 degrees outside with a relative humidity of 60%, a house heated to 65 degrees will have a relative humidity of only about 20%. This will cause real damage to old furniture, particularly furniture having wide panels or veneered surfaces.

The obvious solution is to raise the relative humidity inside the home by adding moisture to the air, and there are a variety of devices, called humidifiers, that do just this. If your home has a forced hot air heating system, the most elegant solution is to add the necessary moisture just downstream from the furnace after the air has been heated — and dried. The desired humidity level is then controlled by a humidistat which monitors the relative humidity, starting up the humidifier as required. Normally the humidistat will be mounted beside the thermostat so that both temperature and humidity can be monitored and controlled from one spot.

Should you instead have a hot water heating system, it is possible to install ducts and a central humidifying system. This is expensive but well worth the cost if you have a really fine collection. Failing this, the normal solution is just to set up portable humidifiers during the dry winter months. These are not very attractive, but if you are conscientious about using them, they do the job. Use a bacteriostat to avoid odor and the nuisance of scrubbing them out every few weeks. Fortunately, humidity spreads fairly evenly throughout a house, so you can place them in inconspicuous locations.

The ideal humidity for antique furniture is somewhere between 45% and 55%, but in older houses you may have trouble keeping it much above 40% in bitter cold weather. However, this should be enough to prevent most damage because you have damped down the large fluctuations associated with cold snaps. Relative humidity is measured with a simple device called a hygrometer, which can be found in almost any hardware store for a few dollars. If you wish to monitor the humidity more closely, you can purchase a hygrograph which will give you a continuous weekly record of the relative humidity on a strip of paper. These are often sold as barographs, which provide a record of barometric pressure, temperature, and humidity.

Under certain conditions, low humidity is not only a winter problem. Furniture stored in an attic can be subject to just as much drying. On a hot summer day the temperature in an unventilated attic can rise to over 140 degrees, quite enough to soften candles. This heating will provide the same temperature/humidity difference as a winter cold snap — and do just as much damage.

Too much humidity is not much of an improvement over too little, for it will both swell wood and soften the old glues. Above 62% it will also support the ubiquitous fungi that give us mildew. Most of the problem centers in basements, particularly near the floor and against walls where there is little air circulation. This is just where furniture is apt to be kept. These problems suggest that furniture is more likely to be damaged in storage than in use, and that the wear and tear of everyday use in a heated home is much preferable to storage in an attic, a basement, or a garage. Not only may these be unsuitable locations, but things kept here seldom receive much attention. Out of sight is out of mind.

The second concern, sunlight, is particularly insidious because its effects are so slow and even. It is all too common to have considerable fading before the damage is noticed. Sunlight, per se, is not the problem. What does the harm is the ultraviolet component of sunlight, the part we cannot see. With time this bleaches out woods and breaks down finishes and fabrics, what is known as photo-chemical damage. The solution here is not so much to darken rooms as to block light in the ultraviolet spectrum. This can be done by using either the transparent window coatings or the special window glazing now sold to protect fabrics. Another, and perhaps simpler solution, is to use translucent shades or Venetian blinds to block direct sunlight. Venetian blinds have the additional benefit of providing a nice period component to your decorating, for they have been in use for over 200 years.

If both you and your spouse are out of the house most weekdays, keep an eye out on weekends to be sure that the change in seasons has not brought direct sunlight where you did not expect it. When possible, decorate with light colors and perhaps some mirrors so that not a lot of sunlight is needed to have bright, cheerful rooms. Not all direct sunlight is bad, for while it rapidly fades watercolor paintings, it tends to brighten oil paintings. It can also be useful if you would lighten something gently. Cherry, in particular, if stained up too dark, can be much improved with a little sunlight.

Furniture beetles require a certain amount of moisture to thrive, and thus are not a serious problem in the north except right along the coast. They infest most woods, but do not attack mahogany, perhaps because it comes from the tropics. These little beetles spend most of their lives as larva, tunneling inside the wood until almost the end of their life cycle. Fortunately, they warn us of their presence by leaving sawdust-like droppings called frass. If you spot some tiny little bits and pieces underneath a piece of furniture, vacuum it up and put down a clean sheet of paper. Then give the piece a firm tap. Should more drop down, or after a short while, the little bits and pieces reappear, you have a problem. If the piece already shows some little exit holes, you can tell if the beetles are still active by looking at the holes. Old holes will look old; they will have rounded edges, be dark on the inside and often filled with dirt and wax. Recent holes have sharp edges and yellow insides. They look new — and they are! Furniture beetles are something that should be attend to promptly, for not only are they slowly ruining the infested piece, but they will soon direct their attention to other nearby furniture.

There are three basic ways to eliminate beetles: poison, suffocation, and freezing. In the past furniture was fumigated with a cyanide compound to kill the larva. However, cyanide is very dangerous, and now professionals fumigate with a product called Vikane which employs a sulfuryl fluoride gas. Although effective, this is expensive, and you might want to try some home remedies first. One alternative is to suffocate the larva by placing the piece in an airtight plastic bag filled with nitrogen. Keep the piece in the bag for about a week, being sure that no air gets in by periodically adding a little more nitrogen. The most simple approach is freezing, putting the piece in a large freezer or perhaps outside on a bitterly cold night. You will have to repeat this a few times, for believe it or not, Mother Nature has provided the beetles with some antifreeze for just such an eventuality.

The amount of attention required by old furniture is a function of its use. Magazine articles will tell you to dust with a spray or treated cloth once a week, and to clean and wax twice a year, but this is much more attention than is necessary. What should you really do? Well, first off, avoid sprays containing silicones. If the silicon compounds work their way down through the finish into the grain of the wood, later refinishing will be a real challenge. Also, lemon oil is, in fact, nothing but mineral oil, a nice scent, and a little coloring. These oils do not feed the wood. Actually, nothing feeds wood. It is a myth. All you are doing is covering your furniture with a fine coat of oil, which makes it look nice for a while, but in the long run will do nothing but darken the wood and attract dust. However, the twice a year wash and wax rule is good advice for areas that are handled a lot; the splats, crest rails, and seat rails of dining room chairs, the tops of tables, and the faces of drawers — any place that has frequent hand or body contact. The oils and salts in our skin generates the sticky coating you find on these surfaces. Given time, the salts eventually break down the finish.

Surfaces that get little handling can be left pretty much alone. Perhaps once a year rub them down with a soft rag, adding a little more wax if the surface seems to have lost its shine. First though, try to work up the existing wax with a brisk rub. The idea here is to keep the film of wax just as thin as possible. There is no advantage in arbitrarily waxing everything, nor in building up many layers of wax.

There are special soaps recommended for furniture cleaning, but just about any soap or detergent will work. One of the best known New York furniture repair and restoration businesses uses nothing more elegant than Spic and Span. Whatever your choice, work with a well squeezed out rag, washing a small area at a time so that the surface does not stay wet. Do not use water on veneered or inlayed surfaces, for any opening or crack will tend to wick up moisture and soften the glue underneath. Here you might want to use mineral spirits, which is usually sold as paint thinner. It is a safe wash for old paint and grime.

Similarly, there is nothing magic about waxes. Although everybody has their favorites, almost any good quality hard paste wax will do. Most have a nice smell, being a mixture of carnuba wax, beeswax, paraffin, and turpentine. Put the wax on quite thin, perhaps repeating from a different direction to avoid missing any areas, then buff up with a soft piece of old towel. You can buff up carved areas with an old shoe brush. Avoid waxing old painted surfaces, as the wax will get into the cracks. The principle virtue of waxes is that they are chemically stable and will not combine with the finish in unfortunate ways. Unlike oil, they will not darken wood and are easy to remove. They should never get you in trouble.

In the past brasses were kept well polished, not only for appearance, but also to brighten up rooms and make it easier to see drawers where the only lighting might have been a few candles. If not guilded, they were generally lacquered to minimize polishing. We know this because there are Federal brasses that still retain traces of the original lacquering. Usually some color was added to the lacquer to give the brass a richer look. In the next chapter we'll find out how to lacquer brasses, but for now let's just talk about polishing.

Most commercial brass polishes are nothing more than a simple mixture of pumice powder and ammonia, which is why they all seem to smell alike. You have to shake the can now and then because the pumice settles to the bottom. All these polishes work, but the pumice abrades away the brass and the ammonia dissolves finishes, so these are not the best polishes for old furniture. Instead, you might try to use a product like Nevr-Dull which also abrades but does not contain ammonia. Unless you are dealing with modern replacements, polish brasses in place, being careful to keep clear of the surrounding finish. If the mount is not absolutely flush with the surface, you can protect the finished surface by slipping a thin little piece of transparent acetate or card stock behind the brass.

The tiny little particles that make up dust are abrasive, so always dust lightly or use a vacuum cleaner with a soft brush attachment. Also, when vacuuming old upholstery, fasten a mesh across the nozzle to avoid pulling at the fabric. Never dust off gilded surfaces with a damp rag. If water gilded, you will literally wipe off the gilding.

Most all of us like to have some pots of flowers around to add a bit of color, particularly during the gloomy winter months. However, these should never be placed on good furniture. The problem here is not the few drops that spill during watering, but rather overfilling or slow seepage that is not noticed until much later. Many vases are not glazed on the bottom, and moisture can penetrate a crack in the glaze and work its way down to the base. You will see this sort of damage all the time at auctions. The solution here is to use silk or dried flowers on fine furniture. They require almost no attention, and in common with Venetian blinds, have been around for a very long time.

Should you be fortunate enough to have a labeled piece, consider if the label requires special care. If it is in an exposed area, or in delicate condition, it might be a good idea to give it a thin clear plastic cover. This should be set out with some little spacers so that it does not contact the surface of label, which will probably be buckled up in places. Giving a label a protective cover has the additional benefit of bringing it to the attention of others, for old labels are not all that obvious if only a fragment remains, or if they have so darkened with age as to merge in with the surrounding surface.

Keep up with the minor repairs that come part and parcel with old furniture. If something comes off, and cannot be fixed immediately, keep it with the piece if at all possible. If it goes into a desk drawer, or perhaps into the basement, its chances of being reunited are just that much less. Also, the older a break or crack, the more difficult it will be to repair, due to both shrinkage, and to dirt and wax working into the opening.

While old furniture should never be a millstone, it does need a certain amount of attention to remain functional and beautiful. For the most part these are easy, pleasant jobs, good chores for a rainy day. Periodically, pieces will require more than just dusting and waxing, perhaps some work on the finish or reupholstery. You may wish to follow a regular program of improvement, every year selecting one or two pieces for additional work.

As you see, proper care is not difficult. It just requires a little time and thought. However, it also requires perseverance, for by its very nature, it is a long term activity. Period furniture is at its best when first brought home from a dealer, or just back from some cleanup and repair. It will be in as good condition as it will ever be. The trick is to keep it that way, to keep it from imperceptibly sliding downhill with time and wear. Here periodic waxing, in addition to improving appearance and protecting the finish, has the further virtue of forcing you to regularly examine your old furniture. This is when you are most likely to notice the small things that need attention, the little bit of loose molding, the spot of lifted veneer, the section of slightly buckled stringing. This is when you spot problems. At the end, you do not want your cherished antiques to be inventoried as they were a great many years ago in Edward Shippen's best parlor:

"A Clock out of Order & a Case ye Key lost
an old ffashioned glass & a pr of Sconces one broke
An old Scriptore with Some broken China & earthenware
one large & 1 small oval Table old & rotten
an old Decanter & 1/2 Dozn broken glasses on ye Mantle ps
10 glass pictures 2 of wch are broken
2 old laquer'd fram'd pictures & 4 fram'd pictrs much Spoiled by ye flys & Smoke"

# Chapter 26

## Clean-up and Repair

When furniture is purchased from a dealer, it will be in good condition and ready to use, but if bought at auction, or perhaps inherited, it is likely to require some further attention. Repairing and restoring old furniture is very different from collecting, and this one short chapter will do no more than help you to get started. It is not intended as a guide for more than the most simple, straightforward projects, and it will not even begin to make you an expert, but hopefully, it will keep you from getting into trouble, or worse, adding further injury to existing wear and tear.

Before getting started, though, there are some general principles to keep in mind when working with period furniture. When considering any job, large or small, always:

- Think very carefully before doing anything.
- Do no more than the minimum necessary to put the piece back in good condition.
- Whenever possible, employ techniques that are both true to period and reversible.

Working with period furniture is the antithesis of the usual home repair job where we just pick up a hammer and a screwdriver and set to work. Here we want to consider first what needs to be done, and then how this might be accomplished. Sometimes there is more than one solution. Approach every job as a new problem, for it is just that. One of the things that makes period furniture so interesting is that no two pieces are the same, and similarly, no two clean up and repair jobs will be the same. Each presents its own problems. Therefore, always start slowly, first going over what you plan to do, perhaps experimenting a little with the finish in an out of the way spot. If you start to get into trouble, stop and think about what is going wrong. Try to determine the why of the problem. Blindly pushing ahead will almost always make things worse.

The basic rule in reconditioning period furniture is to never do more than necessary to put things back to right. You want to avoid damaging the basic "antiqueness" of an old piece, the evidence of handwork, wear, and patina. Excessive cleanup will not only reduce charm — it will reduce value. Consider what is the minimum that might be done to make the piece good looking and useable again. If the finish is only poor in one area, try to correct just that area. For example, the tops of tables are usually in much worse shape than the legs and stretchers. If the top must have a new finish, see if you can get by with no more than a little touch up on the legs, perhaps just where they have been scuffed at the bottom.

Do not be too hasty to clean up early repairs, for they add a certain charm and contribute to the provenance of an old piece. Here we are talking about neat repairs, not the plastic wood and finishing nail variety. In the past most furniture was easy to repair, being fastened with wood pins and water soluble glue, and then generally having a simple finish. Every town had one or two cabinetmakers, much of whose day to day business was keeping this sort of furniture in good repair. Therefore, it is not uncommon to find repairs that in themselves may be quite old. I have seen a Chippendale period side chair in which the mortise-and-tenon joint that fastened a stretcher to a leg had been pinned with a nail, evidently because glue would not hold. Now this is not the most professional fix, but I would not have touched it, for the joint was pinned with a rose-headed nail which itself must have been close to 200 years old. This casual little fix made so long ago contributed much charm to an otherwise fairly ordinary old chair.

You will find that restoration is one of your most trying problems. When faced by your first restoration, you will realize that no matter how thorough your research, and how careful your approach, you can never really know what the original looked like. Aside from the simple problem of ending out a few inches of feet or replacing a chair spindle, you can never be sure that what you are doing is really correct, for even among very standard types of furniture there are dozens of variations. Your best effort will be no more than an educated guess. This is partly why restoration, however carefully researched and executed, never recovers more than a portion of original value, and why you always want to be sure that what you do is reversible.

When considering restoration, it is helpful to remember that there are, in a rough way, four classes of work. In the first case we know exactly what the original looked like and how it was made. Such would be a front or rear foot of a chest of drawers. Here the opposite foot provides a mirror image of the missing foot, and the restoration can be just about perfect. In the second class we have no role model, but have a very good idea of what the original looked like. This would be the case if our chest of drawers were missing both front feet or both rear feet, but the chest is a common type for which there are similar examples. Here a good restorer will often play around a bit, perhaps mocking up the feet out of scrap in an effort to achieve the harmony and balance of the original. While both feet are missing, the critical dimension of length can be determined from the remaining feet. Any such work is helped by considering as many examples as possible, and in addition to reference books, we might try to obtain pictures of similar pieces from the extensive decorative arts picture collection at Winterthur. In the third class, so much is missing that restoration would be no more than an educated guess. Such would be the case if our chest of drawers had lost all four feet and the associated blocking. While the feet could be restored, and perhaps accurately, most serious collectors would not touch such a piece, not only because so much of the original is missing, but because it is hard to be certain that the restoration is really correct. Then finally, there is the case in which so much is missing, and the piece is either so uncommon or so old, that restoration would be based as much on conjecture as on knowledge. Such might be the carved and gilded crest on a Queen Anne mirror. Usually these early pieces are best left alone.

Good furniture restorers always emulate old methods unless the problem is such that only something new will do. They work with hand tools and use hot hide glues and shellac finishes, for not only is this faithful to the original, but repairs done this way unobtrusively blend in with the existing structure. Also, the work can always be redone if the repair does not hold up, or later scholarship reveals an error. At auctions, you will find that well done repairs and restoration are one of your major problems, for they can be remarkably hard to spot, particularly as with time they tend to fade into the original structure.

There are a number of books on repair and restoration of old furniture, some of which I've identified in the appendix. Even if you send out all your repairs, such books are well worth taking the time to read, for they will help you to understand both old construction methods and the techniques involved in repair and restoration. You will find some repairs that appear to be difficult are actually not all that hard, and some that appear relatively easy are a challenge even to the professional. This knowledge is important when considering a bid at an auction, for if a lot will require some repair or restoration before being put to use, you need to have an idea as to just how much trouble you are bidding for. Also, if something is sent out, you want to be able to discuss the repair work intelligently with the cabinetmaker. Unfortunately, none of these books provide the one ingredient you need the most. Experience. All they can do is to guide you as to how things should be done.

Before starting any work, there is a fundamental decision. Should the job be left to an expert? When in doubt, err on the side of the professional. Here the principle is simple: if something is good, then someone good should work on it. If you have inherited a really nice piece, or spent a large sum at auction, it is not logical to then skimp on repairs. The decision must be based on your ability and experience — and you should be careful not to overrate either. As Socrates said, the beginning of wisdom is to "know thyself."

As the interest in antiques has grown, so have the specialists in different types of restoration. Problems that you might think would have to be corrected as best as possible are now the providence of professionals. In addition to the normal cabinet work and the usual clock repair, there are now experts in clock dial restoration, barometer repair, mirror restoration, inpainting, gilding, and reverse painting on glass. This is important to the serious collector, for while an indifferent finish can be improved later, an amateurish touchup of a painted clock dial might be very difficult to correct.

There are two problems in sending out work: first locating a qualified restorer who has time for your job; and second in finding a restorer who thinks as you do about repair, restoration, and finish. If successful in the first, then be sure to take the time to discuss the job in some detail. If there is something special about a piece, such as brasses you don't want disturbed, this is the time to mention it. Go over how repairs will be made and discuss the type of finish you desire. You'll discover that both color and finish are difficult to describe. If the piece needs to be stained, you might bring along a good color photograph of the effect you are after. Failing this, then look around the restorer's shop for a suitable example. Restorers often classify finishes in increasing order of gloss as being either "American," "English," or "French." You want the finish to be appropriate to the subject. A very high finish would be out of place on a simple country table.

You will find that restorers of period furniture almost invariably employ some form of French polish, even though, as we saw earlier, much furniture was just given a little oil and then waxed; and in any event, the technique of French polishing does not appear to have become common until well into the 19th century. However, it has the great merit of allowing the restorer to quickly build up a beautiful shellac finish to the desired amount of gloss without having to resort to endless rubbing down. Just as in the past, furniture restorers have to work quickly if they are to make a decent living.

When something goes out for repair, put something else in its place, for it may not be back for a while. Restorers provide their best service to their best customers, and these will be dealers who can be quite demanding when stock is not on display in their shop, or is needed for an upcoming show. One way to minimize the time away from home is to not actually deliver the piece until the cabinetmaker is ready to start the job. This will also mitigate the nagging fear that something will happen to your cherished antique when it is not under your care and protection. In any event, don't push the restorer, for the last thing you want is a rushed job. The dealer's piece may go out of his shop within a few months, but yours will be with you for many years. Pay bills promptly, for restorers also like to eat, and are likely to be just that much more receptive to your next project.

Upholstering presents its own set of problems. First off, call around to locate a firm that has had experience with period furniture. Again, go over the job in some detail. Try to bring along a picture of a similar piece that has been correctly upholstered, for period upholstering is very different from modern, generally having cleaner lines and much less stuffing. The cushions on wing chairs are an exception. They should be quite deep and filled with down. On over upholstered Federal side chairs examine the outside of the rails for a pattern among the nail holes that would indicate that the original upholstery was embellished with a row or swag of brass-headed cast tacks.

Be absolutely sure that the upholsterer understands that nothing is to be done to the frame of the chair. Over upholstered side chairs were often made with the upper outside corners of the front legs sloped up to help keep the padding in place, and modern upholsterers are apt to cut these off flush, which may make the upholstering easier, but does nothing but reduce the value of your chair. Many years ago in New York City a very good chair was sent out for recovering. One of the seat rails was somewhat broken up, so the upholsterer put in a new rail. This thoughtful idea cost the insurance company $18,000! 

Before getting into repairs, something should be said about shops and tools, for both are important if you are to do good work. The best possible shop is just what most cabinetmakers had in the past, a large room at ground level with a lot of windows to provide natural light. Better yet might be a separate building where fire hazard is minimized and the odor of alcohol and shellac does not get into the home. For most of us, though, the only available space will be somewhere in the basement, so let's see what might be done here. First off, try to use a separate room well clear of the dirt of the furnace and the lint of the dryer. You will inevitably be working with volatile and flammable solvents, so unless there is natural ventilation, install an exhaust fan. Try to get enough room for a good sized work bench, a separate table for leveling and gluing, and then enough area to work all around a large chest of drawers. Provide a lot of light to help get a good match on colors and to avoid holidays. Position the light above you, not above the bench. If you can, have additional lighting on either side so that there are no shadows.

Comfort is important if jobs are not to be hurried, and every shop should have both a comfortable chair and a padded stool. Because the work involves a lot of standing, try to make the floor easy on the feet, perhaps investing in one of the cushioned mats that are used behind store counters. Dig out an old radio or stereo system; it can be lonely there all by yourself. Also, put in a telephone extension, for you want to be able to answer a call without having to run up the stairs.

Woodworking magazines advertise all sorts of beautiful and expensive work benches, and you may be able to charm your spouse into giving you one for Christmas. Failing this happy event, almost any strong, level table will serve the purpose. If the bench is not heavy, bolt it to the wall to keep it from moving around. Whatever the structure, you will need a flush mounted wood vise on one end. You might also want a small metal vise at the other end that can be unbolted in a few minutes to provide a clear surface. In addition to the bench, it is useful to have a separate table for clamping and gluing up. This can be made of almost anything so long as it is level. A carefully selected flush panel door set across a couple of sawhorses will do just fine.

Repair work on old furniture does not require many tools, but what you have should be good quality and kept very sharp. Blunt saws, dull chisels, and worn files all but guarantee poor work, and will get you into trouble in more ways than you would care to count. Fortunately, there are people who resharpen saws and chisels, so you don't have to worry about learning this additional trade. Files should be simply discarded when they loose their edge.

Most amateurs have more tools hung up on a pegboard than are ever used — in addition to a few old wooden ones that are displayed with no purpose but to add a certain period flavor to the shop. However, you will find that the following tools are used fairly regularly:

- Several sizes of hammers and a wooden mallet
- Chisels, perhaps ⅛", ¼", ½", and 1" to start
- Small hand drill and a wide assortment of bits
- Assorted screwdrivers, including some inexpensive ones whose blades can be filed down for special jobs
- A set of small taper punches
- A variety of small diagonal, long nose, and end nipper pliers
- A selection of wood and metal files
- Try square and sliding bevel

- Scratch awl
- Straight edge
- Clamps of every possible size and type
- Two panel saws, one for cross cutting, the other for ripping
- Back saws, at least one with very fine teeth
- Coping saw, adjustable frame fret saw, and an assortment of blades
- Hacksaw with assorted blades
- Smoothing plane
- Small block plane
- Glue injector
- X-ACTO knife and assorted blades
- Package of single edge razor blades
- A pair of sawhorses about 18" high with wide tops to bring work up to a convenient height

The one tool you never have enough of are clamps. Although they would appear to be practical, the common cast iron "C" clamp is actually not all that useful. What you want are handscrews, deep throat "C" clamps, three-way edge clamps, bar clamps, and band clamps. Handscrews are often called "Jorgensen" clamps.

Now that we have some tools and a place to work, we can get started on our project. Unless the finish is obviously beyond repair, the first step is just a thorough cleaning. You will be surprised at the amount of dirt and old wax that can build up over the years. Often the old finish under all this accumulation will still be in good condition. Therefore, first get out the Spic and Span, or your favorite equivalent. Working carefully with a well squeezed out rag, tackle a small area at a time. Sometimes it will take three or four passes to get everything off. You can tell grime from old finish because the former will come off black on your rag. When the rag shows a little brown, stop, for you are down to the old finish. However, there is an exception to this simple rule. Should the piece have spent a long time in a room with a lot of smoking, it will be covered with a layer of tobacco tars, which also comes off brown.

If this procedure does not seem to have much effect, or if working with veneered or inlaid surfaces, use mineral spirits or turpentine. Both are safe and effective in cutting old wax. Mineral spirits are somewhat less smelly. If there is a really bad accumulation, use fine 4.0 steel wool to help things along, always rubbing gently with the grain. Should the cleaning leave you with a presentable surface, just apply a thin coat or two of wax, and then quit. There is no gain in going any further.

In the past, everyone had their own wonderful formula for cleaning and "feeding" old wood. You will find many of these in early books on antiques. Most were a mixture of turpentine and boiled linseed oil. The turpentine would clean off the grime and the oil would darken bleached surfaces and bring up the figure in the wood. While it worked, this treatment is no longer thought to be a good idea, for linseed oil soaks into the grain of the wood and tends to darken with time, a condition for which there is no cure short of radical scraping and sanding.

The time will come when you will want to take something apart. If at all possible, avoid this. Not only does disassembly make the piece just that less original, but it is very likely to induce further damage. Even if it looks easy, it may open up a Pandora's box of problems. Just as a doctor always tries to avoid surgery, we want to avoid disassembly.

Now that I've told you not to take things apart, I'll tell you how to do it safely, for there are times when it cannot be avoided if we are to have a good repair. The most common task is to loose a mortise-and-tenon joint, so we'll use this as a model for all joints. First off, inspect the joint very carefully for signs of nailing, for nails are the all time favorite way to fix a loose joint. Small finishing nails are commonly used, often countersunk and puttied over so as to not show. Sometimes X-rays are used to spot the location of nails on really fine pieces of furniture. Simpler yet, just check with a small magnet, for if there is a nail, it will very probably be either iron or steel. Keep in mind that there may be more than one nail buried in an area where successive generations have tried to tighten up the joint. If you find a nail, it must come out before the joint is taken apart. If the head shows, try to get a grip on it with a small pair of diagonal or end nipper pliers. If not, then the best approach may be to push it right through with a very fine taper punch. Failing this, see if there is some way to avoid taking the joint apart, for you will almost surely do more damage in the process. Should the reason for disassembly simply be reglueing, you might consider boring a very small hole in from the back and using a glue injector to force new glue into the joint.

Wooden pins always taper in from the front, and if you can get at the back, they are generally easy to tap out. If the hole for the pin was not drilled right through, you can drill a small hole in from the back and then use a thin taper punch to pop out the pin. Save and mark the position of each pin so you can put them back in the same position in the same hole.

Old glue is usually brittle, and professionals often loosen a joint with a sharp tap from a mallet. Use a soft wood block so you don't damage the surface. If nothing budges, try drilling a small hole in from the rear and injecting water into the joint to soften the glue. Add a little alcohol to the water to reduce surface tension.

Always try to ease or wedge a joint apart, particularly when working with chairs. The problem is not that you cannot provide a steady pull, but that once the joint comes free there is no way to immediately check the force and motion of your arm. The result, all to often, is a loosened or broken joint somewhere else. If you just stop and think for a minute, you can rig up a simple wedge and lever mechanism from scrap wood. Better yet, buy a tool called a spreader clamp, which is a bar clamp that works in reverse.

Should a joint refuse to budge after a reasonable application of force, see if there is some other alternative. The tenon may be locked in so firmly that nothing short of failure will move it. Apply more force and all you will gain is a broken tenon. If a joint is loose and seems as though it should come apart, but will not, then stop and try to figure out why. There may be a hidden nail that you did not spot, or perhaps the joint has been fox wedged as shown in Figure 5-1. These clever joints were popular on later Windsor chairs when the makers did not want to have the legs project up through the seat. Remember that in taking a joint apart, you are trying to do just what the cabinetmaker wanted to avoid.

Sooner or later you will be faced with an old screw that must be eased a bit or removed. Now here you want to be very careful, for not only do you not want it broken off, but also you don't want to damage the slot or patina on the head. This takes a little planning. You'll remember that when I talked about tools, I suggested screwdrivers that could be filed down for special jobs. The first step is to select a screwdriver of the correct width, then file the point to a perfect parallel fit with the slot. This may be quite thin, for old screws slots were cut with a saw and are often quite narrow. What you are after is a perfect fit that applies an even force across both faces of the slot. Now gently try to turn the screw. If it doesn't want to start, give the head of the screwdriver a firm tap with a hammer. If still no luck, try heating the head of the screw with a soldering iron. If still no luck, then stop and think of way to make the repair without removing the screw. If more than one screw is removed, remember where each came from, for no two screws, and no two holes, will be quite alike.

While on the subject, I'll tell you how to make an "old" screw, for there are times when you will need one. Restorers often have a collection of old screws, but most would rather trade away their soul than give one up, so it's generally make your own or nothing. First off, always clamp the work. Don't ever try to pull things together with a screw, particularly if the screw is at an angle, for this will inevitably bend the shaft.

You will probably have to go a couple of sizes larger with the new screw because the old hole will be somewhat enlarged. This is all right. In fact, it's just what you want. Put the screw in and tighten up snug. Be careful that the point does not push up through a finished surface. If working with a thin table top, you will probably have to file the point down quite a bit to keep it from coming through. This will further improve the period look.

Because the new screw is oversize, all or part of the head will be too high for the original beveled hole. Mark the high side, remove the screw, and file this area down. You will remove the modern turning marks, and if fortunate, end up with an old fashioned looking off-center slot. If this treatment pretty much files the slot away, all the better, for restoring the slot with a thin hacksaw blade will be true to period. Now put your "old" screw out in the rain for a few weeks to acquire some patina, then rub a little oil on the rusted head to get the right aged effect. The result will not fool a dealer for a minute, but it will look right and will be a neat repair.

Although you may not want to tackle any repair work more complicated than a little simple gluing up, we might discuss two common structural failures, a broken leg and a broken tenon. The methods employed in these two repairs are typical of the cabinetmaker's approach to all sorts of structural repairs, but may be very different from what you think would be done.

If one is very lucky, a leg will fail at an oblique angle, and the repair will be no more than a simple clamp and glue job. However, legs generally break just about straight across the grain. As no amount of glue will provide strength to such a break, the normal solution is to bore out the center of the leg and install a hardwood dowel. While this may appear simple, it requires very careful aligning and centering of the drill hole. If the remaining stump of the leg is short, the easiest way to do this is to first glue the leg together, then to bore the dowel hole in from the top of the stump. Otherwise, the restorer will normally remove the stump of the leg, glue the two pieces together, then cut the leg straight across near the break, preferably in the groove of a turning where the cut will not show. The reason for this is that there is no way to obtain a precise center at the ragged break. Then the only problem is how to drill a perfectly aligned hole into both pieces of the leg. This is usually done on a lathe where the head and tail stock are in alignment, and it is possible

**315**

to chuck up the drill bit so that that it will bore an absolutely true hole. When gluing up, the dowel will be a snug fit, and some provision must be made to let air and excess glue escape as the dowel is driven into place. This can be done either by slotting the dowel or by drilling little vents at the bottom of the holes.

Repairing a broken tenon is a good deal easier, although you also may not realize how it is done. Here again, simple gluing will not work, for not only do tenons carry considerable load, but the break will also usually be across the grain. The solution is surprisingly simple. The broken tenon is cut off flush and a second mortise, the mirror image of the first, is worked out at the shoulder of the cut off tenon. Then a new tenon is made up that fits snugly into both mortises. This is called a loose tenon, but if carefully done, will result in a new joint almost as strong as the original.

Aside from missing blocking, probably the most common restoration to secondary structure is replacing the rails of overupholstered chairs, for if they are not broken up by the nails from many upholsterings, they may be suffering from beetle damage. However, replacing rails is the last thing we want to do, for the result is the loss of some of the original structure — and inevitably, some of the value of the chair. Here is where you want to employ some artful repair and stabilization, which is not difficult, particularly as your efforts will not show under the new upholstery. Broken tenons can be replaced with the loose tenon discussed earlier, being careful to get the angle correct, for while the joints on chairs appear to be at right angles, most are not. The rails themselves can be stabilized by gluing and clamping, and if edges have broken off, then by wrapping in strips of linen soaked in glue. Be sure to use a water soluble glue so that later generations will be able to work on the rails again.

In this day and age you may have to deal with a cigarette burn. This can be a real problem, for not only do these burns have a singular lack of charm, but they may not be easy to remove. The damage is mostly due to an additive which keeps the cigarette burning while not being smoked, and unfortunately, they continue to burn very hot indeed. A cigarette burn is often a deep burn, and if you try to scrape or sand it out you are likely to end with a depression far more obvious than the burn itself, particularly as the surfaces that suffer from burns are often viewed from a shallow angle. Should light sanding have little effect, I would suggest that you leave things as they are. Dealers usually insist that cigarette burns be removed, even at the cost of some wood, but this sort of drastic scraping down requires real skill if it is not to show. In the end, perhaps time will help, for now that we understand more about the long term effects of smoking, cigarette burns may eventually join water rings and sewing-bird clamp marks as just another charming little sign of the past.

There are times when you want to trim down a patch or cut a pin flush with the surface. This requires a special flush cutting saw with an offset handle and no set to the teeth. These are well worth their small cost, for nothing else will work. Try cutting off a pin with an ordinary back saw and you are in for no end of trouble, for the width of the spline will prevent a parallel cut and the set of the teeth will tear up the surrounding surface.

Another little trick is to do any required patching before removing the old finish. A certain amount of old stain is always shifted around when refinishing, and this will tend to fill in the new areas. With luck, very little extra stain will be needed.

The important thing to remember about gluing is that the two surfaces must be wood to wood if there is to be any strength in the joint. If not, then take the time to fit a thin wood shim so that there is no gap in the joint. Filling an opening with glue does just that — it fills the opening with glue, and by itself, glue has little strength. The other thing to remember is to always do a dry run on the clamping. Don't ever just squirt on some glue and then start clamping, for in all probability, things won't clamp up the way you thought. Sometimes the solution will involve making up little jigs out of soft scrap wood so that tightening the clamp will exert an even pressure across the glue joint. Another thing to keep in mind is that if you clamp a diagonal break, the lubrication of the glue will cause the two pieces to slide past each other as you tighten things up. Before such clamping, figure out some way to inhibit this lateral movement. Remember that the problem will not be evident in the dry run because there is not yet any glue in the joint. If adding a little glue to drawers, be very careful that everything is level and square. Introduce even a little twist and the drawer will never run smoothly. Here is where the level table we mentioned earlier is particularly useful. If you always remember to put most of your time into the planning, you will generally end up with a successful glue job.

Much gluing involves stabilizing loose veneer, so let's cover this aspect in a little more detail. Loose veneer, if not obvious, can be located by tapping with your fingernail. Areas that are not solid will give back a "hollow" sound. Unless very loose, try to glue veneer back down without removal, for old veneer is brittle and easily broken. The simplest fix is to work in a little moisture to soften the old glue, then add a little new glue. A very thin splint of wood or a small artist's spatula with a thin offset blade is useful for working in the glue. Clamp the veneer down with a little softwood or Plexiglas pad, what is known in the trade as a caul. Put wax paper between the caul and the surface so that the caul does not become attached if glue is forced out by the clamping. Also, keep a small bucket of warm water and some rags handy, for you will find glue gets all over the place. When the glue has set up and the caul is taken off, you will generally find a little glue eased out underneath the wax paper. This will wipe off with a damp rag.

Always use water soluble glues. Not only are they historically correct, but they are reversible. The only thing worse than a joint out of alignment is a joint out of alignment that you cannot correct. Also, you never want to do anything that will preclude later improvement. Not all your small repairs will be as good as they might be, but this is not too important if they can be redone later by someone better. Professionals keep hide glue liquid in a heated pot, but if you do too little work to justify an electric glue pot, then liquid hide or fish glues are a good substitute. Invest in a fresh bottle about once a year, for they have a limited shelf life.

If an old shellac or varnish finish is so deteriorated that cleaning does little good, and the finish does not appear to be original, then it should probably be taken off and replaced. What you want to do is to gently ease off this finish, for the aged surface of the wood underneath the finish is very thin. The key word here is gently. Strypeeze and its host of methylene chloride cousins are much stronger than is needed, and should only be used if nothing else has any effect. All old clear finishes will be either wax, linseed oil, shellac, or some form of varnish. Wax will just wash off. Oil you cannot do much about but to rub down as much as possible with fine 4.0 steel wool, always working gently with the grain. In the old days just a thin coat of oil was used to bring up the figure of the wood before waxing, so these pieces will have very little build up under what will probably be a more recent shellac or varnish finish. However, some 20th century finishes consisted of repeated coats of boiled linseed oil, and it is very difficult to remove this darkened old finish once the oil has polymerized. One well known instruction was to oil "once a week for a month, once a month for a year, and once a year for the rest of your life," so you can see what you are up against.

Fortunately, nine out of ten old finishes will be shellac, and here we should have no problem, for no matter how old, shellac resins will dissolve in alcohol. After washing down to get off the dirt and wax, start with a rag soaked in denatured (ethyl) alcohol. If this seems to work, but only very slowly, use a pad of 4.0 steel wool soaked in alcohol, again always working gently with the grain. If this doesn't seem to have much effect, you are probably dealing with a later varnish. Here you might try a 50-50 mixture of lacquer thinner and denatured alcohol, or a product called lacquer wash thinner, which is a recycled lacquer thinner. Always start with a light hand. You may not have to remove all the finish. Sometimes it is possible to save old alligatored shellac by gently dissolving and blending in the old finish.

Once the old finish is off, or reduced enough to ensure a good base for a new finish, you have the choice of three replacements: wax, shellac, or varnish. If a rural or a simple urban piece, then the correct finish will be no more than several coats of wax. In the past this was usually just beeswax dissolved in a little turpentine. If you like the smell of beeswax and want to be historically correct, you can make some up, but don't ever do it over an open flame! Instead, use a double boiler, adding just enough turpentine to dissolve the beeswax. In the old days the resulting soft paste was worked into the grain of the wood with a bundle of rushes tied together to provide firm pad, then buffed up with a rag or stiff bush — much the way we now polish shoes. Then, as now, a good finish was built up with a number of thin coats, with a rub down between each to remove any excess. The result is a relatively soft, easily patched finish. Much the same effect, but with a tougher finish, can be obtained with any good quality modern floor or furniture wax. Although this simple process may sound too good to be true, wax finishes are both historically correct and can be very attractive.

Should the color of the wood be too light or lack figure, you may want to first add some stain, or perhaps a coat of shellac. Wet the surface with a little mineral spirits or alcohol to see if just shellac will have the desired effect. If this doesn't do enough, then consider staining, which was common on period furniture. Unless employed for light contrasting veneers, both maple and birch were usually stained. Use water or alcohol based stains. Always experiment first on a piece of scrap to get color you want. In the old days this was generally something resembling a better and more fashionable wood — walnut prior to 1750, then mahogany.

Shellac is a just a resin dissolved in alcohol, what used to be called a spirit varnish. It is the only survivor of a large group of alcohol based varnishes that were used throughout the 18th century to obtain a high gloss finish. A well done shellac finish is not only beautiful, but is quite unlike anything else. It contributes much to the warm look of period furniture. Professionals buy shellac in the raw form of flakes, then dissolve the flakes in alcohol and strain the result through cheesecloth to get out the impurities. However, we can get shellac already made up from the local paint or hardware store, where it is generally sold as either orange or white shellac in a 3 lb. cut, which is about 30% resin and 70% ethyl alcohol. Use orange shellac on dark woods such as walnut and mahogany, white or clear shellac on all others. The shellac in the can is much too thick for the many thin coats we need, so pour some into a jar and add about an equal amount of denatured alcohol. Try this mixture out on a piece of scrap, wait a few minutes, then check to see that it is dry. Shellac has a limited shelf life because the dryers tend to evaporate, and old shellac will never set up properly. The can will usually be dated and have a warning message or a warranty to this effect.

A good shellac finish is made up of many very thin coats. Professionals do this fairly rapidly with a technique called French polishing, but this method requires a lot of time and experience to do correctly, so we'll go the simpler route and apply the shellac with a soft brush. Perhaps the best brushes to use with shellac are made of badger hair, but they are expansive and not always easy to find. What we want to do is to build up a number of thin coats that slowly fill the pores in the wood. When working with open grain woods such as walnut and mahogany, you may wish to save time by first using a filler. If you do this, be sure to give the filler at least 72 hours to dry before applying the first coat of shellac. Between each coat, rub down well with 4.0 steel wool. Because shellac is more fun to brush on than to rub down, most beginners spend far too little time with the steel wool. If your first few coats look great and then things look progressively less great, you are probably building up too much shellac. Adding more coats will only make things worse. Instead, rub down until very little shellac comes off in the steel wool. This will take a while, but little by little things will start to look right again. The more coats, the glossier the finish, as you slowly fill in the pores with shellac. A thin "American" finish will have many pores still showing, a somewhat heavier "English" finish only a few, and a high "French" finish none at all. In Victorian times it was popular to add coloring to the shellac, but this tends to hide the natural figure and beauty of the wood. The effect you are after is that of looking down through a translucent finish to the figure of the wood below.

When you have built up the desired number of coats, give a final light rub down to provide some grip to the wax that follows, then apply a couple of thin coats of wax and you are done. Get everything to your satisfaction before this last step, for you will find that wax does not fix problems in a finish — it only makes them shiny. Be careful to not miss any spots on this last rub down, or you may have places where the wax does not adhere. These can be a fooler, for they will look shinier than the waxed areas — just the opposite of what you would think. The new shellac may be a little soft for a while, so don't put anything heavy on the surface for a couple of weeks.

Aside from being a resin dissolved in oil, modern varnishes have little in common with the old oil based varnishes, but they are reversible, and there are places, such as the tops of dining room tables, where their toughness and resistance to alcohol are desirable. However, we want to use a good quality furniture varnish, not a marine spar varnish which is formulated to not fully harden; and never the modern bar top or polyurethane varnishes, which are actually plastics. Apply varnish the same general way as shellac, using a number of thin coats and sanding with fine wet-or-dry paper between each coat. Always do all table leaves as one job. Otherwise, they are apt to end up slightly different — if indeed, all of them ever get done. Remember that the time when you want them to look their best is likely to be when they are all use. When done, rub down gently with a mixture of pumice and oil to cut the high gloss and obtain a soft luster. The result will not be shellac, but it will be almost as good, and only an expert will know the difference.

If a previous owner used silicone wax sprays, you may have inherited an interesting problem. Silicones work their way down through the finish into the wood below, and when you apply varnish they alter the surface tension so that you end up with little circular depressions known as "fish eyes." No amount of sanding will correct this condition. Spend hours sanding out the depressions and most will reappear with the next coat. Fortunately, there are a fixes to this problem. If you suspect that silicone compounds may be present in the surface of the wood, then use a silicone wash before the first coat of varnish. Should they appear later, all is not lost. Woodworking and paint supply shops carry flowout additives that will reduce the surface tension in the varnish, which may solve the problem without having to start all over again. These are often called "fish eye killers."

Painted surfaces present their own unique problems, for here you cannot remove a deteriorated finish and have anything left. Later coats can be lifted off, but this is best left to experts. When dealing with an old or perhaps original paint layer, you first want to determine if the paint requires stabilization. Should the paint be chipping and lifted, you need to restore the adhesion between the paint and the underlying surface. Professionals do this with a picture varnish called Soluvar. Get a small bottle of satin finish Soluvar from an art supply store, and with a very fine brush, work it under the lifted paint. You'll find that satin finish Soluvar dries absolutely clear, so much so that it is easy to forget where you have been. To remember the areas that have been treated, you might want to use little masking tape tabs. Once the finish is stabilized, you can give the piece a gentle wash to remove dirt and oily hand marks. If soap and a well squeezed out rag don't seem to have much effect, you may wish to try mineral spirits or turpentine, but start in an out of the way place to be sure that the paint does not come off also.

Sometimes there will be chipped or worn places that might be improved with a little touchup. This should always be done with water based paints, such as Japan colors, which can be removed later. Here patience is really a virtue, for most of your time will be spent playing around to obtain an adequate color match. After a while, you'll understand why inpainting is so expensive — and why it is perhaps best left to experts. The long-term problem with inpainting is that the original paint is old and stable, while the inpainting is new and unstable. With time the inpainted areas may not quite match the original surface. The same problem also affects staining, which is why patched drawer lips are often so obvious.

In the last chapter it was noted that in the past brasses were lacquered to inhibit tarnishing. This is still a good idea, not just to reduce maintenance, but because it will slow the inevitable loss of material each time you polish. This is significant, particularly when dealing with very old brasses and the rather thin stamped Empire period brasses. The important decision here is not so much as to whether or not to lacquer, but whether or not to lacquer in place, for it is tempting to simplify the job by taking off the brasses. If the brasses are both original and appear to have never been off, they are best left in place, for something of the original will inevitably be lost if you move them. Cotter pin mounts should always be left in place, for removing them will probably ruin the old cotter pins and perhaps result another set of clinch holes when the mounts are replaced. Worse, you will then have a problem in convincing others that the brasses are indeed original

Polishing and lacquering brasses in place is tedious, but it is not all that difficult. If possible, slip a thin little piece of card stock or plastic under the edges of the brasses to protect the surrounding wood finish. Cotton swabs are handy when working with liquid polishes on small areas. When you have the shine you want, clean off any residue with some acetone on a clean swab, then apply the lacquer with a fine brush. Be careful not to miss any areas, or there will later be dark spots when these areas tarnish. It is slow work, and you might work on just one drawer at a time.

If you choose to remove the brasses, remember the positions of both the brasses and the nuts, not only to preserve the original, but also because nuts are not always interchangeable on early brasses. Pad the jaws of the pliers so that they don't leave marks on the nuts. Resist the temptation to remove any slight ridges in the drawer fronts around the edges of the brasses. This may just make the brasses look like replacements.

Should the brasses be modern replacements, you may decide to obtain better. Here though, you want to be very careful that what you are replacing is actually new. Pulls made after about 1780, when thread forming equipment had been developed and rolled sheet brass was in use, often appear quite modern, particularly if they have been removed at some time and the piece refinished. There are two other aspects to keep in mind. Furniture was kept for a long time, and it was not uncommon for a piece to be returned for repairs and upgrading with new, more stylish brasses. Thus we sometimes find old furniture with replaced pulls that are, in themselves, very much period, although perhaps not the period from which the piece was made. The other thing is that original brasses may be one style newer than the case. This is particularly common in American furniture where Chippendale style desks and chests of drawers made after the Revolution were often fitted with Hepplewhite pulls. Unfortunately, a lot of these have since been replaced with "correct" Chippendale designs.

There are two major sources of good quality replacement brasses, Ball and Ball in Exton, Pennsylvania, and Horton Brasses in Cromwell, Connecticut. Both firms offer a wide range of authentic reproduction brasses, and from their catalogs you can get a good idea of what is appropriate to any period. They will also make up brasses to order if you send them one of the originals, which allows you to save any remaining brasses and still have a good match. If all the original brasses are missing, you can still get a good ideal of the original by considering the period and by any signs left in the drawer faces by the originals. Also, take a good look at the escutcheons. They are more likely to be original than the pulls, for not being subject to the pulling forces that eventually separate most handles, they are less likely to have been lost or replaced. In addition to information gleaned from earlier handle holes, it is often possible to detect the faint outline of the original brasses on the drawer faces, even of the piece has been completely refinished. You may find these to be smaller that you thought, for there is a tendency to employ grander brasses than are warranted. As noted earlier, aside from better than average work, brasses on American Colonial furniture were often small and skimpy. However, the reverse may be true on late Federal work, where large, flashy brass rosettes and colorful glass knobs were very much in style.

With this we come to the end of clean up and repair. Before ending, though, it might be noted that even if you do no more than a little cleaning and gluing, working with old furniture is a priceless opportunity to study both period workmanship and the cabinetmaker's trade at close hand. Here we get a close look at beautifully leveled boards, at carefully fitted inlay, and at innumerable strong, neat joints. In addition to the satisfaction of doing our bit to preserve our heritage, working with old furniture provides an understanding and an appreciation of past that we will never get from museums and seldom get from books.

## Chapter 27

## Documentation and Insurance

### Documentation

Before ending, we should discuss documentation and insurance. Neither topic requires more than a few pages, and since they are in some measure related, we'll cover them together in one short chapter. However, brevity should not diminish stature, for both are an important adjunct to any serious collecting.

Nothing will enhance the value of your collection more than careful documentation. Keeping the brasses polished is not nearly so important as knowing where the brasses came from. Good documentation, particularly the purchase receipts that link the items in your collection with known dealers or auction houses, provide a prospective owner with a feel for quality and a basic provenance. It will always help to maintain the value of your collection. At its simplest, documentation may be nothing more than maintaining a record of these receipts. At its best it is a record of everything that you know about your old furniture, including additional information that has come your way since the items came into your home. Whether maintained on file cards, in a loose leaf binder, or on a computer, documentation should include a clear description of each piece, all known provenance and any additional data that could be of interest. This information might be organized as shown on the following page. There is nothing special about this sample entry; you can employ any format that seems complete and easy to use. Whatever you choose, try to keep all associated receipts and photos together in one place. One way is to use slash folders, perhaps kept together in large three-ring binders. You don't know what is going to happen in life, so don't forget to let others know where you keep your documentation.

The data can be typed up or entered in a computer. Whatever the medium, you want to plan for variable length entries and the addition of later information. This is where a computer based system, with its variable length fields, page control, and easy text modification will prove very handy. Once you get started you'll find that your documentation is anything but static; information will be added and changed as you add to your collection and learn more about old furniture. Also, you will end up with more data than is found in any but the very best appraisals — and without having to pay for it.

In this example I've used "PROVENANCE" rather than "PURCHASED" to allow this field to also cover pieces obtained through inheritance. This entry may be quite extensive — and impressive — if something has been passed down for three or four generations. It is the perfect place to maintain a record of family ownership, and a sure way to pass information on to you heirs without it getting muddled in the process.

The cryptic little number in the upper right hand corner is an accession number. This is what connects the documentation with a specific piece in your collection. Museums have used accession numbering systems for years, and since your collection is, in effect, a small private museum, you might wish to do the same. Normally, accession numbers consist of the year the item was acquired followed by the order acquired in that year. Just the tens part of the year will do. Thus, the first piece you acquire in 1998 would be identified 98.1, the second 98.2, etc. To make things a little more personal, you might want to start off with some initials (JFK-98.1). With the millennium approaching, you might want to use a four digit date. Accession numbers are a much more effective identifier than just a simple sequence of numbers, because they identify the year the object came into your collection; and if the collection spans several generations, just who acquired each piece.

A simple and unique numbering system is more important than you might realize, for there will possibly be similar items in your collection, and while their differences are obvious to you, they may not be at all obvious to your children. It is particularly important if your collection has a particular focus; if, for example, it contains a number of Shaker chairs.

Now you ask, how do I write a number on furniture without harming the surface? How do I write on brass candlesticks? The obvious answer, a stick-on label, is not a good idea, for with time the adhesive breaks down and the label is lost. Worse yet, as the adhesive deteriorates, it will leave a mark on the wood. A better solution is to encase the numbers in a lacquer sandwich. If you don't have any lacquer handy, just use clear nail polish. It is also lacquer, and comes equipped with a little brush that doesn't need to be cleaned afterwards. First brush on a little rectangle of lacquer. When dry, add the accession number, then cover it with another coat of lacquer. To ensure a neat job, practice first on a scrap of wood. You may need two or three coats of lacquer to obtain a smooth writing surface. A very fine black felt tip pen seems to give the best results. Remember that in a confined area you may have to letter upside down. If a dark surface, you may want to use white nail polish to get the numbers to stand out against the background. Give the ink plenty of time to dry hard before adding the final protective coat. Put the accession number where it doesn't show but is not too hard to find. On desks and chests of drawers the common location is just inside the top drawer; on chairs, perhaps the underside of a rail or a stretcher. Neatly done, accession numbers not only provide a positive identification, but will add a professional look to your collection.

In your enthusiasm for your collection, remember to be honest in your documentation. Include only information you know to be correct and note any restoration you are aware of. If a piece has problems, then note them. You may kid yourself now, but you don't want to deceive your children later. Worse yet, they may think you didn't know any better.

---

**Acc. No.** 98.3

**Description:** Chippendale maple slant lid desk, New England, c.1760 – 80.

**Dimensions:** H. 40¾" W. 35¾" D. 17"  **Value:** $5,000 (1998)

**Finish:** Shellac

**Inscriptions:** The four small interior drawers are numbered in pencil "1" to "4" (left to right).

**Present Location:** Living Room  **Photographed:** No

**Provenance:** Skinner, Inc. Sale 1850, Lot 21

**Construction & Condition:** Condition good. Primary wood maple, secondary wood white pine. Present brasses not original. Minor drawer lip repairs, two glue blocks missing from base.

**Comments:** Nice old honey brown color. Fan carved propect door.

---

# Chapter 27

## Insurance

After acquiring your first few antiques, you will probably start to wonder about insurance. Upon inquiry, your insurance agent may tell you not to worry, your homeowners policy covers the household furnishings up to one half the value of the property. However, there are a couple of problems here. If you take the time to add up the actual replacement cost of all your household furnishings, not just the big and obvious items like the living room sofa and the dining room table, but the lamps, the linens, the curtains, and your clothing, you may find this already equals about half the insured value of the house. This may not leave much additional coverage if you do more than just occasional collecting. The other problem is more serious. A homeowner's policy is not intended to cover fine arts. There is no appraisal of the furnishings or the collection, and even with good documentation you may have a hassle when you submit a claim of $3000 for a small candlestand. But there is another catch. Most policies set a dollar limit on any one item. You may only receive $1000 for the stand.

Now if the value of most of the antiques in your collection is less than the dollar limit, and you keep a copy of your documentation, along with some good photographs, in a safe deposit box, then a homeowner's policy should be quite satisfactory. However, if the dollar limit is not adequate, it is time to consider a separate fine arts policy. The good news is that fine arts insurance is relatively inexpensive, for houses do not often burn, and period furniture is not often stolen.

The bad news is two-fold. First, to issue a fine arts policy, most insurance companies now require the home to be equipped with an alarm system that is linked to a central station. However, this is not the major investment it once was, for competition has reduced both the cost of installation and the monthly monitoring charge. Also, the sensors have become much smaller and more reliable. In addition, the alarm system can be fitted with a low temperature sensor, so that if far away at an auction in midwinter, you do not have to worry about the pipes freezing.

Secondly, to provide fine arts coverage, the insurer will require a current appraisal of your collection. This must be done by a certified appraiser. Here the estimates of your friend, the proprietor of the local antique and collectibles shop will not do. Neither are bills of sale accepted, although you might want to show them to the appraiser. Since a fine arts appraisal requires the clear and accurate identification of each item, insist on an appraiser who is experienced in period furniture. Appraisers that specialize in fine art are usually either employees of auction houses or antique dealers. Given a choice, I would select the former, not only for their breadth of current market knowledge, but also because a dealer, as both an appraiser and a potential buyer, has an inherent conflict of interest. If less than honest, there will be the temptation to estimate low on something that might later be subject to an offer.

Appraisals are normally costed by the hour or as a percentage of the appraised value. If the former, organize things as much as possible. Work up a list, by room, of what needs to be appraised. Don't worry about minor items, the actual chance of loss is so small that they are not worth the time and cost to appraise.

When your appraisal arrives in the mail, you may be pleasantly surprised at the value of your collection. However, fine arts are appraised at replacement value, what it would cost to purchase items of similar quality from a dealer. It is perhaps twice fair market value — the price that a dealer might offer. Reviewing the appraisal, you will find some items appraised at less than your estimate of their worth, and others that are agreeably high. This is not a problem, so long as the overall evaluation appears to be reasonable. Unless you feel that the appraisal is fundamentally wrong, accept it as is. Remember that the purpose of all this is simply to obtain insurance coverage, not to brag to your friends about your great collection.

As you grow your collection, new pieces can be added to the policy just by sending your agent a copy of the purchase receipt. If acquired at auction, this may be less than the full replacement cost, but it will provide coverage. Every so often, perhaps every four or five years, consider if market prices have changed enough to justify the expense of another appraisal. Unfortunately, you cannot just tell your agent that prices have gone up by about 30%, and to increase your coverage by a like amount. However, appraisals are now kept on computers, so it should not be difficult to adjust the valuation. It should also be considerably less expensive.

# Chapter 28

## Inheritance

*"For we brought nothing into this world,*
*and it is certain we can carry nothing out." – 1 Timothy*

When first starting to collect, we are proud of our new possessions. Here we have lovely old furniture, the likes of which is ours alone. Sunlight, time, and wear have made each one truly unique. Like paintings, there will be similar versions, but none will be quite like ours. However, with time there comes an awareness of another, more subtle, aspect of our collection, an aspect more significant than just simple possession. While we think of period furniture as being valuable, a better word would be precious, for like us, each piece of old furniture is unique. Once gone, it can never be replaced. No reproduction, however perfect, will ever be the original.

In addition, this old furniture is a lasting tribute to generations of mostly unknown craftsmen who worked in the furniture trades. They, along with the customers they served so well, are now long gone. None of us are even close to being the original owners of these things. Nor should we ever be the last. We are but one in many generations who have loved and cherished them, contributing our small record of wear and repair before they pass on to others. While we are collectors, we are also stewards. As such, it is not only our responsibility to look after these things while they are in our custody, but to see that they end up in good hands that will also appreciate and care for them. What then should we do?

Well, the first thing is to consider this question reasonably early, for none of us knows when we will exit the stage. If a simple will and an equal division of property will not provide a good home for your collection, you need to think about the future. Now is the time for a little thought.

In general, there are three ways to pass on a collection. It may be left to children or other individuals, or given to museums or institutions, or sold and the proceeds transferred to the estate or to a charitable organization. None of these approaches is intrinsically any better than the others. Depending on individual circumstances, all have merit and can prove successful.

The majority of furniture collections are simply disbursed among one's children, so let's consider this first. Leaving your collection to your children is not only appealing, but can be good stewardship, for you are in the enviable position of knowing the recipients, their tastes, and their homes. Old furniture that has been in the family for a generation or more is a wonderful inheritance, for it brings not only value, but also beauty and fond memories. A handsome old desk left to a child or grandchild, although lacking the immediacy of money, will surely be enjoyed far longer.

Should you follow this approach, there is one thing you must always do — and one thing you must never do. First, always leave good documentation. In addition to matters of family or historical interest, the information that a piece was handled by a knowledgeable dealer, or was once part of a well known collection, suggests that it has had the approval of experts. Such pieces always do better in the market. Mislay this provenance and what you leave will be that much the less — you will have taxed your children's inheritance. In addition, your heirs need to know about what they have inherited, particularly if they do not have your knowledge of old furniture. The more they appreciate what has been left them, the more they will enjoy it, and the more they are likely to give it good care.

The antique business abounds in stories of wonderful things sold for almost nothing in yard sales and at small estate auctions. Sadly, these stories are true. Sadly, because for each wonderful find, there was a seller who, out of sheer ignorance, just about gave something away. This is where your documentation may be most critical, for your children need to understand what they have inherited. Even if they later wish to sell some things off, they need to know exactly what they are doing. They need to know which pieces are not very good, which are good, and which are very good indeed.

Secondly, don't ever divide up pairs and sets of furniture, even though it may seem fair, and indeed, it may be the path of least resistance. Pairs and sets were originally purchased together and were intended to be seen together and used together. Quite aside from the historical loss in separation, there is almost sure to be a loss in value. Except for really grand pieces, which can stand alone on their merits, dividing up does nothing but reduce value. At auctions you will see innumerable nice side chairs selling for a fraction of what they would bring as a set. Worse yet, what few labels were used in the old days were used sparingly. Often only one piece of a set is labeled. Break up such a set and there is a double loss.

Perhaps the major difficulty in leaving things to children is that each piece of old furniture is very much unique, and while the division may be fair, it will never be equal. Unlike stocks and bonds, a collection of period furniture cannot be divided evenly. Compounding this problem is the inevitability that some pieces will be favorites, and other pieces, perhaps because of size or style, nobody will want. However, in spite of this, should all your children be interested in your collection, and can provide it with a good home, there is no reason why it should not be divided up as a part of your estate.

When things are not equal among children you are faced with a more difficult problem. Here you might sound out your children to see how they felt about the collection. Try to do this individually, so you don't end up with "me too" replies from those worried that they might be left out; and emphasize that none will get short shifted if they are less than interested in the old furniture. What you want are not "correct" answers, but honest answers. When doing this, you might consider giving each of them a copy of any appraisals or documentation you have put together. This way they will all know something about the collection. It should eliminate, or at least mitigate, the misconceptions that seem to lie at the heart of so much family discord.

It will also save endless misunderstanding and hard feelings to have an appraisal of the collection by a specialist in period furniture. This should prevent such misleading and divisive terms as "priceless" and "museum piece." The appraisal need not even be current, but it must be good enough to be accepted by all the children. Note that this appraisal will almost always be a replacement value appraisal that was made to obtain insurance coverage. It is different from the fair market value appraisal that may be required to settle your estate. The latter is required to establish the taxable value of all your property. Here your collection will be appraised at market value, which should be significantly less than replacement value.

Dividing up things ahead of time sounds logical and sensible, but it can have a number of pitfalls. First off, if you give valuable pieces to children as gifts, you must really give them away. Merely leaving a note to the effect inside a drawer of your Chippendale secretary leaves the Internal Revenue Service singularly unimpressed when your executor then tries to leave the secretary out of the estate. Unfortunately, you may find that dividing up early is a constant source of family friction. Perhaps though, this is inevitable when dealing with old furniture.

Lawyers sometimes dislike adding specific bequests to wills, for they add complications which, in turn, can lead to problems. If you feel that you must have specific bequests, be sure that they are carefully worded as to clearly identify the item in question. Describing a very good desk as simply "the old desk in my bedroom" is just asking for trouble.

In the event that any sort of dividing up seems to promise endless family discord, consider leaving everything to auction, the proceeds then going to the estate. This is more common than you would think, for an auction is an open market where all the heirs have an equal chance to bid on their favorite things. They may not end up with all they had wished for, but they cannot blame you for playing favorites. This approach has the additional merit in that a piece that none really want does not end up, unused and unloved, gathering mildew in a damp basement. It may have been a very good piece — in fact, it may have been your favorite. Remember, though, that auctions are full of surprises, and there is always the chance of your children being outbid on something they love by an enthusiastic collector. Also, this solution will always be at the cost of the auction house's expenses and profit.

Should there be no interested children, consider leaving your collection to other family members, or perhaps to younger friends. You still will know the recipients and can direct things to where they are most likely to be understood and appreciated. Failing this, there only remains to disburse the collection either through sale or gift to an institution. If sold, you or your executor should deal with the best auction house that will accept your collection, not only to maximize the proceeds, but also to direct the collection toward the best possible new homes. Here we might note that American period furniture should be sold at an Americana auction, for things sell best when in company with similar things. While they are not family, auctioneers and dealers are very much professionals. They will take good care of your collection.

Although some will disagree, leaving period furniture to museums or to historical societies should perhaps be your last choice, for there are too many nice things tucked away in museum basements, or sitting neglected and mostly unappreciated in minor historical society exhibits. They might very well be better off used and enjoyed in private homes. To be successful with gifts to institutions, you need to take a realistic look at the potential recipient. When considering a museum, ask yourself if your collection would be an asset to their collection, whether they have the experienced staff to give it good care, and if your pieces are really good enough to be displayed, for most museums have much more art than they have display room. Keep in mind that museum holdings are generally far finer than the average private collection. It is a truly remarkable collection that is actually museum quality. Most museums eventually sell off average pieces to provide the funding for better, but it may be years before this is done. Until then, it usually stays in storage.

Historical societies vary widely in assets and quality from those having extensive holdings and professional staffs to small local weekend operations. Perhaps when donating to these institutions, you might consider dividing the collection; tailoring your bequests to the appropriate institution, the grand to the grand, the simple to the simple. Don't worry about splitting up your collection; one way or another, almost all collections are eventually separated.

Now in spite of the potential difficulties in dividing up things early, there is a time when it should be done. This time arrives when you can no longer use all or part of your collection, or can no longer provide it with a good home. Old furniture generally deteriorates more in its last few years in a collection than in all the other time put together. As noted earlier, furniture is in the most danger when it is put away in an attic or a basement, which may happen if you move to a smaller house or into a condominium. Unless you have access to really good storage, this might be the time to start disbursing part of the collection.

Also, your collection may be damaged if you need to keep the heat well up during the cold winter months. At estate auctions you will often see the result of this environment; dried out glues, severe shrinkage, and missing veneer. If you cannot maintain humidity in winter, it is perhaps time to start distributing things, particularly case work with wide panels or a lot of veneer. There is no need to dispose of everything; candlestands, beds and chairs tolerate some dryness quite well, and chairs can be reglued if necessary.

Should you have a large breakfront bookcase with the cornice in storage, or perhaps a tall clock with the finials removed, be sure that others know about this. Better yet, note it clearly in your documentation. Death can be a separator in more than one sense. Another thing to consider is pairs and sets of chairs that are in different rooms, particularly if as a result of sunlight or redecoration they now have different coloring or different upholstery. In the confusion of dividing things up, it is all too easy for these to get separated.

Period furniture should not end up in the wrong hands, and sadly, the wrong hands can be someone very near and dear. Leaving a veneered chest of drawers to a son or daughter living in a dry climate, or a very good desk to an uninterested child, will be a waste of all your years of love and care. This can be difficult, for we are all drawn by family — blood is indeed thicker than water. Should you acquire some really fine pieces and your children show little real interest beyond a certain low snobbery in having old things around, consider leaving your collection to auction and to others. There is no real reason why your collection must go to your children. Never forget that the greatest enemy of old furniture is neither fire, nor water, nor sun — but slow everyday neglect. Remember that in the long run you are no more than the good steward, and these pretty things from the past, in some measure, are no more your children's than they were yours. In passing on your collection, your primary objective should always be to see that it ends up in good hands. Hopefully, the new owners will care for and enjoy your lovely old furniture as much as you have.

# Chapter 29
## Period Furniture Collections

Quite the best way to acquire a feel for period workmanship is to observe a lot of it, and nowhere is this easier to do than by visiting museums and historical societies. While you will not be able to pull out drawers and turn things over, you will get to see a great deal of genuine old furniture, and if in a museum setting, then furniture that is also identified as to origin and date of manufacture.

To start off, we might note that furniture is classified as a decorative art, and should you call a museum for information, the operator will generally direct your inquiry to this department. Also, a number of the listed collections are displayed in period rooms or in period houses. This is an added bonus, for these exhibits suggest where old furniture was used, and may provide some useful ideas on displaying your own collection.

Needless to say, when planning a visit, wear comfortable clothes, and particularly, comfortable shoes, as viewing a collection invariably involves a lot of walking and standing on hard floors. Be sure to take the time, even if there may be a line, to check coats and bags. Bags will have to be checked anyhow, and carrying a heavy topcoat around for two or three hours will dampen any visit. Although it may seem heartless, try to avoid bringing along friends who do not share your interest in old furniture, even if, in other circumstances, they are very good friends. To get the most from a visit, you want to take plenty of time and really think about what you seeing, and you may find chatter, even if light and clever, inimical to thoughtful observation. Should children have to be included, go out of your way to keep them well fed and happy, remembering to check their coats also.

When viewing a major collection, always try to split your tour with lunch, or at least a snack; then rested and fed, go back for a second and more careful look. You will spot all sorts of interesting little details that you missed the first time through.

Some distinction should be drawn between nearby museums, which can be seen at any time, and those far away, where visits may be very infrequent. For the latter, you should do a little planning as it may be a while between visits. First off, be sure to call ahead to find out not only location and hours, but also if the decorative arts galleries are open to the public. Good museums are continually upgrading their displays, and it is not unusual for a gallery to be closed for remodeling. When calling, inquire if guided tours are available, for an hour in the company of a well trained docent will provide far more information than you will ever get from the little cards beside each exhibit. In particular, if you plan to visit the remarkable American furniture collection at Winterthur in Delaware, try to call a few weeks ahead to arrange for one of the small guided tours; where you can spend half a day with a party of no more than four, seeing just William and Mary, Queen Anne, Chippendale, or Federal furniture.

# Chapter 29

The more that you know about a collection the more rewarding will be your visit. The next chapter identifies some excellent books covering a number of the more important collections. In addition, many of the collections have been the subject of articles in *Antiques Magazine*. These are noted in the listing of museums. Most of the public libraries that subscribe to this magazine save the issues, often for twenty years or more. If your library does not have back issues, they may be able to direct you to a nearby library that does.

Major collections display the finest, and often the rarest, of old furniture. They are not at all representative of what you will see at shops and auctions — or for that matter, are ever likely to own. Do not let this discourage you. This high style furniture served as model for a great many others in the trade. It should be in a museum collection, just as should a Rembrandt, who also had a host of competent but lesser followers. When visiting a major collection, in addition to appreciating the superb design and workmanship, look for stylistic features and period motifs that appear in all furniture of the period. Although the pieces you see will probably be far better than you can ever hope to afford, you will probably find they are more similar than not to things in your own collection.

The listing that follows is no more than compendium of the better known exhibits, and does not include a great many fine historical societies and period houses. These are usually open only on a limited schedule during the milder weather. However, if local to your area, they are well worth investigating. Some of the exhibits are very good indeed. Should you find yourself in coastal New England, you might wish to contact the Society for the Preservation of New England Antiquites (SPNEA) in Boston. They maintain historic houses all over New England, a number of which are beautifully illustrated in the March 1986, issue of *Antiques Magazine*.

**California**
> Los Angeles County Museum of Art, Los Angeles
> M. H. De Young Museum, San Francisco

**Connecticut**
> Connecticut Historical Society, Hartford
> Lyman Allyn Museum, New London
> Hitchcock Museum, Riverton (*Antiques*, May 1984)
> New Haven Colony Historical Society, New Haven
> Wadsworth Atheneaum, Hartford (*Antiques*, May 1979, and October 1984)
> Webb-Deane-Stevens Museum, Wethersfield (*Antiques*, March 1976, and May 1984)
> Yale University Art Gallery, Mabel Brady Garvan and Related Collections, New Haven (*Antiques*, June 1980)

**Delaware**
> Historical Society of Delaware, Wilmington and New Castle
> Henry Francis du Pont Winterthur Museum, Winterthur (*Antiques*, June 1978)

**Georgia**
> High Museum of Art, Atlanta
> Telfair Academy of Arts and Sciences, Savannah (*Antiques*, May 1995)

**Illinois**
> Art Institute of Chicago, Chicago (*Antiques*, October 1988)

**Indiana**
> Indianapolis Museum of Art, Indianapolis

**Kentucky**
  Shaker Village of Pleasant Hill, Harrodsburg (*Antiques*, May 1990)
  Shakertown at South Union (*Antiques*, May 1997)
**Louisiana**
  Anglo-American Art Museum, Louisiana State University, Baton Rouge (*Antiques*,
    March 1984)
**Maine**
  Maine Historical Society, Portland
  Portland Museum of Art, Portland
  United Society of Shakers, Sabbathday Lake, Poland Springs
**Maryland**
  Baltimore Museum of Art, Baltimore (*Antiques*, February 1977)
  Historic Annapolis Foundation, Annapolis
  Maryland Historical Society, Baltimore
  Hampton National Historic Site, Towson
**Massachusetts**
  Concord Antiquarian Museum, Concord
  Essex Institute, Salem (*Antiques*, May and December 1977, and March 1990)
  Hancock Shaker Village, Pittsfield (*Antiques*, October 1981)
  Historic Deerfield, Deerfield (*Antiques*, March 1985, and December 1992)
  Museum of Fine Arts, Boston (*Antiques*, September 1981, and May 1986)
  Old Sturbridge Village, Sturbridge (*Antiques*, October 1979)
  Pilgrim Hall, Plymouth (*Antiques*, May 1985)
  Society for the Preservation of New England Antiquities, Boston (*Antiques*, March 1986)
  Worcester Art Museum, Worcester
**Michigan**
  Henry Ford Museum and Greenfield Village, Dearborn
**Minnesota**
  The Minneapolis Institute of Arts, Minneapolis
**Missouri**
  Saint Louis Art Museum, St. Louis (*Antiques*, May 1982)
**New Hampshire**
  New Hampshire Historical Society, Concord
  Currier Gallery of Art, Manchester
  The Museum at Lower Shaker Village, Enfield
  Strawbery Banke, Portsmouth (*Antiques*, July 1992)
**New Jersey**
  Monmouth County Historical Association, Freehold (*Antiques*, January 1980)
  Newark Museum, Newark
  New Jersey State Museum, Trenton
**New York**
  Albany Institute of History and Art, Albany (*Antiques*, May 1981)
  Brooklyn Museum, Brooklyn (*Antiques*, May 1979, and October 1984)
  Historic Hudson Valley, Inc., Tarrytown
  Hudson River Museum, Yonkers
  Margaret Woodbury Strong Museum, Rochester
  The Metropolitan Museum of Art, The American Wing, New York (*Antiques*, May 1980, and
    May 1986)
  Museum of the City of New York, New York

New York Historical Society, New York
New York State Museum, Albany (*Antiques*, May 1981)
Shaker Museum, Old Chatham (*Antiques*, May 1989)
Sleepy Hollow Restorations, Tarrytown (*Antiques*, December 1985)
**North Carolina**
Museum of Early Southern Decorative Arts, Winston-Salem
**Ohio**
Cincinnati Art Museum, Cincinnati
Western Reserve Historical Society, Cleveland
Toledo Museum of Art, Toledo
**Pennsylvania**
Carnegie Institute, Pittsburgh
Chester County Historical Society, West Chester
Philadelphia Museum of Art, Philadelphia
William Penn Memorial Museum, Harrisburg
York County Historical Society, York
**Rhode Island**
The Preservation Society of Newport County, Newport (*Antiques*, April 1995)
Newport Historical Society, Newport
Rhode Island School of Design, Museum of Art, Providence (*Antiques*, July 1980)
Rhode Island Historical Society, Providence
**South Carolina**
Historic Charleston Foundation, Charleston
**Texas**
Dallas Museum of Art, Dallas
Museum of Fine Arts, Bayou Bend Collection, Houston (*Antiques*, September 1985, and September 1993)
San Antonio Museum of Art, San Antonio
**Vermont**
Shelburne Museum, Shelburne (*Antiques*, February 1988)
Bennington Museum, Bennington (*Antiques*, August 1993)
**Virginia**
Colonial Williamsburg Foundation, Williamsburg (*Antiques*, August 1978, January 1981, January 1983, and August 1985)
Virginia Museum of Fine Arts, Richmond
**Washington, D.C.**
Daughters of the American Revolution Museum (*Antiques*, April 1976)
Diplomatic Reception Rooms, United States Department of State (*Antiques*, July 1987, and May 1992)
National Gallery of Art
National Museum of American History, Smithsonian Institution
**Wisconsin**
Chipstone Foundation, Fox Point
Milwaukee Art Museum, Milwaukee (*Antiques*, May 1977)

# Chapter 30
## Suggested Reading

Reading is so important in collecting old furniture that we will finish with a small bibliography of books on the subject. It is limited to those volumes most likely to be helpful to the novice and occasional collector, the most readable and informative books. As such, a number of well known early works by Nutting, Lockwood, and Miller have been omitted because they lack the detailed information so needed by the beginner. Later, however, as one gains experience and can identify styles and regional variations, they become more interesting reading.

Similarly, there are none of the large illustrated coffee table type books, nor any of the popular price guides. While these are interesting to peruse, they are not a great deal of actual help in collecting. Coffee table books tend to illustrate the very best in period workmanship, discussing lovely period furniture that is only found in the grandest collections. Their beautiful color illustrations bear little relation to the market seen by the average collector.

As a beginner, you will probably pick up a price guide or two, and while these books are a useful survey of what is on the market, they poorly serve their stated function. Unlike coins or stamps, which were mass produced, and are very similar one to another, there is so much variation in design, quality, and condition among old handcrafted furniture that relating price to a tiny sketch or small photo doesn't work very well. At best, they provide only a rough guide to average market prices. However, they do provide a broad feel for what is available, what sort of furniture you can expect to find in shops and at auctions.

In the last 30 years there has been a great deal of scholarship in period furniture, and you will find that newer books much more informative. Many of the earlier are very light on detail. Also, ideas on repair and restoration have changed a lot over the years, and early writings on this subject should be treated with care.

Many of the books listed on the following pages are out of print, and can only be found in libraries and used book stores. That a book is out of print does not diminish its merit — our period furniture is also very much "out of print." Most public libraries now have their catalogs linked into regional networks. If a book is not in your local library, there will usually be a computer terminal where you can conduct a search by subject, title, or author; and if successful, have the volume forwarded to your library.

Books on period furniture have a limited audience, and only the major bookstores will stock more than one or two different volumes. However, their staff can easily determine if a book is still in print, and if so, order a copy from the publisher. Should a book no longer be in print, try some used bookstores. Even if they do not have it, they will often be able to locate a copy for sale on the Internet.

Most collectors acquire small libraries of reference books, if for no other reason than to be able to do a little quick research when something interesting is seen at a dealer's shop or at an auction preview. You will find that you tend to purchase just about every good book in your particular area of interest, even if there is a great deal of overlap in subject matter between books. There is always something new and interesting to be learned. You will also find that as you gain experience, rereading books you have read before can be rewarding. You will pick up things you missed, or perhaps did not appreciate the first time through.

# Chapter 30

I would also suggest spending some time at a library leafing through back issues of *Antiques* magazine, or to use the correct name, *The Magazine Antiques*. You will find that the major advertisements for period furniture tell you much about dates, periods and regional variations, and provide a feel for not only what is on the market, but for the best in period furniture. In addition to articles dealing with museum exhibits, notable private collections, and regional furniture types, the May issue is devoted to American furniture. If time is limited, concentrate on this issue. Keep a note of articles of particular interest. The only thing worse than missing a useful article is forgetting where you read it! *Antiques* magazine is such a useful reference that many dealers and collectors keep a complete set of back issues, and you will sometimes see these sold at auction.

### General Information

Damato, H. H. *How to Collect, Refinish & Restore Antique & Country Furniture*. Tab Books, Inc., 1982.

Green, Jeffery P. *American Furniture of the 18th Century*. The Taunton Press, 1990.

Jenkins, Emyl. *Emyl Jenkins' Guide to Buying and Collecting Early American Furniture*. Crown Publishers, Inc., 1991.

Kirk, John T. *American Chairs — Queen Anne and Chippendale*. Alfred A. Knopf, 1972.

_____. *Early American Furniture — How to Recognize, Evaluate, Buy and Care For the Most Beautiful Pieces — High-Style, Country, Primitive, and Rustic*. Alfred A. Knopf, 1974.

_____. *The Impecunious Collector's Guide to American Antiques*. Alfred A. Knopf, 1982.

Koval, Ralph and Terry. *American Country Furniture 1780 – 1875*. Crown Publishers, Inc., 1965.

Newmann, George. *Early American Antique Country Furnishings — Northeastern America 1650 – 1800*. McGraw-Hill Book Company, 1984.

Marsh, Moreton. *The Easy Expert in American Antiques*. J. B. Lippencott, 1978 (1st edition in 1959 titled *The Easy Expert on Collecting and Restoring American Antiques*).

Michael, George. *Antiquing with George Michael*. Greene Press, 1967.

_____. *The Treasury of New England Antiques*. Hawthorn Books, 1969.

Sack, Albert. *Fine Points of Furniture — Early American*. Crown Publishers, Inc., 1950.

_____. *The New Fine Points of Furniture — Early American: Good, Better, Best, Superior, Masterpiece*. Crown Publishers, Inc., 1993.

Smith, Nancy A. *Old Furniture — Understanding the Craftsman's Art*. Bobbs Merrill, Indianapolis, 1975.

Watson, Aldren A. *Country Furniture*. Thomas Y. Crowell Company, 1974.

Way, Nelson E., and Constance Stapleton. *Antiques Don't Lie — (How to Make Antique Furniture Tell Everything, Including Its Age)*. Doubleday and Company, 1975.

Weinhagen, Robert F. *Assume Nothing — A Manual For Buyers of American and English Antique Furniture*. Highland House Publishers, Inc., 1993.

### Clocks and Barometers

Bailey, Chris H. *Two Hundred Years of American Clocks and Watches*. Prentice-Hall, Inc., 1975.

Battison, Edwin A., and Kane, Patrica E. *The American Clock 1725 – 1865 — In the Mabel Brady Garvan and Other Collections at Yale University*. New York Graphic Society (Little, Brown and Company), 1973.

Goodson, Nicholas. *English Barometers 1680 – 1860 — A History of Domestic Barometers and Their Makers*. Clarkson N. Potter, Inc., 1968.

Harris, Henry Gordon. *Collecting and Identifying Old Clocks*. Emerson Books, 1977.

Schwartz, Marvin D. *Collectors' Guide to Antique American Clocks*. Doubleday & Company, 1975.

**Collections – Museums and Historical Societies**

Barquist, David L. *American Tables and Looking Glasses (in the Mabel Brady Garvan and Other Collections at Yale University)*. Yale University Press, 1992.

Downs, Joseph. *American Furniture — Queen Anne and Chippendale Periods in the Henry Francis du Pont Winterthur Museum*. Bonanza Books, 1952.

Jobe, Brock., and Myrna Kaye. *New England Furniture — The Colonial Era*. Houghton Mifflin Company, 1984.

Kane, Patricia E. *300 Years of American Seating Furniture — Chairs and Beds from the Mabel Brady Garvan and Other Collections at Yale University*. New York Graphic Society (Little, Brown and Company), 1975.

Montgomery, Charles F. *American Furniture — The Federal Period in the Henry Francis du Pont Winterthur Museum*. The Viking Press, 1966.

Rogers, Mary-Alice., and Richard Cheek. *American Furniture in the Metropolitan Museum of Art — Late Colonial Period: The Queen Anne and Chippendale Styles — Vol II*. Random House, 1985.

Ward, Gerald W. R. *American Case Furniture — In the Mabel Brady Garvan and Other Collections at Yale University*. Yale University Press, 1988.

**Field Guides**

Butler, Joseph T., and Ray Skibinski. *Field Guide to American Antique Furniture*. Facts on File Publications, 1985.

Miller, Judith and Martin. *The Antiques Directory — Furniture*. G. K. Hall & Co., 1985.

Petraglia, Patricia P. *Sotheby's Guide to American Furniture*. Simon & Schuster, 1995.

Ormsbee, Thomas H. *Field Guide to Early American Furniture*. Little, Brown and Company, 1951. Bantam Books (paperback), 1961.

Voss, Thomas M. *Antique American Country Furniture — A Field Guide*. J. B. Lippincott Co., 1978. Bonanza Books, 1981.

**Miniatures**

Schiffer, Herbert F. and Peter B. *Miniature Antique Furniture*. Livingston Publishing Company, 1972.

**Fakes and Frauds**

Hayward, Charles H. *Antique or Fake?* Evans Brothers, Limited, 1970. St. Martin's Press, 1971.

Kaye, Myrna. *Fake, Fraud, or Genuine?* Little, Brown and Co., 1987.

**Repair and Restoration**

Damato, H. H. *How to Collect, Refinish & Restore Antique & Country Furniture*. Tab Books, Inc., 1982.

Hayward, Charles H. *Antique Furniture Repairs*. Charles Scribner's Sons, 1976.

Rodd, John. *Repairing and Restoring Antique Furniture*. Van Nostrand Reinhold Company, 1981.

**Shaker**

Muller, Charles R., and Rieman, Timothy D. *The Shaker Chair*. The University of Massachusetts Press, 1992.

Meader, Robert F. W. *Illustrated Guide to Shaker Furniture*. Dover Publications, Inc., 1972.

Sprigg, June. *Shaker Design*. W. W. Norton and Company, 1986.

**Windsor Chairs**

Evans, Nancy Goyne. *American Windsor Chairs*. Hudson Hills Press, 1996.

Ormsbee, Thomas H. *The Windsor Chair*. Hearthside Press, Inc., 1962

Santore, Charles. *The Windsor Style in America*. Running Press, 1981.

_____. *The Windsor Style in America, Volume II*. Running Press, 1987.

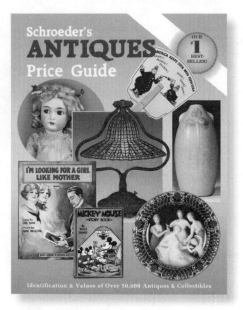